W9-AXU-583

GREGG SHORTHAND FOR COLLEGES DIAMOND JUBILEE SERIES

volume two

LOUIS A. LESLIE
COAUTHOR DIAMOND JUBILEE SERIES
OF GREGG SHORTHAND

CHARLES E. ZOUBEK
COAUTHOR DIAMOND JUBILEE SERIES
OF GREGG SHORTHAND

RUSSELL J. HOSLER
PROFESSOR OF EDUCATION
UNIVERSITY OF WISCONSIN

SHORTHAND WRITTEN BY
CHARLES RADER

SHORTHAND

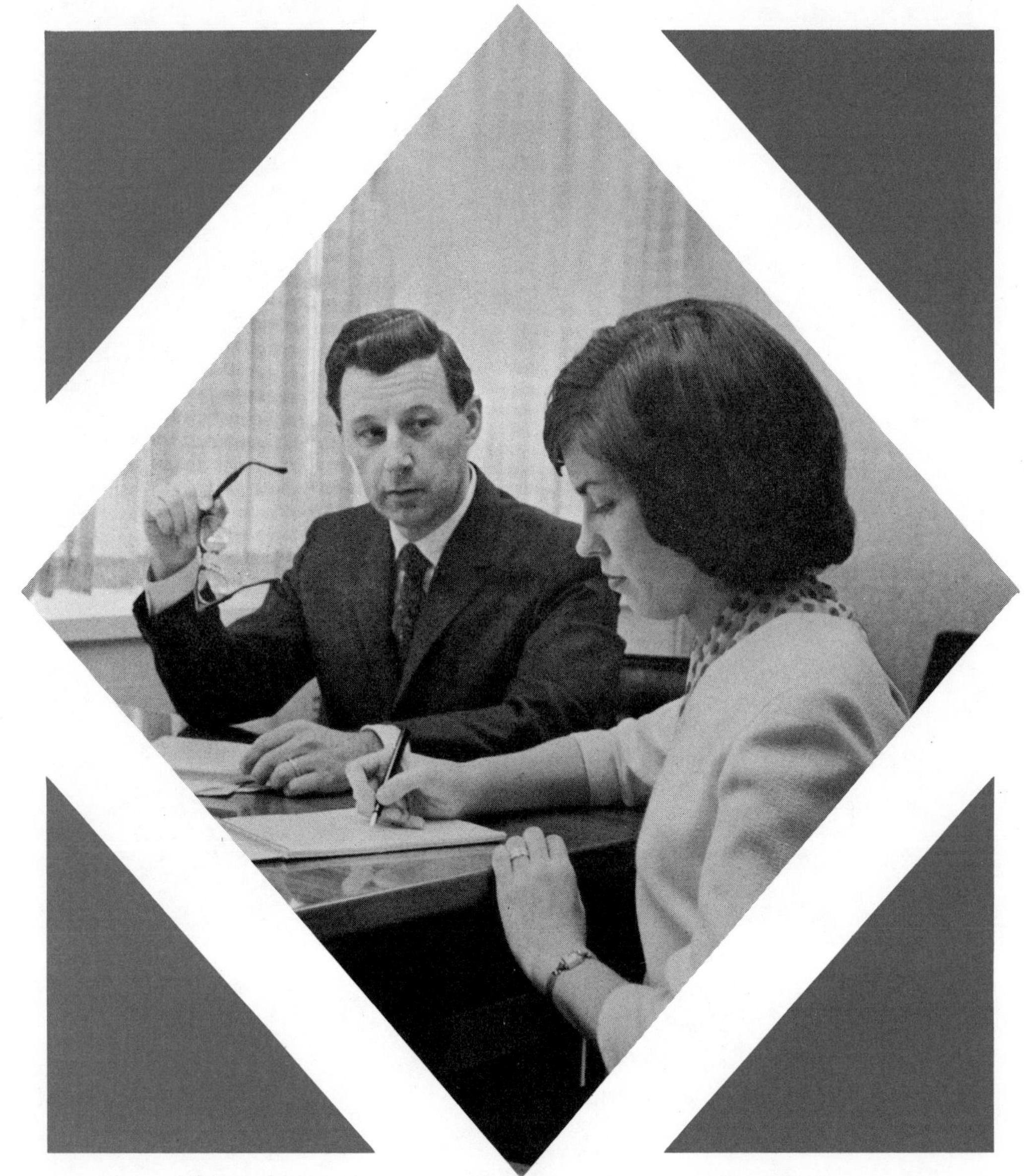

FOR COLLEGES VOLUME TWO

DIAMOND JUBILEE SERIES

75

GREGG DIVISION McGRAW-HILL BOOK COMPANY

NEW YORK ST. LOUIS DALLAS SAN FRANCISCO TORONTO LONDON SYDNEY

Design by BARBARA DU PREE KNOWLES

Chapter illustrations by **Steve Antonakos**

GREGG SHORTHAND FOR COLLEGES, DIAMOND JUBILEE SERIES
VOLUME TWO

Copyright © 1965, 1958 by McGraw-Hill, Inc. All Rights Reserved. Copyright 1953 by McGraw-Hill, Inc. All Rights Reserved. Printed in the United States of America. This book, or parts thereof, may not be reproduced in any form without permission of the publishers. Library of Congress Catalog Card Number 64-8974.

9 10 11 12 13 14 15 DODO 0 9 8 7 6 5 4 3 ISBN 07-037321-3

As its title indicates, *Gregg Shorthand for Colleges, Diamond Jubilee Series, Volume Two,* is planned for use after the completion of Volume One. It is designed to help the student to

1▸ Review the principles of Gregg Shorthand.

2▸ Develop his ability to construct outlines for unfamiliar words under the stress of dictation.

3▸ Develop his dictation speed to the highest possible point.

4▸ Extend his knowledge of the basic elements of transcription, including spelling, punctuation, word usage, and typing style.

5▸ Handle the problems of office dictation.

There are 16 chapters in the book, each containing 5 lessons – a total of 80 lessons. Each lesson consists of three parts:

1▸ Developing Word-Building or Phrasing Power

2▸ Building Transcription Skills

3▸ Reading and Writing Practice

DEVELOPING WORD-BUILDING OR PHRASING POWER

Each chapter contains a carefully planned cycle of word-building or phrasing drills that provide a quick, intensive recall in list form of the major components of Gregg Shorthand.

Lesson 1 in each chapter opens with a brief-form chart that reviews brief forms and their useful derivatives.

Lesson 2 in each chapter concentrates on building phrasing power. The major phrasing principles of the system are reviewed several times in these lessons through carefully constructed phrase lists. In addition, each second lesson contains a helpful list of frequently used first and last names.

Lesson 3 in each chapter is devoted to shorthand word families. These shorthand word families enable the student to take advantage of a very effective aid in word building – analogy. These shorthand word families are an important factor in helping the student construct outlines for unfamiliar words.

Lesson 4 of each chapter is devoted to an intensive drill on word beginnings and endings. Through these drills the student reviews all the word beginnings and endings of the system at least once; some of the more important ones, several times. Lesson 4 also provides drills on common geographical expressions.

Lesson 5 of each chapter contains a shorthand vocabulary builder that provides drills on major principles of Gregg Shorthand — blends, vowel combinations, omissions of vowels, etc.

BUILDING TRANSCRIPTION SKILLS

It is a well-known fact that the weakest link in the transcription chain is the student's ability to handle the mechanics of the English language. In Volume One, a number of features are introduced to strengthen this weak link. Drills are provided to enable the student to improve his ability to spell, to punctuate, and to build his vocabulary concurrently with the development of his mastery of the system.

In Volume Two, the emphasis on the mechanics of the English language is intensified beginning with the very first lesson. Volume Two contains the following transcription skill-building features:

SPELLING

Marginal Reminders • As in Volume One, words selected from the Reading and Writing Practice have been singled out for special spelling attention. These words, correctly divided, appear in the margins of the shorthand material. The words and their shorthand outlines are printed in color.

Spelling Families • Just as shorthand word families are helpful in building shorthand skill, spelling families are useful in developing spelling mastery. Spelling families appear frequently in the lessons of Volume Two.

PUNCTUATION

In Volume One, the student studied ten of the most frequent uses of the comma. In Volume Two, he continues to drill on these uses of the comma. In addition, he studies other important punctuation marks, including the semicolon, the colon, the hyphen, and the apostrophe.

To test the student's grasp of the punctuation rules studied, each lesson (except the fifth in each chapter) contains a Transcription Quiz in which the student must supply all internal punctuation. The Transcription Quiz also teaches the student to supply from context words that have been omitted in the shorthand.

VOCABULARY DEVELOPMENT

Business Vocabulary Builder • In each lesson, several important words and expressions, selected from the Reading and Writing Practice, are highlighted for special study.

Similar-Words Drill • The Similar-Words Drills make the student aware of common groups of words that are responsible for many transcription errors — *there-their,* for example.

Language Studies • The Language Studies deal with common Latin and Greek prefixes and suffixes and are an effective device for developing the student's vocabulary.

GRAMMAR CHECKUP

A number of lessons contain drills dealing with common errors in grammar that the unwary stenographer often makes.

TYPING STYLE STUDIES

In the Typing-Style Studies of Volume Two, the student is taught how to handle numbers, quantities, dates, addresses, and times of day. He is also taught how to type correctly titles of books, magazines, booklets, etc., in business letters.

OFFICE-STYLE DICTATION

Beginning with Lesson 41, the student is taught how to handle the problems that he will meet when he takes dictation from a businessman. Each problem is explained and illustrated.

READING AND WRITING PRACTICE

Volume Two contains 59,199 running words of practice material in the form of business letters and interesting, informative articles.

To give the student the dictation "flavor" of many different kinds of business, each chapter is devoted to a specific business or a department of a business.

The authors wish to acknowledge with gratitude the many helpful suggestions they have received from college teachers who have used previous editions of this book. Wherever possible, these suggestions have been adopted.

LOUIS A. LESLIE
CHARLES E. ZOUBEK
RUSSELL J. HOSLER

contents

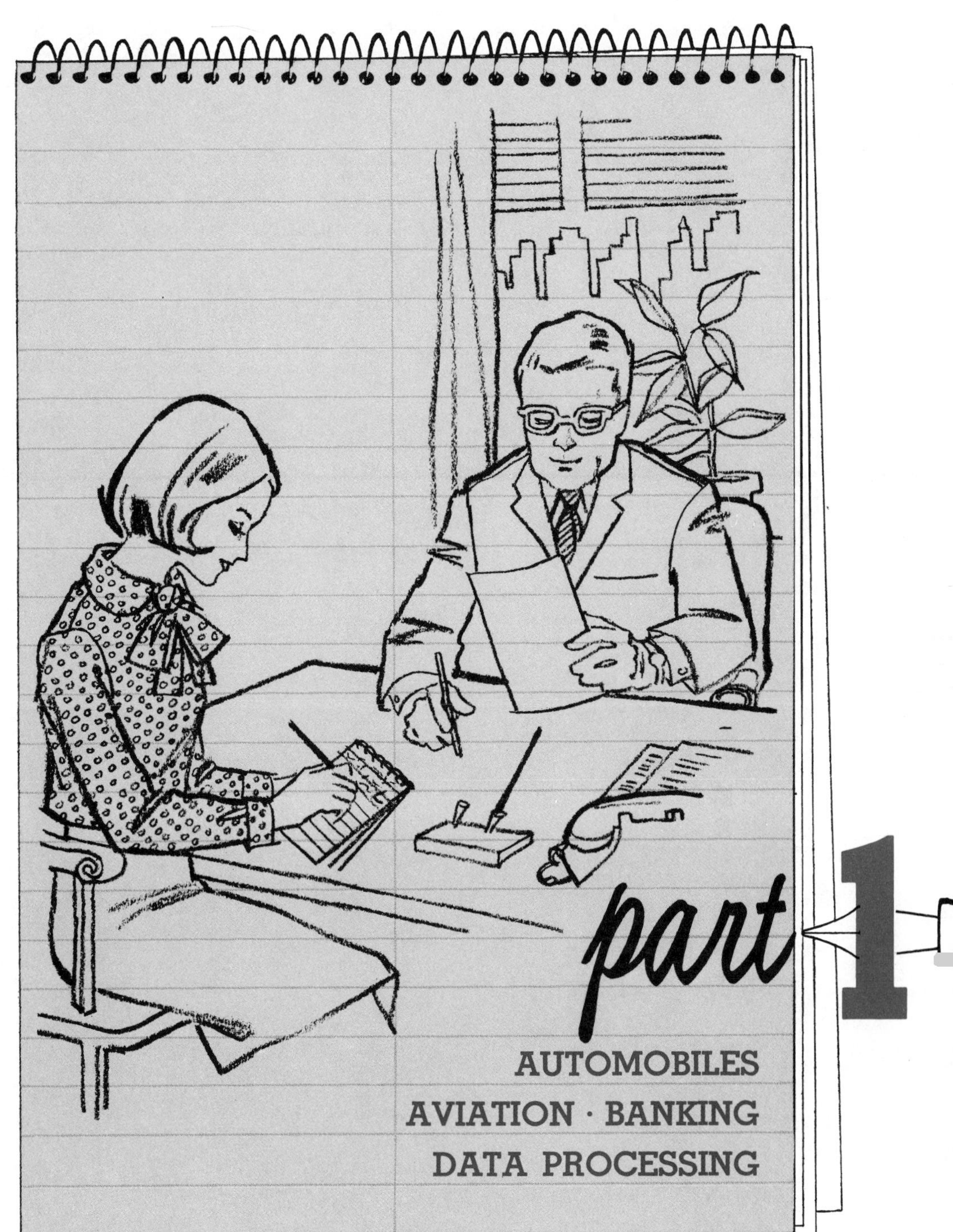

part 1

AUTOMOBILES AVIATION · BANKING DATA PROCESSING

▶ Before you begin the second phase of your shorthand training—speed building—it might be helpful to take inventory of what you have accomplished thus far. Upon your completion of *Gregg Shorthand for Colleges, Diamond Jubilee Series, Volume One,* you made considerable progress toward your goal to become a stenographer and secretary.

▸ You have learned the alphabet of Gregg Shorthand; consequently, you have the means with which to construct an outline for any word in the language.

▸ You have learned many useful abbreviating devices, such as brief forms, word beginnings and endings, and phrases that will help you write more easily and rapidly.

▸ You have improved your command of the nonshorthand elements of transcription – spelling, punctuation, word usage, and grammar.

You now have a firm foundation for your task ahead—developing your ability to take dictation on unfamiliar material rapidly and transcribing accurately on the typewriter. With this foundation, and an efficient practice program, you will experience the thrill of watching your shorthand speed grow and your ability to handle the mechanics of the English language improve almost from day to day!

YOUR PRACTICE PROGRAM

Outside of Class

Your assignments outside of class will consist largely of reading and copying well-written shorthand. This reading and copying will help your shorthand speed develop rapidly. Your work at this stage of your shorthand study should be easy and pleasant, for you have no new shorthand principles or abbreviating devices to learn.

To get the most out of your outside-of-class practice, follow these suggestions:

Read the word and phrase drills that are given at the beginning of each lesson.

Study Building Transcription Skills.

Read and copy the Reading and Writing Practice in this way:

1▸ Always read a letter or article from the shorthand before you copy it. If you cannot immediately read an outline, spell the shorthand characters in it. Usually this spelling will give you the meaning; but if it does not, refer to your Transcript if you have been provided with one. If not, write the shorthand outline you cannot read on a card or slip of paper and find out its meaning in class the next day. *Do not spend more than a few seconds trying to decipher an outline.* At this stage, there will not be many outlines that you cannot read.

2▸ After you have read the material from the shorthand, make a shorthand copy of it.

3▸ If time permits, read what you have written.

YOUR PRACTICE PROGRAM

In Class

In class most of your time will be devoted to taking dictation at constantly increasing speeds. Your instructor will see to it that you get the proper kind of dictation at the proper speeds so that your dictation skill will increase steadily and rapidly.

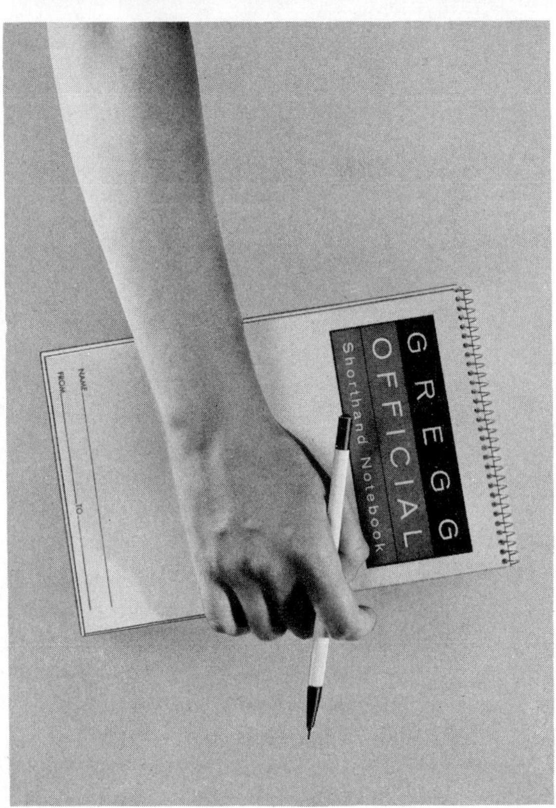

PUNCTUATION BRUSHUP

As you learned in *Gregg Shorthand for Colleges, Diamond Jubilee Series, Volume One,* the competent secretary must be able to do more than take her employer's dictation and read it back. Among other things, she must be able to punctuate correctly if she is to produce letters that her employer will sign.

In Volume One, you studied ten of the most frequent uses of the comma. In Chapter 1 of Volume Two you will "brush up" on these uses of the comma. Then, beginning with Chapter 2, you will be introduced to new and more advanced points of punctuation.

PRACTICE PROCEDURES

To be sure that you derive the greatest benefit from your study of punctuation and spelling in each Reading and Writing Practice, follow these suggestions:

1▸ Read carefully each punctuation rule and the illustrative examples.

2▸ Read the Reading and Writing Practice. Each time you see an encircled punctuation mark, note the reason for its use, which is indicated directly above the encircled mark.

3▸ Make a shorthand copy of the Reading and Writing Practice. As you copy, insert the punctuation marks in your shorthand notes, encircling them as in the textbook.

4▸ When you encounter a shorthand outline printed in color, that indicates the word has been singled out for spelling attention. Finish reading the sentence in which it occurs. Then glance at the left margin of the shorthand, where the word appears in type. Spell the word aloud if possible, pausing slightly after each word division. (The word divisions indicated are those given in *Webster's Seventh New Collegiate Dictionary.*)

In Chapter 1 you will review:

, parenthetical

In order to make his meaning absolutely clear, a writer sometimes inserts a comment or an explanation that could be omitted without changing the meaning of the sentence. These added comments and explanations are called *parenthetical* and are separated from the rest of the sentence by commas.

If the parenthetical word or expression occurs at the beginning or end of a sentence, only one comma is needed.

I want to urge you, however, not to worry.

We shall miss you, of course.

Each time a parenthetical expression occurs in the Reading and Writing Practice, it will be indicated thus in the shorthand:

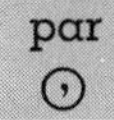

, apposition

Sometimes a writer mentions a person or thing and then, in order to make his meaning perfectly clear to the reader, says the same thing again in different words. This added explanation is known as an expression in *apposition*.

An expression in apposition is set off by two commas, except at the end of a sentence, when only one comma is necessary.

Your secretary, Miss Smith, tells me you are improving.

I met Mr. Smith, president of Smith and Company.

Each time an expression in apposition occurs in the Reading and Writing Practice, it will be indicated thus in the shorthand:

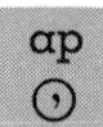

, series

When the last member of a series of three or more items is preceded by *and*, *or*, or *nor*, place a comma before the conjunction as well as between the other items.

Please accept my best wishes for your success, prosperity, and happiness.

I can see him on March 1, on March 18, or on April 10.

Each time a series occurs in the Reading and Writing Practice, it will be indicated thus in the shorthand:

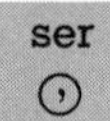

, conjunction

A comma is used to separate two independent clauses that are joined by a conjunction:

> I am proud that you are one of us, and I want you to know that I appreciate your work.

Each time this use of the comma occurs in the Reading and Writing Practice, it will be indicated thus in the shorthand:

, and omitted

When two or more adjectives modify the same noun, they are separated by commas.

> He was a quiet, efficient worker.

However, the comma is not used if the first adjective modifies the combined idea of the second adjective plus the noun.

> She wore a beautiful green dress.

Each time this use of the comma occurs in the Reading and Writing Practice, it will be indicated thus in the shorthand:

Introductory Commas

Introductory commas will be treated under the four headings listed below. Next to each of these headings is the indication that will appear in the Reading and Writing Practice exercises for that use of the comma.

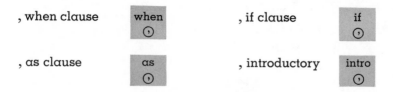

, when clause — when ⊙

, if clause — if ⊙

, as clause — as ⊙

, introductory — intro ⊙

All introductory dependent clauses beginning with words other than *when, as,* and *if* will be classified as ", introductory."

When the original shipment is located, we will make the necessary adjustments.

As you know, we guarantee our cameras for a year.

If you are in urgent need of the notebooks, wire us.

Unless we receive our supplies soon, we shall be in difficulty.

When the main clause comes first, however, no comma is usually necessary between the main clause and the dependent clause.

We shall be in difficulty unless we receive our supplies soon.

Wire us if you are in urgent need of the notebooks.

A comma is also required after introductory words and explanatory expressions such as *frankly, consequently, on the contrary, for instance.*

Frankly, I cannot wait any longer.

On the contrary, you are the one who made the error.

, nonrestrictive

Nonrestrictive clauses and phrases are set off by commas. A nonrestrictive clause or phrase is one that may be omitted without changing the meaning of the sentence. The nonrestrictive clause or phrase might be classified as parenthetical. It is important that you follow the meaning of the dictation in order to be able to identify the restrictive and the nonrestrictive clauses and phrases and to punctuate them correctly.

RESTRICTIVE—NO COMMAS: All persons who are old enough to vote should register.

NONRESTRICTIVE—COMMAS: John Smith, who is old enough to vote, should register.

In the first sentence above, *who are old enough to vote* is a restrictive clause and must *not* be set off by commas. The expression *who are old enough to vote* identifies the persons who should register. In the second sentence, *who is old enough to vote* is a nonrestrictive or descriptive or parenthetical clause that must be set off with commas. It is not needed to identify the particular person who should register; it could be omitted without changing the meaning of the sentence.

Each time the nonrestrictive use of the comma occurs in the Reading and Writing Practice exercise, it will be indicated in the shorthand thus:

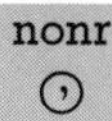

CHAPTER ONE

1

automobiles

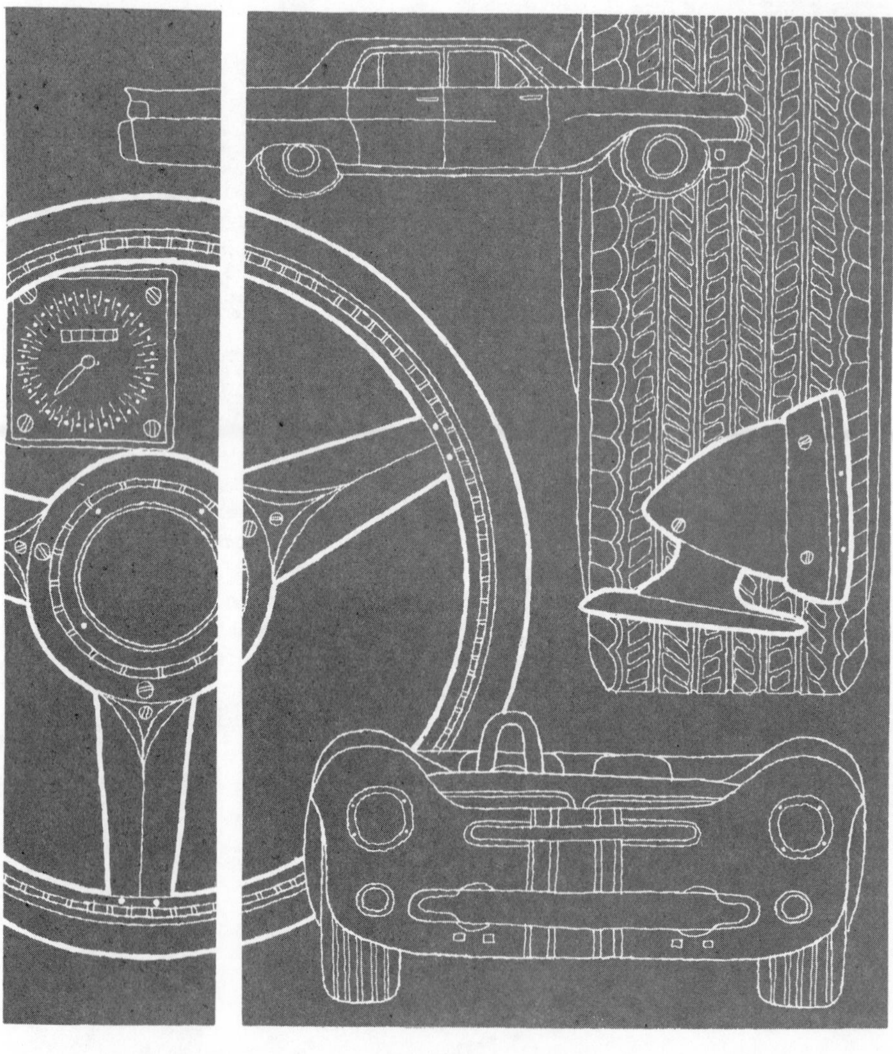

DEVELOPING WORD-BUILDING POWER

1 ▸ Brief Forms and Derivatives • There are 36 brief forms and derivatives in the following chart. You have already read and written these brief forms many times; consequently, you should be able to read these words rapidly. First read each line of brief forms from left to right; then read each line from right to left. Finally, read down each column. Reading Goal: 30 seconds.

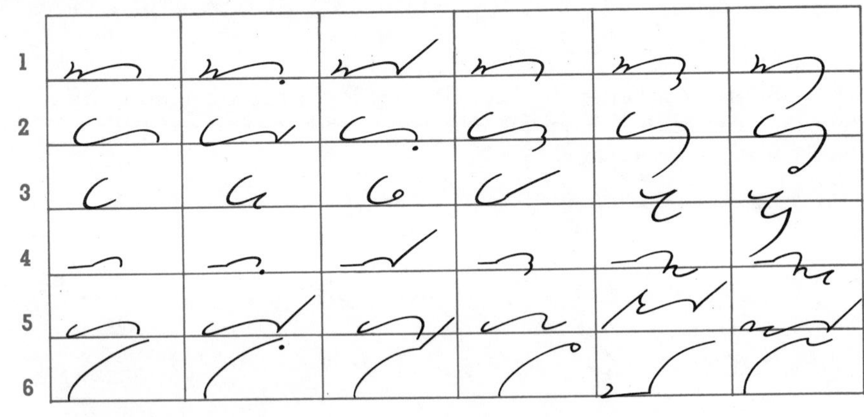

—— ♦ ♦ ——

1 Suggest, suggesting, suggested, suggestion, suggestions, suggestive.
2 Progress, progressed, progressing, progresses, progressive, progressively.
3 Present, presents, presently, presented, represent, representative.
4 Enclose, enclosing, enclosed, encloses, enclosure, enclosures.
5 Organize, organized, organization, organizer, disorganized, unorganized.
6 Time, timing, timed, timely, sometime, timer.

BUILDING TRANSCRIPTION SKILLS

2▸ BUSINESS VOCABULARY BUILDER

The greater command you have of words, the more efficient stenographer or secretary you will be. In the Business Vocabulary Builder that you will find in each lesson, you will continue to build your knowledge and understanding of useful business words and expressions.

Be sure to study each Business Vocabulary Builder before you begin your work on the Reading and Writing Practice in the lesson.

promotion pieces Circulars, booklets, and other printed material designed to build goodwill and increase business for a company.

tentatively Not finally; temporarily.

warranty A document that guarantees the maker's responsibility for the repair or replacement of defective parts of an article.

intervals Spaces of time between events.

READING AND WRITING PRACTICE

3▸ Brief-Form Letter • The following letter contains many brief forms and derivatives. It is ideal for warmup purposes. You can profitably read and copy it many times.

(134)

4

brakes
me·chan·i·cal
re·spon·si·ble

par

if

and o

thor·ough
ad·just
re·plen·ish

ser

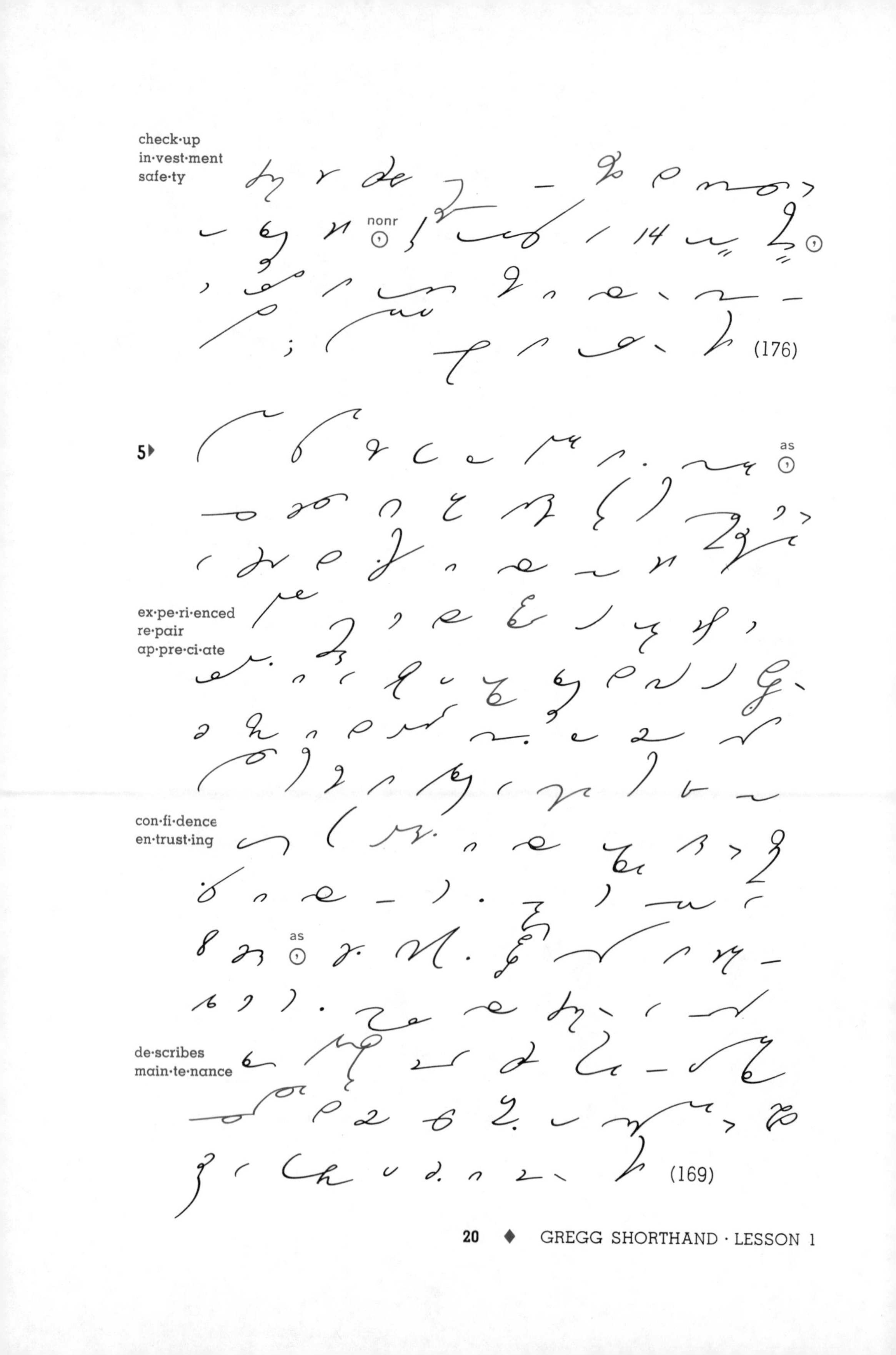

check·up
in·vest·ment
safe·ty

nonr

(176)

5

as

ex·pe·ri·enced
re·pair
ap·pre·ci·ate

con·fi·dence
en·trust·ing

as

de·scribes
main·te·nance

(169)

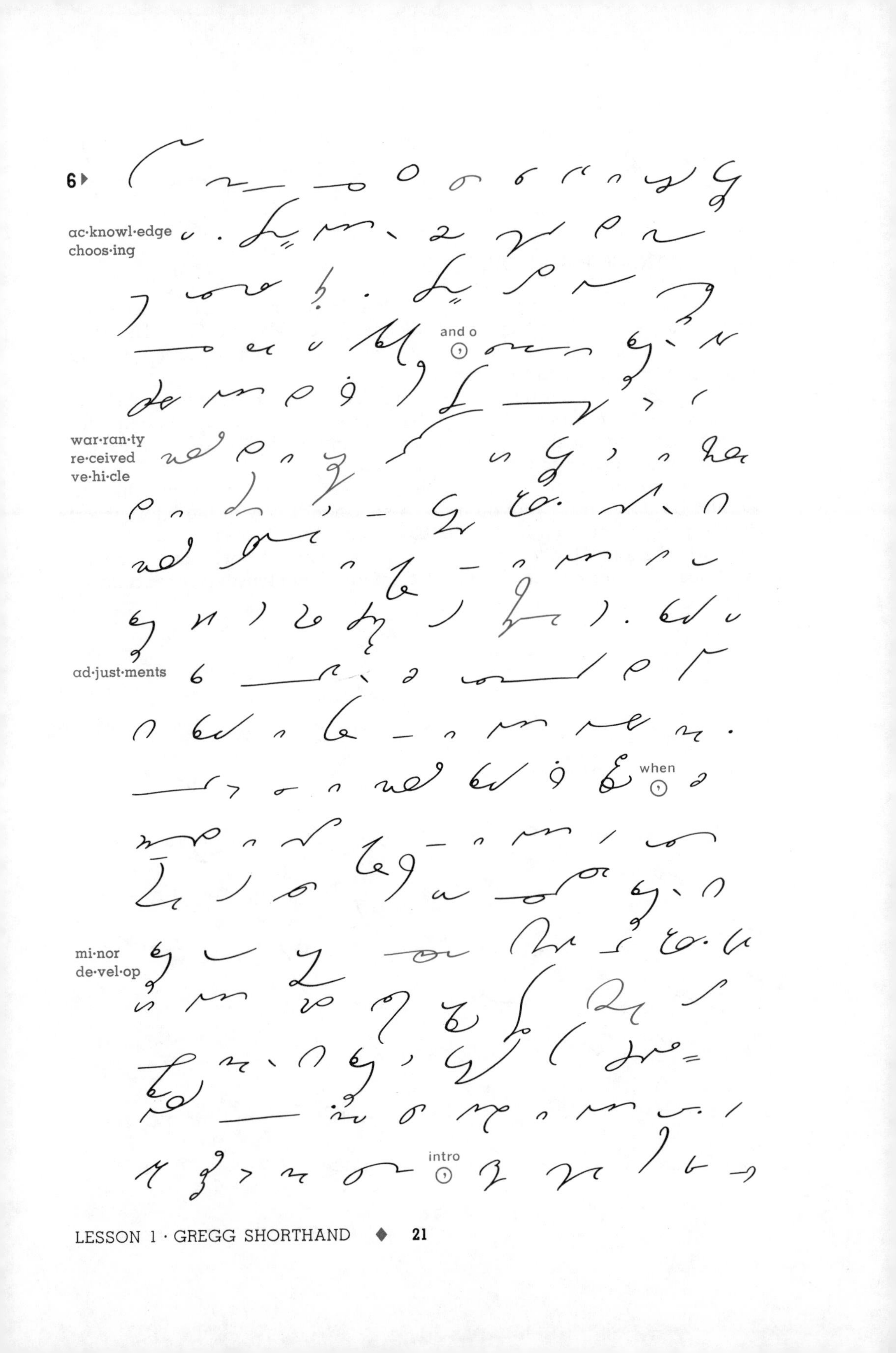

6

ac·knowl·edge
choos·ing

and o

war·ran·ty
re·ceived
ve·hi·cle

ad·just·ments

when

mi·nor
de·vel·op

intro

(221)

7▸ TRANSCRIPTION QUIZ

You are already familiar with the Transcription Quiz from your work with *Gregg Shorthand for Colleges, D.J.S., Volume One.* This quiz gives you an opportunity to see how well you can apply the ten comma rules you have studied thus far.

In Lessons 1 through 10 of Volume Two, the Transcription Quiz will contain the same punctuation problems as those in Volume One. In later lessons, as new points of punctuation are introduced, these quizzes will become more advanced, more challenging.

As you read the Transcription Quiz letter, decide what punctuation should be used. Then, as you make a shorthand copy of the letter, insert the correct punctuation in the proper places in your notes.

In the following letter you will have to supply 5 commas – 1 comma *as* clause, 2 commas conjunction, 1 comma *when* clause, 1 comma apposition.

30

(100)

BUILDING PHRASING SKILL

8 ▸ Useful Business-Letter Phrases

We

1

Who

2

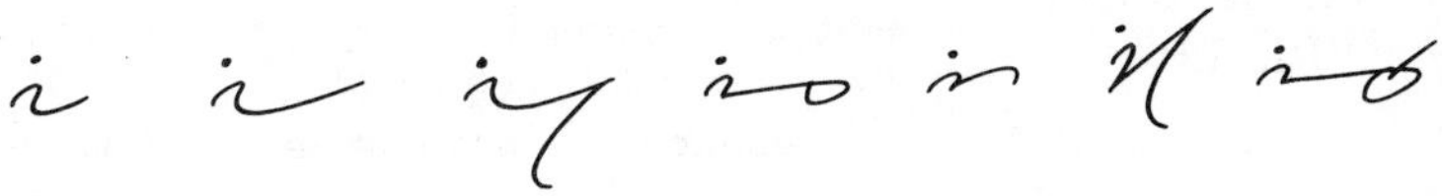

You

3

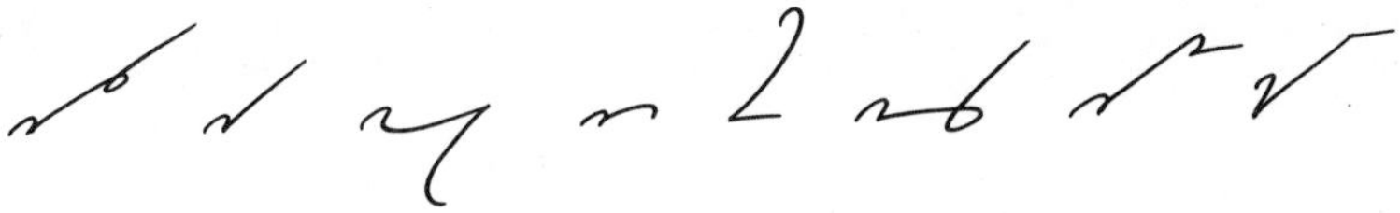

They

4

—— ♦ ♦ ——

1 We are, we will, we can, we may, we should, we have, we did.

2 Who are, who will, who will be, who may, who can, who should be, who might.

3 You did, you would, you will be, you can, you have not, you made, you do not, you should not.

4 They are, they will, they have, they may, they cannot, they would be, they did.

9 ▸ Frequent Names • In the second lesson of each chapter you will find a number of common last names and a number of common men's or women's first names. Read through the list, referring to the key whenever you cannot read a name. Some of these names are used in the Reading and Writing Practice.

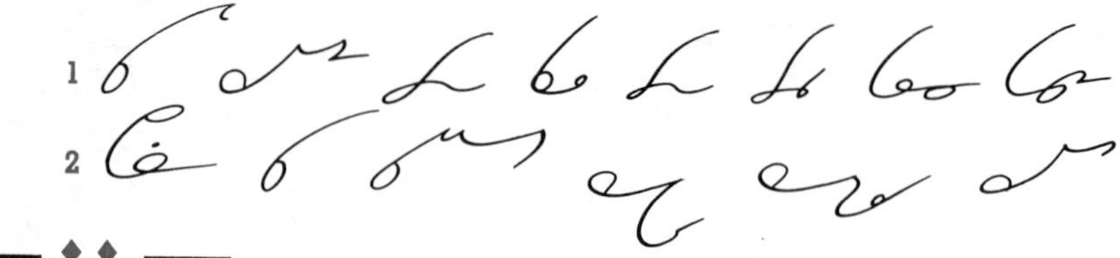

— ♦♦ —

1 Adams, Anderson, Baker, Barry, Becker, Bennett, Brennan, Brown.
2 Abraham, Adam, Adolph, Albert, Alfred, Andrew.

BUILDING TRANSCRIPTION SKILLS

10▸ BUSINESS VOCABULARY BUILDER

treads The top layer of a tire that grips the road.

minimize To keep to the smallest possible number, degree, or extent.

notarized Signed by a public officer who certifies that a document is authentic.

discrepancy A disagreement; a difference.

READING AND WRITING PRACTICE

11▸ Phrase Letter • The following letter is stocked with phrases. You can read and copy it several times with profit.

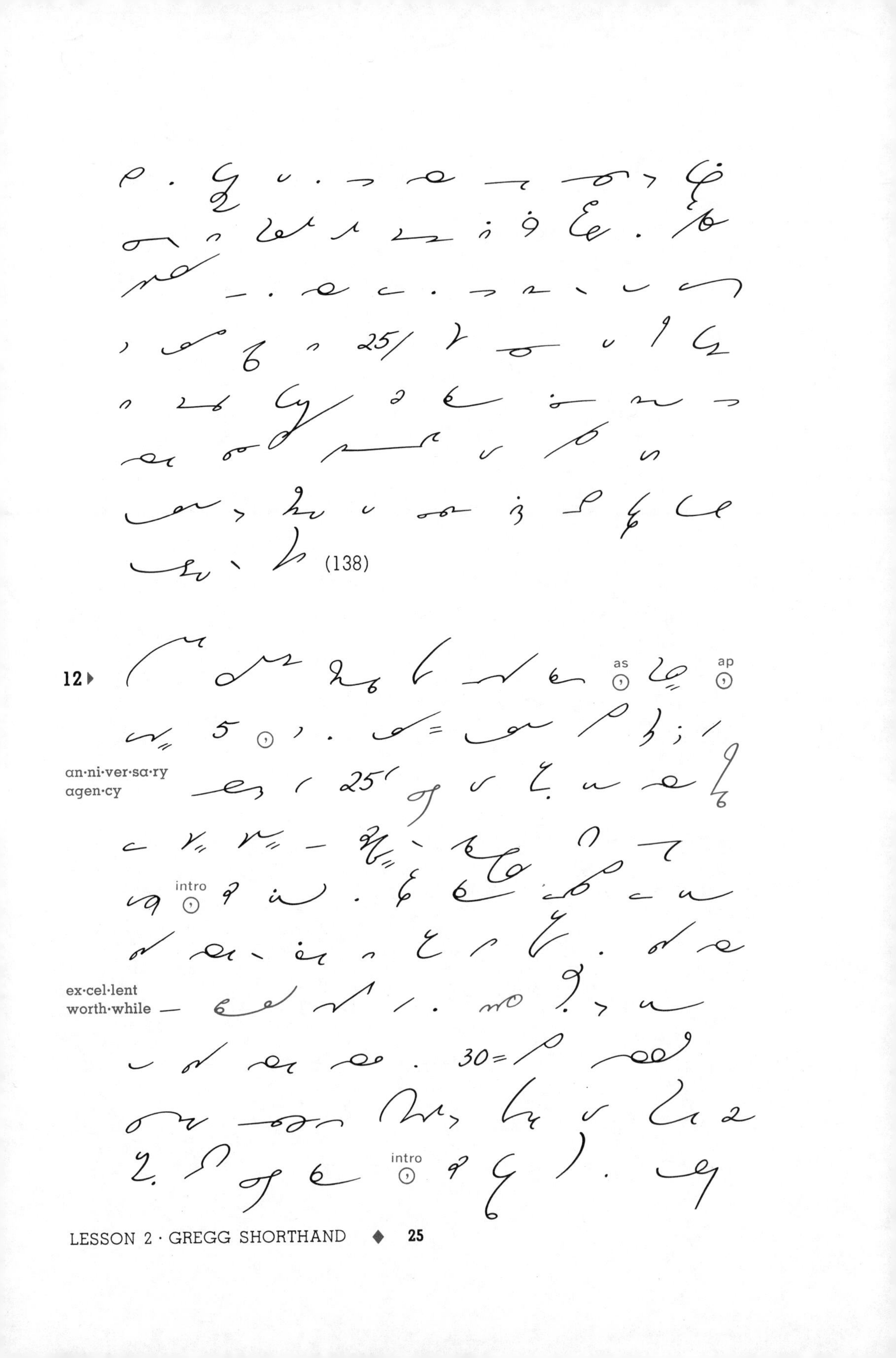

(138)

12 ▸

as

ap

an·ni·ver·sa·ry
agen·cy

intro

ex·cel·lent
worth·while

intro

par

choose
for·ward

(161)

13

ser

skid·ding
trace·able

intro

con·scious
de·pend·able
equipped

par

and o

nonr

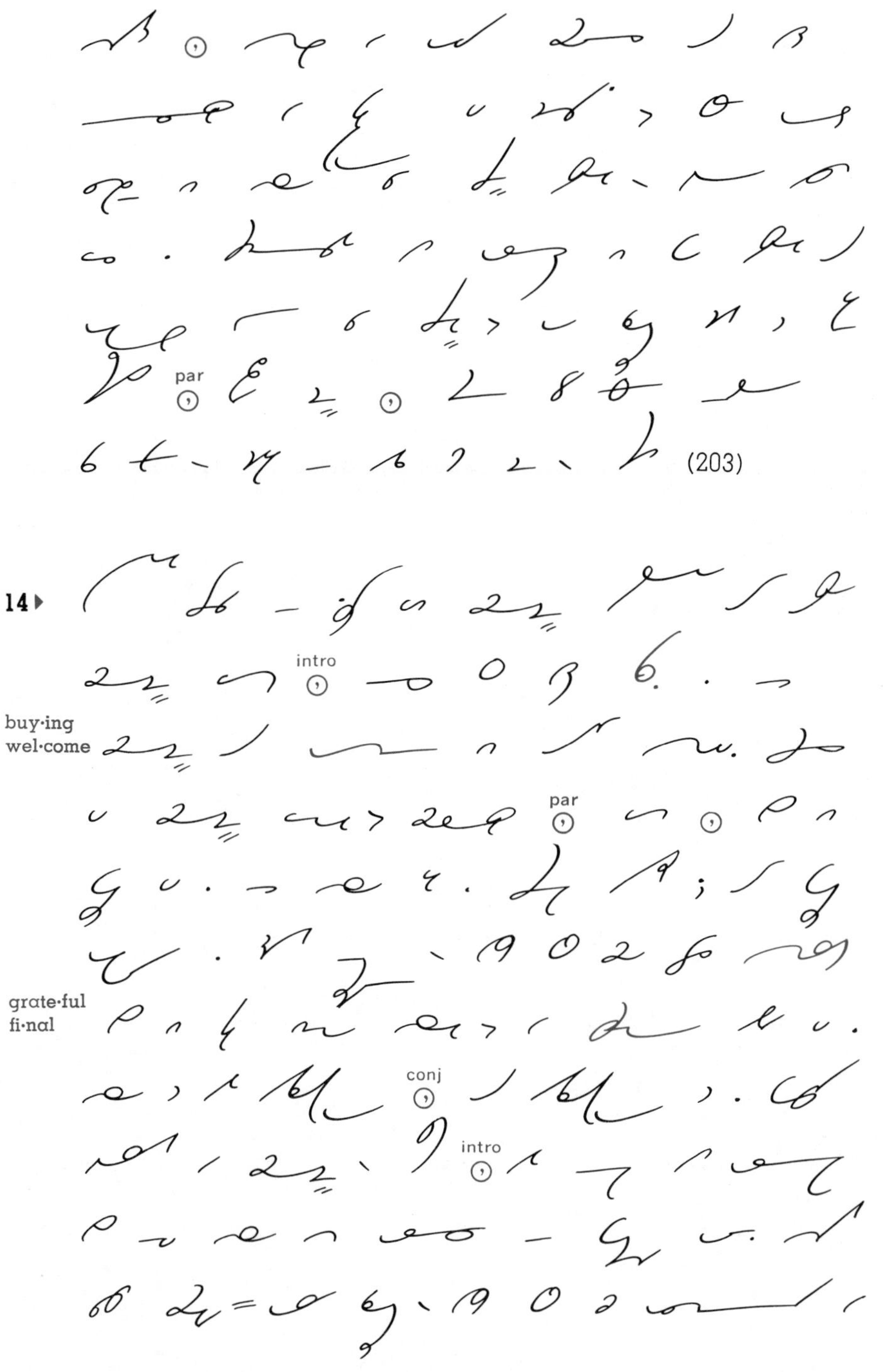
par
(203)
14
intro
buy·ing
wel·come
par
grate·ful
fi·nal
conj
intro

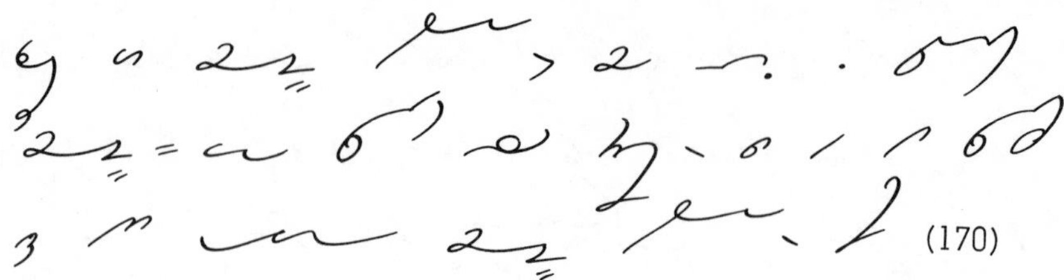

15▸ Transcription Quiz • In this letter there are 5 commas for you to supply—2 commas apposition, 1 comma *when* clause, 1 comma conjunction, 1 comma introductory.

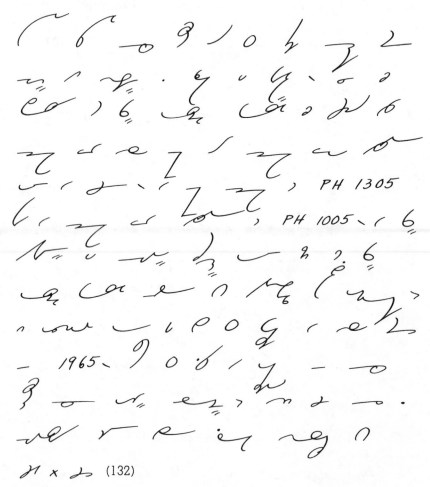

(132)

DEVELOPING WORD-BUILDING POWER

16▸ Word Families • The principle of analogy is of great assistance to the shorthand writer in constructing new outlines. The word families that you will find in the third lesson of each chapter will enable you to take full advantage of this principle.

Read the following Word Families, referring to the key whenever you cannot read an outline.

-er

1

-ection

2

-let

3

-ify

4

Ent-

5

—— ◆◆ ——

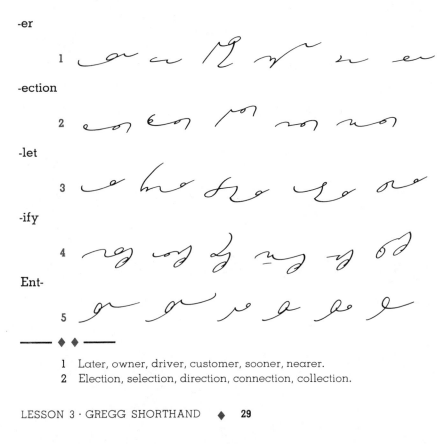

1 Later, owner, driver, customer, sooner, nearer.
2 Election, selection, direction, connection, collection.

3 Let, booklet, pamphlet, leaflet, outlet.
4 Gratify, rectify, verify, qualify, notify, identify.
5 Entitle, entitled, entry, entire, entirely, entail.

BUILDING TRANSCRIPTION SKILLS

17 BUSINESS VOCABULARY BUILDER

personnel The people who work for an organization.
enhances Makes greater in value.
with our compliments Free.
brochures Pamphlets; booklets.

READING AND WRITING PRACTICE

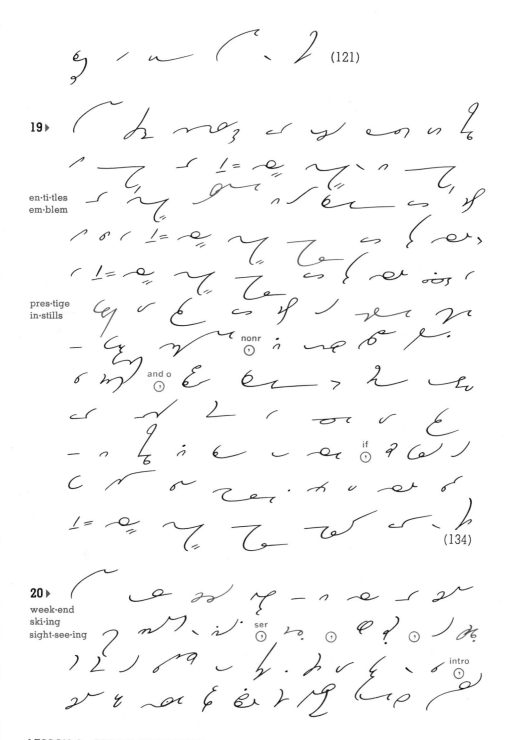

(121)

19

en·ti·tles
em·blem

pres·tige
in·stills

nonr

and o

if

(134)

20

week·end
ski·ing
sight-see·ing

ser

intro

if

me·chan·ics
nec·es·sary

when

brakes
steer·ing
re·act

conj

ser

pail
safe·ty

conj

(222)

21▸

ap

as

lat·er
mod·el

conj

ad·ver·tis·ing
var·i·ous
col·or

ser

if

(147)

22▸ Transcription Quiz • In this letter there are 7 commas for you to supply—1 comma introductory, 4 commas parenthetical, 2 commas apposition.

(153)

▸ *Don't be discouraged if your first invasion of the business world produces only a position that you feel is of a menial nature. No one starts at the top of a ladder. Hard work and an honest interest in your job are still the best aids to success that I know.*—Tom Dodd, New York Regional Director, Manpower, Inc.

DEVELOPING WORD-BUILDING POWER

23▸ Word Beginnings • Can you read this entire list in 45 seconds or less?

Con-

1

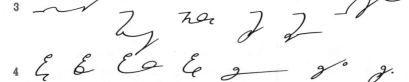

Com-

2

In-

3

Ex-

4

Re-

5

Dis-

6

—— ♦ ♦ ——

1 Consider, convenient-convenience, condition, congratulate, convention, containing, confer.

2 Complete, comfortable, comply, competent, committee, compress.

3 Include, involved, insurance, invite, investment, individual.

4 Expense, expire, explain, express, examine, exceedingly, exciting.

5 Receipt, reside, receive, replacement, repeated, replenish.

6 Discuss, discount, displace, distance, district, dissatisfied.

24▸ Geographical Expressions • Read through this list a number of times, referring to the key whenever you cannot read a geographical expression.

1 Stamford, Hartford, Bradford, Cranford, Bedford, Oxford.

2 Maine, New Hampshire, Virginia, Massachusetts, Connecticut, Rhode Island, New Jersey, New York.

3 United States, United States of America, England, Canada, Mexico, Guam, Hawaii.

BUILDING TRANSCRIPTION SKILLS

25▸ BUSINESS VOCABULARY BUILDER

minor Of lesser importance. (Do not confuse "minor" with "miner," a person who works in a mine.)

lubrication The act of applying oil and grease to parts of a car.

limousines Large luxurious cars, often driven by chauffeurs.

READING AND WRITING PRACTICE

26▸

its
ed·u·ca·tion
dis·cussed

intro

fac·ul·ty
com·mit·tee

when

guid·ance
as·sis·tance

(144)

27▸

intro

ap

mi·nor
trans·mis·sion

par

and o

as

be·gin·ning
sea·son

par

if

per·cent
of·fer·ing
lu·bri·ca·tion

ser

(161)

28

par

op·er·at·ing
main·te·nance

intro

nonr

for·ward
op·por·tu·ni·ties

(183)

29▸

Con·nect·i·cut
com·ing

nonr

fleet
lim·ou·sines

24

conj

sight-see·ing
chauf·feurs

and o

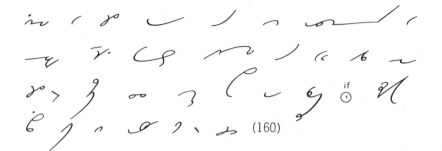

if

(160)

30▸ Transcription Quiz • In the following letter you must supply 5 commas to punctuate it correctly—1 comma conjunction, 1 comma introductory, 2 commas parenthetical, 1 comma *as* clause.

(133)

DEVELOPING WORD-BUILDING POWER

31 ▸ Shorthand Vocabulary Builder

Oi

1

Ow

2

I

3

U

4

—— ♦♦ ——

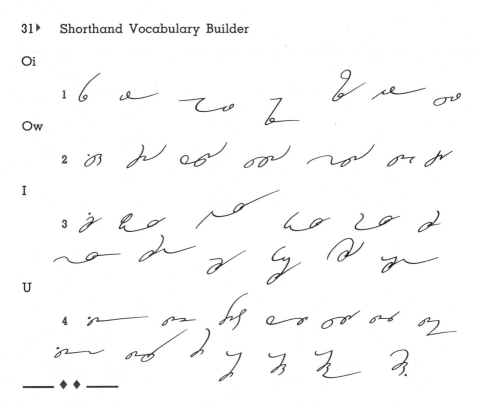

1 Boy, oil, employ, enjoyment, avoid, toil, annoy.

2 House, found, around, account, ground, ounce, shout.

3 White, isolate, delighted, polite, flight, fine, climb, vital, inside, provide, defined, recital.

4 Human, union, beautiful, argue, acute, unit, uniform, humor, united, view, review, refuse, refusal, confusing.

BUILDING TRANSCRIPTION SKILLS

32 ▸ **BUSINESS VOCABULARY BUILDER**

chores Daily or routine jobs of a household or farm.
dominion Absolute authority.
supremacy Complete authority or power.
laborious Involving hard work or effort.

READING AND WRITING PRACTICE

33 ▸ **The Boy Who Put the World on Wheels**

conj

intro

intro

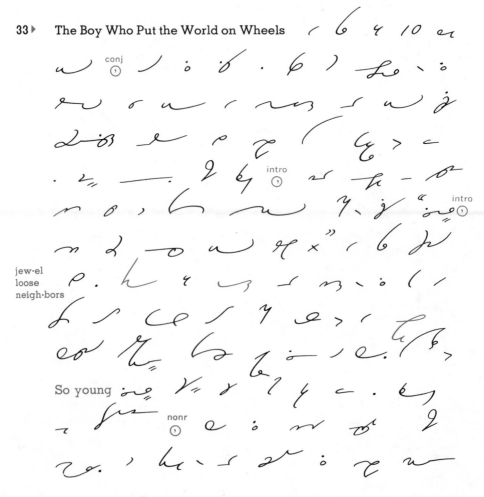

jew·el
loose
neigh·bors

So young

nonr

shin·gle
knit·ting

and o

conj

when

In 1896,

par

al·leys
cyl·in·ders

par

mu·se·um
piece

conj

de·scen·dants

(312)

34 ▸ The Automobile

do·min·ion
hu·man·i·ty

conj

bridged
ig·no·rant

ser

sti·fling
steel

re·union
su·prem·a·cy

nonr

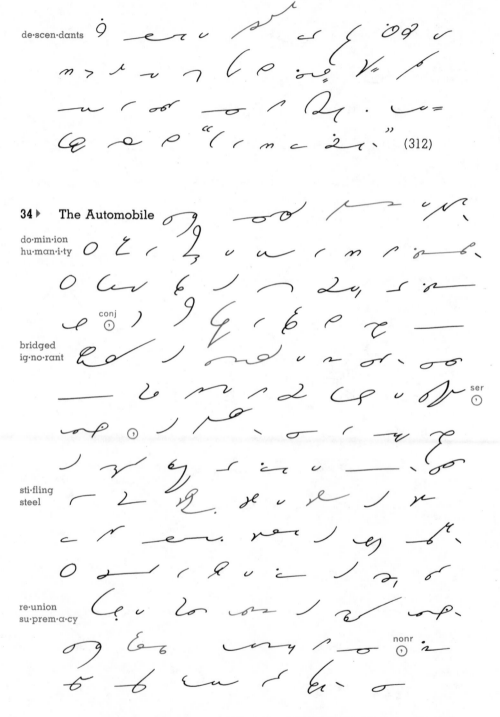

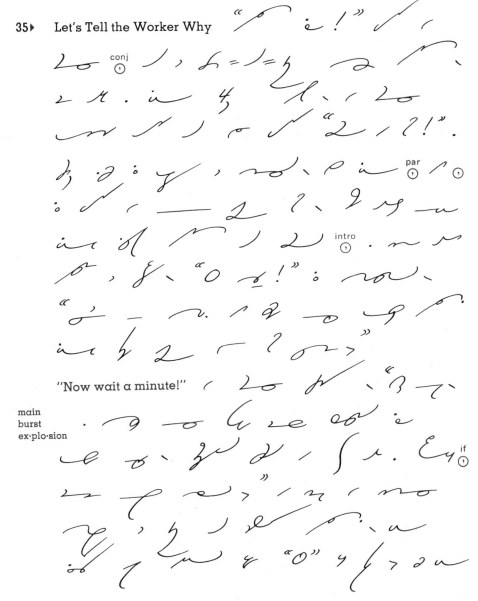

—*John O. Munn* (146)

35▸ Let's Tell the Worker Why

conj

par

intro

"Now wait a minute!"

main
burst
ex·plo·sion

if

ser

gov·ern·ment em·ploy·ee

conj

Recently

ser

and o

REVIEW TIP

Beginning on page 503 you will find complete lists of the word beginnings and endings, phrases, and brief forms of Gregg Shorthand.

You are already familiar with the words and phrases in those lists; but to be sure that they do not become hazy in your mind, you should review them frequently.

Consequently, plan to set aside a few minutes each day to read from those lists. Time spent on those lists will be time well spent.

After you have read all the lists from left to right, read them again from right to left.

At this stage of your shorthand course, you should be able to read the lists very rapidly.

CHAPTER TWO

aviation

DEVELOPING WORD-BUILDING POWER

36 ▸ **Brief Forms and Derivatives** • Can you read these brief forms and derivatives in 40 seconds or less?

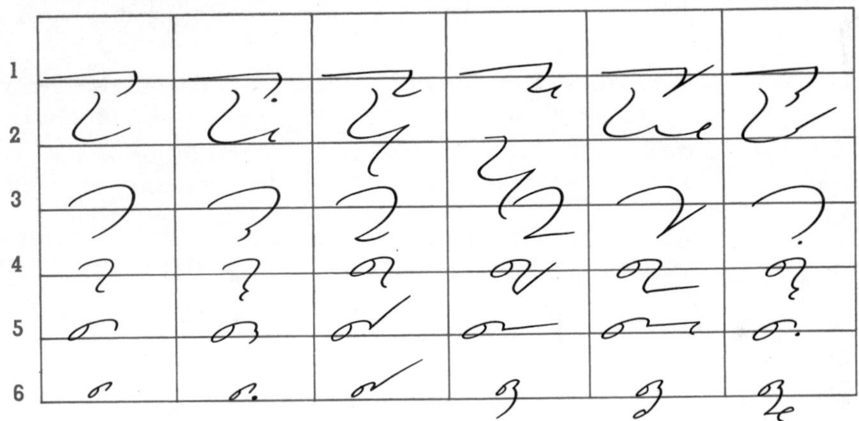

1 Manufacture, manufacturing, manufacturer, manufacturers, manufactured, manufactures.

2 Value, values, valuable, invaluable, valueless, valued.

3 Govern, governs, governor, government, governed, governing.

4 Company, companies, accompany, accompanied, accompaniment, accompanies.

5 Acknowledge, acknowledges, acknowledged, acknowledgment, acknowledgments, acknowledging.

6 Use, using, used, useful, usefully, usefulness.

37 ▸ PUNCTUATION PRACTICE . courteous request

Very often one businessman may wish to persuade another to take some definite action. He could make his request for action with a direct statement, such as:

I wish to hear from you by return mail.

A direct statement of this type, however, might antagonize the reader. Many businessmen, therefore, prefer to make such a request in the form of a question.

May I hear from you by return mail.

Where a request for definite action is put in the form of a question, a period is used at the end of the sentence.

This is the way you can decide whether to use a question mark or a period:

1 If the question calls for an answer in the form of action, use a period.
2 If the question calls for an answer in words, use a question mark.

cr ⊙ Whenever the period is used in this situation in the Reading and Writing Practice, it will be indicated in the shorthand as shown in the left margin.

38 ▸ BUSINESS VOCABULARY BUILDER

suspend To stop temporarily.
accommodate To take care of.
comprehensive Covering completely.

READING AND WRITING PRACTICE

39 ▸ Brief-Form Letter • The following letter contains many brief forms and derivatives. You can profitably read and copy it several times.

(161)

40

ap

18

tem·po·rar·i·ly
re·ceived

and o

per·mis·sion
per·son·nel

intro

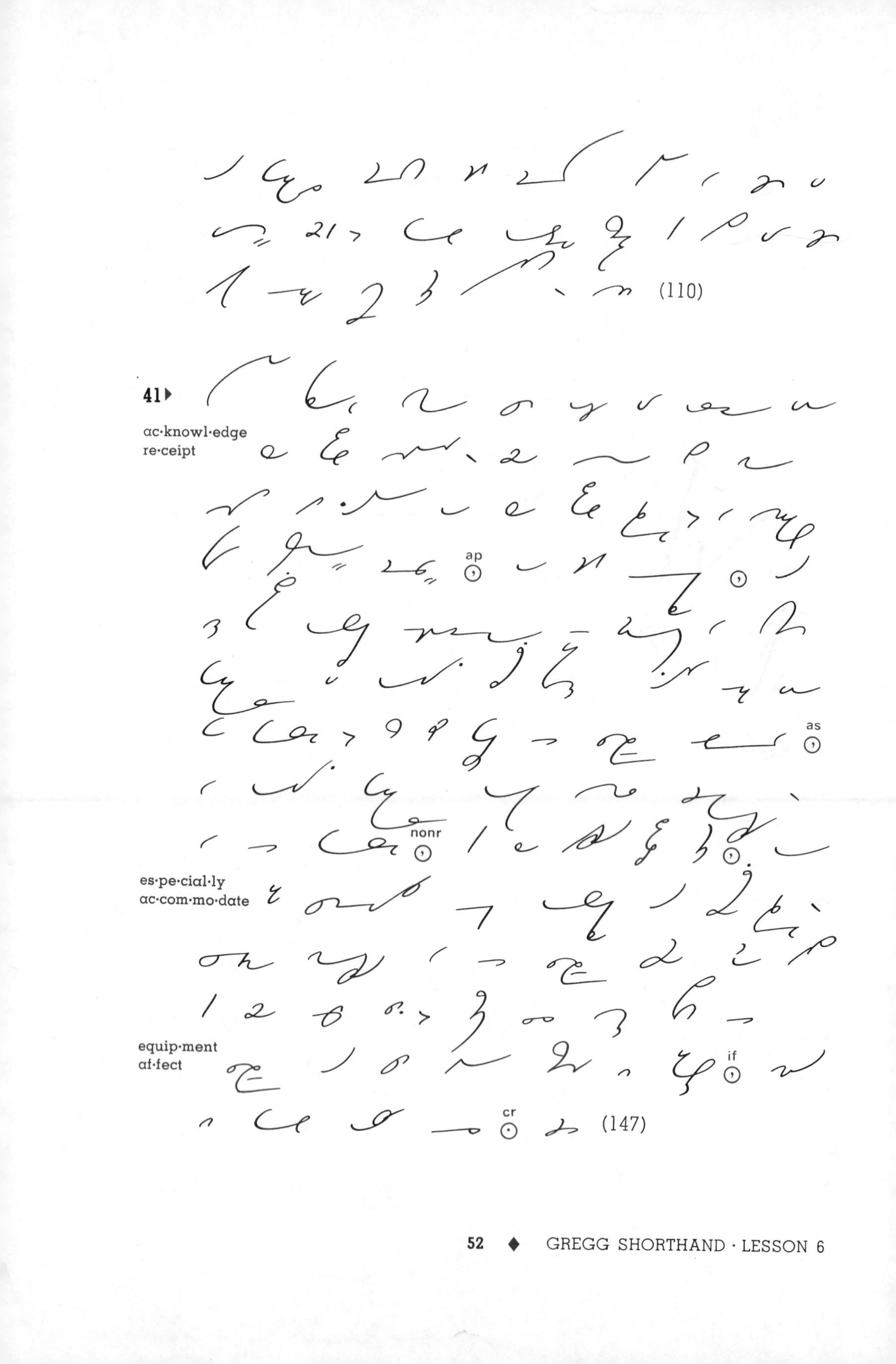

(110)

41

ac·knowl·edge
re·ceipt

ap

es·pe·cial·ly
ac·com·mo·date

as

nonr

equip·ment
af·fect

if

cr

(147)

42 ▸

Di·rec·to·ry
Man·u·al
al·ready

conj

ser

of·fered
fre·quen·cies

par

as

if

cr

(175)

43 ▸ Transcription Quiz • For you to supply: 7 commas—1 comma conjunction, 3 commas apposition, 1 comma *when* clause, 2 commas parenthetical.

9:30

21

(186)

▸ *The girl who stands out head and shoulders above the drones is the one who shows that she can assume responsibility — that she can think for herself and that she possesses the initiative to work out problems on her own.*

BUILDING PHRASING SKILL

44 ▸ Useful Business-Letter Phrases • There are 39 phrases in the following list. Can you read them in 30 seconds?

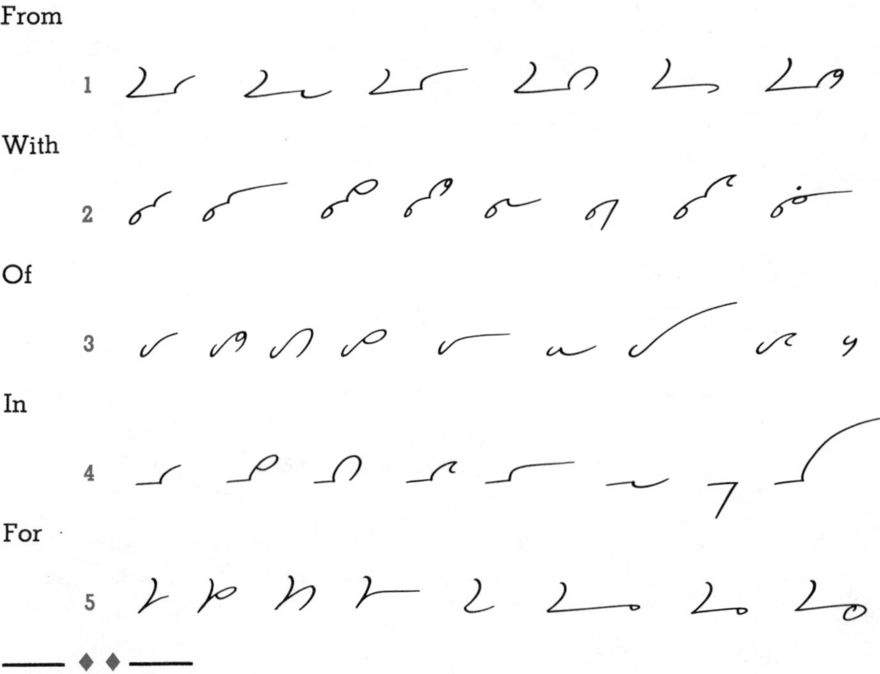

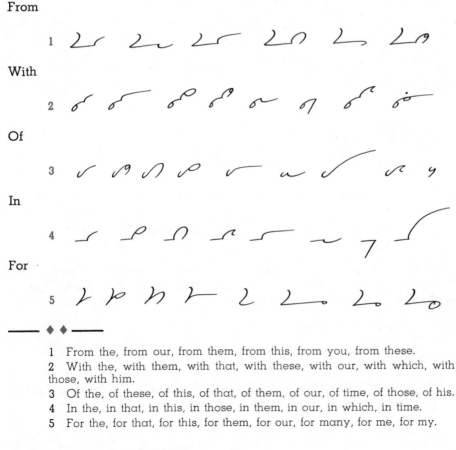

1 From the, from our, from them, from this, from you, from these.

2 With the, with them, with that, with these, with our, with which, with those, with him.

3 Of the, of these, of this, of that, of them, of our, of time, of those, of his.

4 In the, in that, in this, in those, in them, in our, in which, in time.

5 For the, for that, for this, for them, for our, for many, for me, for my.

45 ▸ Frequent Names

— ♦♦ —

1 Burke, Callahan, Cameron, Campbell, Carroll.
2 Adeline, Agnes, Amelia, Annabell, Augusta, Barbara.

BUILDING TRANSCRIPTION SKILLS

46 ▸ PUNCTUATION PRACTICE , introducing short quote

Short quotations are introduced by a comma.

The professor said, "The class will start promptly at nine o'clock."
He replied, "I cannot stay any longer."

isq (,) Each time this use of the comma occurs in the Reading and Writing Practice, it will be indicated in the shorthand as shown in the left margin.

, inside quote

. inside quote

The comma and period are *always* typed inside the final quotation mark.

Mr. Jones said, "You should report for work tomorrow morning."
The booklet, "Ten Ways to Reduce," is out of stock.

iq (,) iq (.) When a comma or period is placed inside quotation marks in the Reading and Writing Practice, it will be indicated in the shorthand as shown in the left margin.

? inside quote

Question marks are placed inside or outside the final quotation marks according to the sense of the sentence.

She said, "Are you going swimming tonight?"

BUT

Did Mr. Allen really say, "This report must be on my desk by four o'clock"?

iq (?) Whenever a question mark is placed inside quotation marks in the Reading and Writing Practice, it will be indicated in the shorthand as shown in the left margin.

47 ▸ **BUSINESS VOCABULARY BUILDER**

substantial Large.
centralized (adjective) All in one place.
resume To start again.

READING AND WRITING PRACTICE

48 ▸ Phrase Letter

(120)

49▸

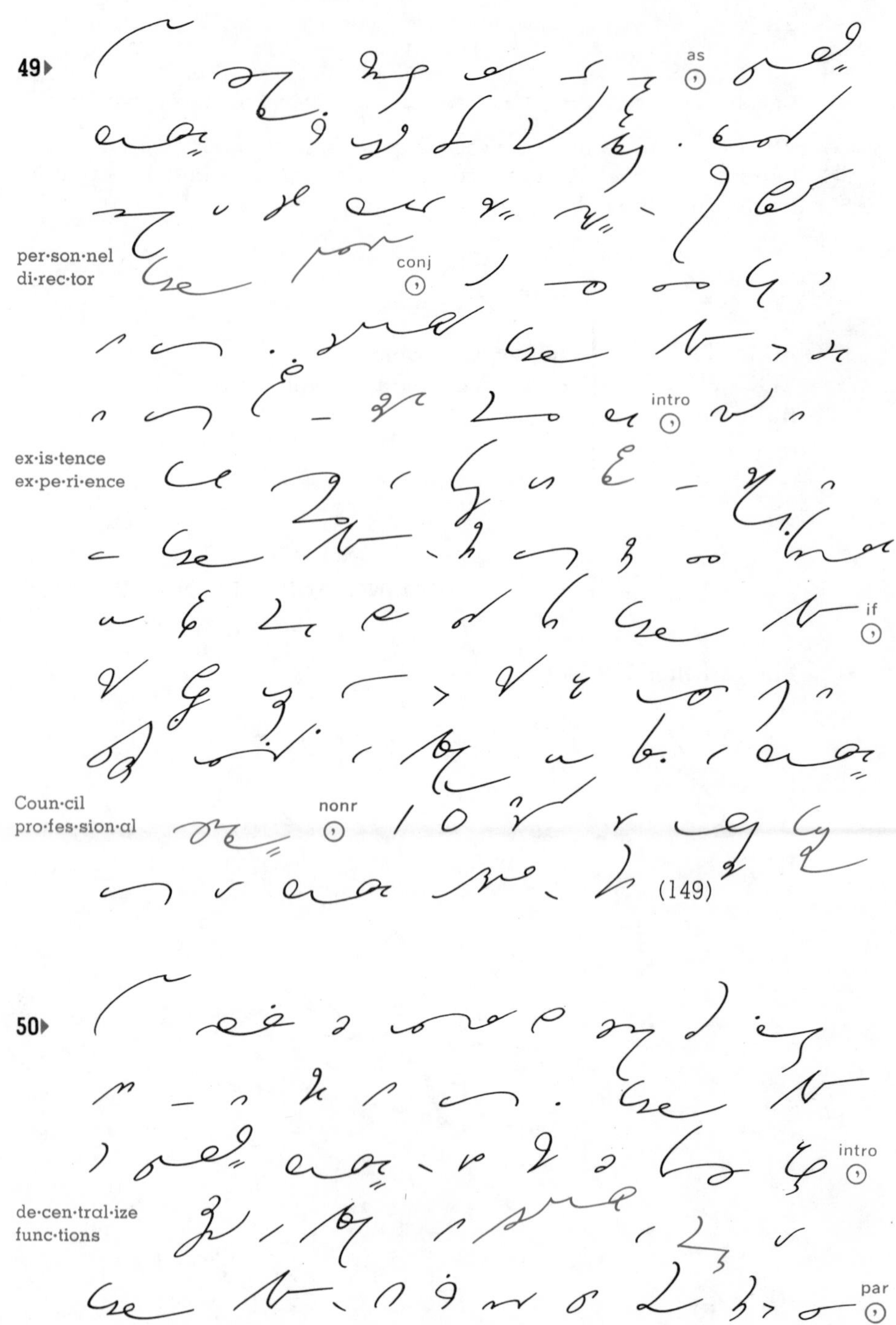
as
per·son·nel
di·rec·tor
conj
intro
ex·is·tence
ex·pe·ri·ence
if
Coun·cil
pro·fes·sion·al
nonr
(149)
intro
de·cen·tral·ize
func·tions
par

50▸

ser

when isq

pres·i·dent
urge

iq

conj

(150)

51 when

ti·tle
Fed·er·al

intro

Aero·nau·tics
re·ceive

isq

if

iq

rec·og·nize
ex·ceed·ing·ly

and o

par

(150)

52▸ Transcription Quiz • For you to supply: 7 commas—1 comma nonrestrictive, 1 comma introductory, 2 commas series, 2 commas apposition, 1 comma *if* clause.

(160)

DEVELOPING WORD-BUILDING POWER

53 ▸ Word Families

-port

1

-serve

2

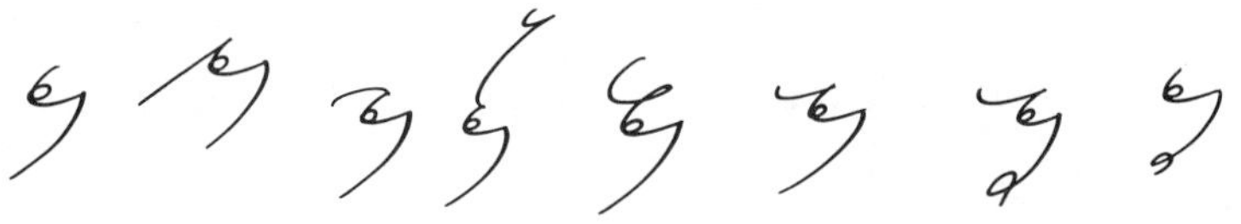

-form

3

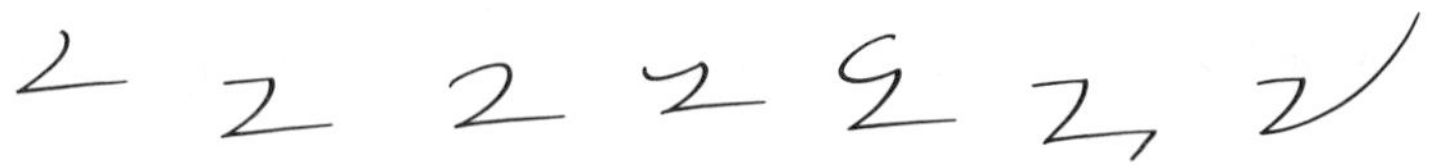

-sure

4

-sult

5

1 Airport, support, report, Westport, import, export, purport, deport, reporter.

2 Serve, deserve, conserve, observe, preserve, reserve, reservation, service.

3 Form, inform, conform, reform, perform, information, informed.

4 Sure, assure, insure, pleasure, measure, immeasurable, reassure.

5 Insult, result, consult, consulted, consultation, consults, consultant.

54▸ PUNCTUATION PRACTICE hyphens

Hyphenated before noun

No noun, no hyphen

No hyphen after *ly*

You can quickly decide whether to use a hyphen in compound expressions like *past due* or *well trained* by observing these rules:

1 If a noun follows the expression, use a hyphen.

We are concerned about your past-due account (noun).
Our well-trained representative (noun) will call on you.

Whenever a hyphenated expression occurs in the Reading and Writing Practice, it will be called to your attention in the margin thus:

past-due
hyphenated
before noun

2 If *no* noun follows the compound expression, do *not* use a hyphen.

Your account is past due.
Our representative is well trained.

Occasionally, these expressions in which a hyphen is not used will be called to your attention the Reading and Writing Practice thus:

well trained
no noun,
no hyphen

3 No hyphen is used in a compound modifier where the first part of the expression is an adverb that ends in *ly.*

He was editor of a widely read magazine.

To be sure that you are not tempted to put a hyphen in expressions of this type, we will occasionally call attention to them in the Reading and Writing Practice thus:

widely read
no hyphen
after *ly*

55▸ BUSINESS VOCABULARY BUILDER

capacity The amount that can be held or accommodated.

immeasurably Incapable of being measured; greatly.

READING AND WRITING PRACTICE

56▸

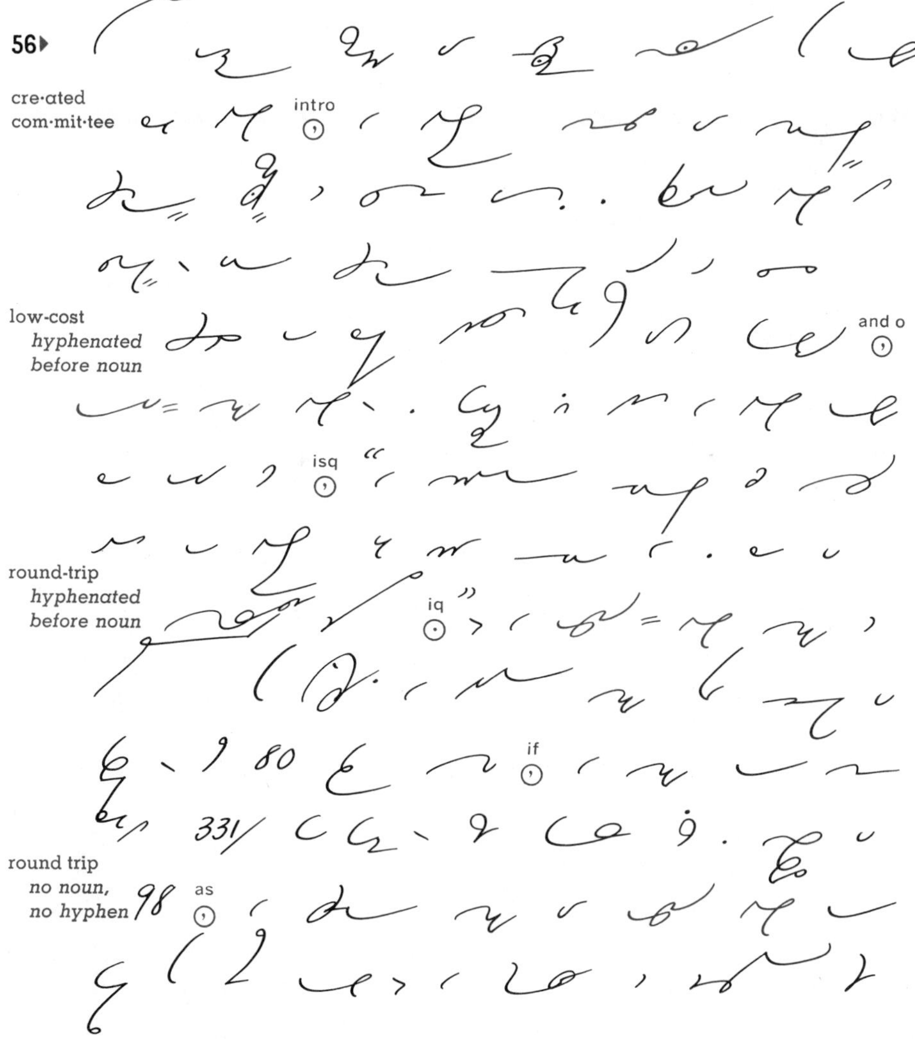

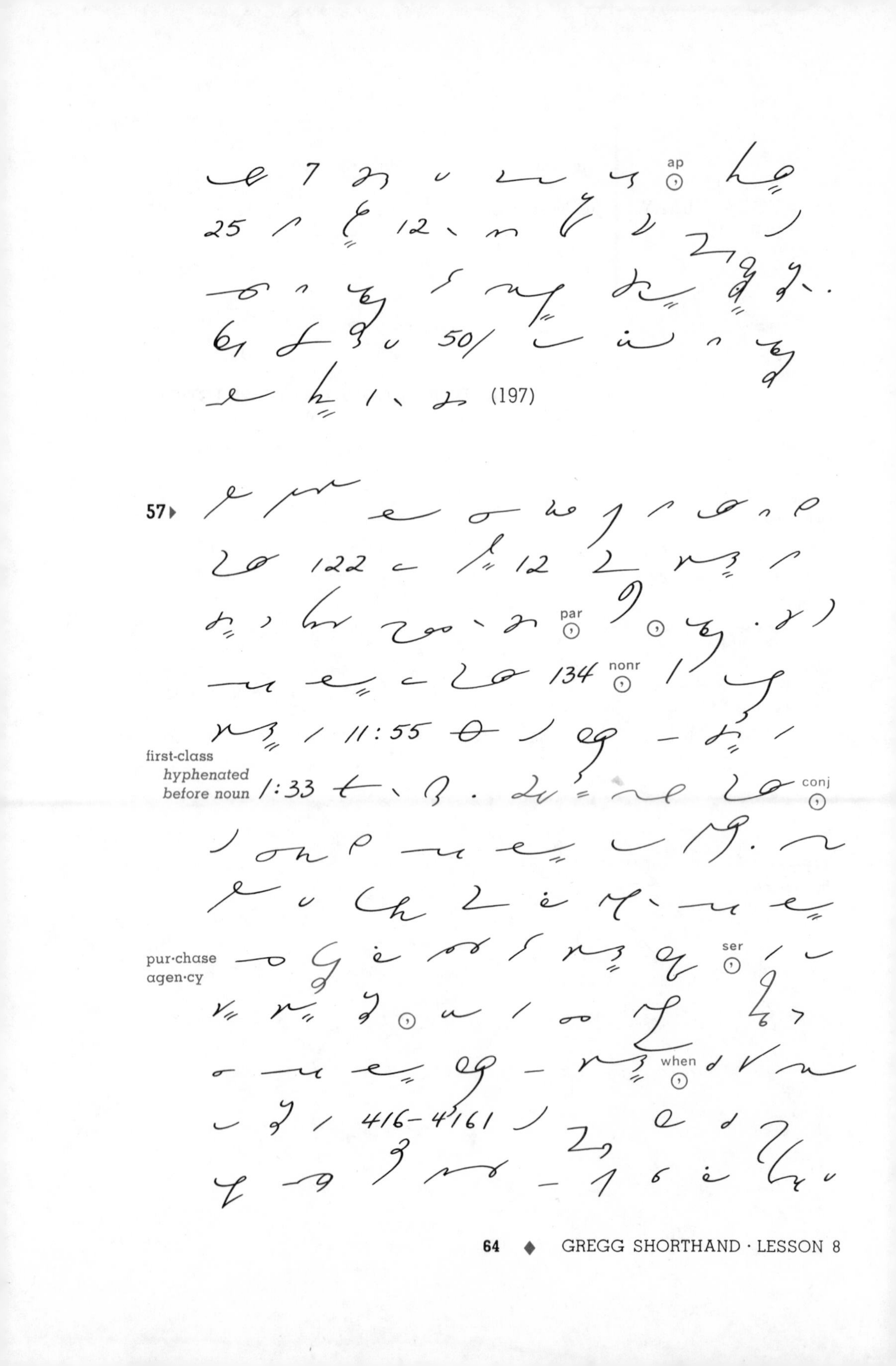

ap

25 12

50

(197)

57▸ 122 12

par

134 nonr

11:55

first-class *hyphenated before noun* 1:33

conj

pur·chase

agen·cy

ser

when

416-4161

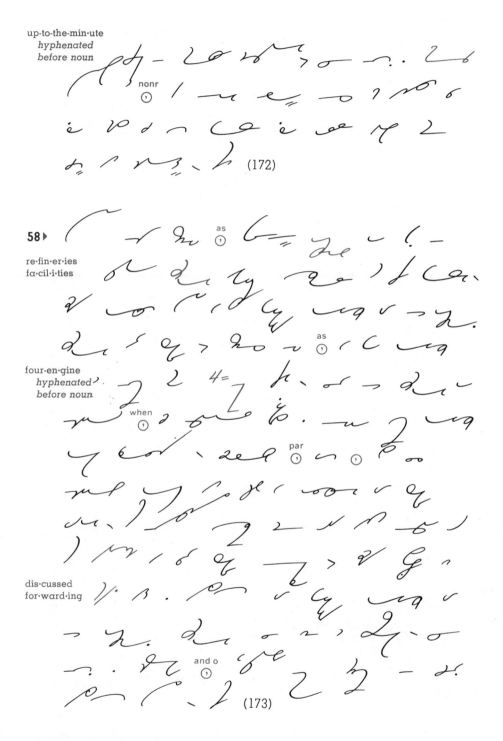

up-to-the-min·ute
hyphenated before noun

nonr

(172)

58 ▸

re·fin·er·ies
fa·cil·i·ties

as

as

four-en·gine
hyphenated before noun

4=

when

par

dis·cussed
for·ward·ing

and o

(173)

59▸ Transcription Quiz • For you to supply: 6 commas—3 commas introductory, 2 commas apposition, 1 comma *if* clause.

(159)

▸ *When you can't say anything nice about another person, you will be wise to follow the example of Calvin Coolidge, who said, "I have never been hurt by anything I didn't say."*

DEVELOPING WORD-BUILDING POWER

60 ▸ Word Endings

-tion

1

-ment

2

-ly

3

-ure

4

-ual

5

—— ◆◆ ——

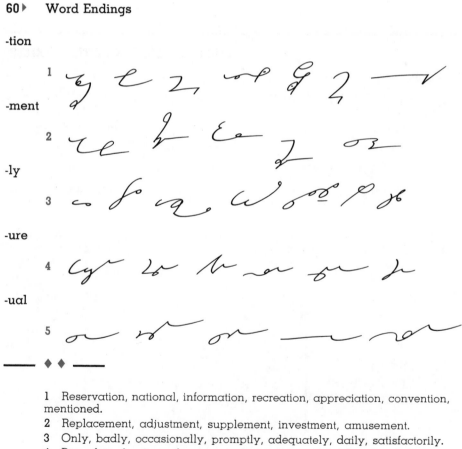

1 Reservation, national, information, recreation, appreciation, convention, mentioned.
2 Replacement, adjustment, supplement, investment, amusement.
3 Only, badly, occasionally, promptly, adequately, daily, satisfactorily.
4 Procedure, furniture, departure, creature, natural, feature.
5 Annual, schedule, actual, manual, gradual.

61 ▸ Geographical Expressions

1 Bloomfield, Greenfield, Westfield, Winfield, Deerfield, Plainfield.

2 Pennsylvania, Maryland, Virginia, West Virginia, North Carolina, South Carolina, Georgia, Florida.

3 Argentina, Australia, Belgium, Bolivia, Brazil.

BUILDING TRANSCRIPTION SKILLS

62 ▸ PUNCTUATION PRACTICE ; no conjunction

A semicolon is used to separate two independent, but closely related, clauses when no conjunction is used to connect the clauses.

I should like to stay; he wants to leave.

The above sentence could be written as two sentences, with a period after *stay*. However, because the two thoughts are closely related, the use of the semicolon seems more appropriate.

nc (;) Each time this use of the semicolon occurs in the Reading and Writing Practice, it will be indicated in the shorthand as shown in the left margin.

63 ▸ BUSINESS VOCABULARY BUILDER

custody Keeping.

roster A roll or list of names.

via By way of.

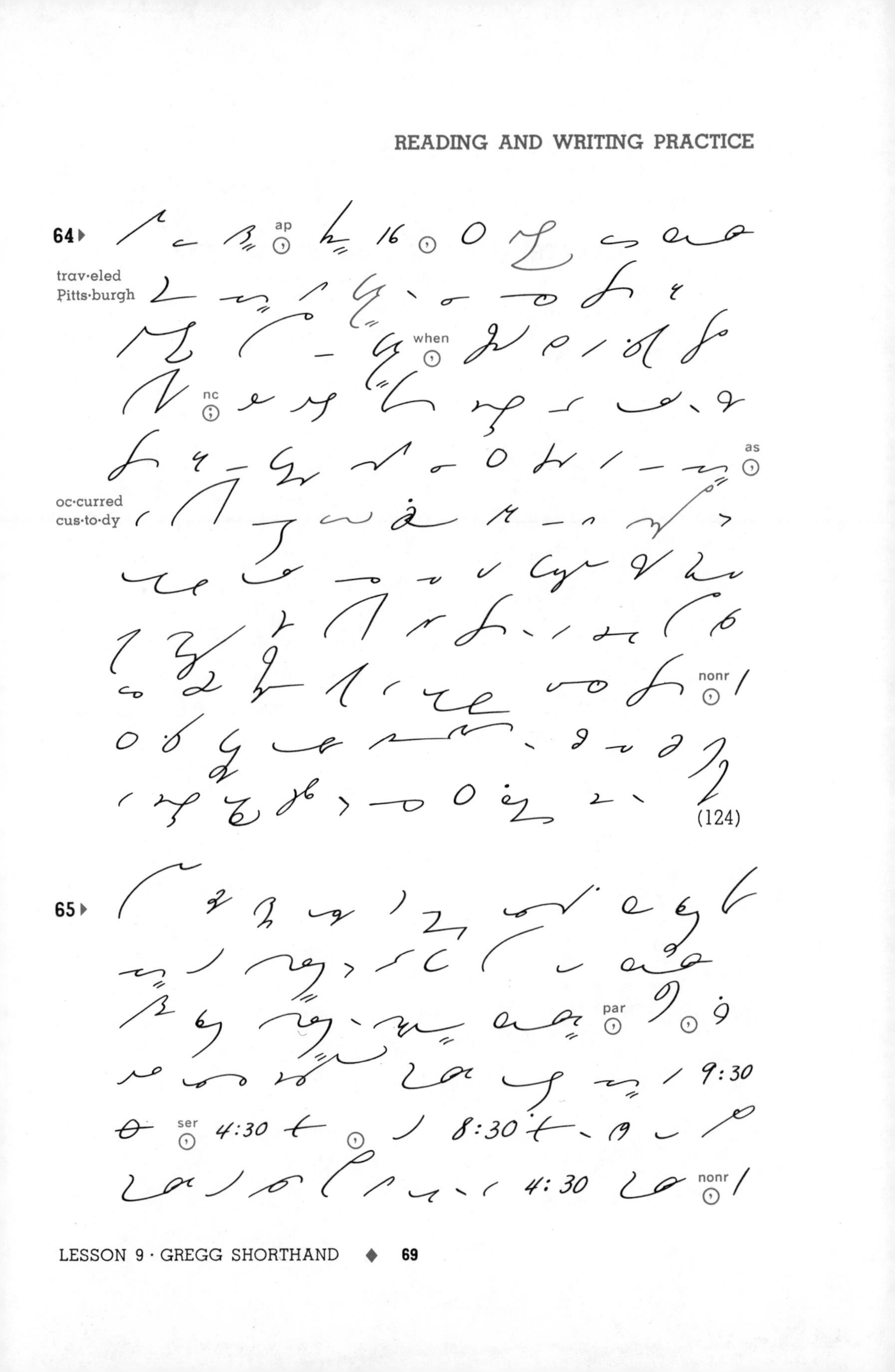

64 ap when nc as nonr

trav·eled
Pitts·burgh

oc·curred
cus·to·dy

(124)

65 par ser nonr

GREATER BOSTON REALTY COMPANY

329 Concord Avenue   Cambridge, Mass. 02138

Telephone:
Area: 617
Local: 547-6097

September 19, 196-

Mr. Edward H. James
316 West Broadway
Milwaukee, Wisconsin 53206

Dear Mr. James:

As I am sure you know, your resignation came as quite a blow to me. I knew, of course, that your health was not the best. I had hoped that a long vacation would be the answer to your problems.

Under the circumstances, I think you are wise to take your doctor's advice to move to a warmer climate.

I do not have to tell you, Mr. James, that I appreciate your years of service and the part you played in building up our organization to its position of leadership in its field.

If you should later decide to return to us, there will always be a place for you on my staff.

Cordially yours,

John H. Moore

John H. Moore
Sales Manager

JHM:LEA

Short Letter
Blocked Style
Standard Punctuation

first-class
hyphenated before noun

round-trip
hyphenated before noun

(135)

66

Ad·ver·tis·ers
an·nu·al

best at·tend·ed
no noun, no hyphen

one-stop
hyphenated before noun

rec·re·a·tion
wheth·er

their

nc

par

(217)

67▸ Transcription Quiz • For you to supply: 5 commas—1 comma conjunction, 2 commas introductory, 2 commas parenthetical.

(109)

DEVELOPING WORD-BUILDING POWER

68 ▸ Shorthand Vocabulary Builder

-ation

1

Tem

2

Ten, Den

3

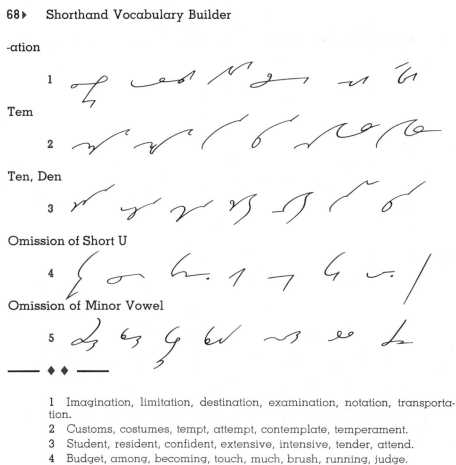

Omission of Short U

4

Omission of Minor Vowel

5

—— ◆◆ ——

1 Imagination, limitation, destination, examination, notation, transportation.

2 Customs, costumes, tempt, attempt, contemplate, temperament.

3 Student, resident, confident, extensive, intensive, tender, attend.

4 Budget, among, becoming, touch, much, brush, running, judge.

5 Various, serious, previous, period, courteous, theory, genuine.

BUILDING TRANSCRIPTION SKILLS

69 BUSINESS VOCABULARY BUILDER

agonizing Very painful.
congenial Agreeable; friendly.
ordinance A law.
allure Attraction; charm.

READING AND WRITING PRACTICE

70 A Trip to Europe by Plane

par

nc intro

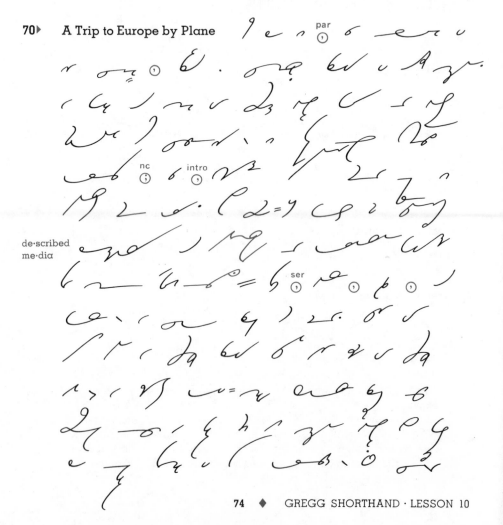

de·scribed
me·dia

ser

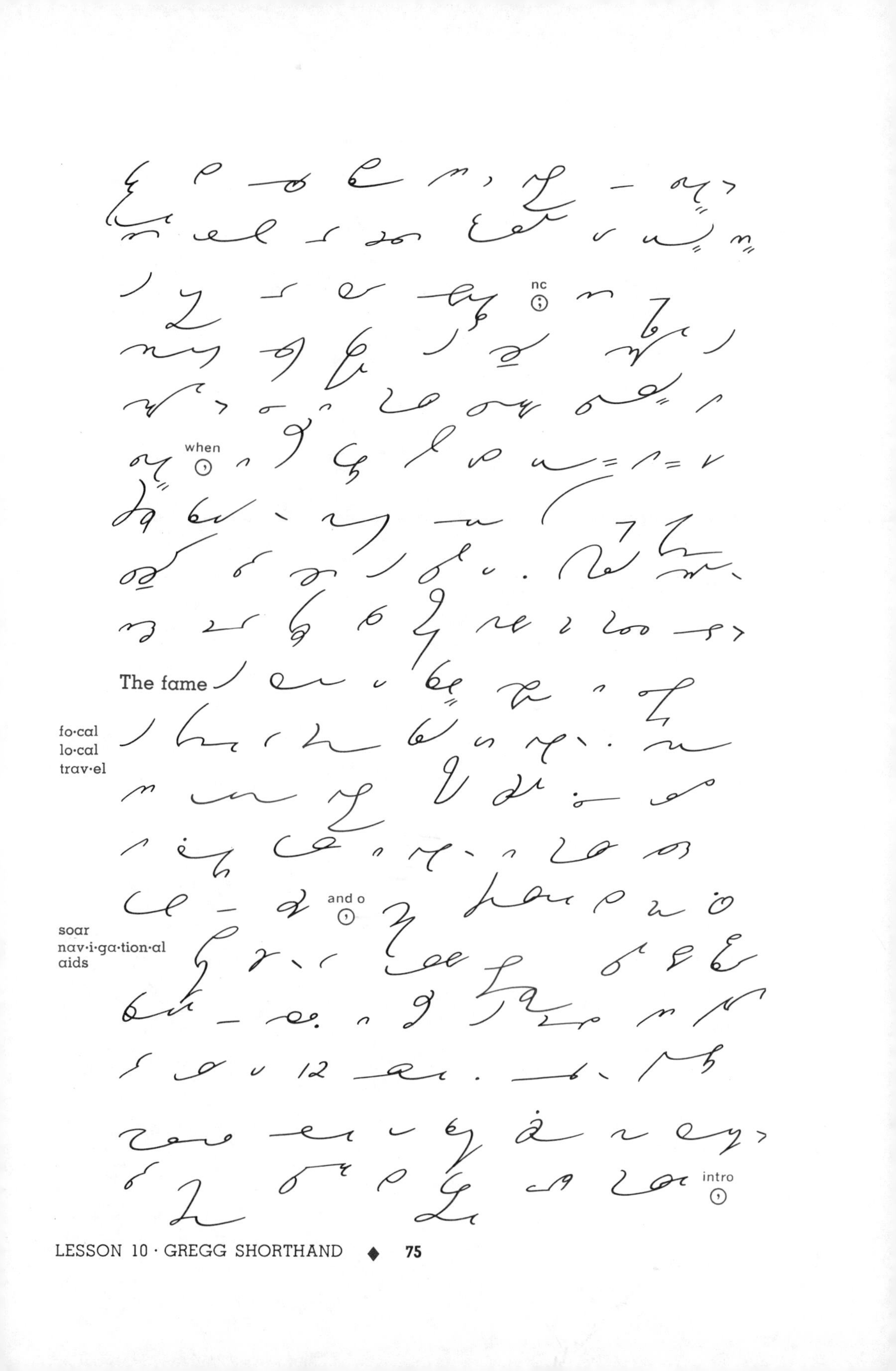

nc

when

The fame

fo·cal
lo·cal
trav·el

and o

soar
nav·i·ga·tion·al
aids

intro

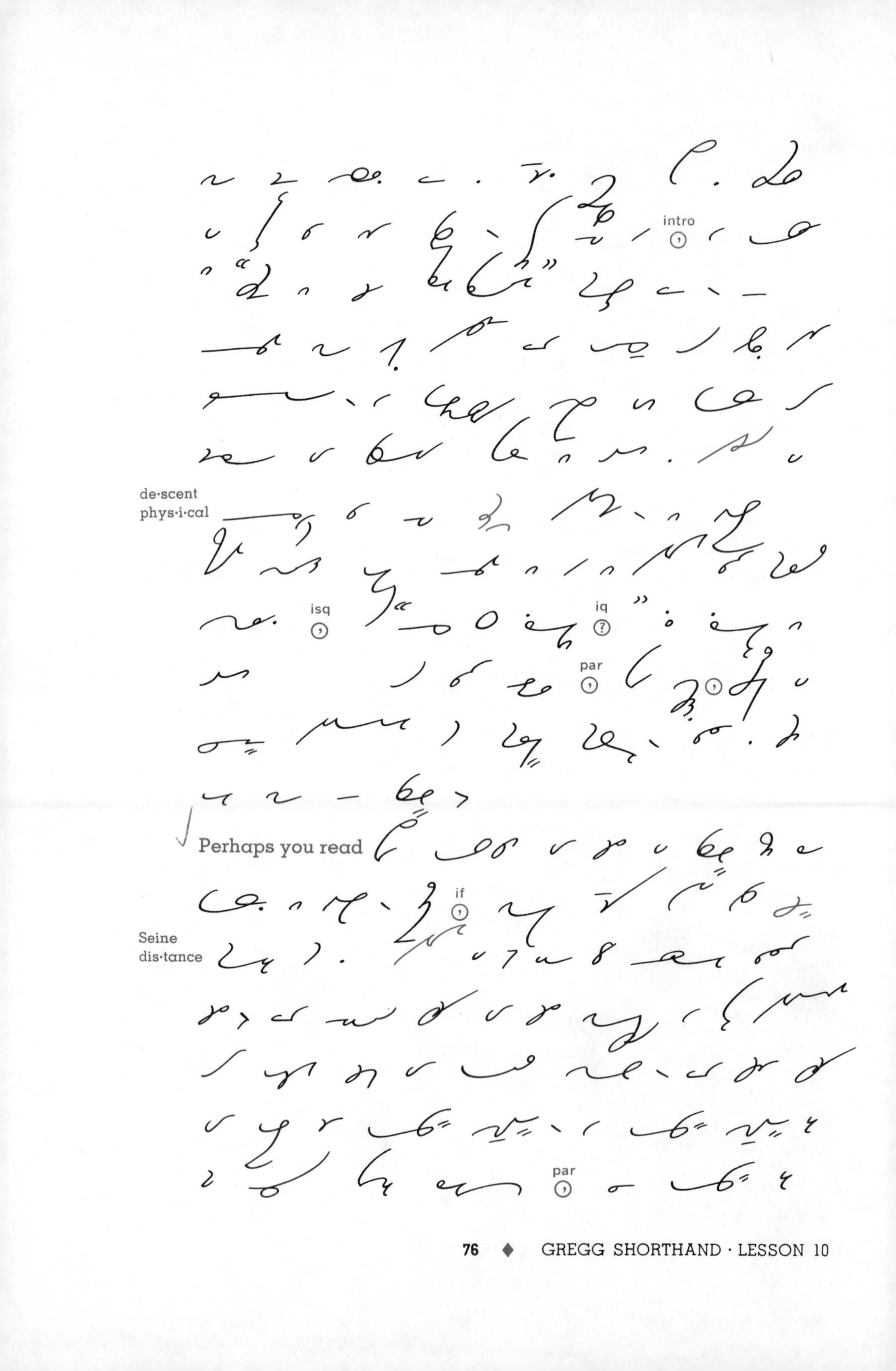

intro

de·scent
phys·i·cal

isq

iq

par

Perhaps you read

if

Seine
dis·tance

par

nc

intro

intro

bar·ri·er

traf·fic

conj

conj

if

Of course,

intro

(760)

CHAPTER THREE

banking

DEVELOPING WORD-BUILDING POWER

71▸ Brief Forms and Derivatives • Can you read the 36 brief forms and derivatives in 30 seconds or less?

1						
2						
3						
4						
5						
6						

—— ◆◆ ——

1 Advantage, advantages, advantageous, disadvantage, disadvantages, disadvantageous.
2 Object, objection, objections, objected, objective, objectively.
3 Over, overcome, overpaid, overlook, oversee, overdo.
4 State, states, statement, misstate, stated, restate.
5 Recognize, recognizing, recognized, recognizes, recognizable, recognition.
6 Out, outside, outcome, outfit, outline, without.

BUILDING TRANSCRIPTION SKILLS

72▸ PUNCTUATION PRACTICE ; because of comma

A comma is used to separate two independent clauses that are joined by a conjunction. However, a comma sometimes occurs within one or both of the independent clauses. When that occurs, a semicolon is used between the independent clauses.

> Our records indicate, Mr. Green, that we filled six orders for you last year; and every one of them was delivered within three days.
>
> He would like to buy the old house; but the owner, Mr. Dane, will not sell it.

The reason for this punctuation rule is simple enough. If there are other commas in the sentence, something stronger than a comma is required to separate the two parts of the sentence.

bc (;) Each time this use of the semicolon occurs in the Reading and Writing Practice, it will be indicated in the shorthand as shown in the margin.

73 ▸ BUSINESS VOCABULARY BUILDER

merger The combining of two or more companies into one.

executor The person or organization designated to carry out the provisions of a will.

stability The quality of being steady; firmness.

semiannually Twice a year.

READING AND WRITING PRACTICE

74 ▸ Brief-Form Letter • This letter is packed with brief forms and derivatives. You can profitably read and copy it several times.

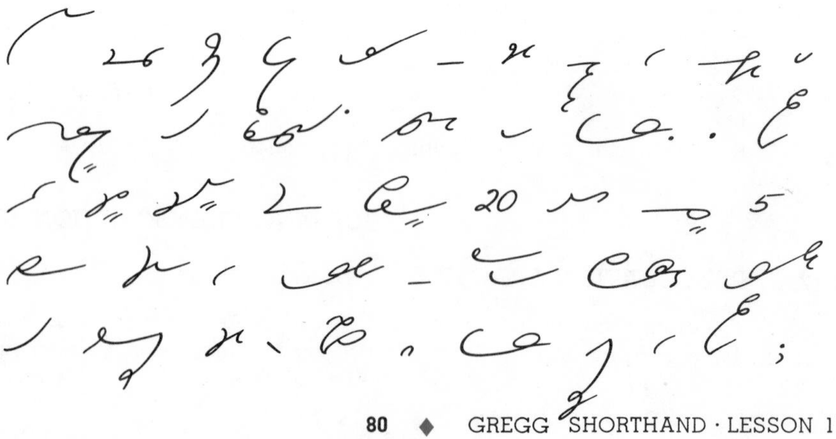

(155)

75

ap

passed

ex·ec·u·tor

bc

415615

nonr

1955

12

nc

in·her·i·tance

for·ward

intro

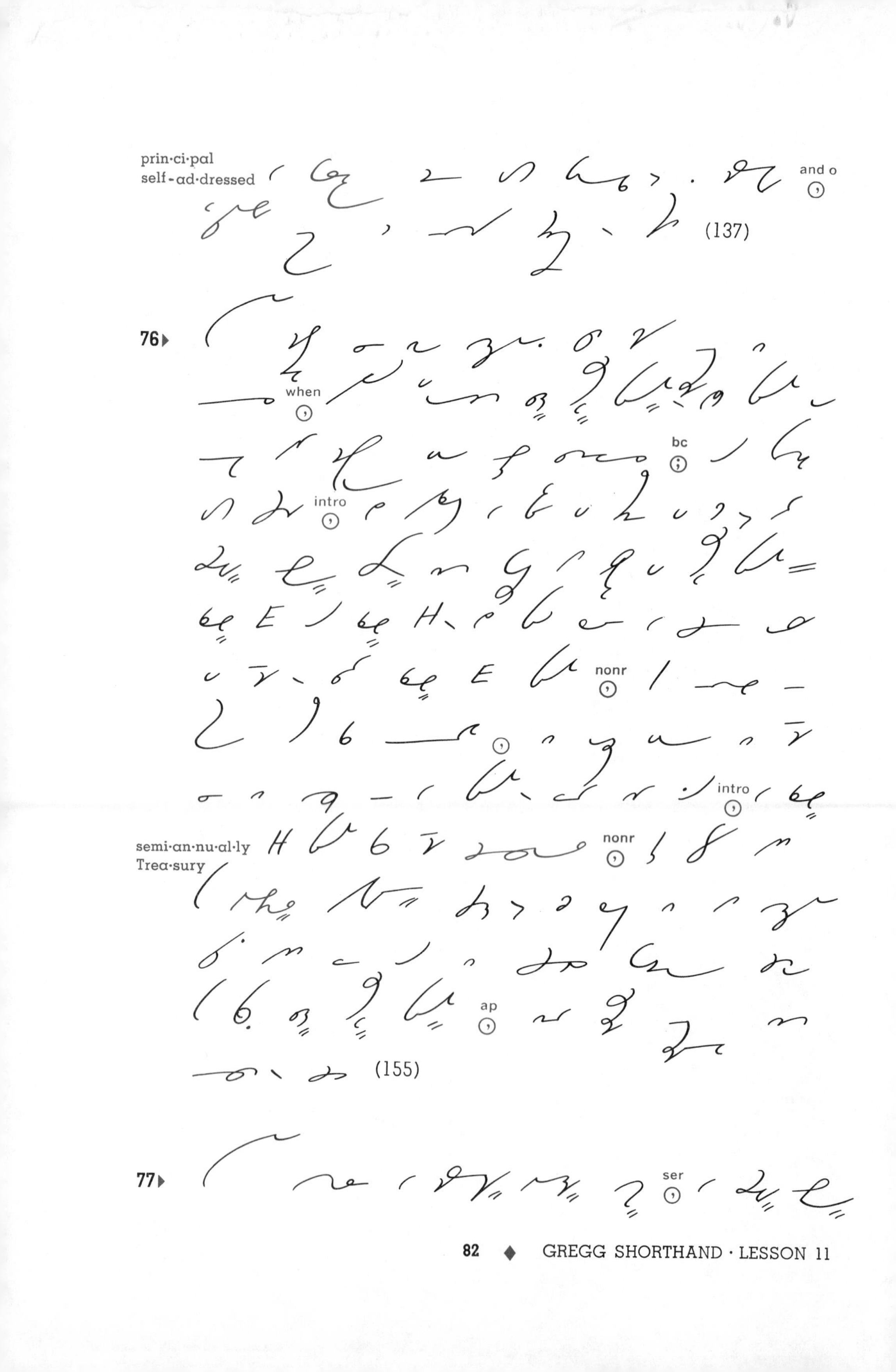

prin·ci·pal
self-ad·dressed

and o

(137)

76▸

when

bc

intro

nonr

intro

semi·an·nu·al·ly
Trea·sury

nonr

ap

(155)

77▸

ser

ex·pe·ri·ence

3

yours
merg·er

par

bc

110 intro

ser

14

1461

de·pos·i·tor
char·ac·ter

intro

(233)

78▸ Transcription Quiz • In this and succeeding Transcription Quizzes, a new factor will be added that will be a challenge to you. In addition to supplying the commas necessary to punctuate the letter correctly, you will have to supply a number of words that have been omitted from the printed shorthand.

Occasionally a stenographer will omit a word when he is taking dictation, either through lack of attention or because he did not hear it. Then, with the help of the meaning of the sentence, he will supply the missing word when transcribing.

You should have no difficulty supplying the missing word in these Transcription Quizzes, as in each case only one possible word makes sense.

As you copy the Transcription Quiz in your notebook, encircle in your notes the punctuation and the missing words that you supply.

For you to supply: 5 commas – 1 comma *and* omitted, 2 commas parenthetical, 1 comma introductory, 1 comma *when* clause; two missing words.

Lesson 12

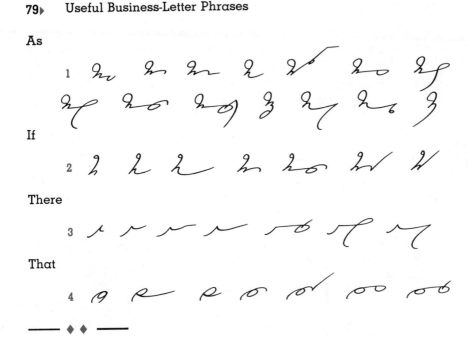

BUILDING PHRASING SKILL

79 Useful Business-Letter Phrases

As

1 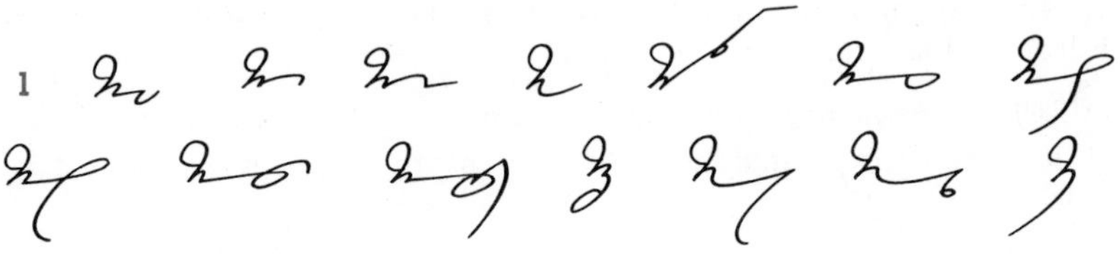

If

2 

There

3 

That

4 

1 As you know, as you can, as you cannot, as you are, as you did not, as you may, as you may have, as you may be, as you make, as you might have, as you say, as you will be, as you will see, as you have.

2 If you, if you are, if you will, if you can, if you make, if you could, if you would.

3 There is, there are, there are not, there will, there might, there may be, there will be.

4 That is, that will, that are, that can, that could, that may, that might.

80▸ Frequent Names

—— ◆◆ ——

1 Clark, Cohen, Cohn, Collins, Connell, Cooper.
2 Beatrice, Belle, Bertha, Bridget, Caroline, Catherine, Celia.

BUILDING TRANSCRIPTION SKILL

81▸ **PUNCTUATION PRACTICE** **; illustrative ,**

When an illustration is introduced by an expression such as *namely, that is, for example,* the expression should be preceded by a semicolon and followed by a comma.

He has an overpowering ambition; namely, to fly a jet plane.

Bill has many talents that most people are not aware of; for example, he has a law degree.

il (;) Each time this use of the semicolon occurs in the Reading and Writing Practice, it will be indicated in the shorthand as shown in the left margin.

82▸ **BUSINESS VOCABULARY BUILDER**

objective (adjective) Based on facts and not on emotions or feeling.

inflation An increase in the amount of currency in circulation resulting in a sudden fall in its value.

deprived Made to do without.

READING AND WRITING PRACTICE

83▸ **Phrase Letter** • The following letter has many useful phrases. Read and copy it several times.

(127)

84

pur·chas·ing
sim·i·lar

as

ser

intro

ser

rec·om·mend
ad·van·tage

il

nonr

bc

in·tel·li·gent
de·ci·sions

and o

ser

intro

(201)

85

intro

bc

new-car
hyphenated before noun

intro

ad·vi·sors
bor·row·ing

intro

il

ser

choose
bud·get

nc
and o

(147)

86▸

il

if

intro

nonr

intro

its
fur·ther·more

intro

ser

stat·utes
fac·tors
bear·ing

(179)

87 ▸ **Transcription Quiz** · For you to supply: 5 commas – 1 comma *as* clause, 3 commas parenthetical, 1 comma conjunction; two missing words.

(133)

DEVELOPING WORD-BUILDING POWER

88 ▸ Word Families

Prove

1

-ount

2

-rate

3

Re-

4

-ic

5

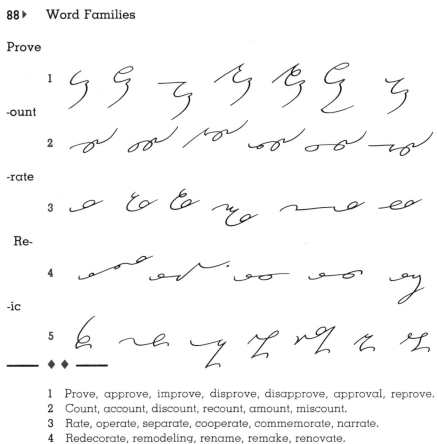

1 Prove, approve, improve, disprove, disapprove, approval, reprove.
2 Count, account, discount, recount, amount, miscount.
3 Rate, operate, separate, cooperate, commemorate, narrate.
4 Redecorate, remodeling, rename, remake, renovate.
5 Basic, classic, logic, tragic, strategic, topic, terrific.

89 ▸ TYPING STYLE STUDIES Dates

1 If the name of the month precedes the day, do not use *th, st,* or *d* after the number. This is the most frequent way that dates are expressed in business letters.

On June 16, 1968, he will be sixty-five years old.

Notice that when a date is expressed in this way, there is a comma both *before* and *after* the year.

2 If the day precedes the month, *th, st,* or *d* should be included.

On the 25th of May he will be able to vote.

When dates appear in the Reading and Writing Practice, they will be called to your attention in the margin thus:

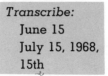

Transcribe:
June 15
July 15, 1968,
15th

Amounts of money

1 When transcribing even amounts of dollars in business letters, do not use a decimal point or zeros.

His check for $152 (not $152.00) was returned by the bank.

2 In business letters use the word *cents* in amounts under $1.

The book cost only 39 cents (not $.39).

When amounts such as the above appear in the Reading and Writing Practice, they will occasionally be called to your attention in the margin of the shorthand thus:

Transcribe:
$515
6 cents

Addresses

1 Always use figures in house numbers.

He lived at 600 (not six hundred) Market Street.

2 Spell out numbers in street addresses from one through ten.

He worked at 330 Fourth Avenue.

3 Use numbers in street addresses over ten.

His address is 18 East 67 Street.

NOTE 1: Always spell out *Street, Avenue, Road,* etc.

NOTE 2: Omit *th, st,* and *d* from numbered street names. The omission of these endings adds to the readability of the address.

When street addresses occur in the Reading and Writing Practice, they will occasionally be called to your attention in the margin of the shorthand thus:

> *Transcribe:*
> 67 Street
> Fourth Street

90 ▸ **BUSINESS VOCABULARY BUILDER**

comptroller A financial officer of an organization.

contemplate To consider; to expect or to look forward to an event.

confidential Given in confidence; not to be shared with others.

READING AND WRITING PRACTICE

91 ▸

comp·trol·ler
opin·ion

intro

bc

(144)

92 ▸

nonr

Transcribe:
15th

isq

ap

1106

1107

iq

Transcribe:
$500
$337

nonr

337

as

1156

Transcribe:
52 Street

52

intro

re·al·ize

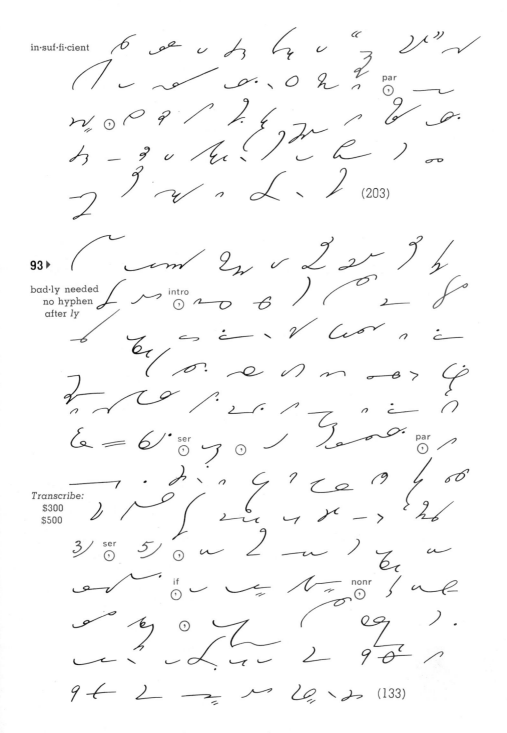

in·suf·fi·cient

(203)

93

bad·ly needed no hyphen after *ly*

par

intro

ser

par

Transcribe: $300 $500

ser

if

nonr

(133)

94▸ Transcription Quiz • For you to supply: 5 commas — 2 commas *when* clause, 1 comma *and* omitted, 1 comma conjunction, 1 comma *if* clause; 2 missing words.

(166)

DEVELOPING WORD-BUILDING POWER

95▸ Word Beginnings

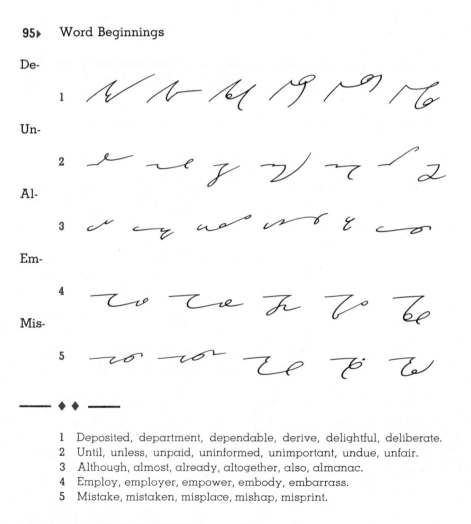

De-

1

Un-

2

Al-

3

Em-

4

Mis-

5

—— ◆◆ ——

1 Deposited, department, dependable, derive, delightful, deliberate.
2 Until, unless, unpaid, uninformed, unimportant, undue, unfair.
3 Although, almost, already, altogether, also, almanac.
4 Employ, employer, empower, embody, embarrass.
5 Mistake, mistaken, misplace, mishap, misprint.

96 ▸ Geographical Expressions

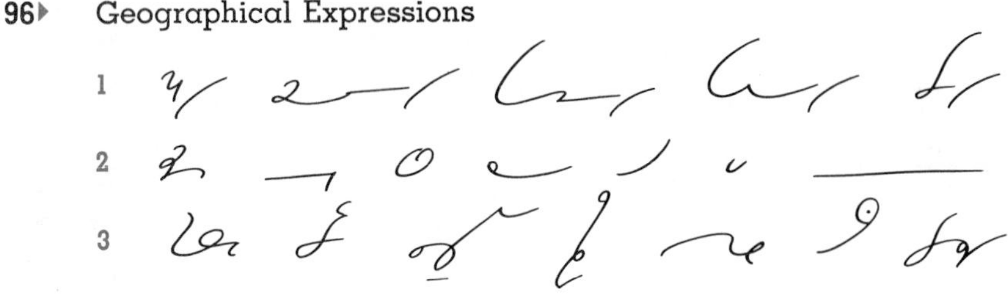

— ♦♦ —

1 Washington, Wilmington, Bloomington, Burlington, Bennington.
2 Wisconsin, Michigan, Iowa, Illinois, Indiana, Ohio, Minnesota.
3 France, Spain, Equador, Egypt, Greece, India, Pakistan.

BUILDING TRANSCRIPTION SKILLS

97 ▸ PUNCTUATION PRACTICE : introducing long quote

Long quotations are introduced by a colon.

The mayor of the city said: "Our city is growing steadily every year as a result of the expansion of our industrial plants and the friendly attitude shown to visitors by the citizens of our city. If our city continues to grow at the same rate for the next ten years, we shall have a population of more than 900,000 people."

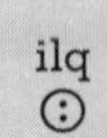

Whenever this use of the colon occurs in the Reading and Writing Practice, it will be indicated in the shorthand as shown in the left margin.

: enumeration

A colon is used after an expression that introduces some following material, such as an explanation of a general statement, a list, or an enumeration.

The job requires the following skills: shorthand, filing, typing, and bookkeeping.

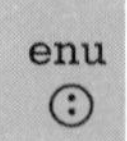

Whenever this use of the colon occurs in the Reading and Writing Practice, it will be indicated in the shorthand as shown in the left margin.

98▸ BUSINESS VOCABULARY BUILDER

necessitated Made necessary.

bank statement A monthly report from a bank indicating the amounts deposited, the amounts withdrawn, and the remaining balance in a bank account.

facilitate To make easy.

READING AND WRITING PRACTICE

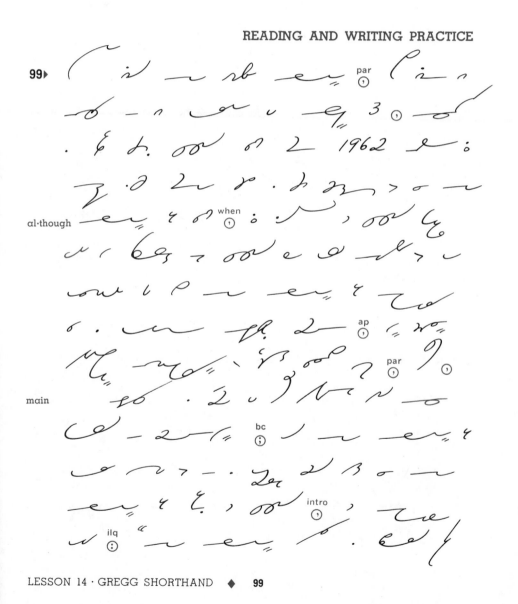

99▸

par

when

al·though

ap

par

main

bc

intro

ilq

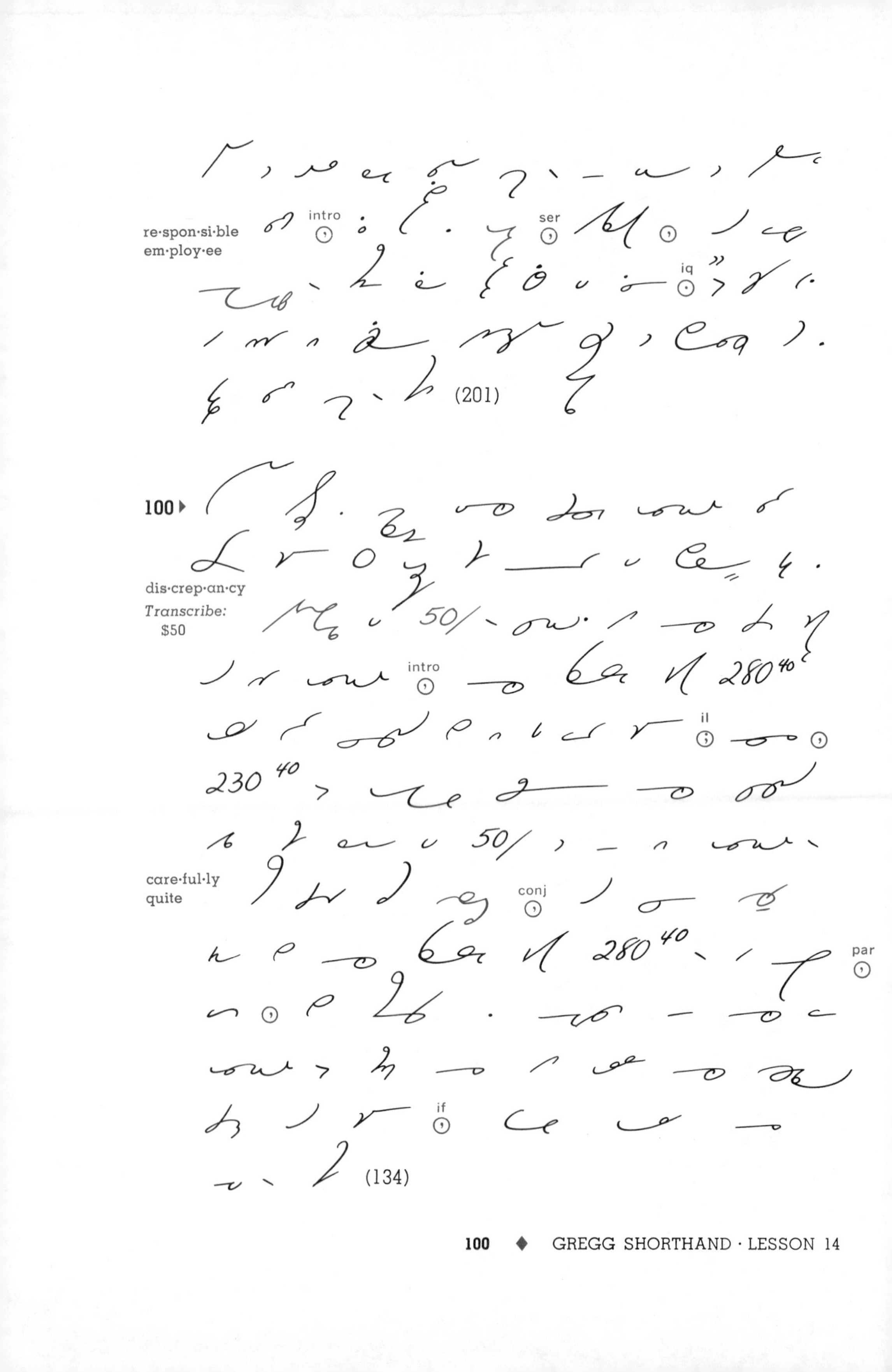

intro

ser

re·spon·si·ble
em·ploy·ee

iq

(201)

100 ▸

dis·crep·an·cy
Transcribe:
$50

50/

intro

280 40

il

230 40

50/

care·ful·ly
quite

conj

280 40

par

if

(134)

101▸

intro

il

drive-in *hyphenated before noun*

enu

de·pos·its with·draw·als

nc

intro

ser

(123)

102▸

nonr

past pre·mi·um

ilq

ser

bc

intro

nc

rea·son
non·pay·ment

iq

as

par

if

(144)

103 ▸ **Transcription Quiz** • For you to supply: 5 commas — 1 comma *as* clause, 3 commas introductory, 1 comma *and* omitted; 2 missing words.

(110)

DEVELOPING WORD-BUILDING POWER

104▸ Shorthand Vocabulary Builder

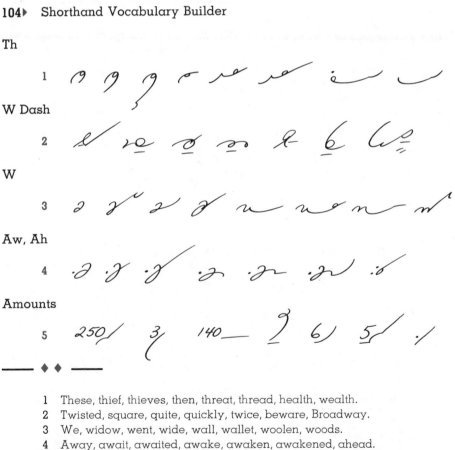

Th

1

W Dash

2

W

3

Aw, Ah

4

Amounts

5 250 3 140 6 5

—— ♦♦ ——

1 These, thief, thieves, then, threat, thread, health, wealth.
2 Twisted, square, quite, quickly, twice, beware, Broadway.
3 We, widow, went, wide, wall, wallet, woolen, woods.
4 Away, await, awaited, awake, awaken, awakened, ahead.
5 $250,000; 3,000,000,000; 140,000,000; several hundred; $600; $500,000; a dollar.

BUILDING TRANSCRIPTION SKILLS

105▸ BUSINESS VOCABULARY BUILDER

stashed away Hidden.
caches (pronounced "kash·es") Hiding places.
hoards Hidden supplies.

READING AND WRITING PRACTICE

106▸ Where Does All the Money Go?

intro

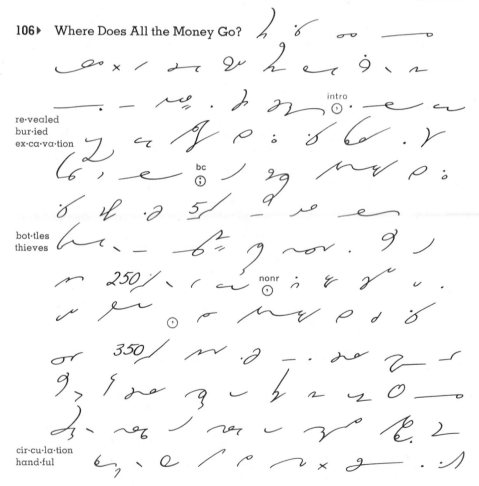

re·vealed
bur·ied
ex·ca·va·tion

bc

bot·tles
thieves

nonr

cir·cu·la·tion
hand·ful

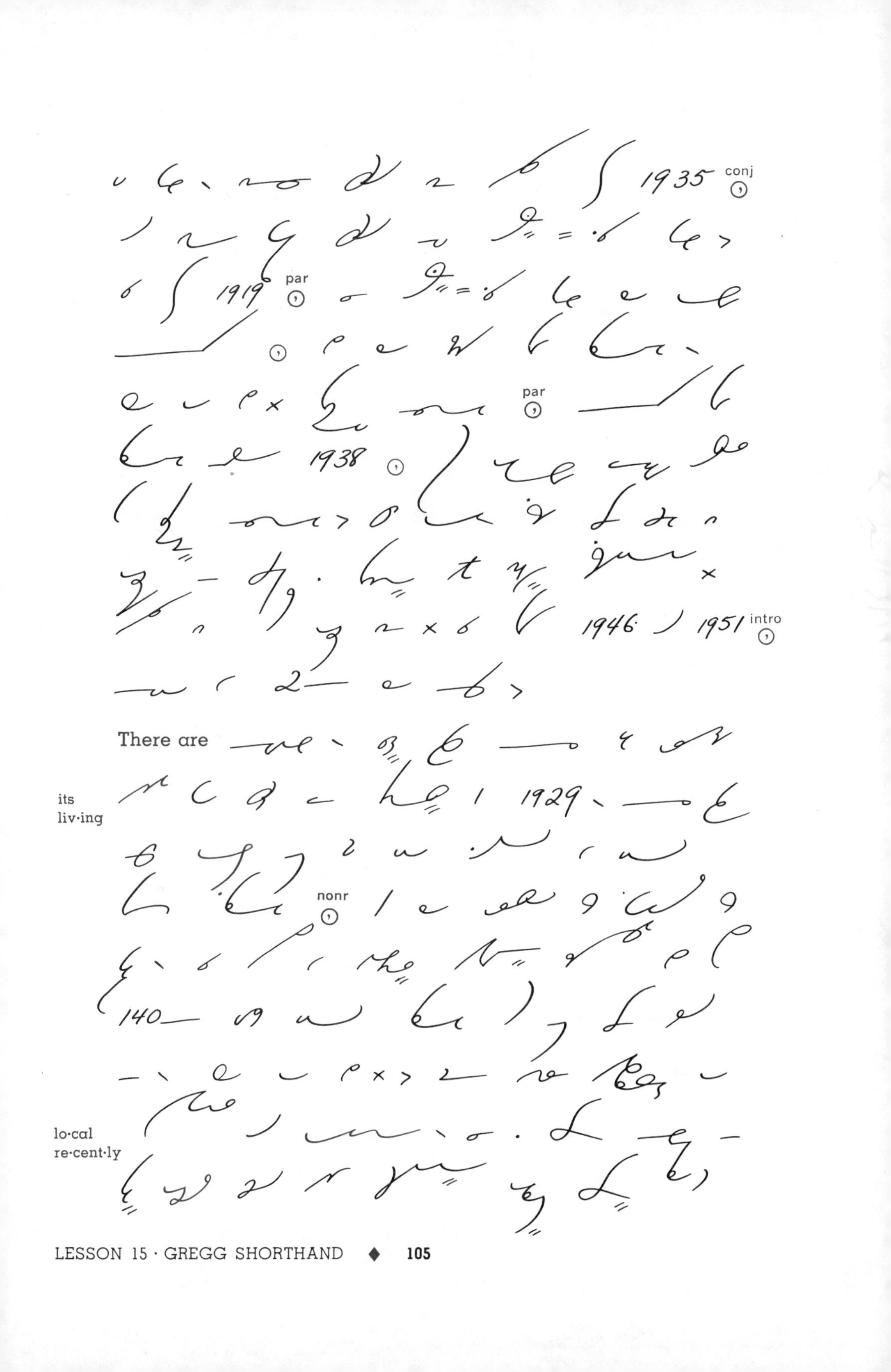

1935 conj

1919 par

par

1938

1946 1951 intro

There are

its
liv·ing

1929

nonr

140

lo·cal
re·cent·ly

nick·els

when nc

par

ripped
cas·cad·ing

when

par

Money

de·stroy
a·board

wear

ser

iq

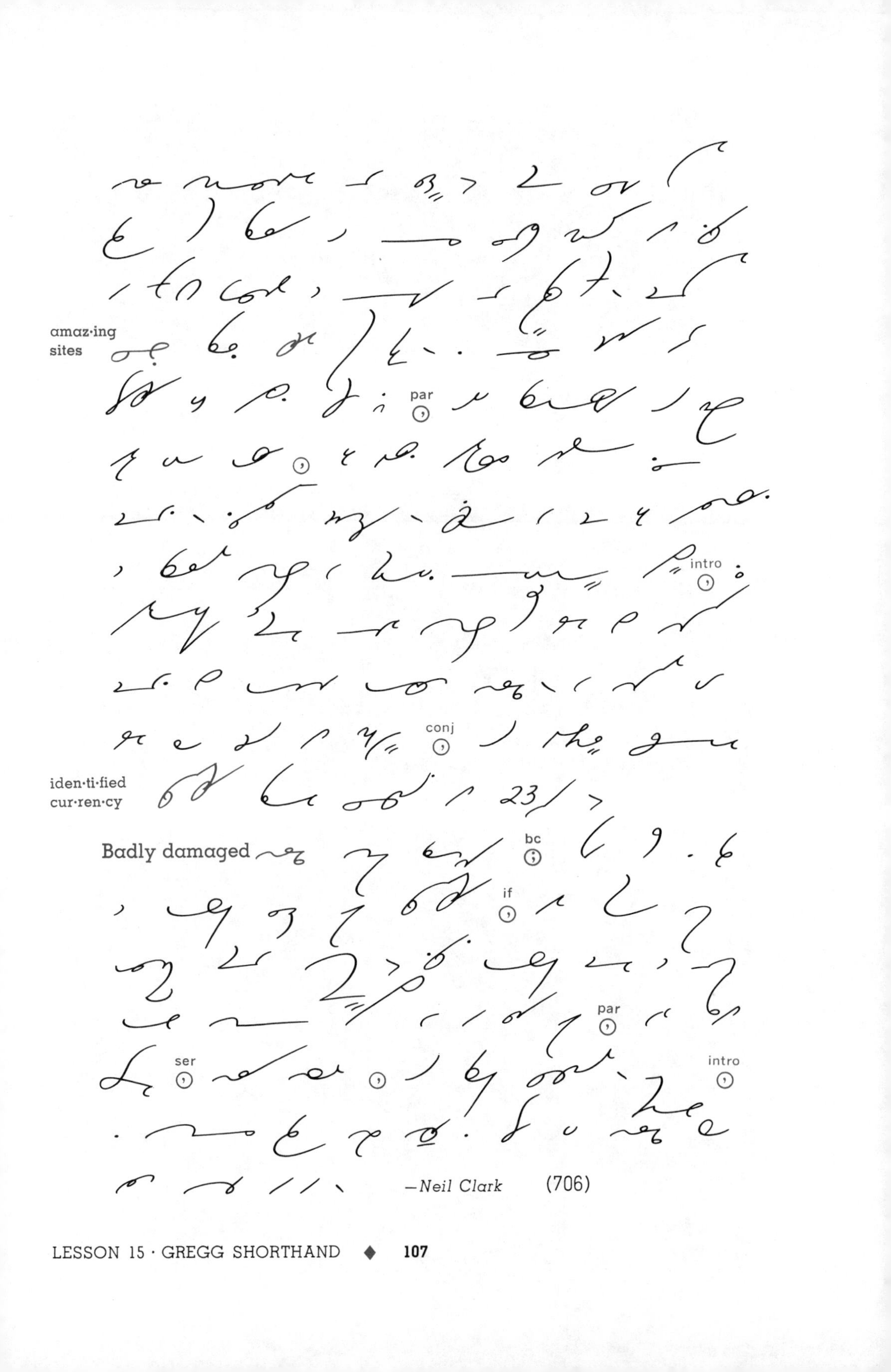

amaz·ing
sites

par

intro

conj

iden·ti·fied
cur·ren·cy

23

Badly damaged

bc

if

par

ser

intro

—*Neil Clark* (706)

CHAPTER FOUR

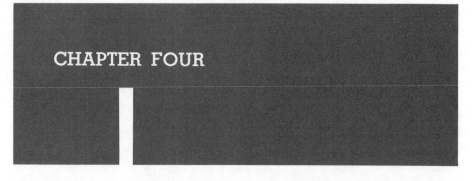

data processing

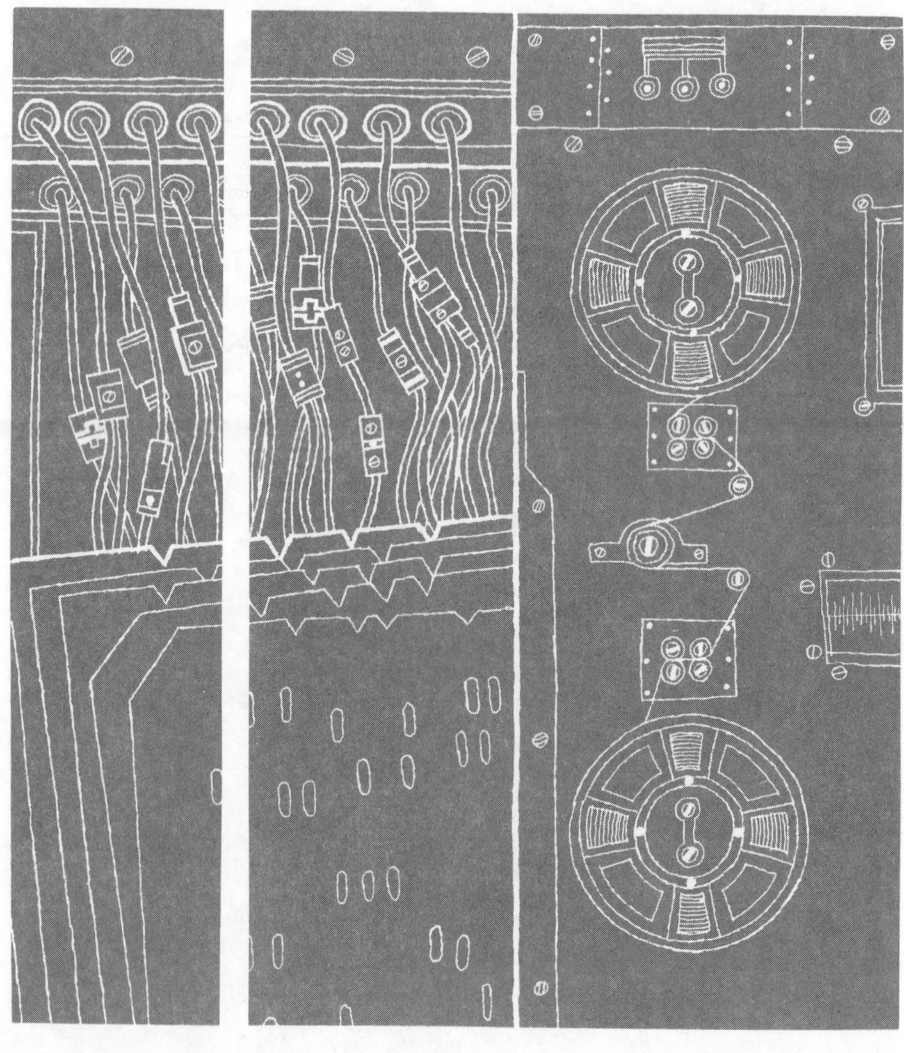

DEVELOPING WORD-BUILDING POWER

107▸ Brief Forms and Derivatives • Can you read the following 42 brief forms and derivatives in 35 seconds or less?

1 Advertise, advertising, advertised, advertisement, advertisements, advertiser.

2 Part, parts, partly-party, parted, depart, department.

3 Short, shorter, shorten, shortly, shortage, shorthand.

4 Send, sending, sender; difficult, difficulty, difficulties.

5 Therefore, thereby, therein; request, requests, requested.

6 Correspond-correspondence, corresponds, corresponded, corresponding, correspondingly, correspondent.

7 Great, greatly, greater; wish, wished, wishful.

108 ▸ TYPING STYLE STUDY Time

1 Spell out the time of day when it is accompanied by *o'clock.* (Remember the apostrophe!)

He came at ten o'clock (not 10 o'clock).

2 Use numbers in expressing time with *a.m.* and *p.m.*

He left at 9:15 a.m. and returned at 9:30 p.m.

NOTE: Write a.m. and p.m. with small letters and no space after the first period.

Occasionally these expressions of time will be called to your attention in the margins of the shorthand in the Reading and Writing Practice thus:

Transcribe:
9 a.m.
ten o'clock

Commas in numbers

1 When a number contains four or more digits, a comma is used to separate thousands, millions, billions.

$1,000 (not $1000)   167,841   1,321,000   4,500,000,000

2 A comma, however, is not used in large serial numbers, room numbers, house or street numbers, telephone numbers, page numbers, and dates.

No. 14568	6314 Third Avenue		Longacre 4-1414
Room 1146	page 1212	1966	214-3141

These uses of the comma in numbers will be called to your attention in the margin of the Reading and Writing Practice thus:

Transcribe:
No. 14568
$1,000

109▸ BUSINESS VOCABULARY BUILDER

allied Related to.
prospective Expected.
exceeds Goes beyond.

READING AND WRITING PRACTICE

110▸ Brief-Form Letter • The following letter has a high concentration of brief forms and derivatives. You can read and copy it several times with profit.

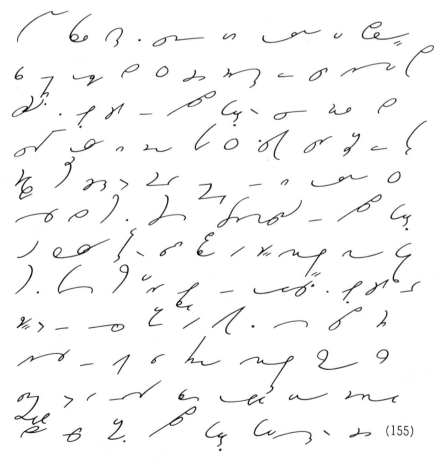

(155)

111 ▸

one-week *hyphenated before noun*

ap

as

Transcribe: Room 1515 1480

15/

1515

1480 35

nonr

Transcribe: nine o'clock

18

18

conj

if

par

ac·com·mo·da·tions ar·ea

nc

intro

(152)

112 ▸

spon·sor·ing pro·spec·tive

nonr

Transcribe:
1616

re·ceiv·able
in·ven·to·ry

enu

ser

per·son·nel
man·a·ge·ri·al

Transcribe:
9 a.m.
4 p.m.

Transcribe:
Room 1106

par

bc

if

par

en·roll·ment
sub·mit·ted
di·rec·tor

ap

(234)

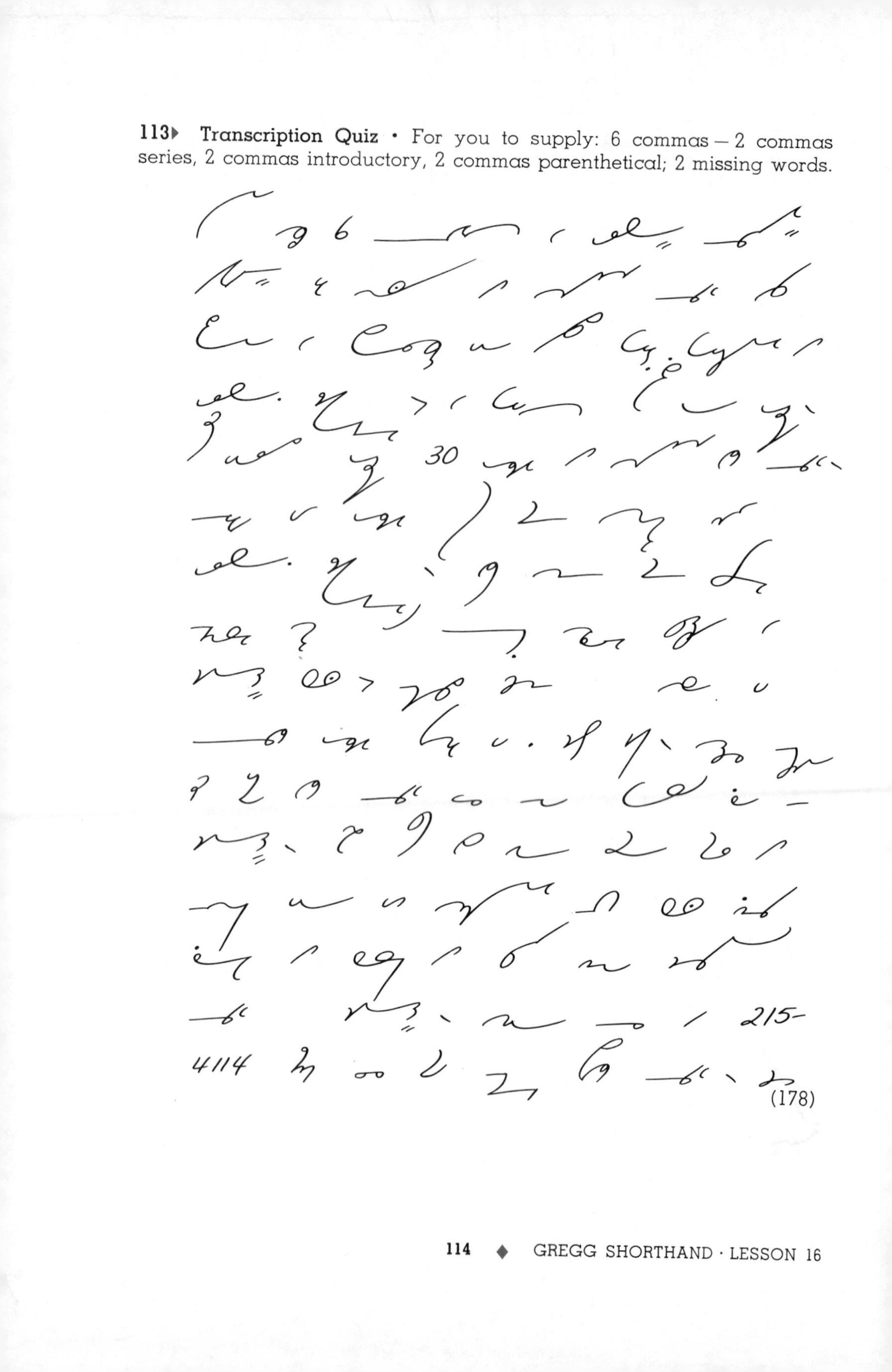

113▸ Transcription Quiz · For you to supply: 6 commas – 2 commas series, 2 commas introductory, 2 commas parenthetical; 2 missing words.

(178)

BUILDING PHRASING SKILL

114 ▸ Useful Business-Letter Phrases

To

1

About

2

Let us

3

I

4

— ♦♦ —

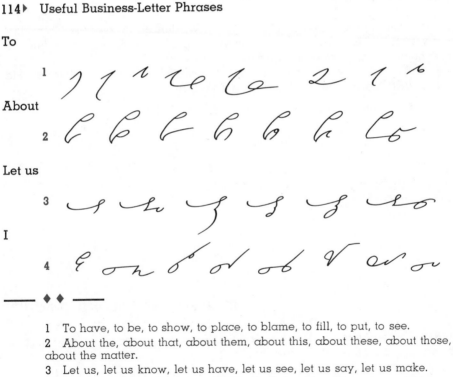

1 To have, to be, to show, to place, to blame, to fill, to put, to see.

2 About the, about that, about them, about this, about these, about those, about the matter.

3 Let us, let us know, let us have, let us see, let us say, let us make.

4 I was, I am sure, I did, I could, I made, I should not, I wrote you, I know.

115 ▸ Frequent Names

1

2

1 Crowley, Daly, Davidson, Davis, Donovan, Doyle.
2 Arthur, Benjamin, Charles, Clarence, Daniel, David.

BUILDING TRANSCRIPTION SKILLS

116 ▸ GRAMMAR CHECKUP all right

This expression should always be written as two words. Some unwary transcribers are tempted to spell it *alright* because of the influence of such words as *altogether*, *always*, and *already*.

A good way to remember that *all right* is spelled as two words is to recall that its opposite is *all wrong*—two words.

John says that it will be all right for us to follow him.

117 ▸ BUSINESS VOCABULARY BUILDER

pursue To follow.
objective (noun) Aim; goal.
instantaneous Immediate.

READING AND WRITING PRACTICE

118 ▸ Phrase Letter • The following letter contains many useful phrases. Read and copy the letter several times.

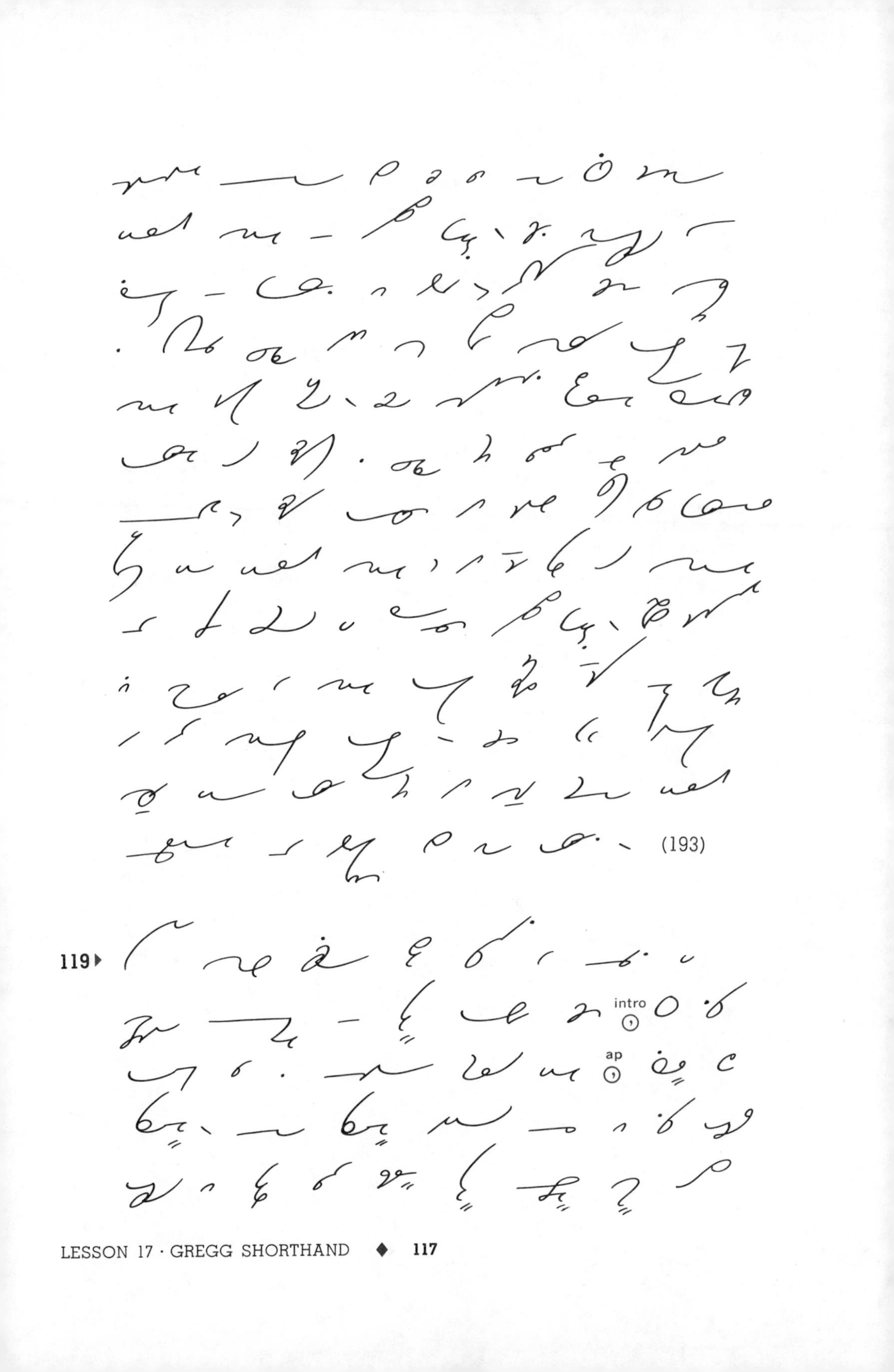

(193)

119

intro

ap

con·nec·tion
all right

nonr

po·ten·tial
op·por·tu·ni·ty

conj

if

of·fi·cers
anx·ious

as

par

(237)

120▸

intro

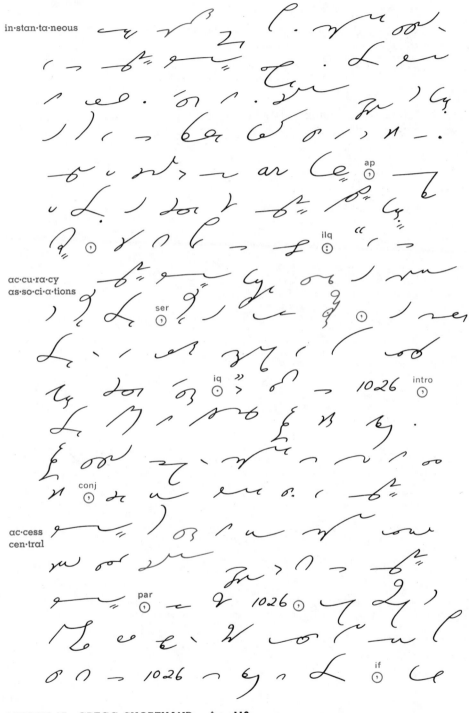

in·stan·ta·neous

ap

ilq

ac·cu·ra·cy
as·so·ci·a·tions

ser

iq 1026 intro

conj

ac·cess
cen·tral

par 1026

1026 if

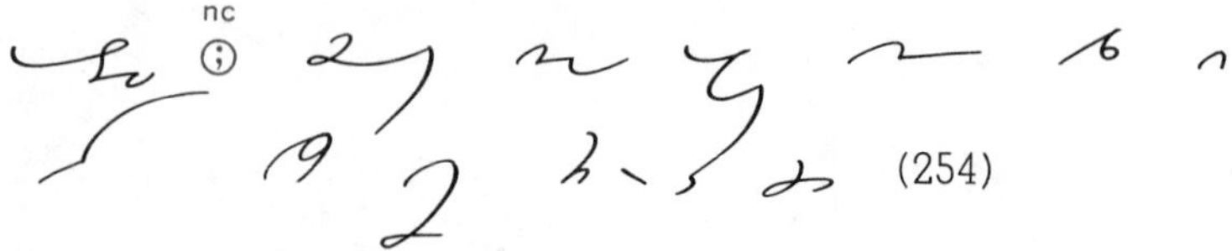

121 ▸ Transcription Quiz • For you to supply: 6 commas — 1 comma introductory, 3 commas apposition, 2 commas parenthetical; 2 missing words.

(157)

THE DARRIS COMPANY

3674 NORRAND BOULEVARD, ST. LOUIS, MISSOURI 63103

November 16, 196-

The New York Insurance Company
221 Broadway
New York, New York 10028

ATTENTION: Mr. Parsons

Gentlemen:

This is just a note to tell you how glad we are that we took your advice a few years ago and purchased business-interruption insurance.

As you know, on May 16 of last year our store was burned to the ground. We could easily have been bankrupted as a result of the fire, which caused considerable damage. Thanks to our policy with your organization, however, everything turned out all right.

Of course, we obtained temporary quarters quickly. However, we suffered operating losses of more than $50,000. In addition, we had extra expenses amounting to $30,000 for fixtures and other items. We recovered this $80,000 because we had invested in your business-interruption insurance.

While I am president of our company, we will never be without business-interruption insurance.

Cordially yours,

Harold G. Green

Harold G. Green
President

HGG:MH

Average-Length Letter
Semiblocked Style, with Attention Line
Standard Punctuation

DEVELOPING WORD-BUILDING POWER

122▸ Word Families

-dent

1

-cate

2

-sive

3

-ser

4

-son

5

—— ♦♦ ——

1 President, resident, incident, confident, evident, indent, prudent.

2 Certificate, complicate, locate, dedicate, indicate, educate.

3 Extensive, intensive, comprehensive, apprehensive, responsive, offensive, defensive.

4 Answer, eraser, closer, condenser, composer, endorser.

5 Person, reason, comparison, season, crimson, arson, unison.

BUILDING TRANSCRIPTION SKILLS

123 ▸ SIMILAR-WORDS DRILL

Words that sound alike and words that sound or look *almost* alike are responsible for many errors that stenographers make when they transcribe. Often they know which word of a similar-sounding pair is the correct one to use in a sentence, but they transcribe the incorrect one because of carelessness or inattention.

Hereafter, in the third lesson of each chapter you will study a Similar-Words Drill that will call to your attention pairs of words that may lead to mistranscription if you are not careful.

Study the definition of each word carefully. As you read the Reading and Writing Practice of the lesson, watch for the similar words; you will find them used a number of times.

Advice, advise

advice *(noun)* Recommendation; suggestion; guidance.

People ask for his advice on many subjects.

advise *(verb)* To guide; to suggest; to inform.

Would you be good enough to advise us what to do.

124 ▸ BUSINESS VOCABULARY BUILDER

simultaneously At the same time.
category Class; group.
ultimate Final.
CPA Certified Public Accountant.

READING AND WRITING PRACTICE

125 ▸

intro

op·ti·cal scan·ning

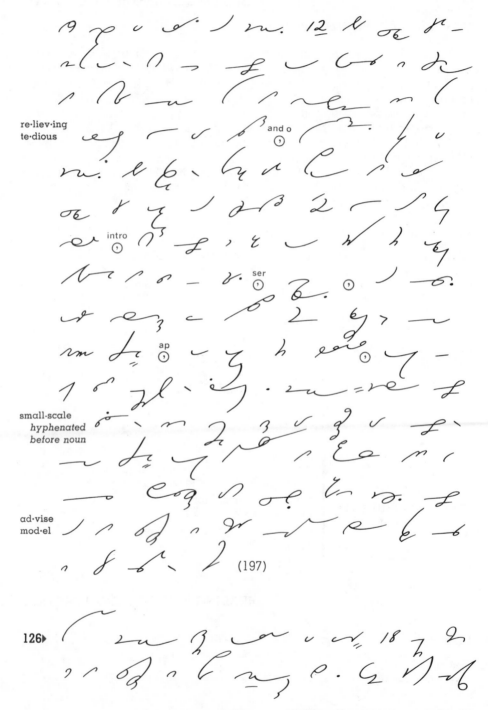

re·liev·ing
te·dious

and o

intro

ser

ap

small-scale
hyphenated before noun

ad·vise
mod·el

(197)

126▸

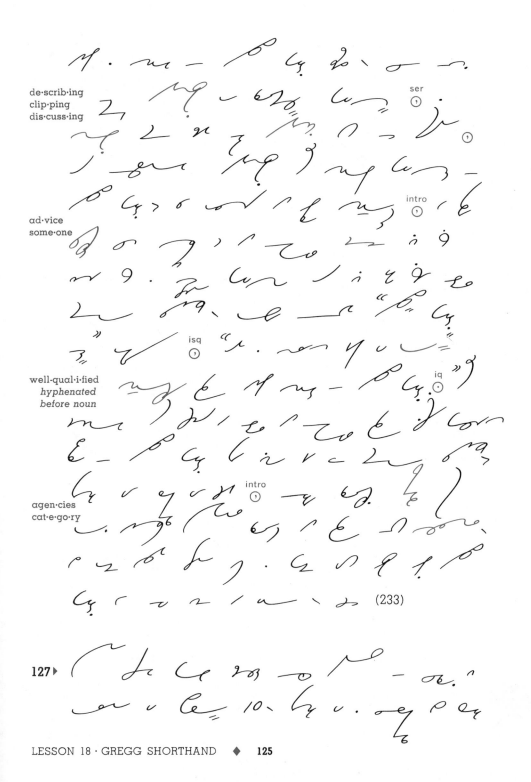

de·scrib·ing
clip·ping
dis·cuss·ing

ser

ad·vice
some·one

intro

isq

well-qual·i·fied
hyphenated before noun

iq

agen·cies
cat·e·go·ry

intro

(233)

127 ▸

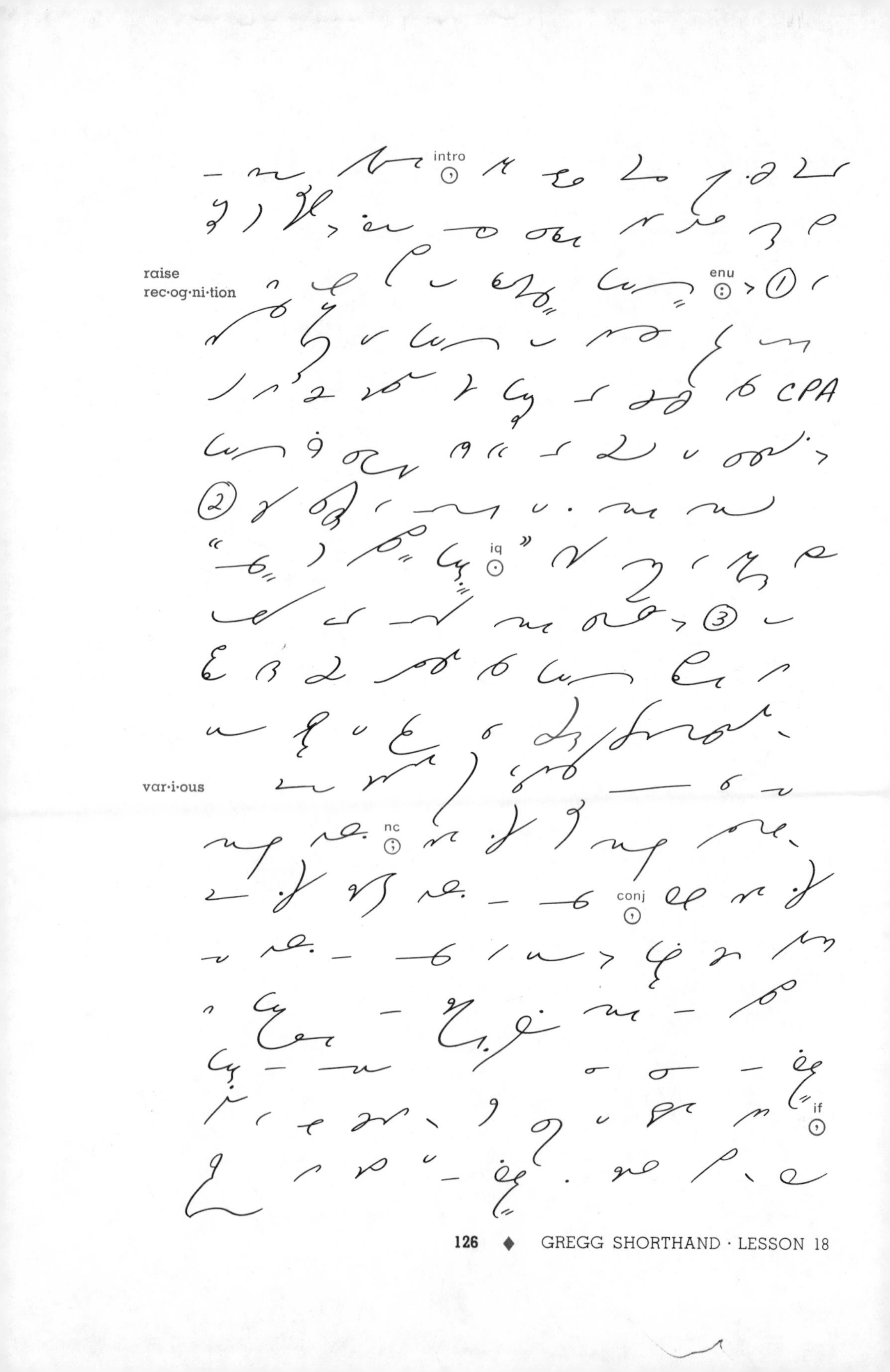

intro

raise
rec·og·ni·tion

enu

CPA

iq

var·i·ous

nc

conj

if

(250)

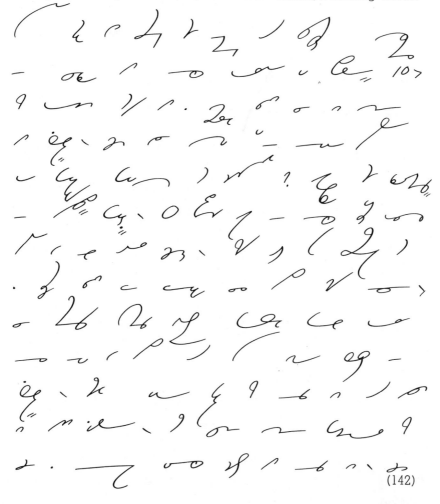

128▸ Transcription Quiz • For you to supply: 5 commas — 1 comma *when* clause, 2 commas parenthetical, 2 commas *if* clause; 2 missing words.

(142)

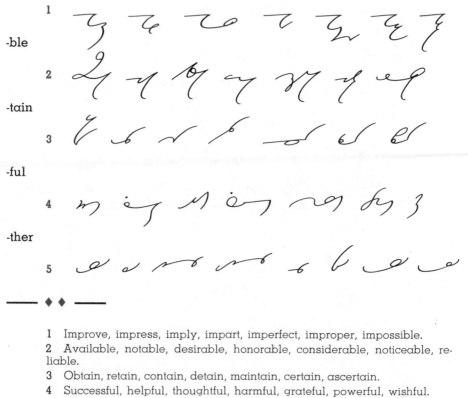

DEVELOPING WORD-BUILDING POWER

129▸ Word Beginnings and Endings

Im-

1

-ble

2

-tain

3

-ful

4

-ther

5

—— ♦♦ ——

1 Improve, impress, imply, impart, imperfect, improper, impossible.

2 Available, notable, desirable, honorable, considerable, noticeable, reliable.

3 Obtain, retain, contain, detain, maintain, certain, ascertain.

4 Successful, helpful, thoughtful, harmful, grateful, powerful, wishful.

5 Rather, either, together, altogether, neither, bother, lather, leather.

130 ▸ Geographical Expressions

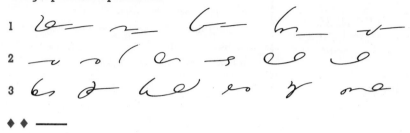

1 Framingham, Cunningham, Birmingham, Buckingham, Nottingham.
2 Missouri, Kentucky, Tennessee, Arkansas, Mississippi, Alabama, Louisiana.
3 Peru, Siam, Poland, Turkey, Sweden, Ukraine.

BUILDING TRANSCRIPTION SKILLS

131 ▸ SPELLING FAMILIES -er, -ar, -or

Be very careful of words ending in the sound of *er* — they may be spelled *er, or,* or *ar.* When in doubt, look them up!

Words Ending in -er

of·fi·cer	train·er	man·a·ger
sub·scrib·er	di·vid·er	reg·is·ter
pro·duc·er	read·er	cus·tom·er
book·keep·er	gar·den·er	con·sid·er

Words Ending in -ar

sug·ar	col·lar	par·tic·u·lar
gram·mar	cel·lar	reg·u·lar
pop·u·lar	sim·i·lar	mor·tar

Words Ending in -or

ma·jor	gov·er·nor	el·e·va·tor
pro·fes·sor	su·per·vi·sor	sen·a·tor
hu·mor	dic·ta·tor	gen·er·a·tor
neigh·bor	in·ven·tor	en·deav·or

132 ▸ BUSINESS VOCABULARY BUILDER

concepts Ideas; thoughts.
administrator One who manages or directs.
inception Origin; start.
nominal Very small or slight in degree.

READING AND WRITING PRACTICE

133 ▸

ap

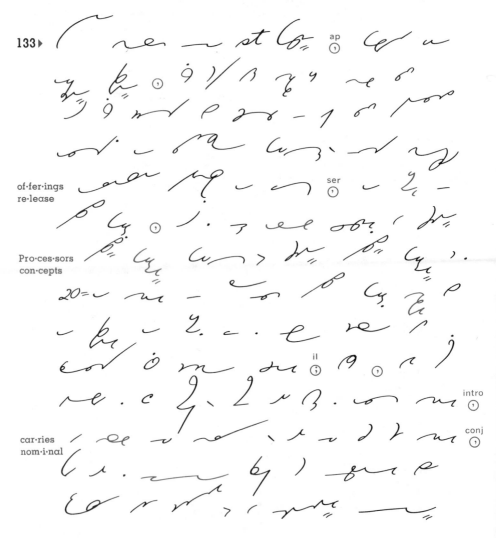

of·fer·ings
re·lease

ser

Pro·ces·sors
con·cepts

il

intro

car·ries
nom·i·nal

conj

for·ward·ing
Man·u·al

if

(207)

134 ▸

two-week
hyphenated before noun

par

sched·uled
by-prod·ucts

intro

and o

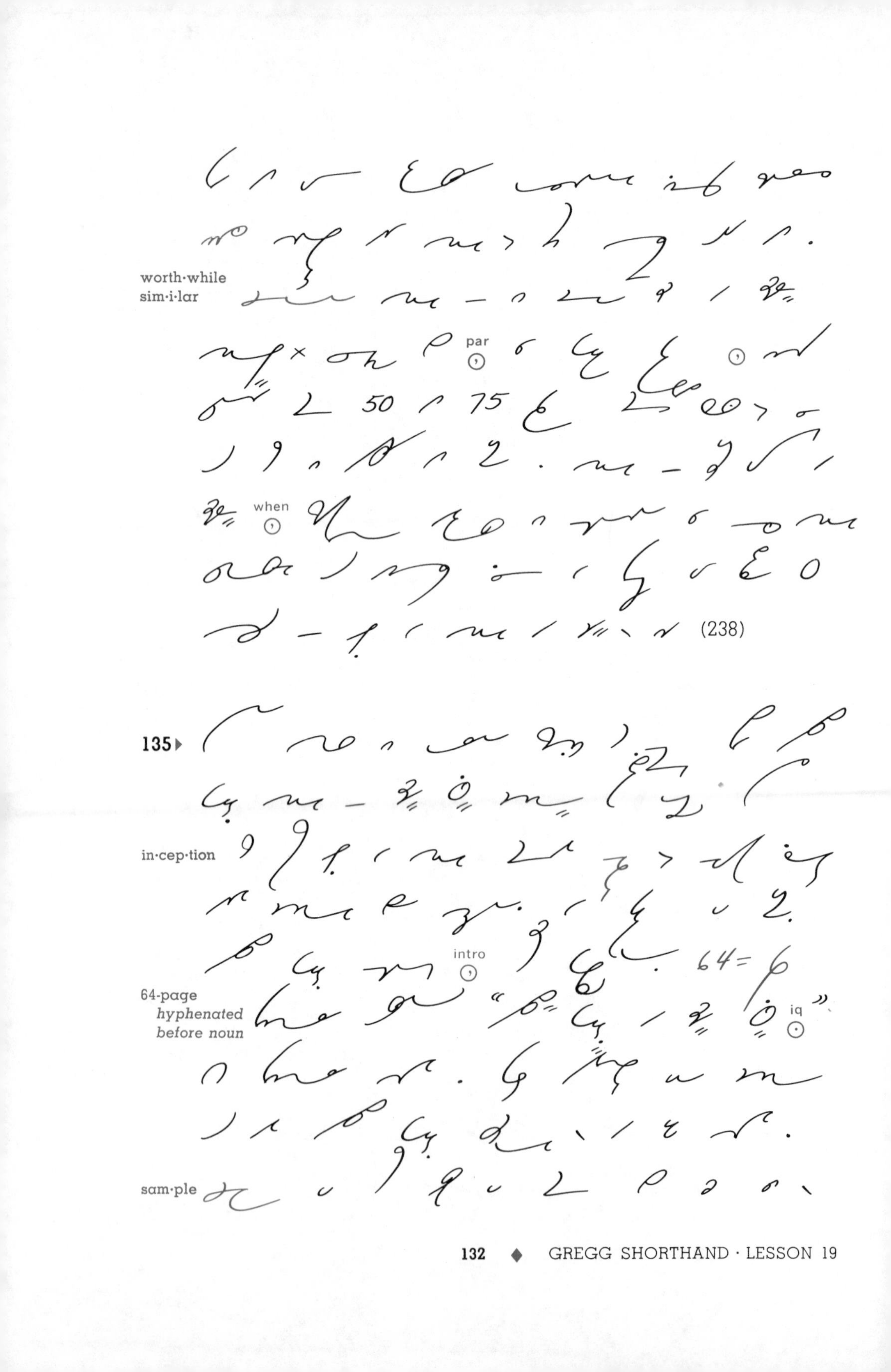

worth·while
sim·i·lar

par

when

(238)

135

in·cep·tion

intro

64-page
hyphenated before noun

iq

sam·ple

136 ▸ Transcription Quiz • For you to supply: 6 commas — 1 comma *as* clause, 1 comma introductory, 1 comma conjunction, 2 commas apposition, 1 comma *if* clause; 2 missing words.

(147)

DEVELOPING WORD-BUILDING POWER

137 ▸ Shorthand Vocabulary Builder

Ses

1

Div, Dif

2

Tern, Term

3

Ult

4

-nd

5

—— ◆◆ ——

1 Offices, glasses, lenses, braces, forces, necessary, basis, sister.
2 Dividend, division, dividing, differ, different, differences, defeat.
3 Turn, return, attorney, turned, term, termed, termination.
4 Consult, consultant, result, insult, ultimate, culminate, culture.
5 Bonds, signed, land, explained, trained, designed, learned.

138 ▸ BUSINESS VOCABULARY BUILDER

decade Ten years.

public utility company An organization that provides water, light, gas, etc.

linking Connecting.

wholly Completely. (Do not confuse with "holey," which means "full of holes.")

READING AND WRITING PRACTICE

139 ▸ Revolution in Office Work

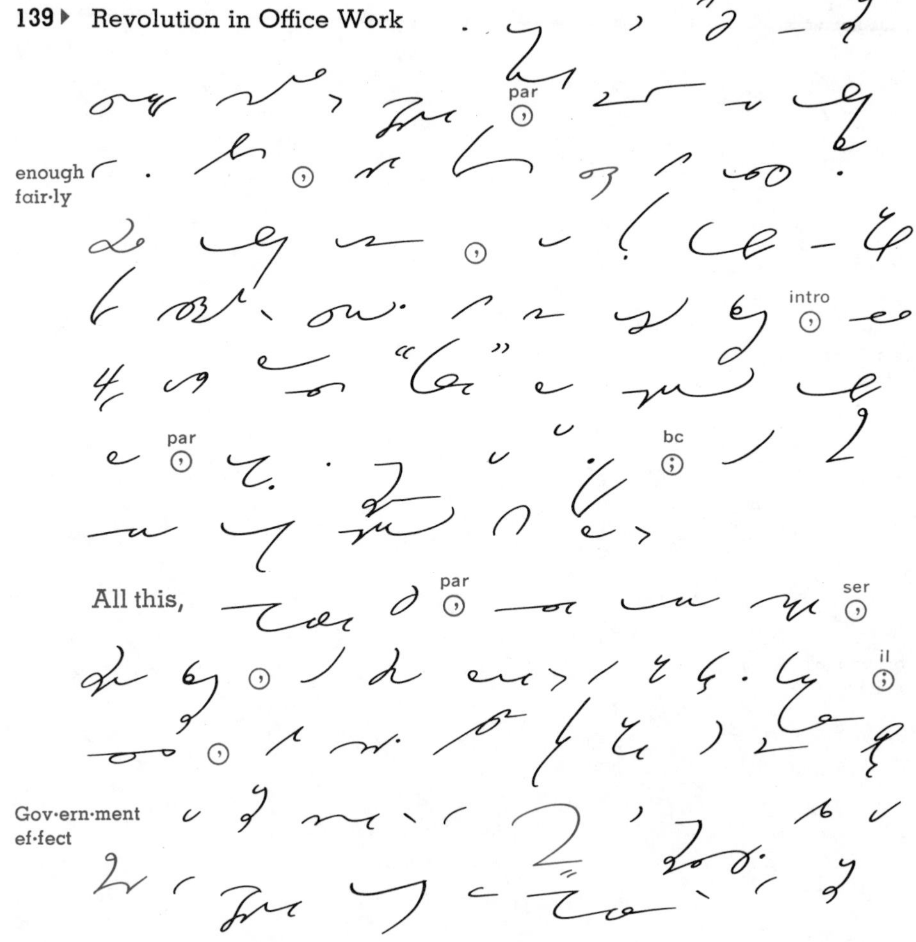

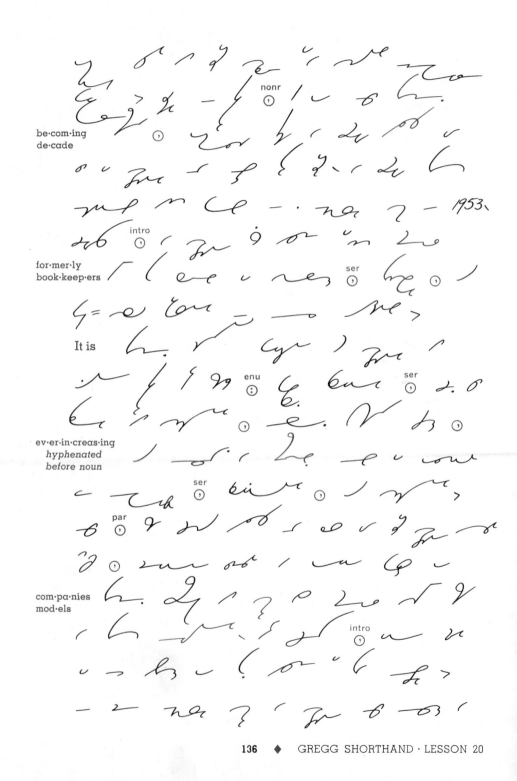

nonr

be·com·ing
de·cade

1953

intro

for·mer·ly
book·keep·ers

ser

It is

enu

ser

ev·er-in·creas·ing
hyphenated before noun

ser

par

com·pa·nies
mod·els

intro

de·ci·sion
wheth·er
qual·i·fies

pure·ly
gad·get

A large

safe·ty
growth
of·fi·cer

ser

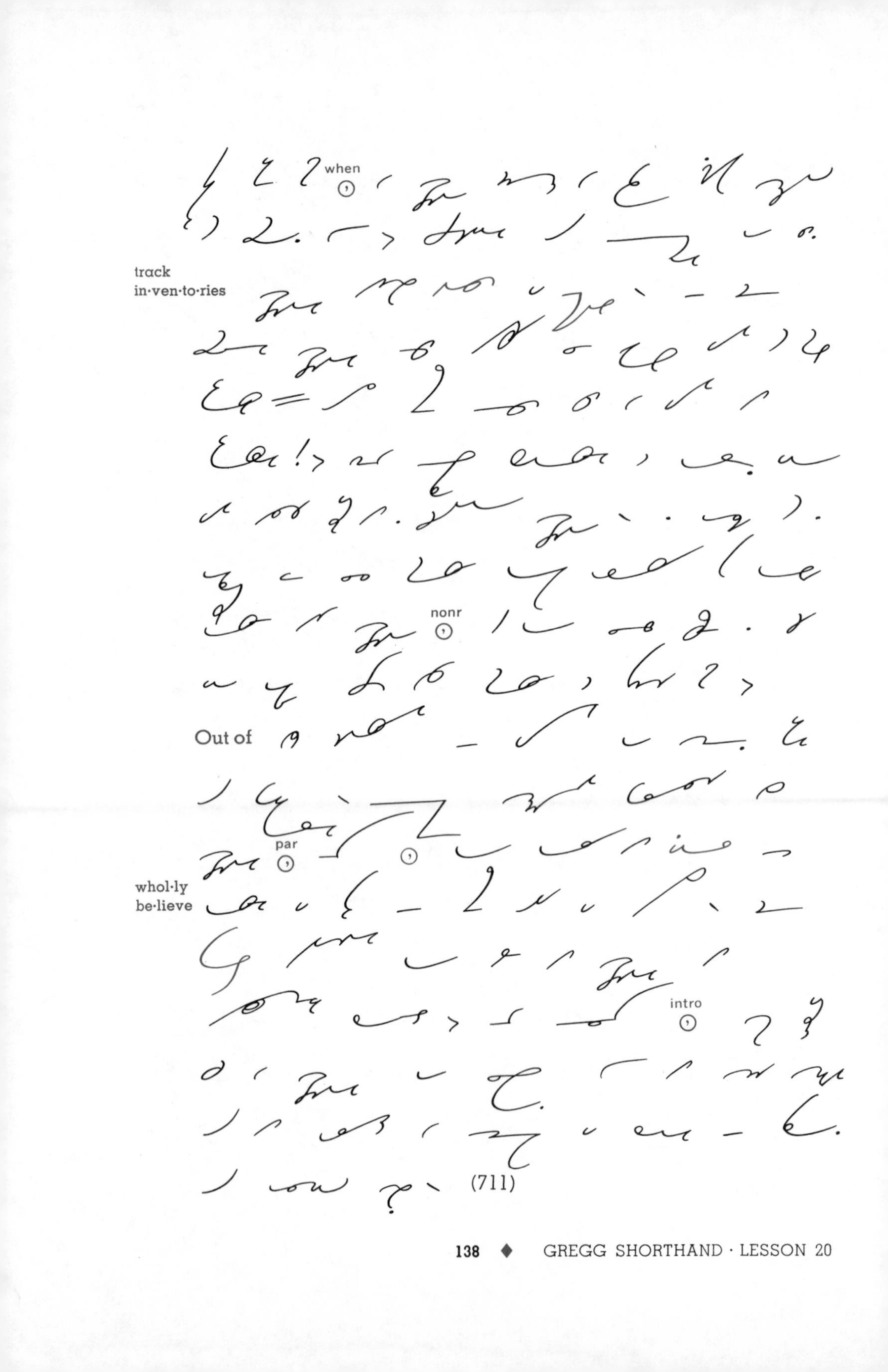

when ,

track
in·ven·to·ries

nonr ,

Out of

par ,

,

whol·ly
be·lieve

intro ,

(711)

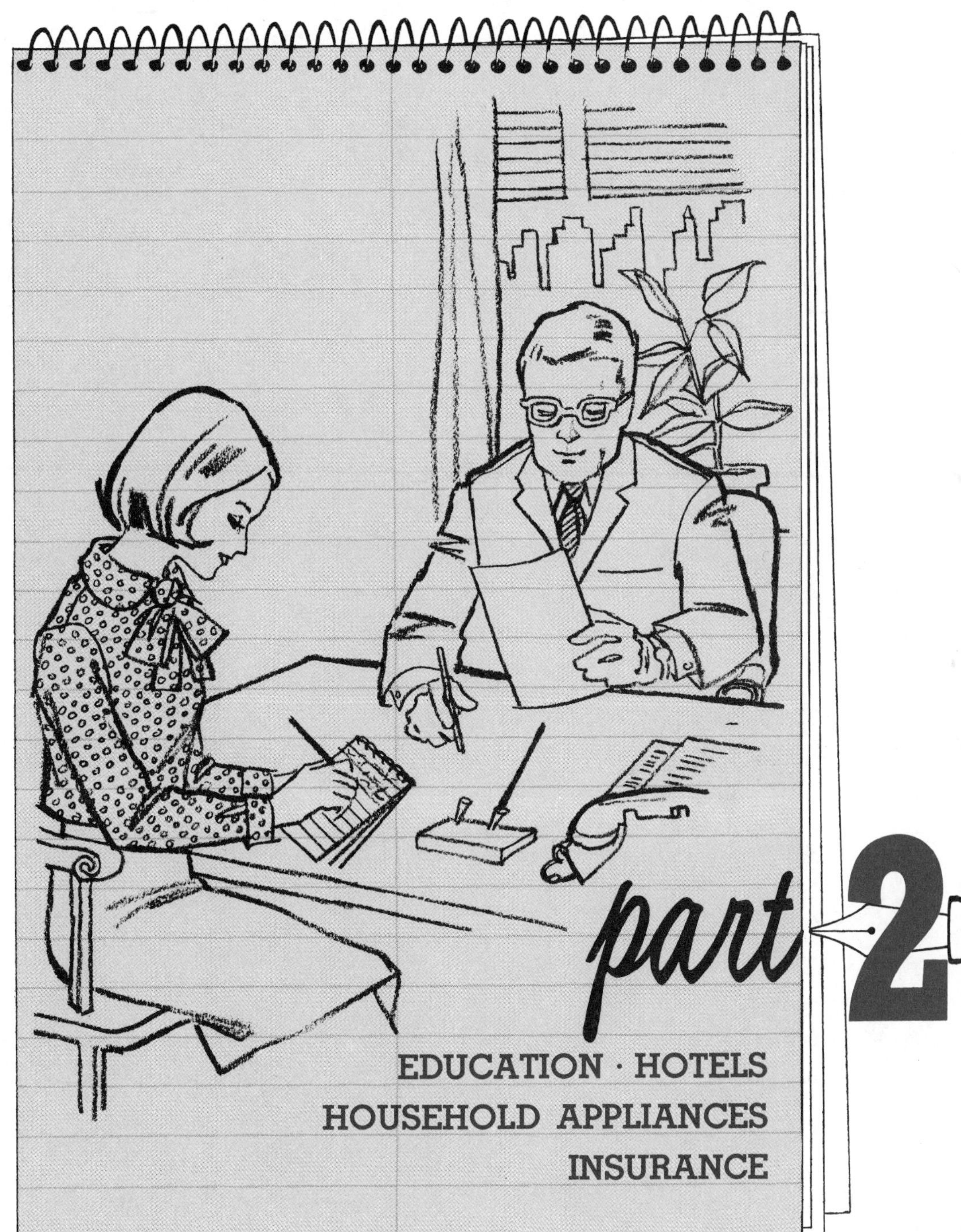

part 2

EDUCATION · HOTELS
HOUSEHOLD APPLIANCES
INSURANCE

In developing speed on new material—material that has not been previously practiced—every shorthand writer at one time or another encounters three problems. Perhaps you have already faced them in your dictation practice.

1▸ He falls behind.

2▸ He is called upon to write an unfamiliar word.

3▸ He does not hear, or mis-hears, a word.

What does the experienced writer do when he meets these problems?

He falls behind

a He "hangs on" as long as he can. He realizes that the dictator may come to his rescue by stopping a few moments to take a breath, to cough, or to clear his throat. Often these few moments enable him to catch up.

b When he falls hopelessly behind, he drops the words he has not written and skips a line or two. This blank space indicates to him the point at which he has a break.

c He picks up the dictation at the new point.

d When he transcribes he tries, with the help of context, to supply the missing words.

He encounters an unfamiliar word

a He tries to write it alphabetically, in full.

b If he cannot write it in full, he tries to write at least the beginning of the word. This beginning often helps him to locate the word in a dictionary when he transcribes.

c If the word completely escapes him, he leaves a space in his notes and continues writing; he does not waste precious moments trying to build an outline for it because he knows that the dictator will not wait for him.

d When he transcribes, he substitutes for the word he missed a synonym that will not change the meaning of the dictated material.

He does not hear, or mis-hears, a word

a When he does not hear a word, either because the dictator did not enunciate clearly or because some noise interfered, he leaves a space in his notes and supplies the word later, with the help of context. He does not stop writing!

b If he thinks he heard a word but knows from context that it could not possibly be the correct one, he writes the word he thinks he heard and encircles it. If he is pressed for time to encircle it, he skips a line in his notes. Often, the outline for the word that he thought he heard will help him supply the correct one.

c On some occasions the word that he did not hear, or mis-heard, will occur to him later during the dictation. He does not take time to insert it in its proper place; he knows that this may cause him to fall behind. He does, however, try to hold the word in his mind and fill it in immediately upon the completion of the dictation.

These suggestions, of course, apply to your work on speed development. On the job, however, you would stop the dictator tactfully when one of these situations arises rather than risk the possibility of turning in an inaccurate transcript.

dictation problems

CHAPTER FIVE

education

DEVELOPING WORD-BUILDING POWER

140▸ Brief Forms and Derivatives

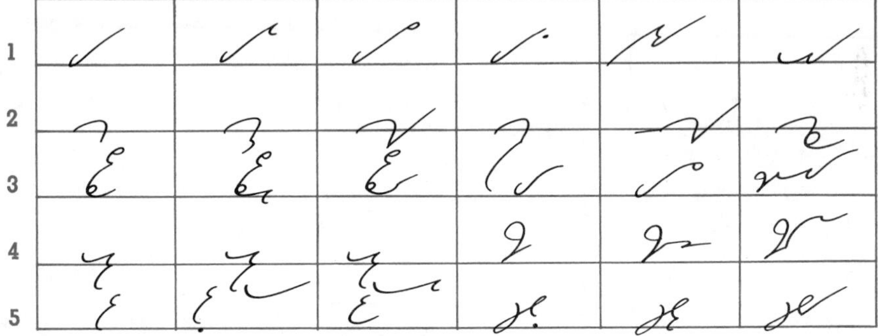

—— ♦♦ ——

1 Order, orders, orderly, ordering, disorder, reorder.
2 Question, questions, questioned, questionable, unquestioned, questionnaire.
3 Experience, experiences, experienced; ordinary, ordinarily, extraordinary.
4 Responsible, responsibility, responsibilities; after, afternoon, afterdinner.
5 Speak, speaking, speaker; satisfying, satisfies, satisfied.

BUILDING TRANSCRIPTION SKILLS

141▸ TYPING STYLE STUDY **titles**

books, booklets, and **pamphlets** In letters, titles of books, booklets, and pamphlets are enclosed in quotation marks.

The textbook that we use, "Modern Economics," is being revised.

"The History of the United States" has been adopted by the city schools.

A copy of our booklet, "Punctuation in a Nutshell," is enclosed.

magazines, newspapers, and **bulletins** In letters, titles of magazines, newspapers, and bulletins are not quoted; they are simply capitalized.

The Daily Cardinal is the name of the newspaper.

The students in our class read Today's Secretary.

The first word and all the other main words in a title are capitalized. Words such as *in, the, and* in the body of the title are not capitalized.

CAUTION: These styles are recommended for general business letters; they are the ones followed in your textbook. However, some employers prefer to have the titles of publications typed in all caps; others prefer to have them underscored. Be sure to find out which style your employer prefers.

142▸ BUSINESS VOCABULARY BUILDER

encountered Met.
significant Important.
convene To meet; to gather.

READING AND WRITING PRACTICE

143▸ Brief-Form Letter

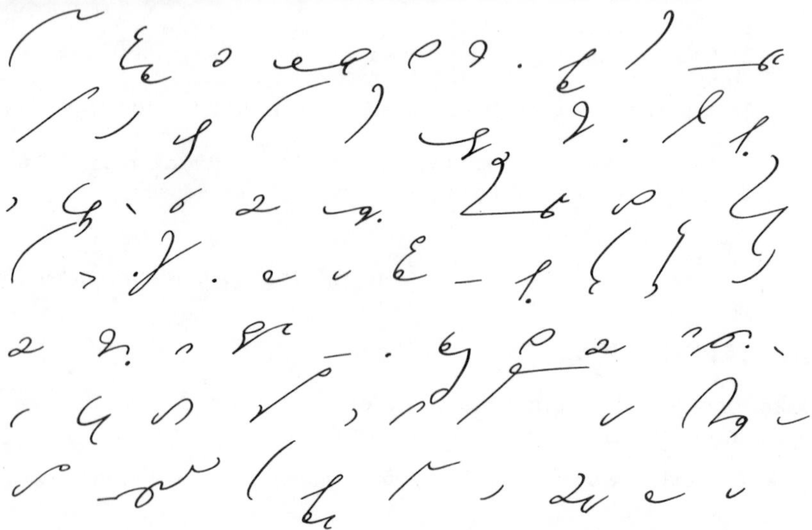

(165)

144▸

intro

ap

rec·om·men·da·tion
ide·al

bc

ilq

conj

iq

intro

re·ceiv·ing
pro·fes·sor

ap

well-known
hyphenated
before noun

ap

iq

ap

Transcribe:
two o'clock

par

dis·cus·sion
em·pha·sized

(243)

145▸

as

nonr

sched·ule
ef·fi·cient·ly

enu

ser

their lei·sure

par

nc

(208)

146

intro

up to date *no noun, no hyphen*

and o

intro

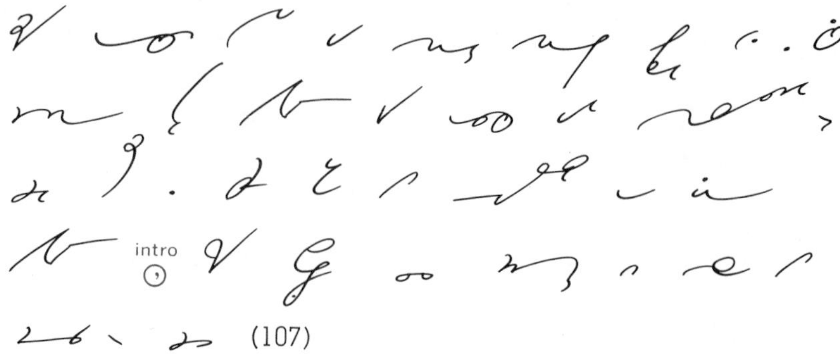

147▸ Transcription Quiz • For you to supply; 5 commas—1 comma apposition, 1 comma *when* clause, 1 comma introductory, 1 comma *if* clause, 1 comma conjunction; 2 missing words.

(125)

BUILDING PHRASING SKILL

148 ▸ Useful Business-Letter Phrases

Been

1

Able

2

Want

3

Or Omitted in Phrases

4

—— ◆◆ ——

1 Has been, it has been, I have been, you have been, you have not been, I have not been, who have been, who have not been, should have been, could have been.

2 I have been able, who have been able, has not been able, would be able, should be able, I have not been able, he will not be able, may not be able.

3 I want, you want, he wants, do you want, if you want, he wanted, I wanted, who wanted.

4 One or two, two or three, three or four, day or two, day or two ago, week or two, week or two ago.

149 ▸ Frequent Names

— ♦♦ —

1 Driscoll, Duffy, Duncan, Dunne, Edwards, Evans, Farrell.
2 Charlotte, Clara, Constance, Cora, Cynthia, Delia.

BUILDING TRANSCRIPTION SKILLS

150 ▸ GRAMMAR CHECKUP may, can

may Implies *permission* or *possibility.*

You may leave at four o'clock if your work is finished. (You have permission.)

I may go to the ball game if the weather is nice. (There is a possibility.)

can Implies *ability* or *power.*

I can read very rapidly. (Am able to.)

He can run faster than John. (He has the power to.)

151 ▸ BUSINESS VOCABULARY BUILDER

imperative Necessary; absolutely essential.
participate To take part.
prestige Standing or estimation in people's minds.

READING AND WRITING PRACTICE

152 ▸ Phrase Letter

(159)

153▸

re·ferred

isq

iq

if

isq

iq

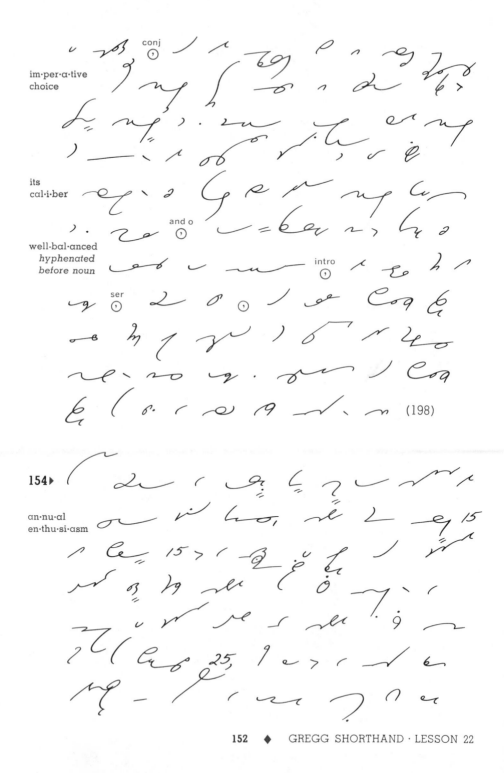

conj

im·per·a·tive
choice

its
cal·i·ber

and o

well-bal·anced
hyphenated
before noun

intro

ser

(198)

154▸

an·nu·al
en·thu·si·asm

15

15

25,

prize
rec·og·ni·tion

if

(117)

155

well qual·i·fied
no noun,
no hyphen

ser

8-week
hyphenated
before noun

intro

bc

if

15

ac·cep·tance
agree·ment

intro

par

nc

Wis·con·sin

(157)

156 ▸ Transcription Quiz • For you to supply: 10 commas—2 commas introductory, 4 commas parenthetical, 1 comma *if* clause, 2 commas nonrestrictive, 1 comma conjunction; 2 missing words.

(181)

DEVELOPING WORD-BUILDING POWER

157 ▸ Word Families

-iance

1

Comm-

2

Come

3

-ply

4

-ses

5

—— ◆◆ ——

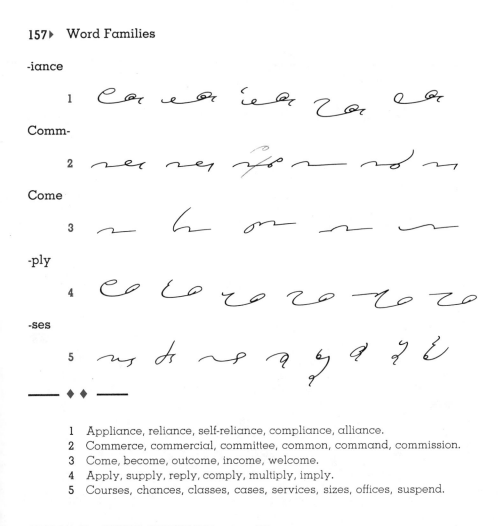

1 Appliance, reliance, self-reliance, compliance, alliance.
2 Commerce, commercial, committee, common, command, commission.
3 Come, become, outcome, income, welcome.
4 Apply, supply, reply, comply, multiply, imply.
5 Courses, chances, classes, cases, services, sizes, offices, suspend.

BUILDING TRANSCRIPTION SKILLS

158 ▸ SIMILAR-WORDS DRILL **sight, site, cite**

sight Vision; mental perception.

Do not lose sight of this important fact.

site A location.

If you are looking for a site for your new plant, let us know.

cite To quote; to name.

We can cite you many instances that prove our point.

159 ▸ BUSINESS VOCABULARY BUILDER	
	enviable Highly desirable.
	recruiting Enlisting new members.
	emphasizes Stresses.

READING AND WRITING PRACTICE

160 ▸

de·scrib·ing
of·fered

as

ser

1912

bc

intro

cite
alum·ni
prom·i·nent

and o

lose
sight

ap

if

nc

its
site

(198)

161▸

ap

as

ap

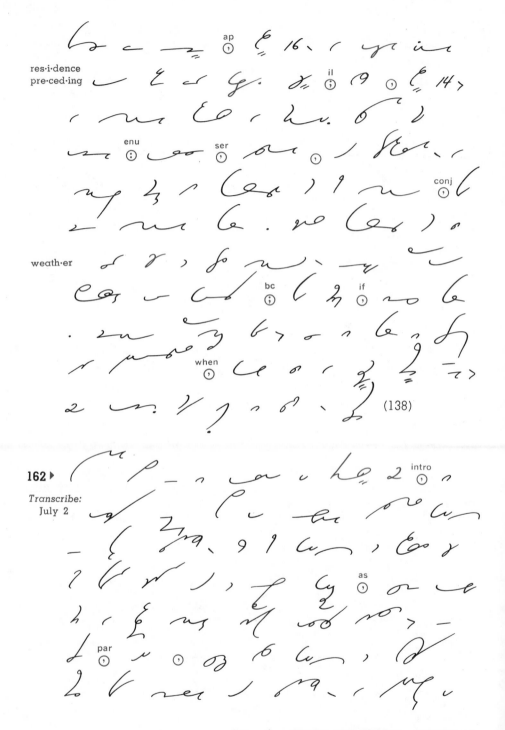

res·i·dence
pre·ced·ing

il

enu ser

conj

weath·er

bc if

when

(138)

162 ▸

Transcribe:
July 2

intro

as

par

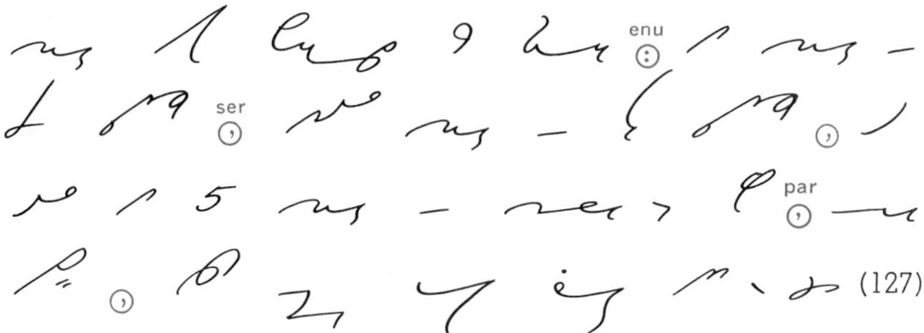

163 ▸ Transcription Quiz • For you to supply: 5 commas—2 commas nonrestrictive, 2 commas introductory, 1 comma *if* clause; 2 missing words.

(146)

DEVELOPING WORD-BUILDING POWER

164 ▸ Word Beginnings and Endings

-ship

1

Inter-

2

Trans-

3

-ification

4

-cal, -cle

5

1 Fellowship, membership, partnership, authorship, relationships, companionship.

2 Interest, interestingly, interview, interfered, internal, intermission, interrupt.

3 Transcription, transcribe, transport, transportation, transparent, translate.

4 Qualifications, classifications, specifications, ratification, modification, notification.

5 Mechanical, chemical, radical, particle, surgical, medical.

165▸ Geographical Expressions

1 Norristown, Tarrytown, Youngstown, Jamestown, Georgetown, Johnstown.

2 Texas, New Mexico, Oklahoma, Kansas, Colorado, Nebraska, Wyoming.

3 U.S.S.R., Uruguay, Venezuela, Yugoslavia, Albania.

BUILDING TRANSCRIPTION SKILLS

166▸ SPELLING FAMILIES ie, ei

One of the most troublesome spelling families in the English language is the *ie, ei* group. Grammarians tell us that:

1 i comes before e

achieve	**brief**	**yield**
piece	**chief**	**friend**
be·lief	**niece**	**re·lief**

2 except after c

de·ceit	**re·ceipt**	**re·ceive**

and when the combination has the sound of a

their	**heir**	**eight**

But, of course, this rule, like any other rule, has its exceptions. Here are a few words that are used with some frequency in business that are exceptions to the rule.

ei·ther	**nei·ther**	**lei·sure**
for·eign	**ef·fi·cient**	**suf·fi·cient**

In your Reading and Writing Practice you will find a number of these words; watch for them.

167 ▸ **BUSINESS VOCABULARY BUILDER**

audiovisual Pertaining to sound and sight.

secondary level Beyond elementary school, usually from the ninth through twelfth grades.

fellowship A position, usually in a university, granting a salary and allowing for advanced study or research.

READING AND WRITING PRACTICE

168 ▸

as·sis·tance
sep·a·rate

be·lief
re·ceived
yield

par

iq

if

ap

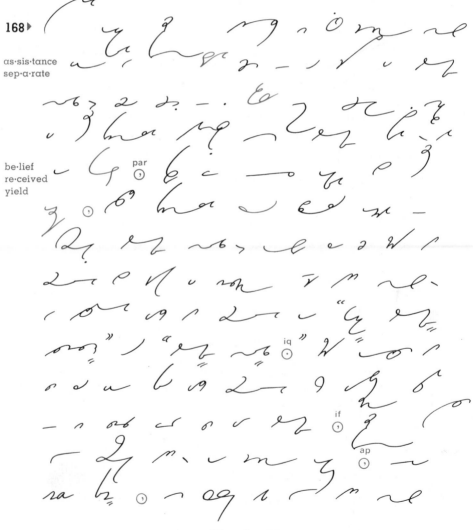

2679 So. York St., Denver, Colorado 80210

April 14, 196-

Mrs. Charles R. Gray
3313 Western Parkway
Denver, Colorado 80210

Dear Mrs. Gray:

I must make a confession. When I came here last fall to take over the Denver branch of McRay Company, Inc., I was sure that it would be easy to sell a great deal of furniture in a short time. The sight of the homes here in Denver must have caused me to be overoptimistic.

In anticipation of the sales that I expected, I bought large quantities of fine furniture. In spite of the quality of the furniture and the appeal of our low prices, however, sales fell far below my expectations. Now I have a warehouse full of merchandise that must be moved. What's more, there are new shipments on the way from several manufacturers.

The time for action has come. On Saturday, May 6, you will see in all the Denver papers an announcement of stock-disposal sales. Prices will be low. In many cases, our furniture will be offered at cost and even less. Of course, we expect a great response. Because of this, I feel that you and a few other preferred customers should have the opportunity to shop in comfort before public announcement is made of the sale.

Therefore, please consider this a personal invitation for you to shop at your convenience on May 3, 4, or 5. When you come, please give the enclosed card to one of our salesmen. He will then take you to the floor on which the sale will be held.

Very truly yours,

McRAY COMPANY, INC.

Martin A. Foster

Martin A. Foster
Manager

MAF:RE
Enclosure

Long Letter
Indented Style
Standard Punctuation

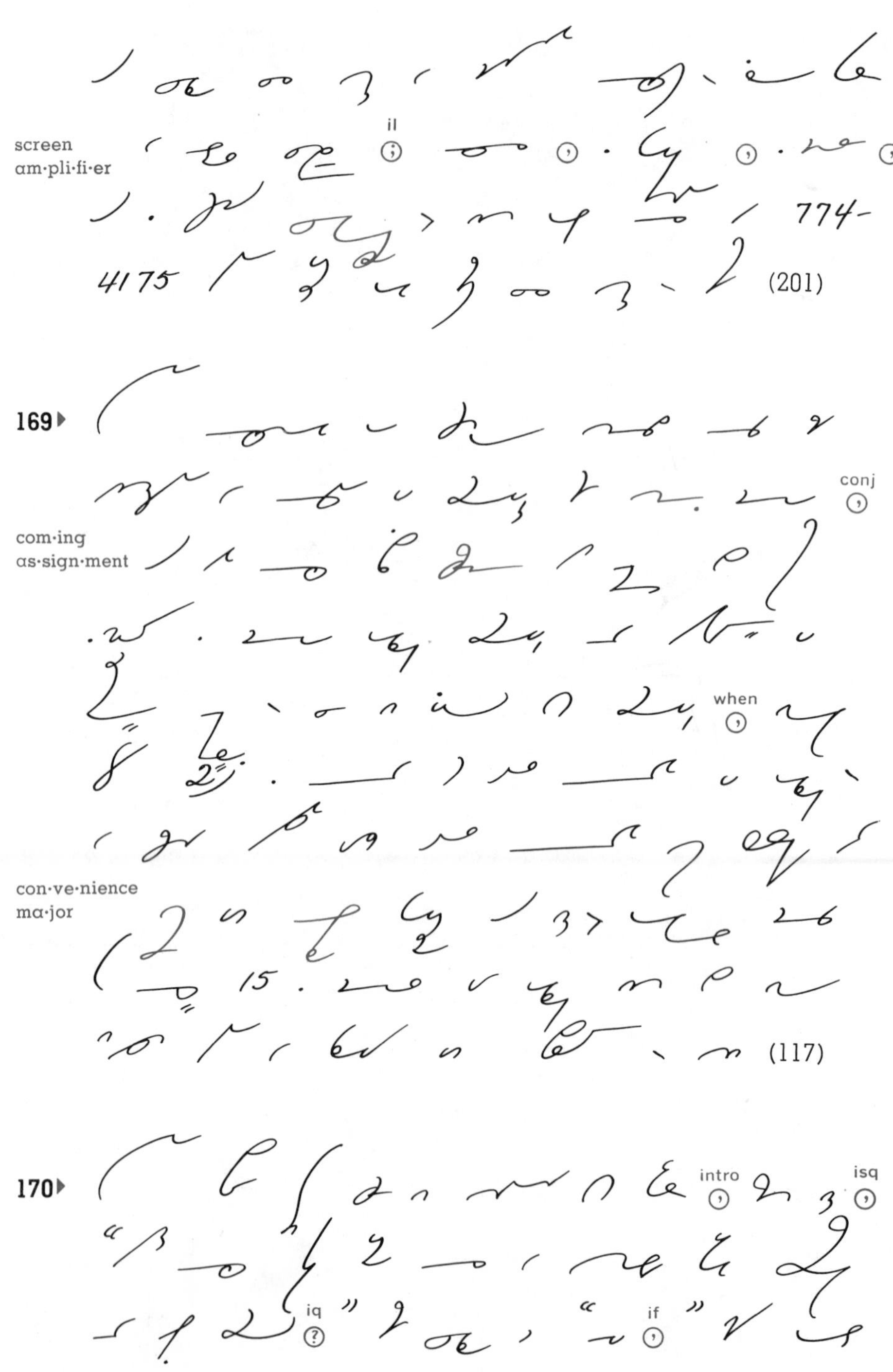
screen
am·pli·fi·er
il
774-
4175
(201)
169
conj
com·ing
as·sign·ment
when
con·ve·nience
ma·jor
15
(117)
170
intro
isq
iq
if

1926 intro

intro

va·can·cies
el·e·men·ta·ry

par

sec·on·dary
ex·cept
com·pe·ti·tion

nc intro

nc

(180)

171

its
ware·house

8:30 4

intro

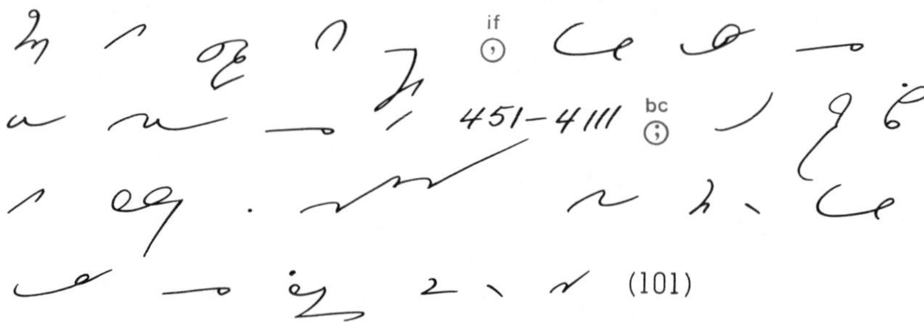

172 ▸ Transcription Quiz • For you to supply: 4 commas—2 commas series, 1 comma *and* omitted, 1 comma introductory; 2 missing words.

17

13

(131)

DEVELOPING WORD-BUILDING POWER

173 Shorthand Vocabulary Builder

Ng

1

Ia, Ea

2

Men, etc.

3

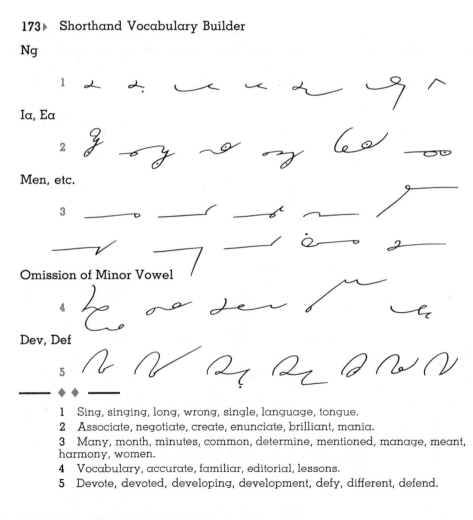

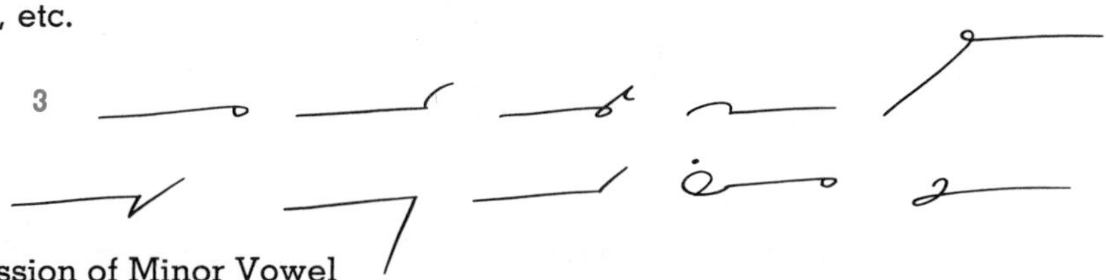

Omission of Minor Vowel

4

Dev, Def

5

1 Sing, singing, long, wrong, single, language, tongue.

2 Associate, negotiate, create, enunciate, brilliant, mania.

3 Many, month, minutes, common, determine, mentioned, manage, meant, harmony, women.

4 Vocabulary, accurate, familiar, editorial, lessons.

5 Devote, devoted, developing, development, defy, different, defend.

BUILDING TRANSCRIPTION SKILLS

174 ▸ **BUSINESS VOCABULARY BUILDER**

primitive Uncivilized; crude; simple.
cultivate To improve by care, training, or study.
adage An old saying or proverb.
articulation Act of speaking clearly, distinctly.
slur To pronounce rapidly and indistinctly.

READING AND WRITING PRACTICE

175 ▸ **The Gift of Voice**

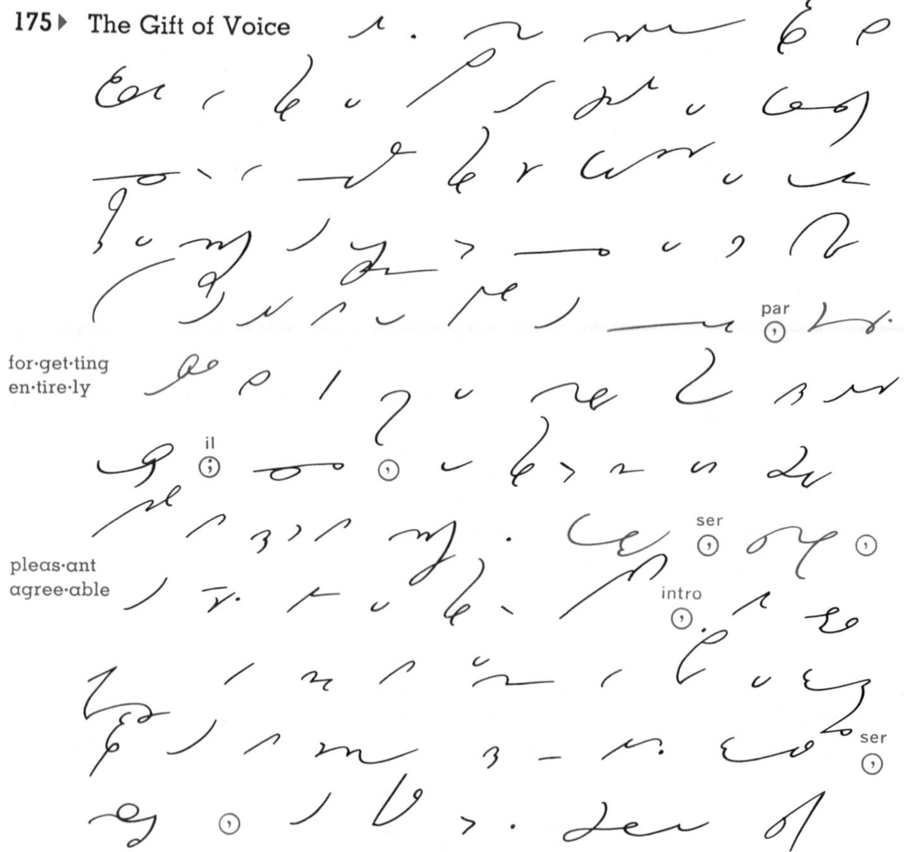

iq

and o

nc

if

par

and o

well-mod·u·la·ted *hyphenated before noun*

nc

sole·ly
re·al·ize

In cultivating

intro

and o

conj

aloud
enun·ci·ate

bc

par

the·ater
ex·am·ple

par

(338)

176 ▸ Developing your Vocabulary

intro

for·mer
rec·og·nize
ac·qui·si·tion

ap

isq

il

ac·cu·rate
tongue

iq

intro

enu

ac·cess
li·brary

conj

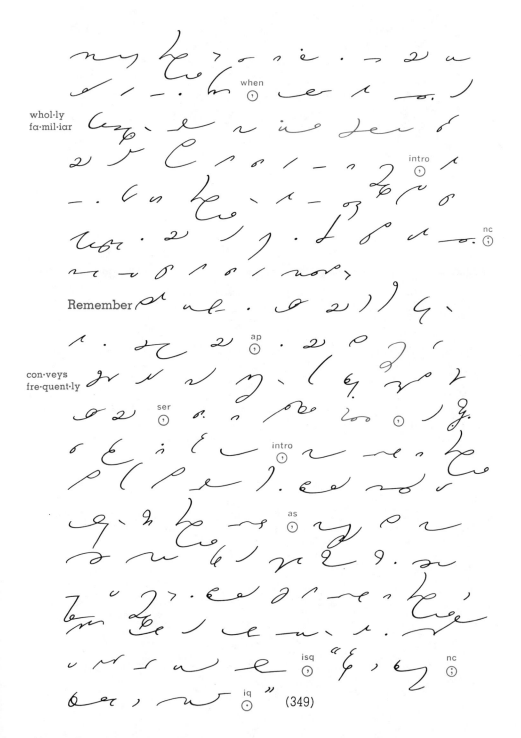

whol·ly
fa·mil·iar

when

intro

nc

Remember

ap

con·veys
fre·quent·ly

ser

intro

as

isq

nc

iq

(349)

CHAPTER SIX

hotels

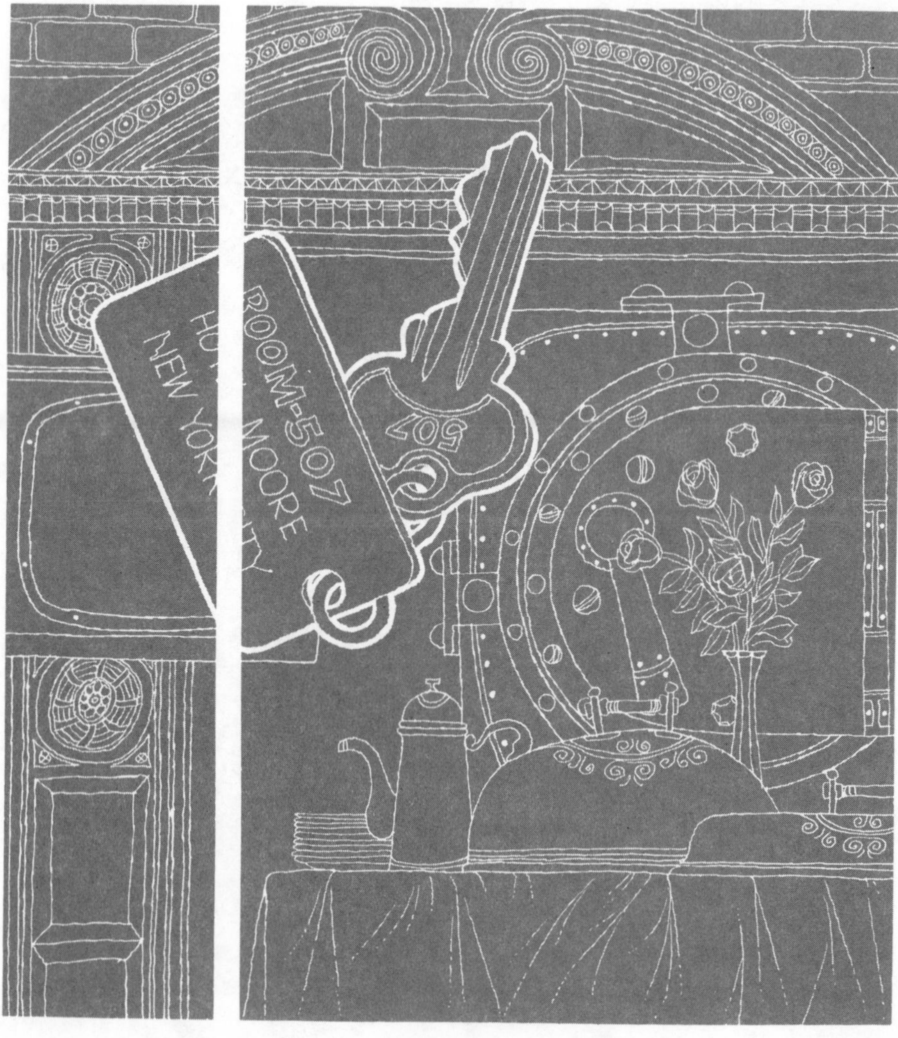

DEVELOPING WORD-BUILDING POWER

177▸ Brief Forms and Derivatives

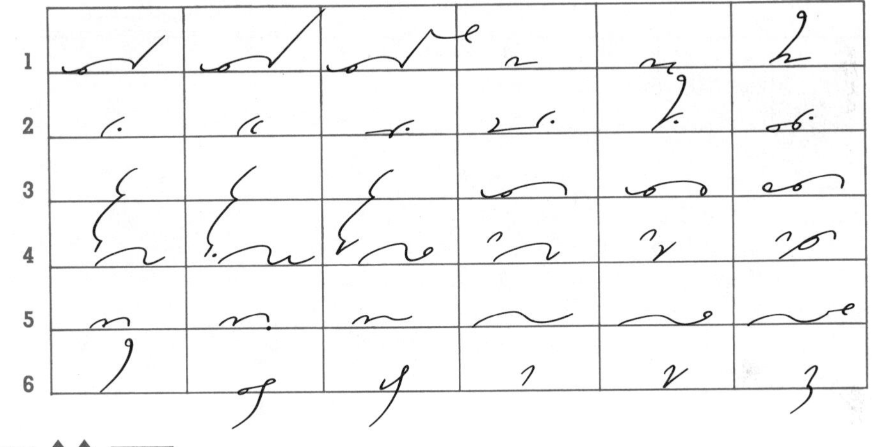

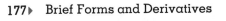

1 Regard, regarded, regardless; one-won, once, everyone.
2 Thing-think, things-thinks, nothing, something, everything, anything.
3 Publish-publication, publishing, published; regular, regularly, irregular.
4 Great, greater, greatly; undergo, understate, undertake.
5 Work, working, worker; glad, gladly, gladness.
6 Ever-every, whenever, whatever; wish, wished, wishful.

BUILDING TRANSCRIPTION SKILLS

178▸ PUNCTUATION PRACTICE the apostrophe

1 A noun that ends in an *s* sound and is followed by another noun is

usually a possessive, calling for an apostrophe before the *s* when the word is singular.

This company's advertising is designed for three colors.

Mr. Green's job will be to look after our interests in television.

2 A plural noun ending in *s* calls for an apostrophe *after* the *s* to form the possessive.

Their employees' wages have been raised.

All students' marks will be issued Friday.

3 An irregular plural calls for an apostrophe *before* the *s* to form the possessive.

We sell children's toys.

He will open a men's clothing store soon.

4 The possessive forms of pronouns do not require an apostrophe.

You will be wasting your time as well as ours.

These papers are theirs, not ours.

179▸ BUSINESS VOCABULARY BUILDER

accessible Easy to reach.
hospitality Cordial treatment.
booked to capacity Full.

READING AND WRITING PRACTICE

180▸ Brief-Form Letter

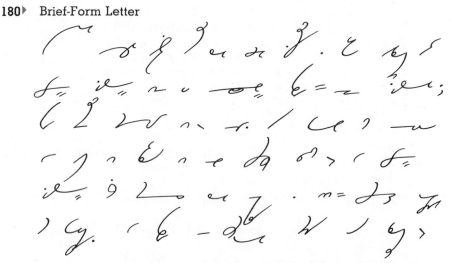

(127)

181 ▸

ho·tel's
ac·com·mo·da·tions

par

Transcribe:
January 10
January 20

ser

if

bu·reau
for·ward
Den·ver's

ap

(142)

182

par

and o

am·ple
halls

ser

intro

ide·al
na·tion's

co·op·er·ate
year's
ac·cept

par

bc

(175)

183

States

18 20

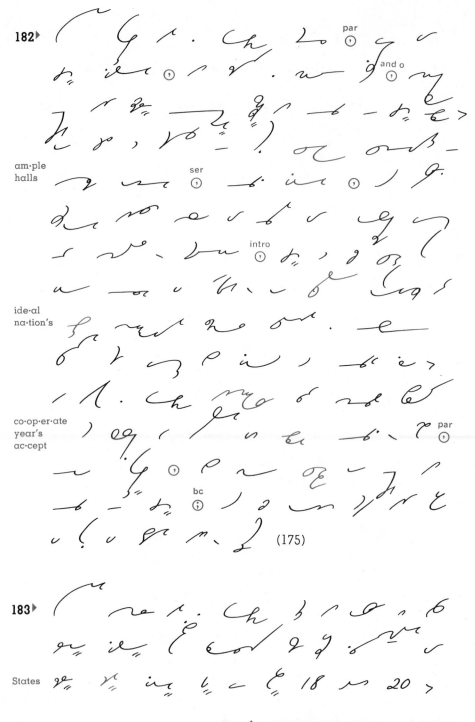

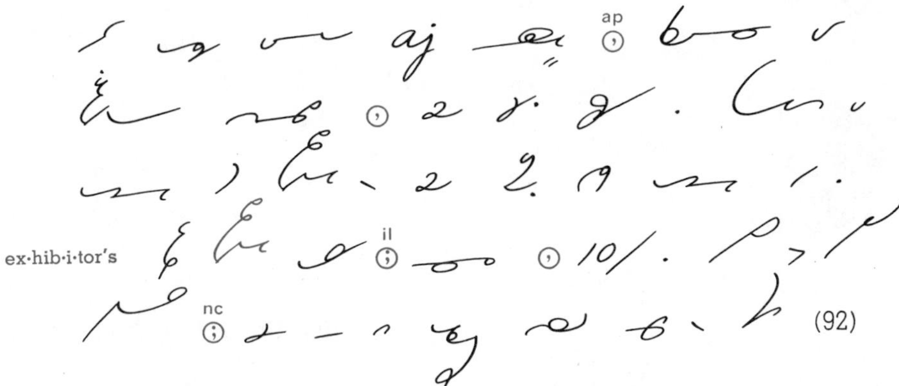

184▸ Transcription Quiz • For you to supply: 5 commas — 1 comma *if* clause, 1 comma apposition, 1 comma conjunction, 1 comma *as* clause, 1 comma *when* clause; 2 missing words.

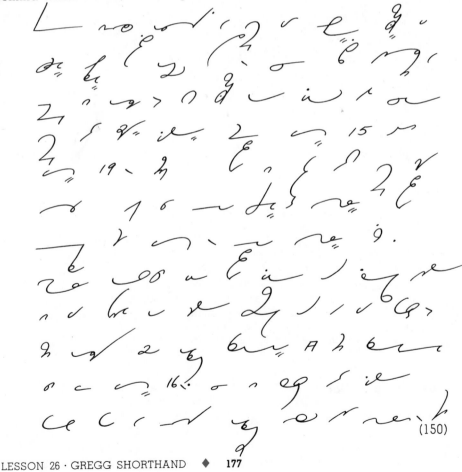

(150)

BUILDING PHRASING SKILL

185▸ Useful Business-Letter Phrases

Ago

1

Few

2

To

3

In addition

4

— ♦♦ —

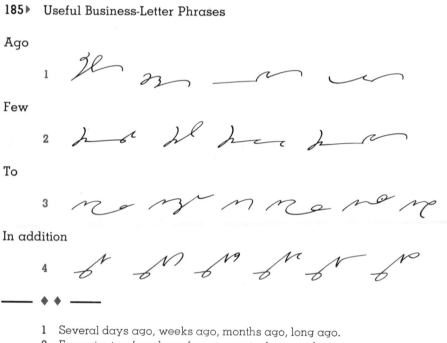

1 Several days ago, weeks ago, months ago, long ago.
2 Few minutes, few days, few moments, few months ago.
3 To complete, to consider, to question, to complain, to create, to keep.
4 In addition to the, in addition to this, in addition to these, in addition to those, in addition to them, in addition to that.

186▸ Frequent Names

1

2

1 Fisher, Fitzgerald, Foley, Fox, Fraser, Gordon.
2 Duncan, Edgar, Edmond, Edward, Ernest, Eugene.

BUILDING TRANSCRIPTION SKILLS

187 GRAMMAR CHECKUP let, leave

Let and *leave* are two words that people often misuse. You will have no difficulty using these words correctly if you will remember these definitions.

leave To move or go away from; to depart.

I will leave home about ten o'clock.

let To permit; to allow.

Let (not leave) me help you.

HINT: If you are in doubt as to whether *let* or *leave* is correct, substitute *permit* and *depart*. If *permit* makes sense, use *let;* if *depart* makes sense, use *leave.*

188 BUSINESS VOCABULARY BUILDER

anthology A collection of literary pieces or writings.
ascertaining Learning; finding out.
superb Extremely good; excellent.
unwittingly Not knowingly.
adjoining Next to.

READING AND WRITING PRACTICE

189 Phrase Letter

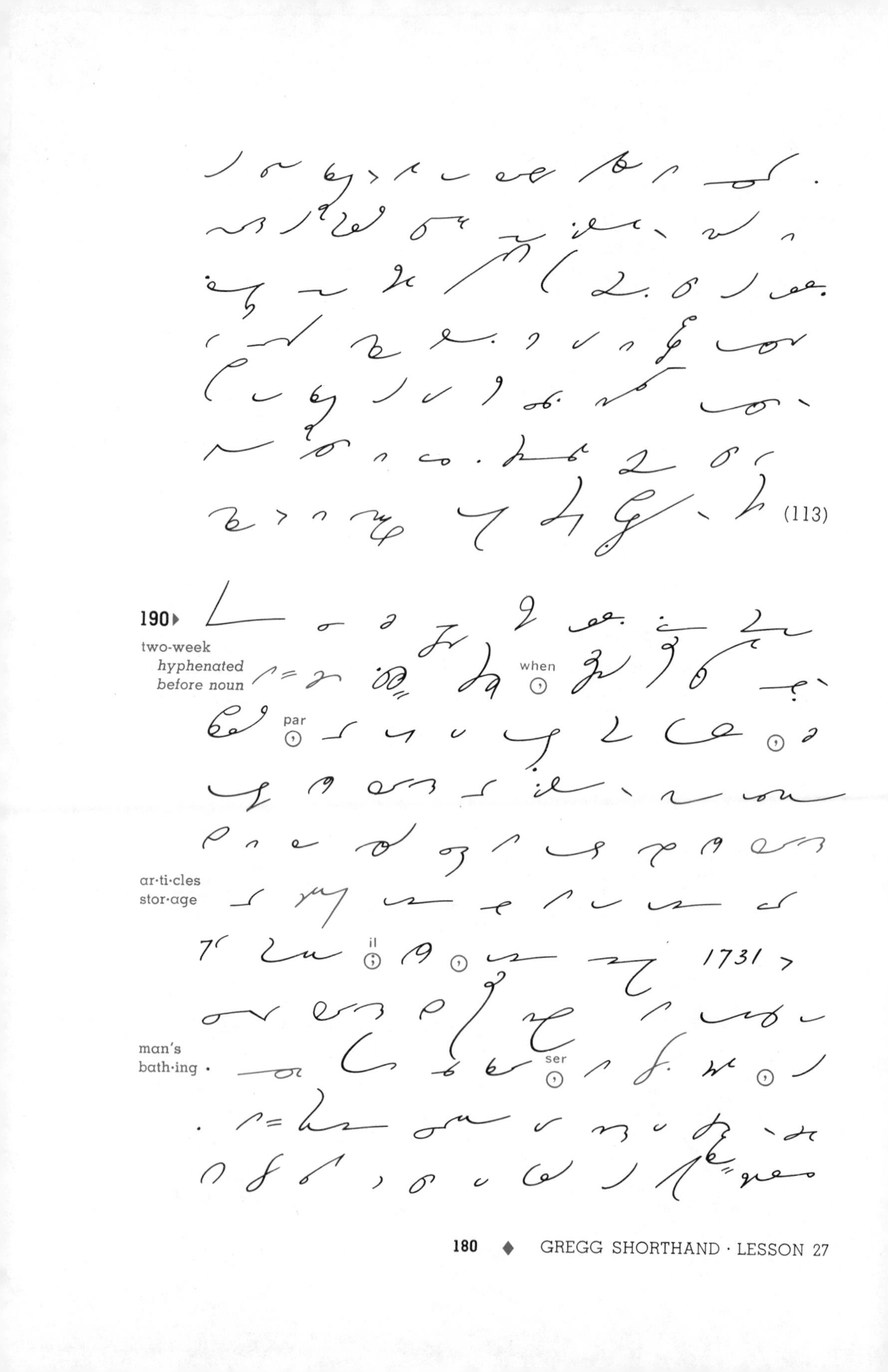

(113)

190

two-week
hyphenated before noun

when

par

ar·ti·cles
stor·age

il

1731

man's
bath·ing

ser

intro

if

par

(152)

191

nonr

27

nc

20 par

6:30 if

Transcribe: five o'clock

5

as

if

(165)

192

25

26 bc par

ex·ten·sive
re·mod·el·ing

intro and o

mod·ern
spe·cial

enu 10

ser 15 20

suite
ad·join·ing

20

25

if

28 isq

iq (210)

193▸ Transcription Quiz • For you to supply: 7 commas — 1 comma *as* clause, 2 commas series, 2 commas introductory, 2 commas conjunction; 2 missing words.

(178)

DEVELOPING WORD-BUILDING POWER

194▸ Word Families

Book

1

-ally

2

-rative

3

-ist

4

-man

5

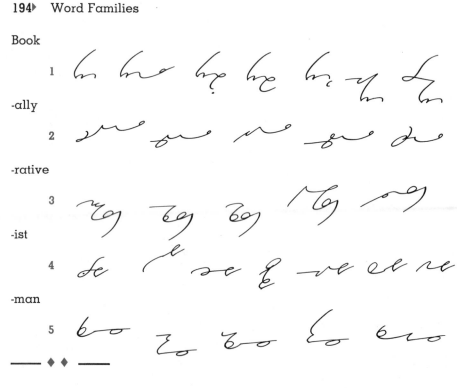

1 Book, booklet, bookkeeping, bookkeeper, bookings, notebook, bankbook.
2 Centrally, naturally, totally, materially, finally.
3 Cooperative, imperative, comparative, deliberative, decorative.
4 Pianist, dentist, chemist, typist, motorist, artist, tourist.
5 Chairman, newspaperman, repairman, businessman, salesman.

195 ▸ SIMILAR-WORDS DRILL suite, suit

suite (pronounced *swēt*) A group of rooms occupied as a unit.

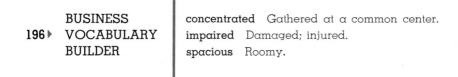

The reception will be held in the Governor's suite on the 10th floor.

suit (*verb*) To answer the requirements of.

The time of the meeting can be arranged to suit your convenience.

196 ▸ BUSINESS VOCABULARY BUILDER

concentrated Gathered at a common center.
impaired Damaged; injured.
spacious Roomy.

READING AND WRITING PRACTICE

197 ▸

com·mit·tee
An·nu·al
suite

intro

con·nect·ing
suit
ide·al·ly

if

anx·ious
cen·tral·ly

conj

(158)

198

Transcribe:
$180
July 14

ap

par

bc

co·op·er·a·tive
de·lin·quent

intro

as

and o

if

intro

self-in-ter-est
prompt-ly

(186)

199 ▸ *Transcribe:*
5855
In-di-an-ap-o-lis

5855

intro

ap

over-night
dis-tance

intro

and o

spa-cious
mod-ern

nc

intro

night's

nc

(198)

200▸

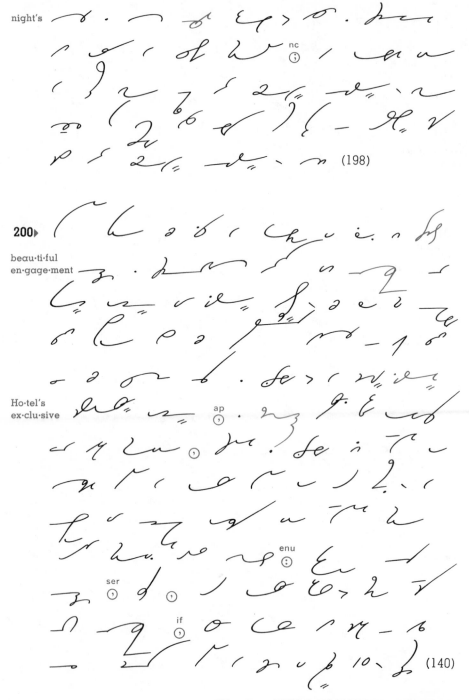

beau·ti·ful
en·gage·ment

Ho·tel's
ex·clu·sive

ap

enu

ser

if

(140)

201 ▸ Transcription Quiz • For you to supply: 8 commas – 4 commas series, 1 comma *when* clause, 2 commas parenthetical, 1 comma *if* clause; 2 missing words.

(156)

DEVELOPING WORD-BUILDING POWER

202 ▸ Word Beginnings and Endings

Sub-

1

For-, Fore-

2

Per-

3

Electric-

4

-ings

5

1 Submit, submitted, subdividing, subway, subcommittee, subsequent, substance.

2 Forget, forgot, formal, foremost, informed, force, enforced.

3 Permit, permission, perform, perhaps, permanent, perpetual.

4 Electric appliances, electric motor, electric wire, electric lights, electric razor.

5 Meetings, gatherings, readings, listings, greetings, sayings.

203 ▸ Geographical Expressions

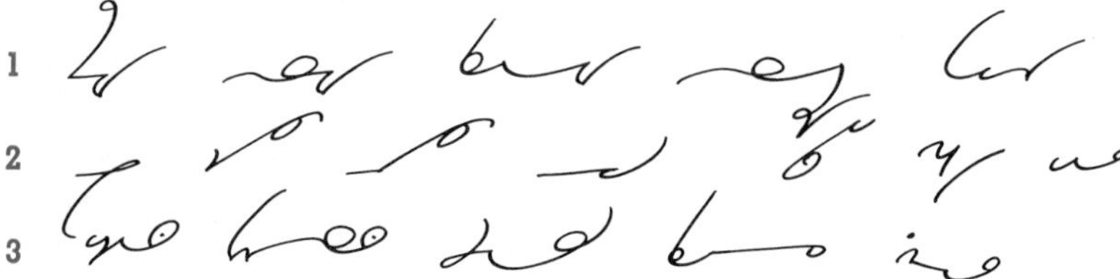

—— ♦♦ ——

1 Evanston, Cranston, Charleston, Galveston, Brockton.

2 Nebraska, South Dakota, North Dakota, Montana, Idaho, Washington, Oregon.

3 Austria, Bulgaria, Finland, Germany, Hungary.

BUILDING TRANSCRIPTION SKILLS

204 ▸ SPELLING FAMILIES -cal, -cle

Whenever you hear the ending that is pronounced "kle," be careful; it may be spelled *cal* or *cle*. Here are examples of each ending.

Words Ending in -cal

med·i·cal	rad·i·cal	po·lit·i·cal
log·i·cal	phys·i·cal	crit·i·cal
sur·gi·cal	mu·si·cal	chem·i·cal
iden·ti·cal	ver·ti·cal	op·ti·cal

Words Ending in -cle

ve·hi·cle	mir·a·cle	bi·cy·cle
par·ti·cle	ar·ti·cle	spec·ta·cle
ob·sta·cle	re·cep·ta·cle	ici·cle

205 ▸ BUSINESS VOCABULARY BUILDER

discriminating (adjective) Having good judgment.
ultimate (noun) Something final.
commend To praise.

206 ▸

el·e·gant
mag·nif·i·cent

sim·i·lar
guest
suites

ex·am·ple
gym·na·si·um

ap ap ser nonr intro isq iq il when

(188)

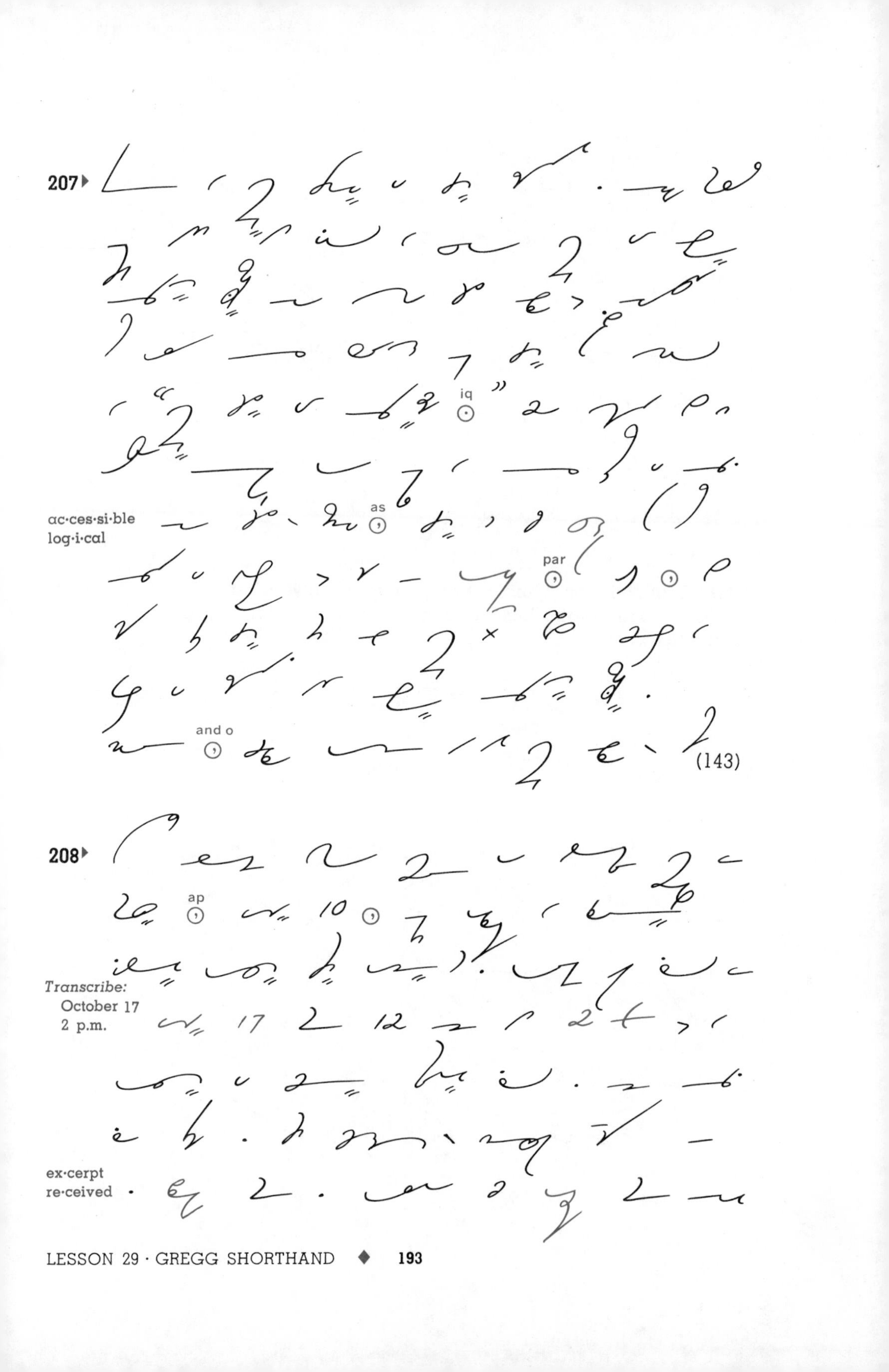

207▸

iq

ac·ces·si·ble
log·i·cal

as

par

and o

(143)

208▸

ap

10

Transcribe:
October 17
2 p.m.

17 12

ex·cerpt
re·ceived

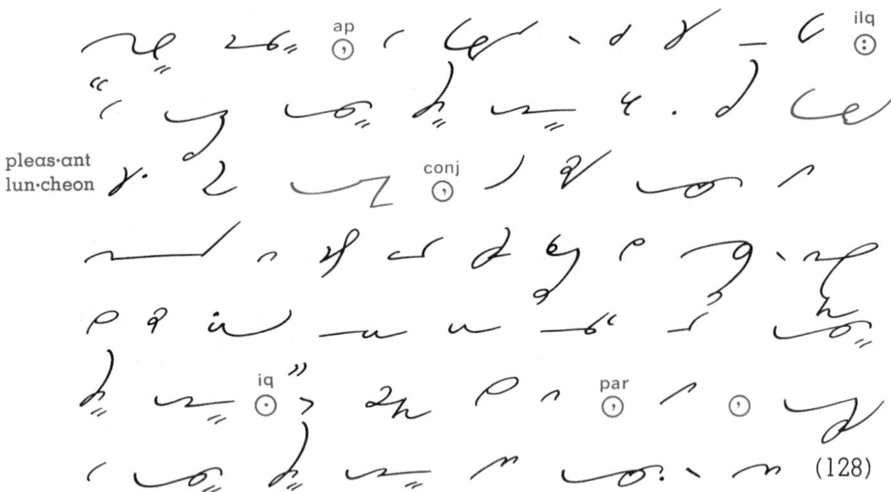

209▸ Transcription Quiz • For you to supply: 6 commas—2 commas series, 1 comma introductory, 2 commas conjunction, 1 comma *if* clause; 2 missing words.

17 18 19

17

17

(130)

DEVELOPING WORD-BUILDING POWER

210 ▸ Shorthand Vocabulary Builder

Rd

1

Ld

2

Moo, Noo

3

Or, Ol

4

Ot, Od

5

— ◆◆ —

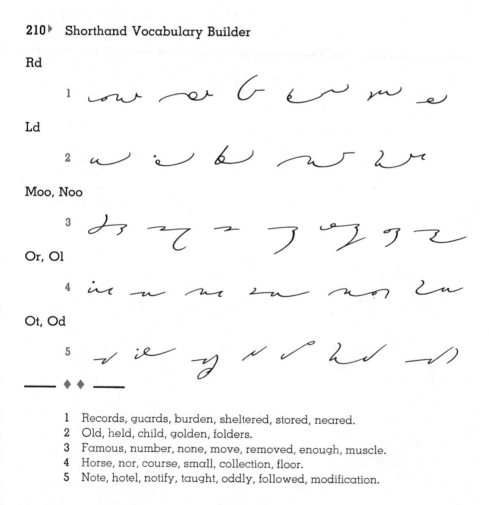

1 Records, guards, burden, sheltered, stored, neared.
2 Old, held, child, golden, folders.
3 Famous, number, none, move, removed, enough, muscle.
4 Horse, nor, course, small, collection, floor.
5 Note, hotel, notify, taught, oddly, followed, modification.

BUILDING TRANSCRIPTION SKILLS

211 ▸ BUSINESS VOCABULARY BUILDER

forerunner Predecessor.
migration Movement from one place to another.
commodious Large and comfortable.
linking Joining.

READING AND WRITING PRACTICE

212 ▸ Speaking of United States Hotels

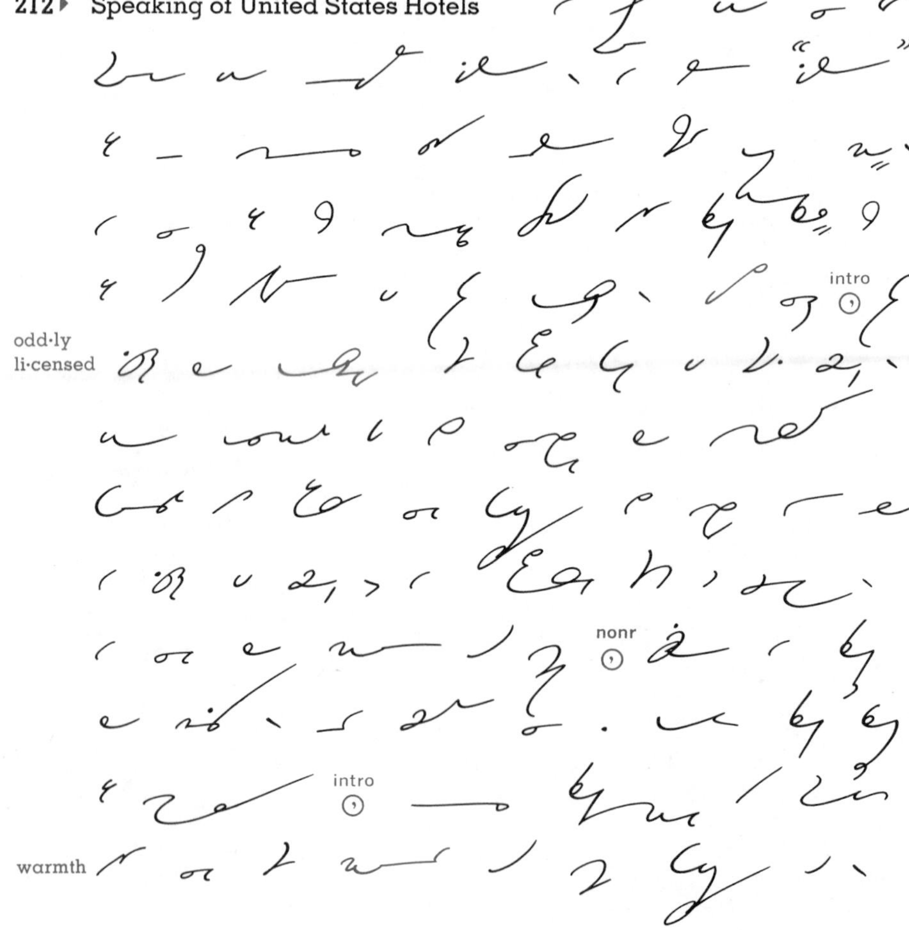

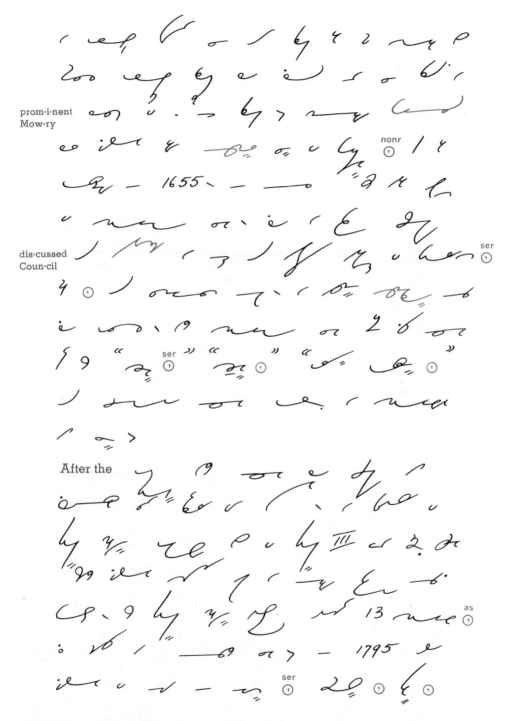

prom·i·nent
Mow·ry

nonr

1655

dis·cussed
Coun·cil

ser

ser

After the

III

13

as

1795

ser

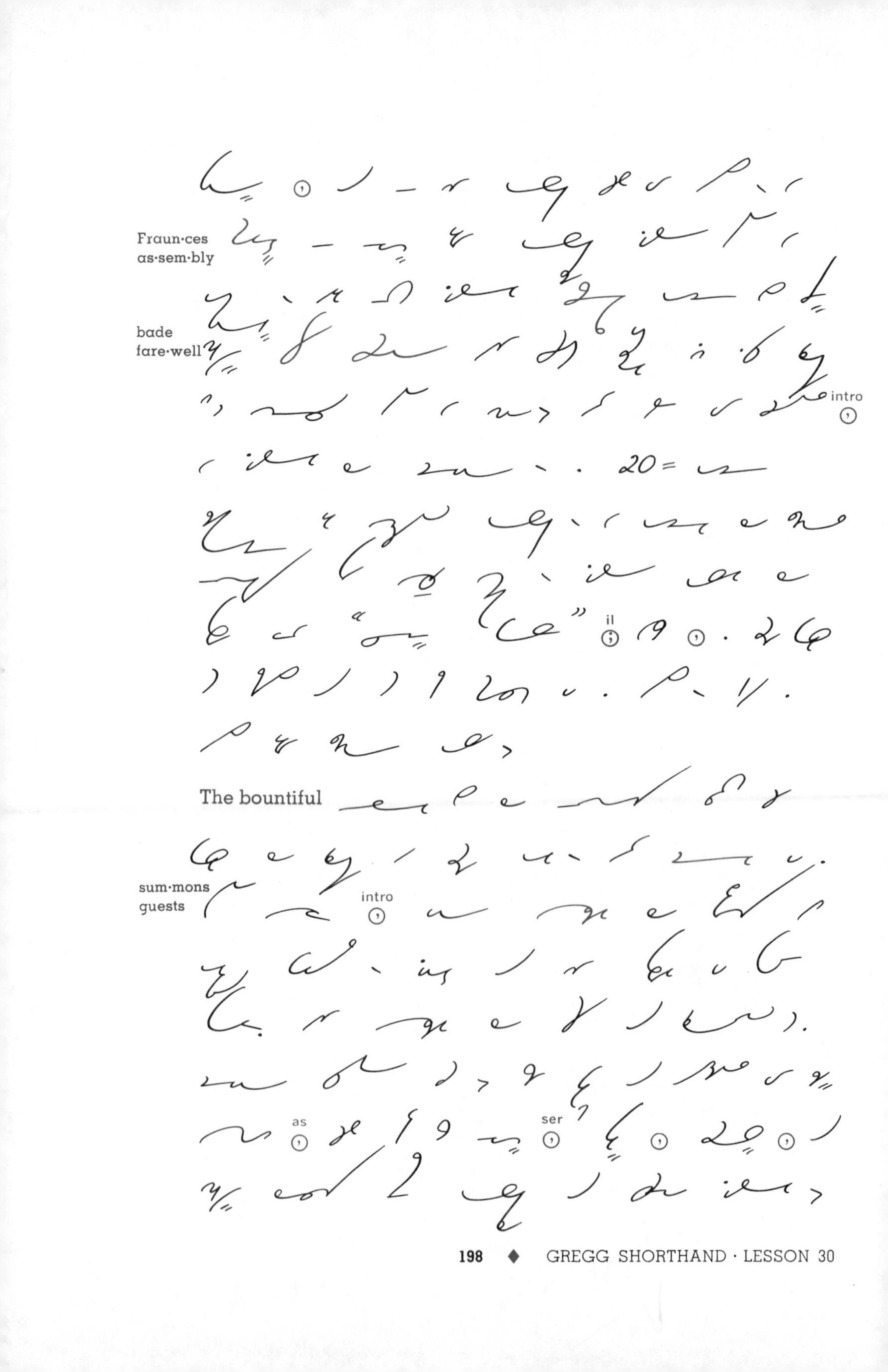

Fraun·ces
as·sem·bly

bade
fare·well

intro

il

The bountiful

sum·mons
guests

intro

as

ser

iq

dai·ly
spa·cious

conj

In 1859

par

el·e·va·tor
com·mo·di·ous

intro

ser

(674)

▸ *People are judged to a large degree by their ability to work with other people.* — Robert F. Black

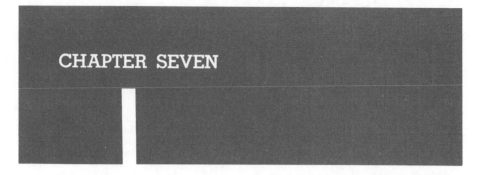

CHAPTER SEVEN

household appliances

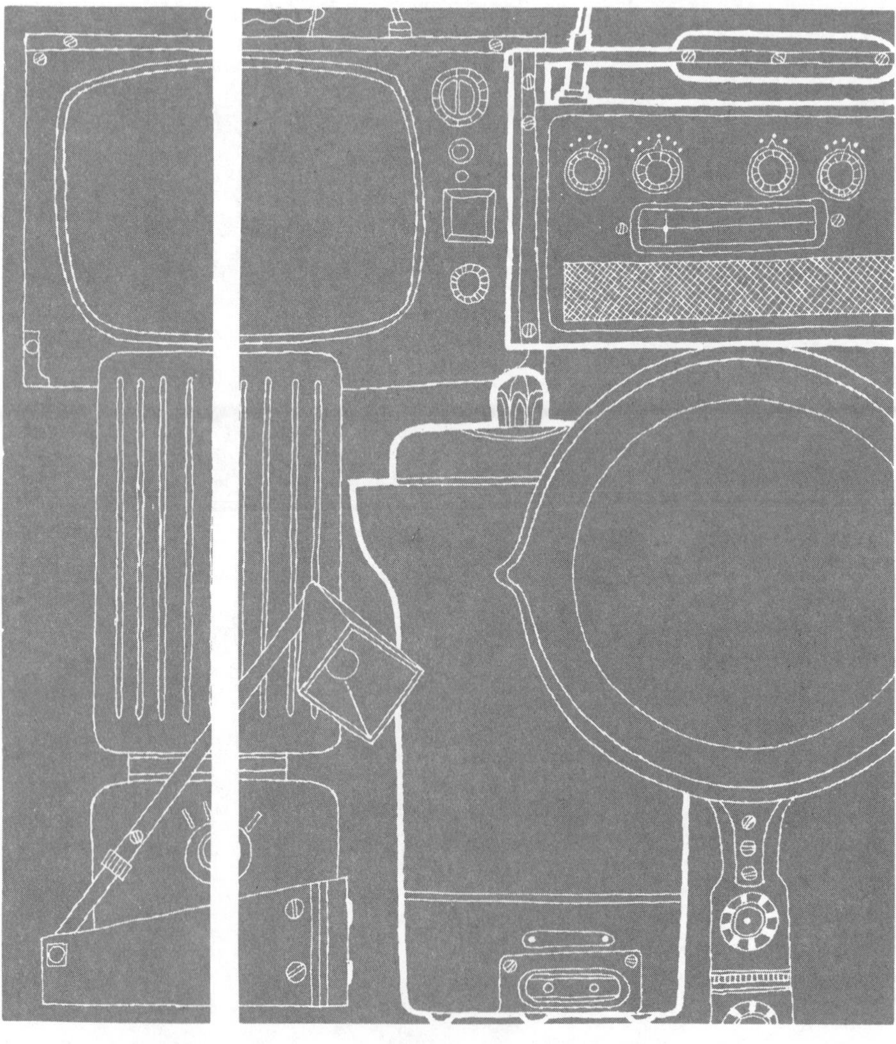

DEVELOPING WORD-BUILDING POWER

213 ▸ Brief Forms and Derivatives

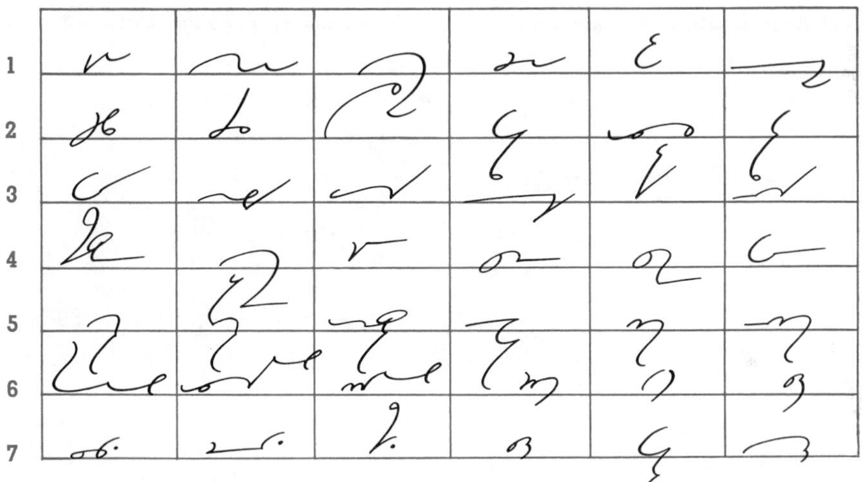

1 Shorter, greater, governor, sender, speaker, manufacturer.

2 Satisfactorily, generally, timely, probably, regularly, publicly.

3 Presented, corresponded, organized, manufactured, subjected, enclosed.

4 Advertisement, government, statement, acknowledgment, accompaniment, presentment.

5 Questionable, objectionable, recognizable, improbable, workable, unworkable.

6 Valueless, regardless, worthless; successful, thankful, useful.

7 Anything, something, everything; uses, purposes, goods.

BUILDING TRANSCRIPTION SKILLS

214 BUSINESS VOCABULARY BUILDER

humidity Moisture; dampness.

franchise The right granted to an individual or group to sell a company's products or services in a particular area.

respiratory Relating to breathing.

humidifier An appliance that regulates the amount of moisture in a room.

READING AND WRITING PRACTICE

215 Brief-Form Letter

(141)

216 di·rec·tor ar·ti·cle

ap

ilq

coughs re·spi·ra·to·ry ir·ri·ta·tions

ser

iq

if

ser

conj

par bc

(197)

217

hu·mid·i·fy·ing
pu·ri·fies

intro ser

breathe
par·ti·cles

nc

if

(187)

218

proud
fran·chise

well known
no noun,
no hyphen

nc

conj

as

intro

nonr

bc

par

bc

(198)

219▸ Transcription Quiz • The Transcription Quizzes hereafter will present a new challenge to you.

Thus far you have had to supply only commas to punctuate a letter correctly; in this and following quizzes you will also have to supply semicolons and colons.

For you to supply: 6 commas—2 commas apposition, 1 comma *when* clause, 1 comma *if* clause, 2 commas introductory; 1 semicolon because of comma, 1 semicolon no conjunction; 2 missing words.

(141)

▸ *Get your day off to a good start by wishing everyone a cheery "Good morning."*

DEVELOPING WORD-BUILDING POWER

220 Useful Business-Letter Phrases

Thank you

1

After

2

So

3

Sure

4

The

5

—— ♦♦ ——

1 Thank you, thank you for, thank you for the, thank you for your order, I thank you, I thank you for, I thank you for the, to thank you, to thank you for.

2 After the, after that, after that time, after these, after those, after them, after that date.

3 So well, so many, so little, so that, so far, so much.

4 Be sure, to be sure, can be sure, may be sure, we are sure, I am sure, you may be sure.

5 With the, by the, when the, is the, on the, into the, in the, that the, and the, of the.

221 ▸ Frequent Names

1 Graham, Griffiths, Hamilton, Hanson, Harris.
2 Dorothy, Edith, Edna, Eleanor, Elizabeth, Esther.

BUILDING TRANSCRIPTION SKILLS

222 ▸ GRAMMAR CHECKUP don't, doesn't

Use *doesn't* in the third person singular, not *don't.*

She doesn't (not don't) work here any longer.
He doesn't have an office at the present time.
That doesn't seem possible.

No one ever seems to use *doesn't* when he should use *don't* – you never hear anyone say, "I doesn't"; but you will frequently hear people incorrectly say, "he don't" and "that don't." Of course *you* never make that mistake!

223 ▸ BUSINESS VOCABULARY BUILDER

thermostat An automatic device for regulating temperature.

ignited Lighted.

reputable Enjoying a good reputation; being in high esteem.

READING AND WRITING PRACTICE

224 ▸ Phrase Letter

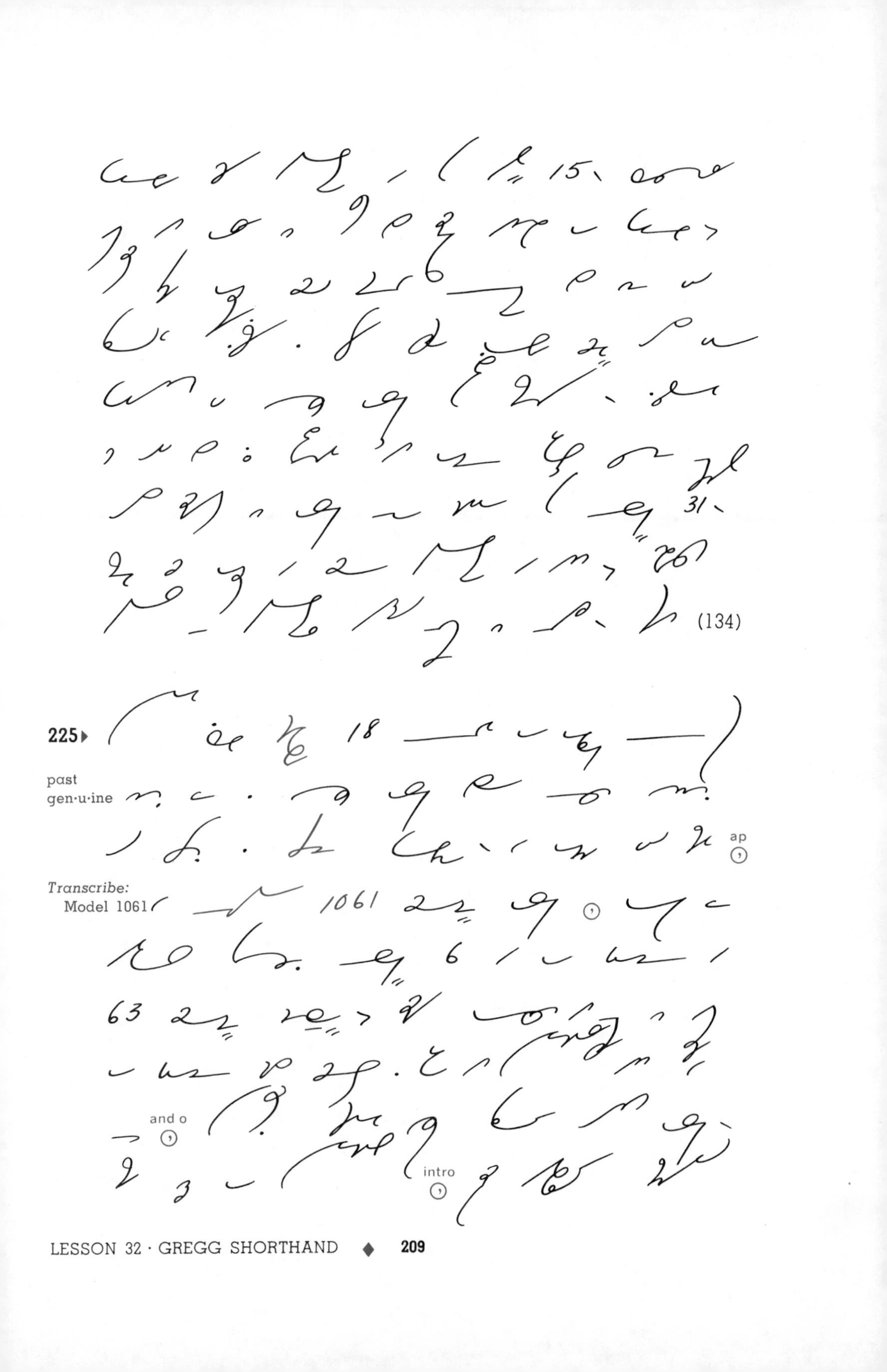

(134)

225▸

past

gen·u·ine

ap

Transcribe:
Model 1061

and o

intro

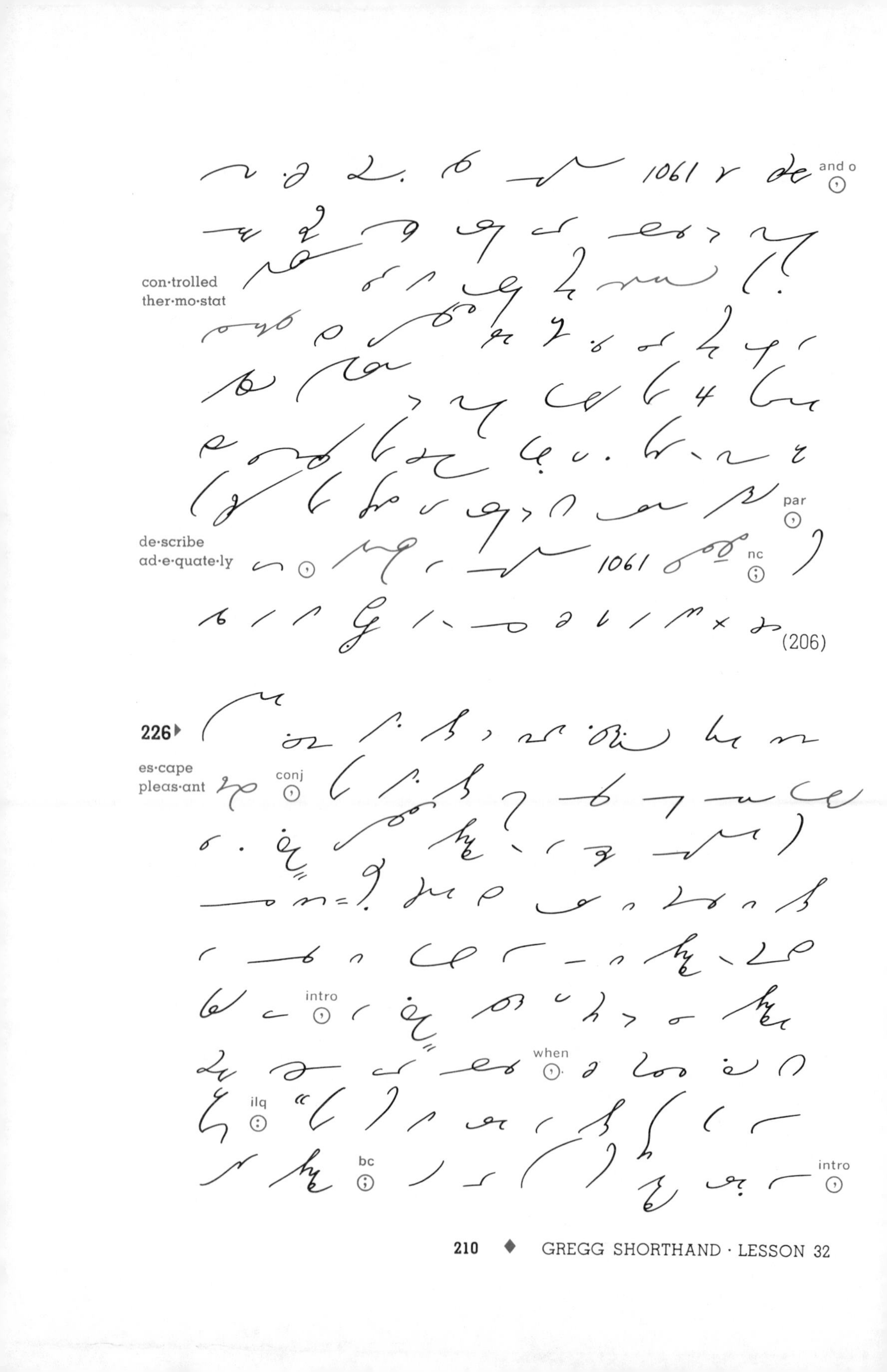

1061 and o

con·trolled
ther·mo·stat

par

de·scribe
ad·e·quate·ly
1061 nc

(206)

226 ▸

es·cape
pleas·ant
conj

intro

when

ilq

bc

intro

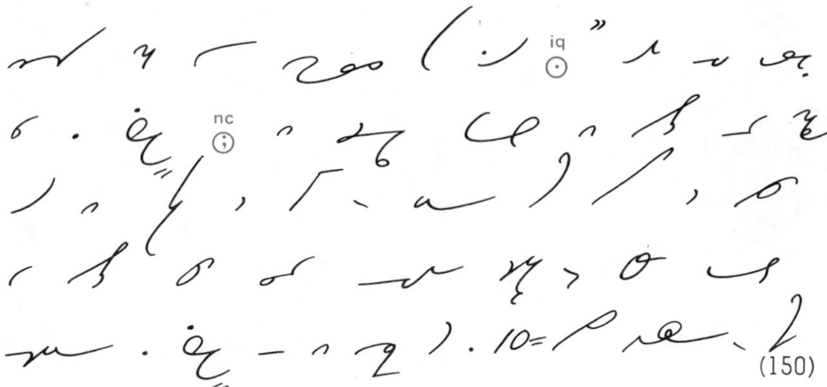

(150)

227▸ Transcription Quiz • For you to supply: 6 commas—2 commas *if* clause, 2 commas parenthetical, 2 commas apposition; 1 semicolon no conjunction; 1 semicolon because of comma; 2 missing words.

(138)

DEVELOPING WORD-BUILDING POWER

228▸ Word Families

Verse

1

-duce

2

-io

3

-rise

4

-tation

5

1 Verse, adverse, reverse, diverse, universe, averse, inverse.
2 Produce, reproduce, introduce, reduce, deduce, induce.
3 Studio, radio, folio, portfolio, trio, Leo.
4 Rise, arise, comprise, enterprise, apprise, surprise, sunrise.
5 Reputation, consultation, hesitation, invitation, notation, quotation, station, recitation.

BUILDING TRANSCRIPTION SKILLS

229▸ SIMILAR-WORDS DRILL affect, effect

affect To act upon; to influence.

These proceedings will adversely affect your credit standing.

effect *(noun)* Result; outcome.

Such action could have an adverse effect on your credit standing.

effect *(verb)* To bring about; to accomplish.

This is the third letter we have written you to effect a settlement of your account.

230▸ BUSINESS VOCABULARY BUILDER

straits Situations of distress; difficulties.
institute legal proceedings To sue.
quandary A state of doubt.
embark To engage in; to set out on.

READING AND WRITING PRACTICE

231▸

Transcribe: $1,200

ser

conj

if il

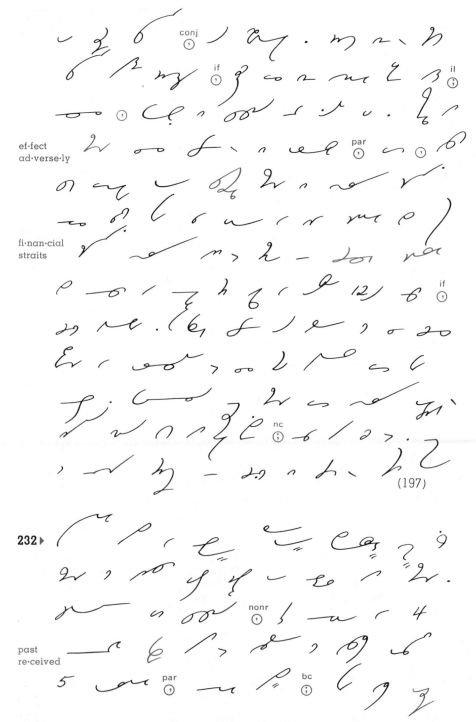

ef·fect
ad·verse·ly

par

fi·nan·cial
straits

if

nc

(197)

232 ▸

nonr

past
re·ceived

par bc

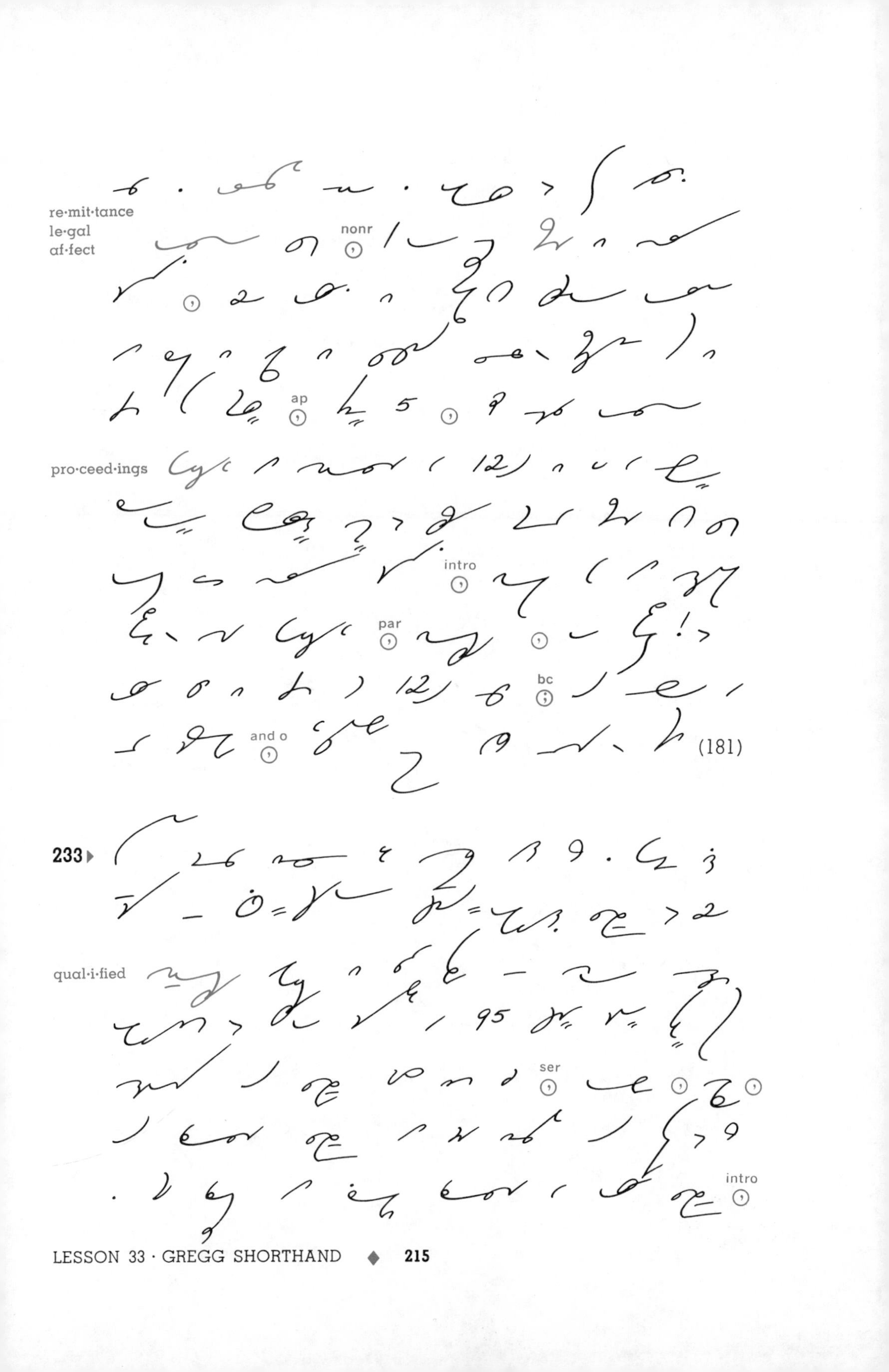

re·mit·tance
le·gal
af·fect

pro·ceed·ings

(181)

233

qual·i·fied

unique
au·dio

iq

intro

if

Transcribe:
8:30 a.m.
5:30 p.m.

8:30 5:30

8:30 (161)

234

par

Transcribe:
Model 1856

1856

par

intro

if

(118)

235▸ Transcription Quiz • For you to supply: 7 commas – 2 commas parenthetical, 1 comma *and* omitted, 2 commas introductory, 2 commas series; 1 semicolon because of commas; 1 semicolon no conjunction; 2 missing words.

(163)

DEVELOPING WORD-BUILDING POWER

236 ▸ Word Beginnings and Endings

Under-

1

-ward

2

-lity

3

Fur-

4

Self-

5

—— ♦ ♦ ——

1 Understand, underpaid, undermine, underestimate, underrated, underprivileged.

2 Forward, backward, onward, outward, inward, reward, rewarded.

3 Quality, ability, inability, desirability, facility.

4 Further, furthermore, furniture, furnace, furnaces, furnishing, furnished.

5 Self-addressed, self-confident, self-assurance, self-contained, self-service, selfish.

BUILDING TRANSCRIPTION SKILLS

237 ▸ SPELLING FAMILIES -cial, -tial

Be very careful when you must transcribe a word ending with the sound of *shal;* sometimes it is spelled *cial;* at other times, *tial.*

Words Ending in -cial

spe·cial	of·fi·cial	ben·e·fi·cial
fi·nan·cial	so·cial	com·mer·cial
ar·ti·fi·cial	cru·cial	su·per·fi·cial

Words Ending in -tial

es·sen·tial	sub·stan·tial	po·ten·tial
con·fi·den·tial	res·i·den·tial	in·flu·en·tial
ini·tial	cir·cum·stan·tial	par·tial

238 ▸ BUSINESS VOCABULARY BUILDER

perpetual Unending; everlasting.

artificial Not real.

overhead Such expenses of running a business as rent, telephone, light, wages, etc.

READING AND WRITING PRACTICE

239 ▸

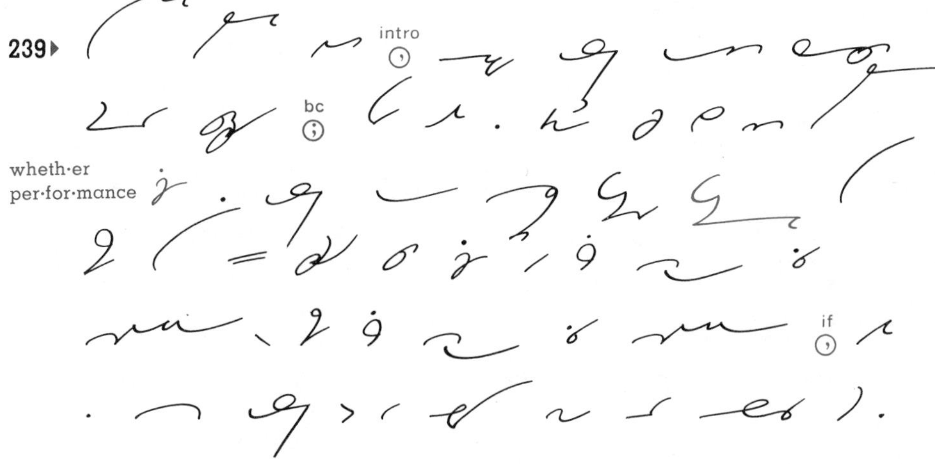

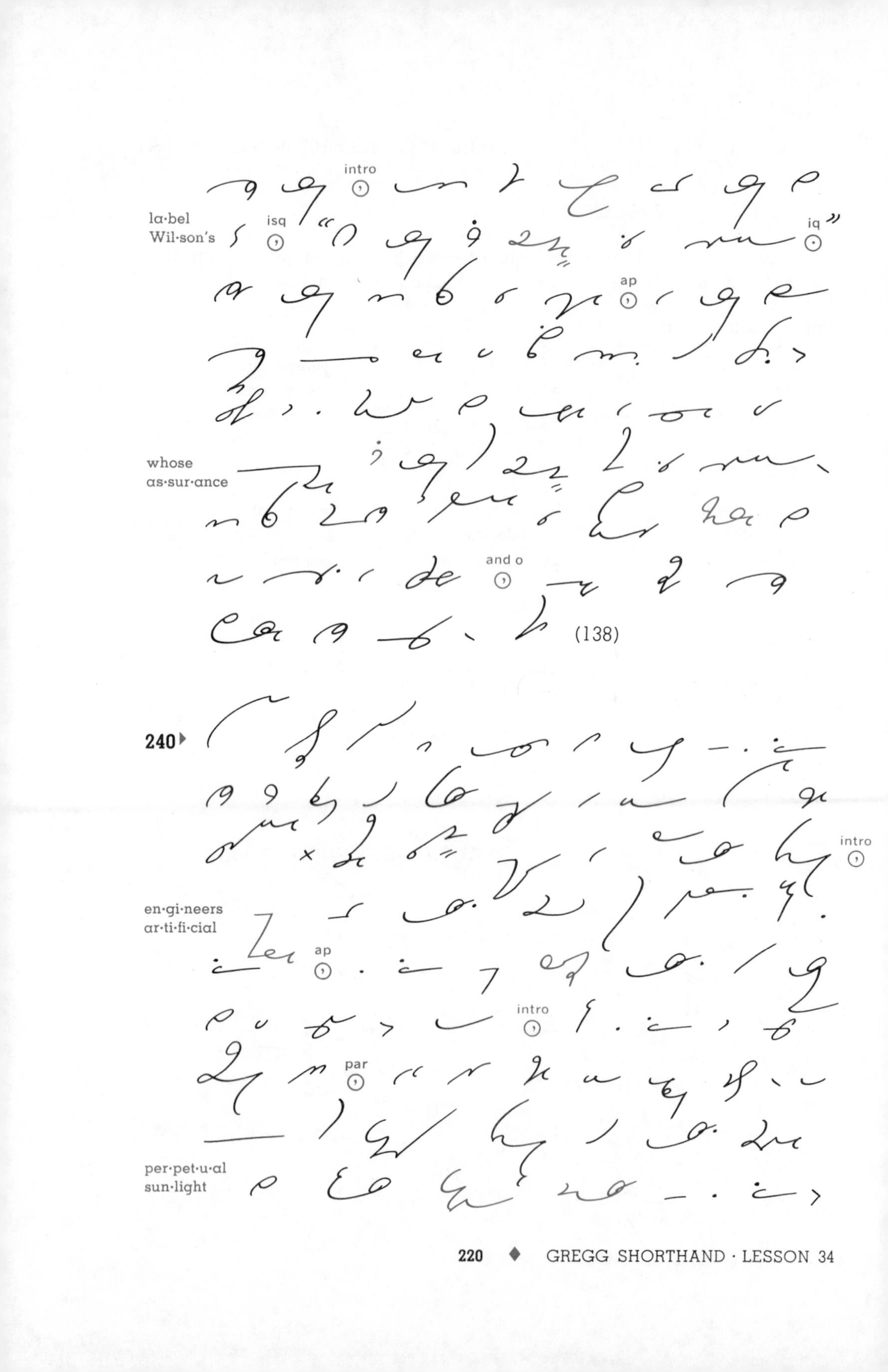

intro

la·bel
Wil·son's

isq

iq

ap

whose
as·sur·ance

and o

(138)

240

intro

en·gi·neers
ar·ti·fi·cial

ap

intro

par

per·pet·u·al
sun·light

de·vel·op·ments

ap

nc

ser

nc

fam·i·ly's
equip·ment

(173)

241

as

com·pet·i·tive

nc

intro

par

when

prompt·ly
com·mer·cial
sub·stan·tial

when

bc

(137)

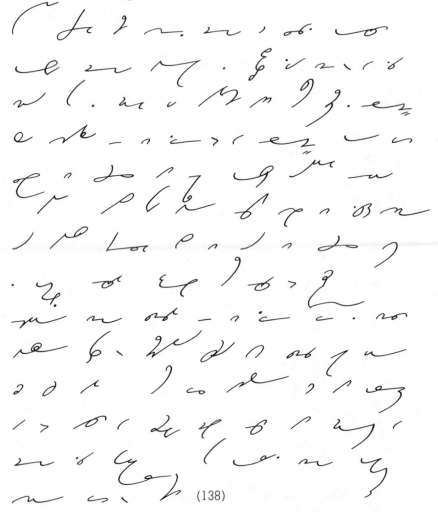

242 **Transcription Quiz** • For you to supply: 9 commas—2 commas *if* clause, 6 commas parenthetical, 1 comma nonrestrictive; 1 semicolon because of comma; 2 missing words.

(138)

DEVELOPING WORD-BUILDING POWER

243 ▸ Shorthand Vocabulary Builder

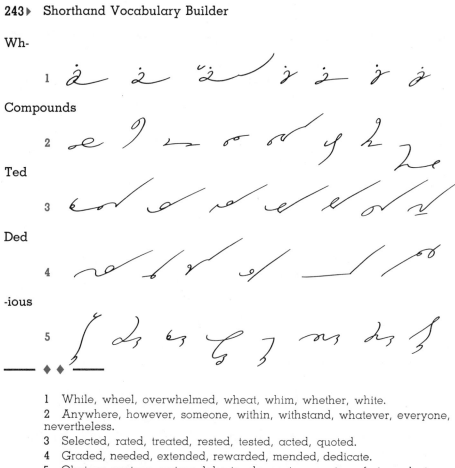

Wh-

1

Compounds

2

Ted

3

Ded

4

-ious

5

— ◆◆ —

1 While, wheel, overwhelmed, wheat, whim, whether, white.

2 Anywhere, however, someone, within, withstand, whatever, everyone, nevertheless.

3 Selected, rated, treated, rested, tested, acted, quoted.

4 Graded, needed, extended, rewarded, mended, dedicate.

5 Obvious, various, serious, laboriously, envious, curious, furious, devious.

244 BUSINESS VOCABULARY BUILDER

servitude Compulsory labor or service.
embossed Raised above the surface.
indifferent Showing no interest or concern.
earmarks Identifying marks.

READING AND WRITING PRACTICE

245 The Typewriter

intro

equal·i·ty
bar·ri·ers

intro

of·fered
ca·reer

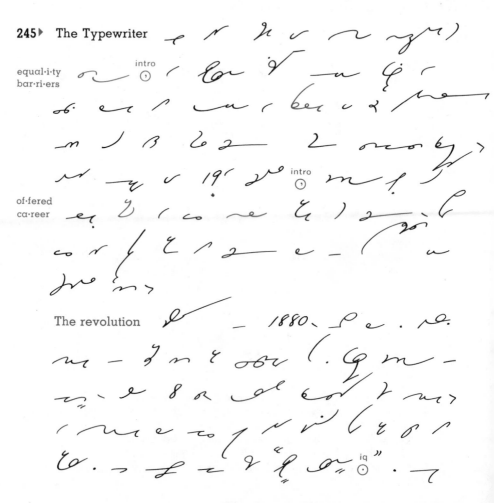

The revolution

iq

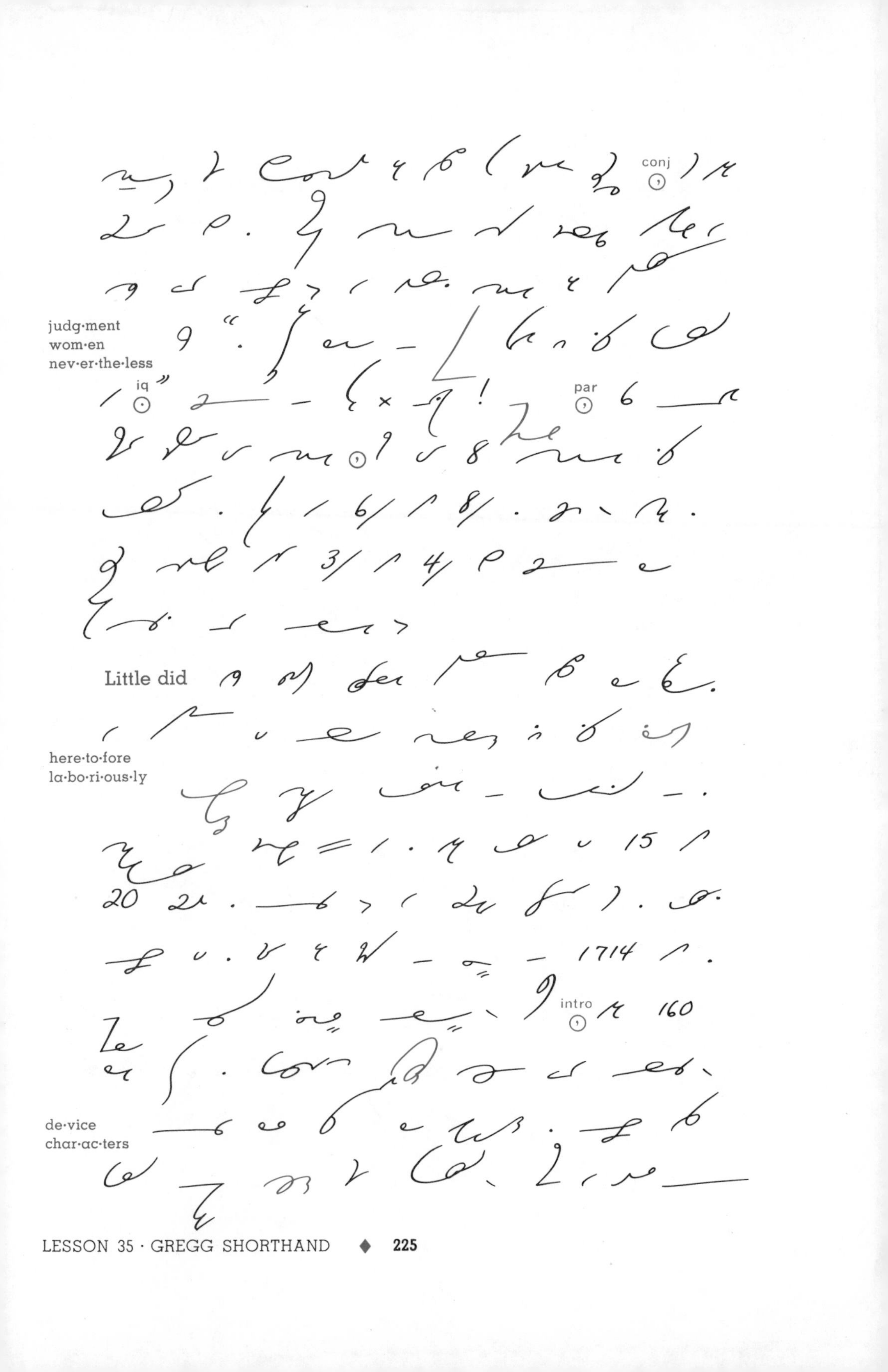

conj

judg·ment
wom·en
nev·er·the·less

iq

par

Little did

here·to·fore
la·bo·ri·ous·ly

intro

de·vice
char·ac·ters

se·ri·al·ly
clum·sy
ser

Glid·den
Soulé
Sholes
nonr

1867

Six years 30 intro

il

ap

when
flaws

ap

ap·pa·ra·tus
re·fine·ments

intro

1874

The world

nc

12

steel
pur·chased

intro

125

intro

intro

(681)

▸ *The person who reads a good newspaper every day and who keeps up on what is going on in the world (and in town, too) can't help but be a more valuable employee as well as a more interesting person.*

CHAPTER EIGHT

insurance

DEVELOPING WORD-BUILDING POWER

246 ▸ Brief Forms and Derivatives

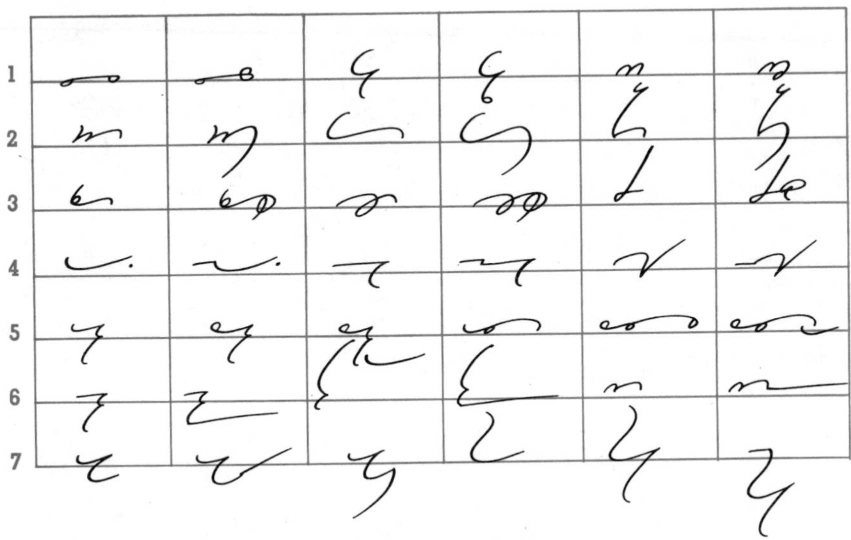

— ◆◆ —

1 Immediate, immediately, purpose, purposely, world, worldly.

2 Success, successive, progress, progressive, object, objective.

3 Circular, circularize, character, characterize, general, generalize.

4 Willing, unwilling, important, unimportant, questioned, unquestioned.

5 Responsible, irresponsible, irresponsibility, regular, irregularly, irregularity.

6 Newspaper, newspapermen, business, businessmen, work, workmen.

7 Represent, represented, representative, value, valuable, invaluable.

247 ▸ BUSINESS VOCABULARY BUILDER

casualty An unfortunate occurrence; an accident.
involuntary Not done willingly or through choice.
cash value The refund that a life insurance policyholder receives when he cancels his policy.

READING AND WRITING PRACTICE

248 ▸ Brief-Form Letter

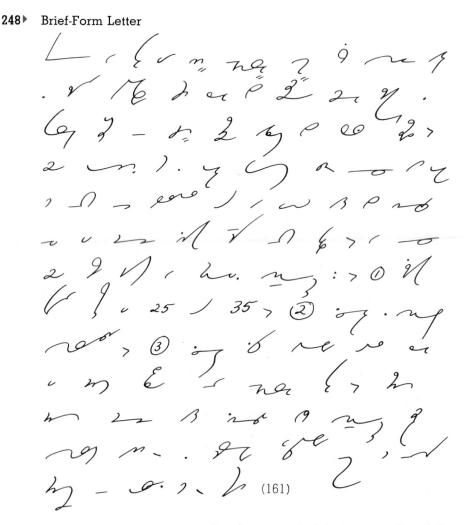

(161)

249

com·pa·nies
ac·ci·dent

ser

bc

isq iq

nc

thou·sands
dol·lars

nc intro

conj

com·pe·tent
ad·vise

nc

if

(214)

250

spur
loss

par

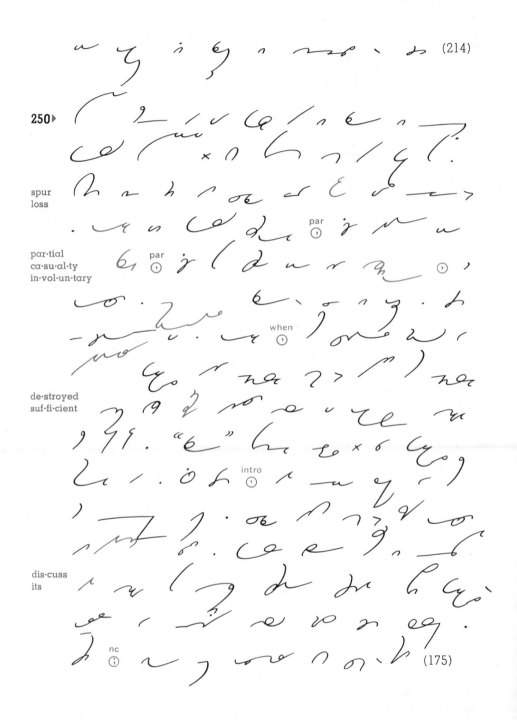

par·tial
ca·su·al·ty
in·vol·un·tary

par

when

de·stroyed
suf·fi·cient

intro

dis·cuss
its

nc

(175)

251 ▸ Transcription Quiz • For you to supply: 5 commas — 4 commas parenthetical, 1 comma *if* clause; 1 colon enumeration; 2 missing words.

(164)

▸ *In almost any group of people — offices being no exception — you will find petty annoyances. The idea is to make sure they remain just that — petty.*

BUILDING PHRASING SKILL

252 ▸ Useful Business-Letter Phrases

Several

1

Hope

2

Time

3

Omission of Of

4

—— ♦ ♦ ——

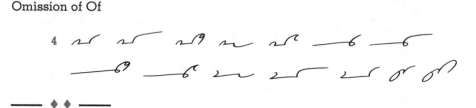

1 Several days, several days ago, several months, several months ago, several times.

2 I hope, I hope that, I hope you will, I hope you can, we hope, we hope you will, we hope you can, we hope that.

3 At this time, at that time, in time, on time, at the time, of time, this time.

4 One of the, one of them, one of these, one of our, one of those, many of the, many of them, many of these, many of those, some of our, some of them, some of the, out of the, out of this.

253 ▸ Frequent Names

1 Henderson, Hoffman, Hughes, Hunter, Jackson, Johnson, Johnston.
2 Felix, Francis, Frederick, George, Gilbert, Godfrey.

BUILDING TRANSCRIPTION SKILLS

254 ▸ GRAMMAR CHECKUP common errors in grammar

The writer who is careful about his grammar never uses:

party for **person**

NO The **party** who called left no message.
YES The **person** who called left no message.

writer for **I**

NO The **writer** appreciates your thoughtfulness.
YES **I** appreciate your thoughtfulness.

try and for **try to**

NO Try **and** be on time.
YES Try **to** be on time.

the reason is because for **the reason is that**

NO The reason for his action was **because** he was confused.
YES The reason for his action was **that** he was confused.

different than for **different from**

NO The movie was different **than** any other I have ever seen.
YES The movie was different **from** any other I have ever seen.

those kind for **those kinds**

NO Those **kind** of toys appeal to children.
YES Those **kinds** of toys appeal to children.

255 BUSINESS VOCABULARY BUILDER

lapse To expire; to cease to exist.
current Belonging to the present time.
dedicated (adjective) Devoted.

READING AND WRITING PRACTICE

256 Phrase Letter

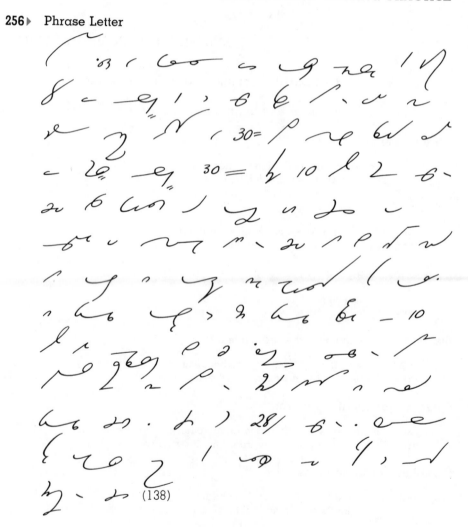

30= 30= 10 10 28/ (138)

257 ▸ conj

growth
na·tion's

and o

par

in·sis·tence
re·ceived

161518.

Transcribe:
No. 161518

nonr

(139)

258 ▸

dol·lars'
past

and o

nc

Ha·waii
achieve·ment
proud

intro

Per·son·nel
thor·ough·ly

par

as

fi·nan·cial
fam·i·lies

peace
mind

bc

intro

(183)

259

to·day's

intro

par

year's

ser

bank·rupt·cy

conj

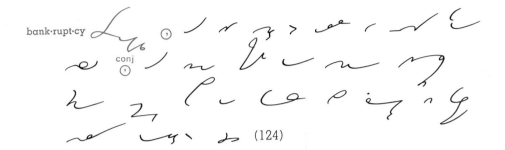

(124)

260 ▸ Transcription Quiz • For you to supply: 4 commas — 2 commas introductory, 2 commas series; 1 semicolon because of comma; 1 semicolon illustrative; 2 missing words.

40,

(141)

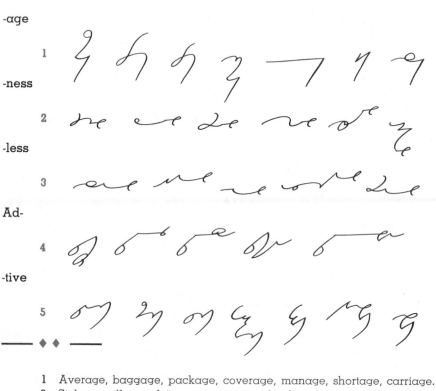

DEVELOPING WORD-BUILDING POWER

261▸ Word Families

-age

1

-ness

2

-less

3

Ad-

4

-tive

5

1 Average, baggage, package, coverage, manage, shortage, carriage.
2 Sickness, illness, fairness, greatness, kindness, reasonableness.
3 Careless, thoughtless, unless, regardless, fearless.
4 Advice, admit, admire, adventure, administer.
5 Attractive, effective, active, prospective, positive, descriptive, captive.

262▸ SIMILAR-WORDS DRILL apprised, appraised

apprised Informed.

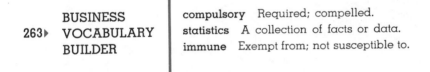

He was apprised of our decision last Wednesday.

appraised Set a value on.

The house was appraised at $40,000.

263▸ BUSINESS VOCABULARY BUILDER

compulsory Required; compelled.
statistics A collection of facts or data.
immune Exempt from; not susceptible to.

READING AND WRITING PACTICE

264▸

ap·prised
dis·con·tin·u·ing

as

nonr

be·gin·ning

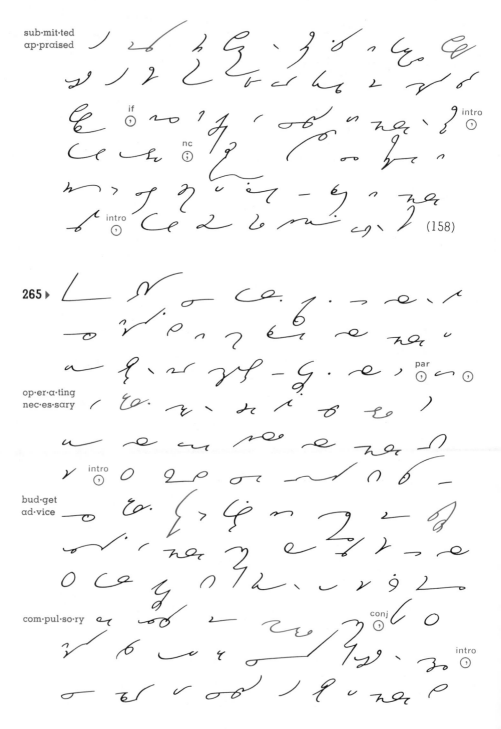

sub·mit·ted
ap·praised

if
intro

nc

intro
(158)

265

par

op·er·a·ting
nec·es·sary

intro

bud·get
ad·vice

com·pul·so·ry
conj

intro

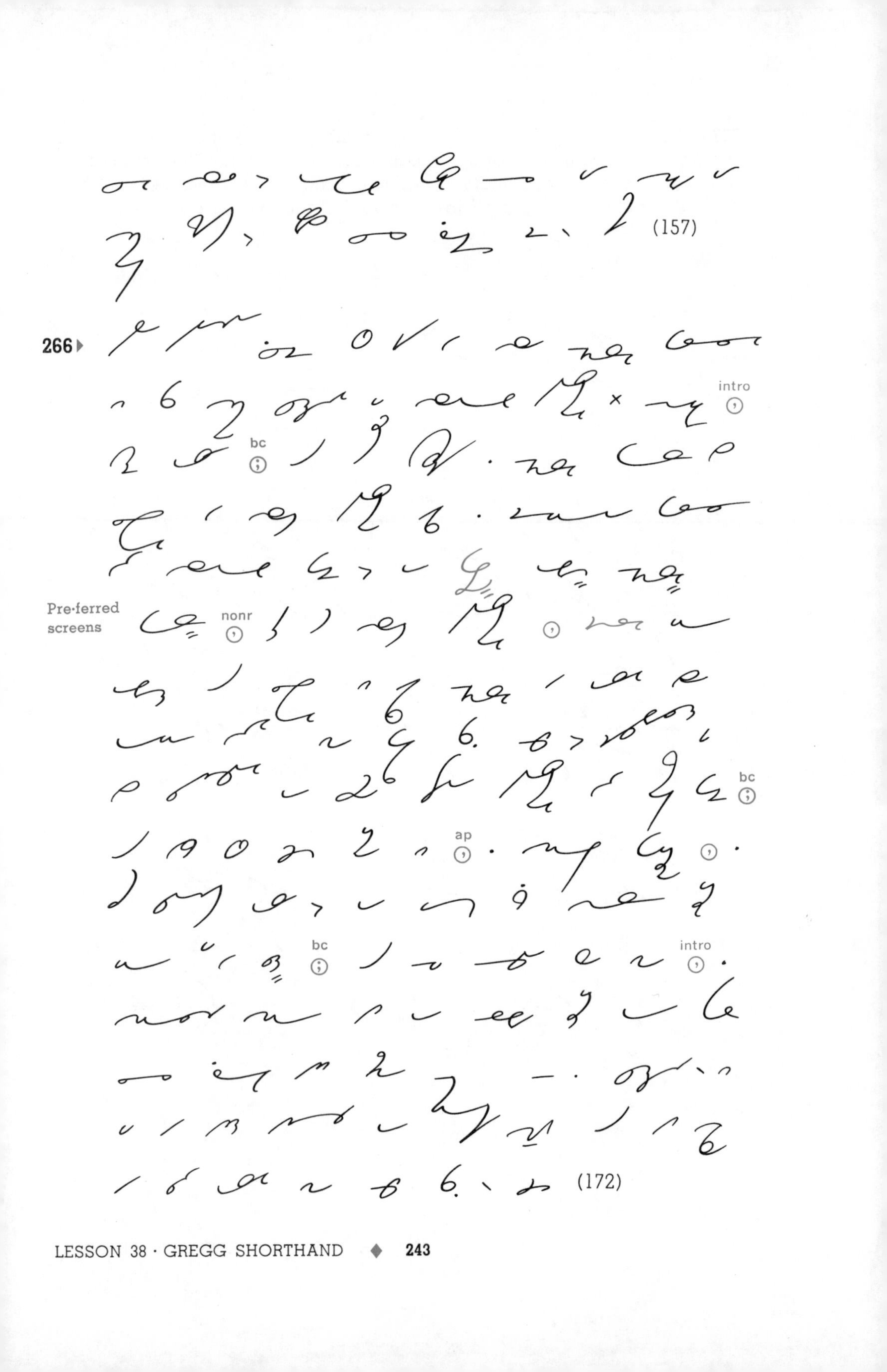

(157)

266

intro

bc

Pre·ferred screens

nonr

bc

ap

bc

intro

(172)

267 ▸ Transcription Quiz • For you to supply: 10 commas — 1 comma conjunction, 6 commas parenthetical, 1 comma *if* clause, 1 comma *when* clause, 1 comma introductory; 1 semicolon no conjunction; 1 colon introducing long quote; 1 period inside quote; 2 missing words.

(162)

DEVELOPING WORD-BUILDING POWER

268 ▸ Word Beginnings and Endings

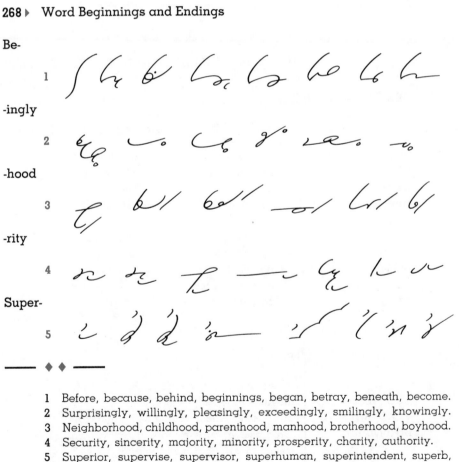

Be-

1

-ingly

2

-hood

3

-rity

4

Super-

5

—— ♦♦ ——

1 Before, because, behind, beginnings, began, betray, beneath, become.
2 Surprisingly, willingly, pleasingly, exceedingly, smilingly, knowingly.
3 Neighborhood, childhood, parenthood, manhood, brotherhood, boyhood.
4 Security, sincerity, majority, minority, prosperity, charity, authority.
5 Superior, supervise, supervisor, superhuman, superintendent, superb, superstition, supersede.

269 Geographical Expressions

1 New Orleans, New York, New London, New Bedford, New Britain, Newark.

2 Alaska, Arizona, Arkansas, California, Colorado, Connecticut, Delaware.

3 Portsmouth, Scotland, Wales, Ireland, Belfast.

BUILDING TRANSCRIPTION SKILLS

270 SPELLING FAMILIES

Words in Which Y Is Changed to I in the Past Tense and in the S-Form

ap·ply	ap·plied	ap·plies
re·ply	re·plied	re·plies
im·ply	im·plied	im·plies
sup·ply	sup·plied	sup·plies
re·ly	re·lied	re·lies
com·ply	com·plied	com·plies
mul·ti·ply	mul·ti·plied	mul·ti·plies
typ·i·fy	typ·i·fied	typ·i·fies
ac·com·pa·ny	ac·com·pa·nied	ac·com·pa·nies
car·ry	car·ried	car·ries

271 BUSINESS VOCABULARY BUILDER

adequate Sufficient; enough.

devastate To lay waste.

irrefutable Incapable of being disproved.

progressive Moving forward; advancing.

reimbursed Paid back; repaid.

272 ▸

conj

be·lieve
ad·e·quate

and o

intro

par

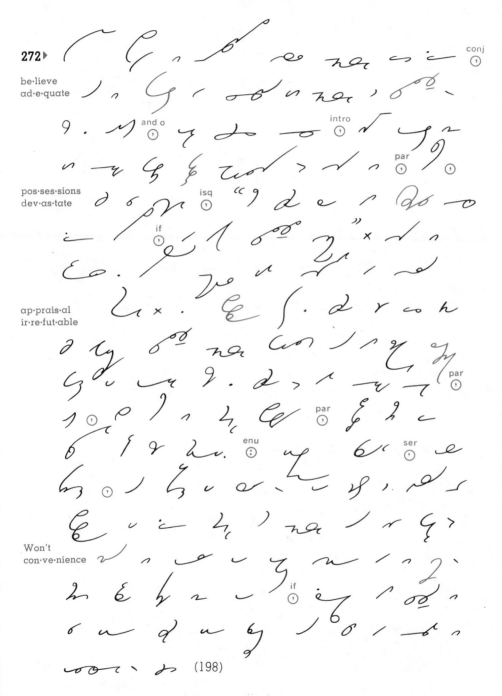

pos·ses·sions
dev·as·tate

isq

if

ap·prais·al
ir·re·fut·able

par

par

enu

ser

Won't
con·ve·nience

if

(198)

273 ▸

if

par

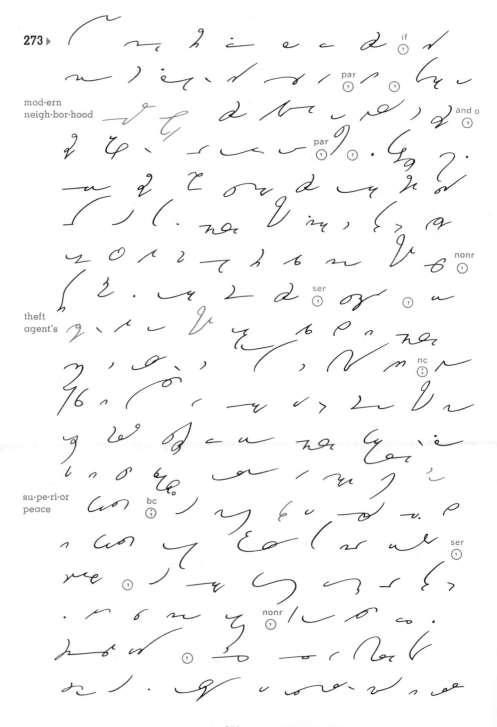

mod·ern
neigh·bor·hood

and o

par

nonr

ser

theft
agent's

nc

su·pe·ri·or
peace

bc

ser

nonr

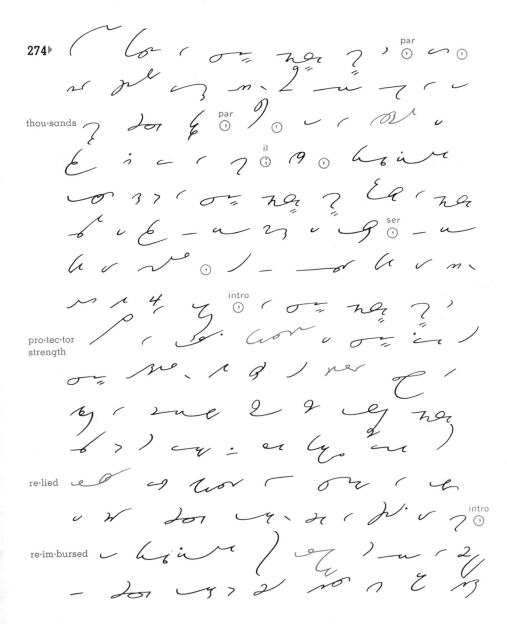

(225)

274

par

thou·sands

par

il

ser

intro

pro·tec·tor

strength

re·lied

intro

re·im·bursed

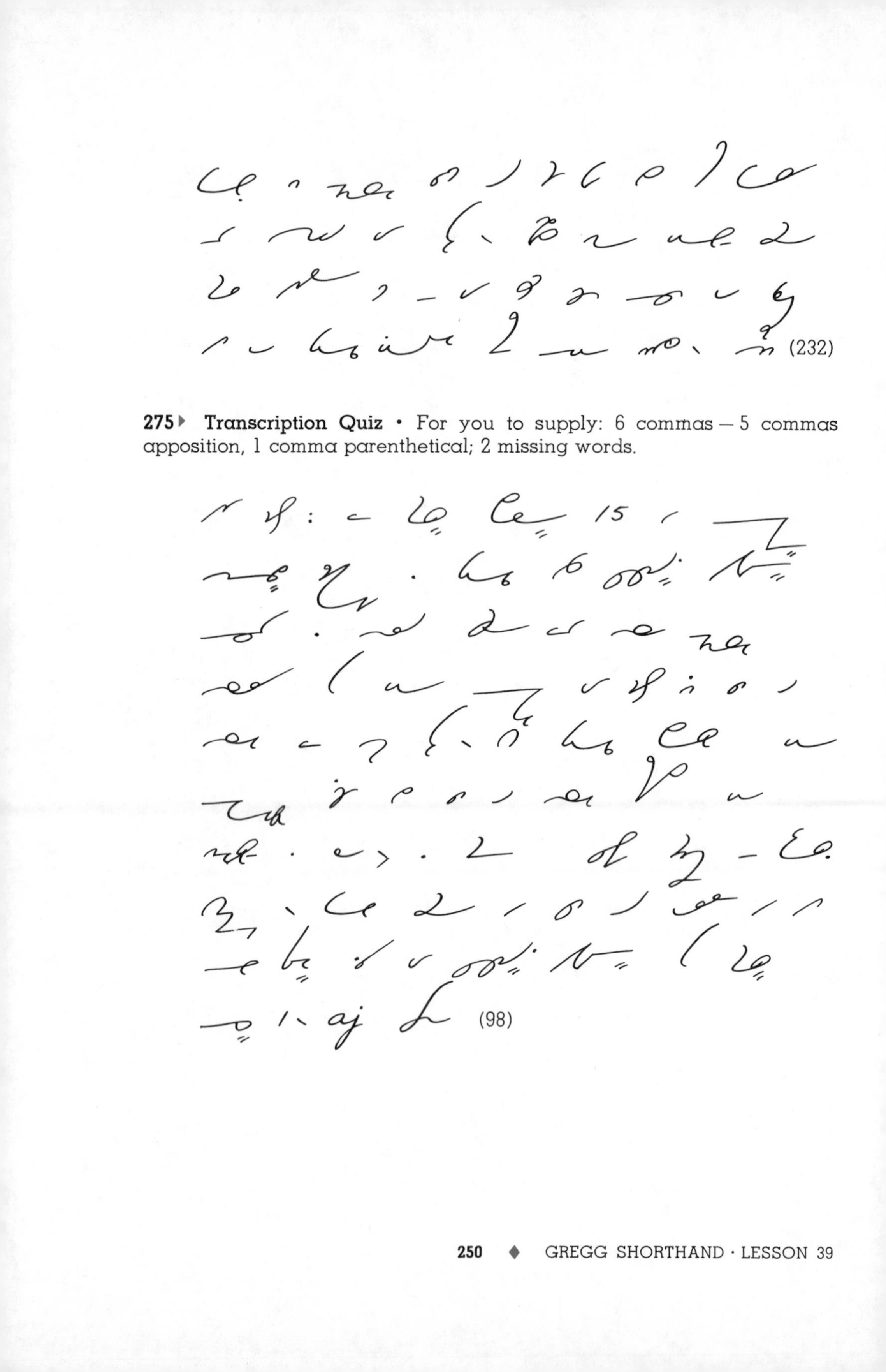

(232)

275 ▸ **Transcription Quiz** • For you to supply: 6 commas – 5 commas apposition, 1 comma parenthetical; 2 missing words.

(98)

DEVELOPING WORD-BUILDING POWER

276 ▸ Shorthand Vocabulary Builder

Md, Mt

1

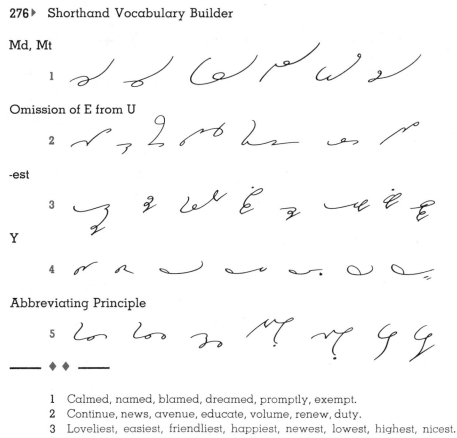

Omission of E from U

2

-est

3

Y

4

Abbreviating Principle

5

—— ◆◆ ——

1 Calmed, named, blamed, dreamed, promptly, exempt.

2 Continue, news, avenue, educate, volume, renew, duty.

3 Loveliest, easiest, friendliest, happiest, newest, lowest, highest, nicest.

4 Youth, young, yield, yellow, yearning, yard, Yale.

5 Frequent, frequently, consequently, distributing, contributing, privilege, privileged.

BUILDING TRANSCRIPTION SKILLS

277▸ BUSINESS VOCABULARY BUILDER

vowed Solemnly promised.
coping Overcoming problems and difficulties.
impelling Urging forward; driving.
recipient One who receives.

READING AND WRITING PRACTICE

278▸ Why Does a Man Buy Life Insurance?

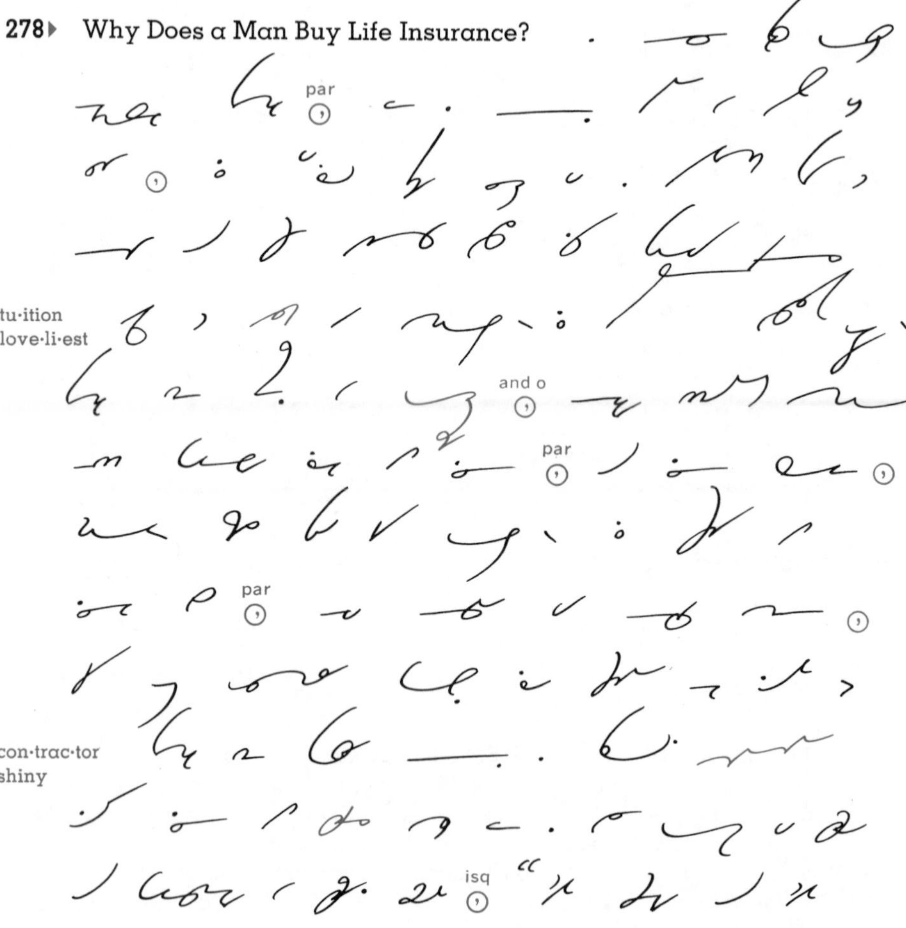

iq

ap

calmed
sol·emn

conj

pledged
theirs

Because

conj

de·ceased
whol·ly

intro

and o

im·pel·ling
re·spon·si·ble

nc

(328)

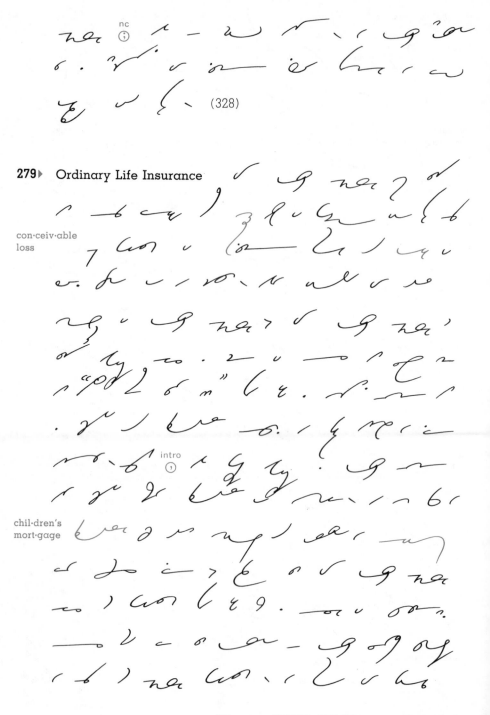

279 Ordinary Life Insurance

con·ceiv·able
loss

intro

chil·dren's
mort·gage

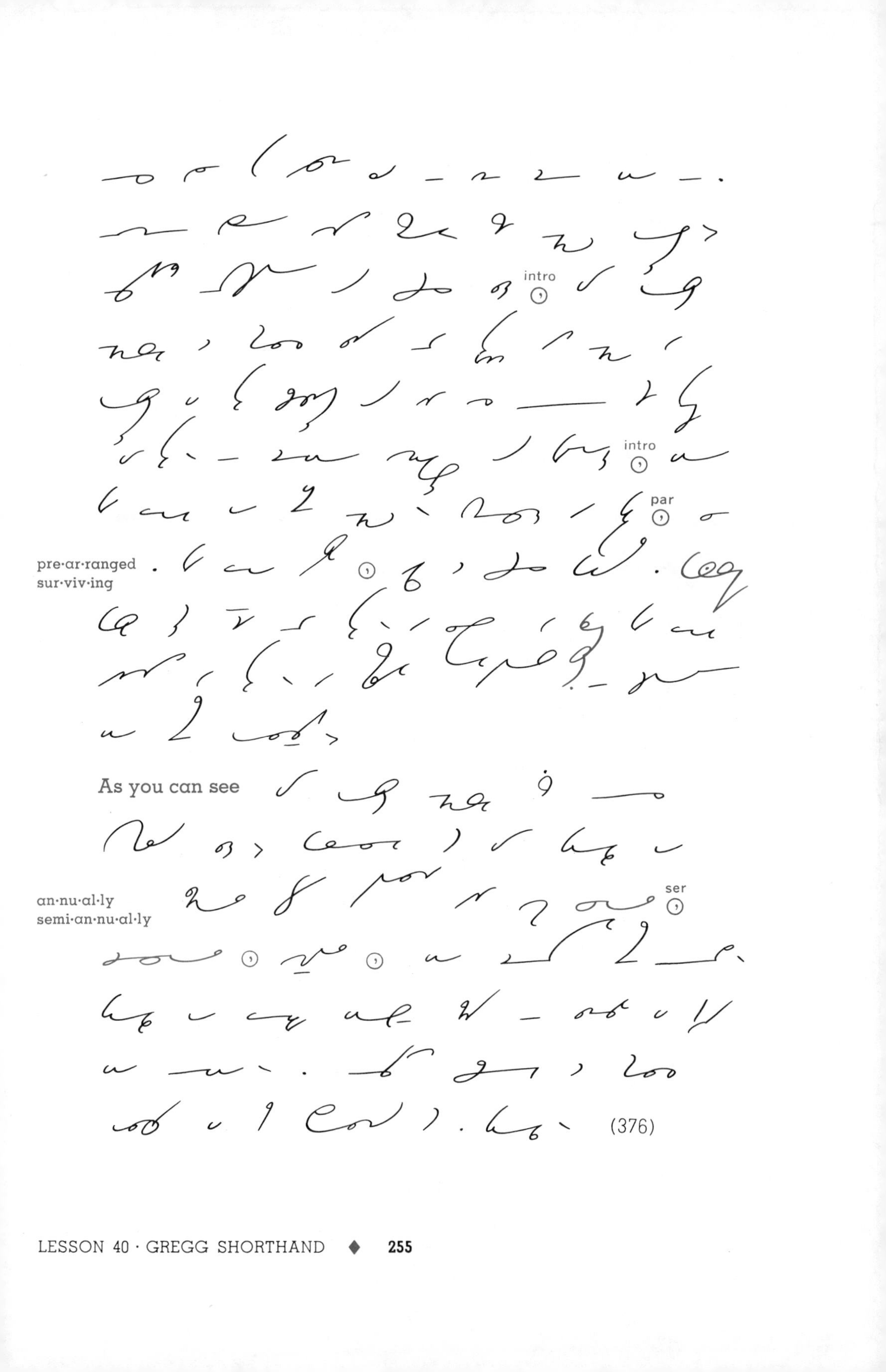

intro

intro

par

pre·ar·ranged
sur·viv·ing

As you can see

an·nu·al·ly
semi·an·nu·al·ly

ser

(376)

280 ▸ Industrial Life Insurance

1854

sim·i·lar

and o

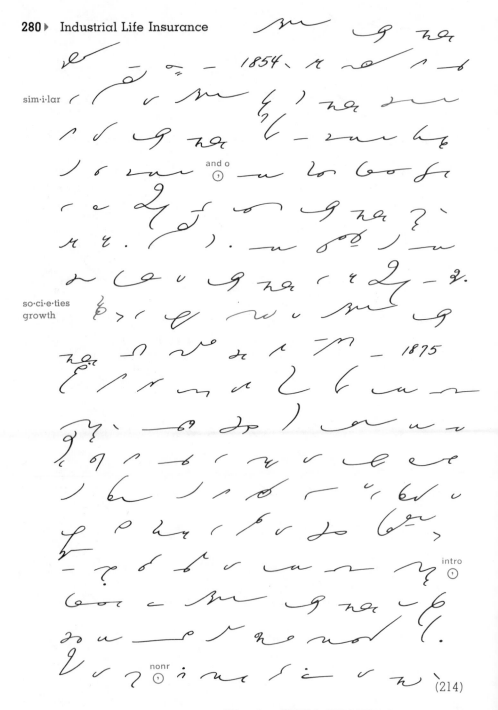

so·ci·e·ties
growth

1875

intro

nonr

(214)

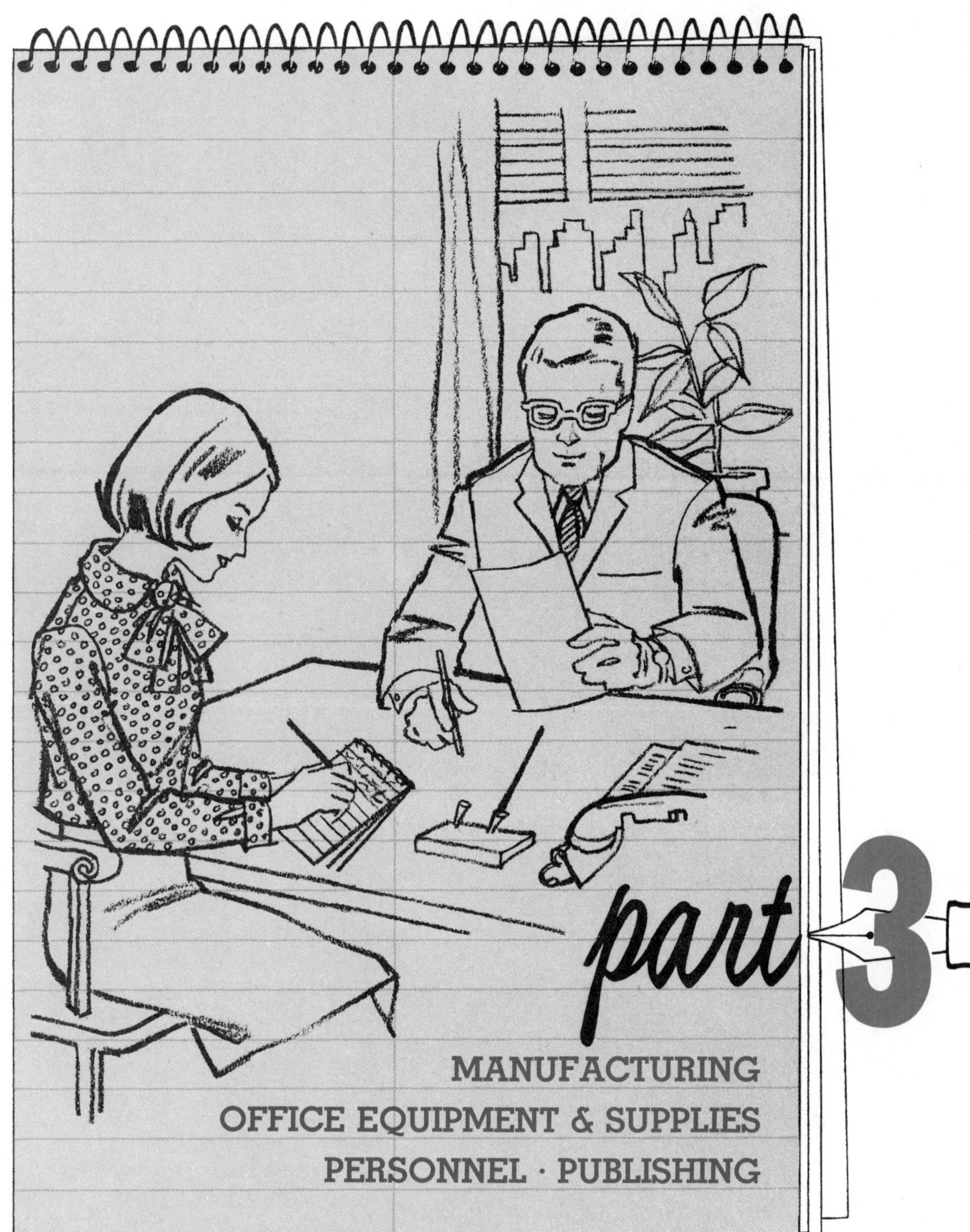

part 3

MANUFACTURING
OFFICE EQUIPMENT & SUPPLIES
PERSONNEL · PUBLISHING

At this stage of your shorthand course, you have already read and copied and taken from dictation thousands upon thousands of words not only in practiced material but in material you have never seen before. As a result, you possess considerable skill, perhaps more than you realize. In fact, if you had to, you could take dictation from a businessman, provided his dictation were not too difficult or too fast.

You would find, however, that taking dictation in the business office is somewhat different from taking dictation in class.

Your teacher realizes that during the learning stages your skill will develop

dictation in the office

most rapidly under ideal working conditions. Consequently, his dictation is smooth and even and distinct. Most of it is carefully timed because that is the only way your skill development can be accurately measured.

OFFICE-STYLE DICTATION

The businessman, however, is not concerned with the development of your skill; he assumes that you are already skilled. His dictation will not always be smooth and even. Depending upon the flow of his thoughts, it may be slow at times, fast at others. He may change his mind about a word, a phrase, or even a sentence and substitute another. He may delete and he may insert. His dictation will never be timed!

You will quickly become accustomed to this type of office-style dictation if you have sufficient shorthand speed. The more speed you possess, the easier office-style dictation will be for you. Therefore, strive to build your shorthand speed to the highest point possible; you will always be glad that you did!

Beginning with Lesson 41 — and in the first lesson of each chapter thereafter — you will study some of the problems you will meet when you take office-style dictation. You will be given suggestions on how to handle each problem and shown how to treat it in your shorthand notes.

CHAPTER NINE

manufacturing

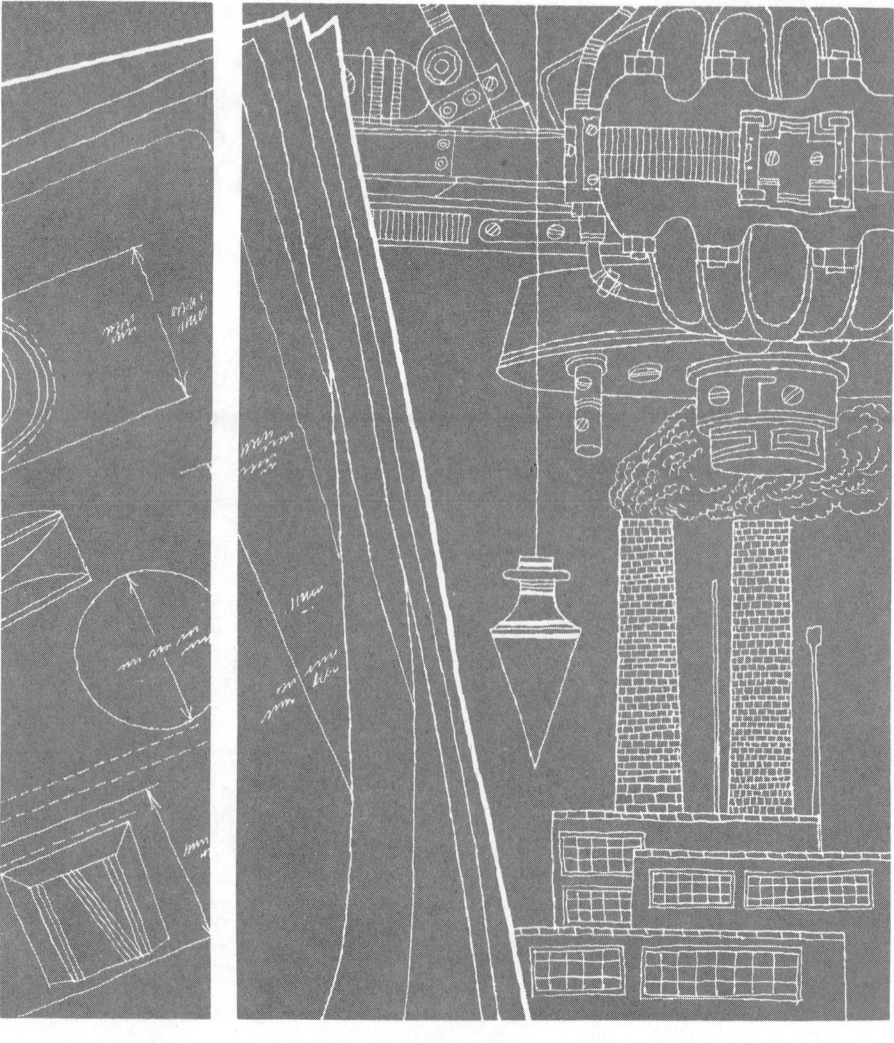

DEVELOPING WORD-BUILDING POWER

281 ▸ Brief Forms and Derivatives

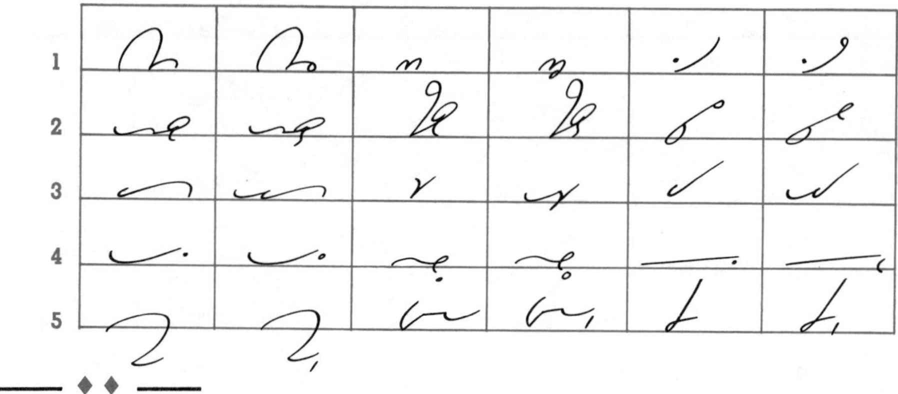

1 Difficult, difficulty; world, worldly; hand, handy.
2 Recognize, recognizes; advertise, advertises; idea, ideas.
3 Organize, reorganize; state, restate; order, reorder.
4 Willing, willingly; corresponding, correspondingly; morning, mornings.
5 Governor, governorship; partner, partnership; general, generalship.

BUILDING TRANSCRIPTION SKILLS

282 ▸ BUSINESS VOCABULARY BUILDER

depot Station.
diligence Attention; care.
furthering Advancing.

283 ▸ Brief-Form Letter

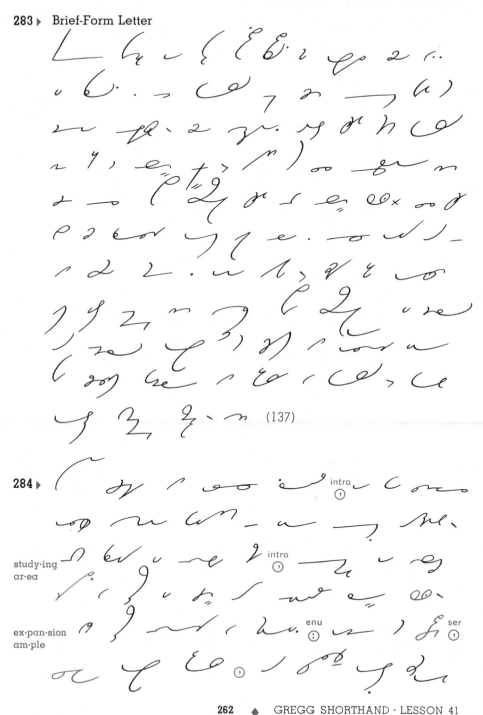

(137)

284 ▸

intro

studying
area

intro

expansion
ample

enu

ser

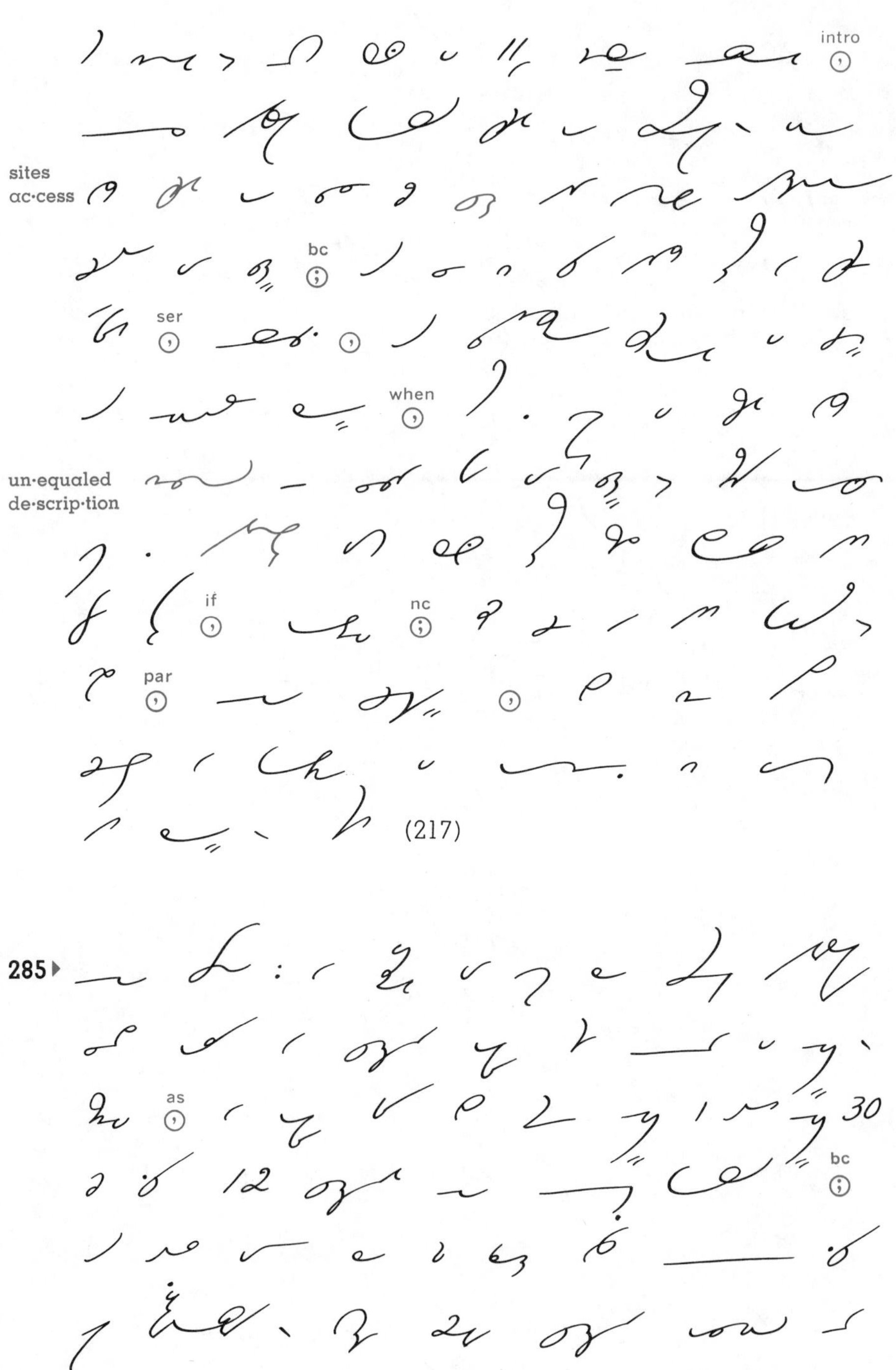
intro
sites
ac·cess
bc
ser
when
un·equaled
de·scrip·tion
if
nc
par
(217)
285
as
30
12
bc

20

some·one's
ex·er·cised

il

dil·i·gence
su·per·vi·sor

par

when

intro

(201)

286

as

intro

(81)

287▸ Transcription Quiz • For you to supply: 7 commas—2 commas nonrestrictive, 3 commas series, 2 commas parenthetical; 1 semicolon illustrative, 1 semicolon no conjunction; 2 missing words.

1943

(184)

OFFICE-STYLE DICTATION, 1

Deletions

A businessman will occasionally decide to delete — take out — a word or a phrase or even a sentence that he has dictated. For example, he may say:

> The pamphlet describes completely the investments we suggest—take out **completely.**

To indicate this deletion, you would simply strike a heavy downward line through the word thus:

Sometimes he may simply repeat the sentence without the word or phrase that he wishes to omit. He may say:

> The enclosed pamphlet describes and illustrates what we have in mind — no, **the enclosed pamphlet describes what we have in mind.**

To indicate this deletion, you would mark out in your notes not only the word *illustrates* but the word *and* as well.

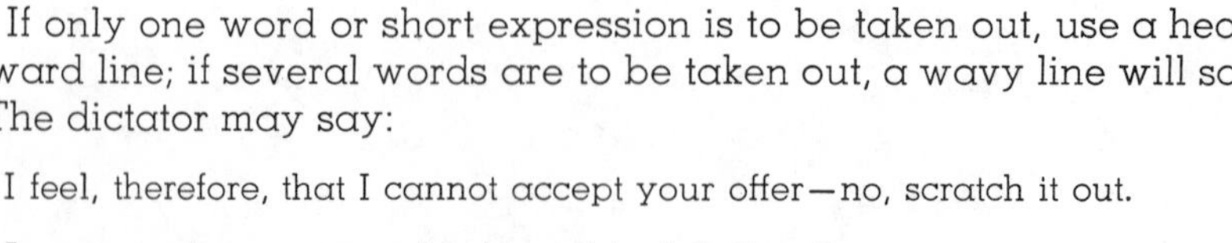

If only one word or short expression is to be taken out, use a heavy downward line; if several words are to be taken out, a wavy line will save time. The dictator may say:

> I feel, therefore, that I cannot accept your offer—no, scratch it out.

In your notes you would show this deletion thus:

288 ILLUSTRATION OF OFFICE-STYLE DICTATION

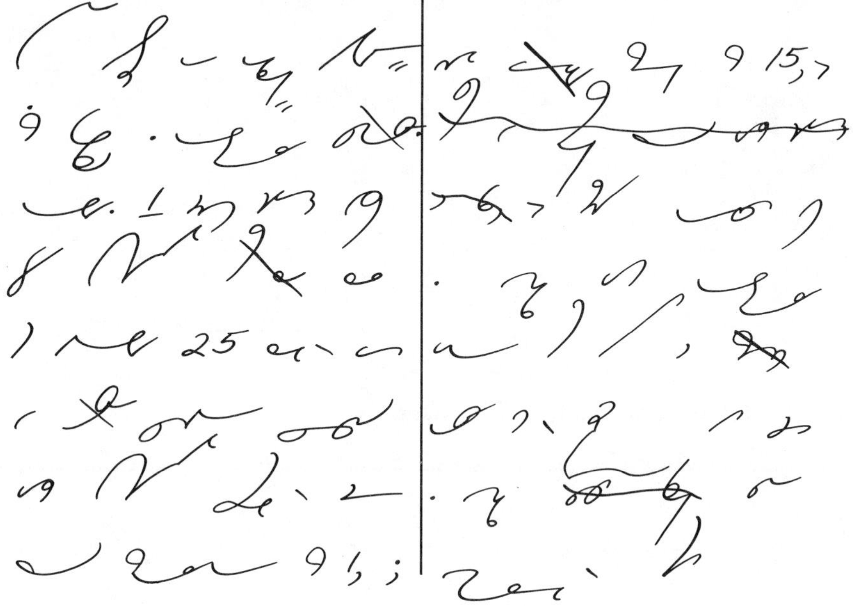

In keeping with the increased pace of business, the executive finds that he no longer has time to attend to much of his own detail work. He must now depend on his secretary to take care of many important matters that he formerly handled. He wants a truly competent and responsible assistant. If you can meet these requirements, many a harried executive will be eager and ready to roll out the red carpet for you—wall to wall!

BUILDING PHRASING SKILL

289 ▸ Useful Business-Letter Phrases

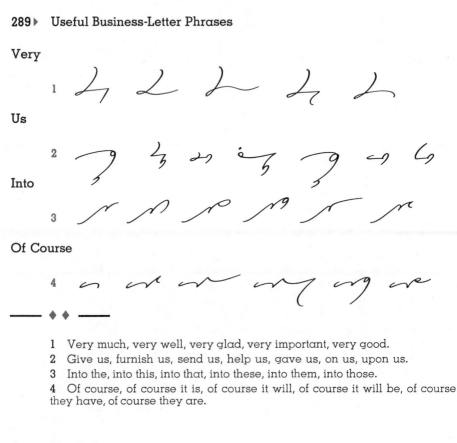

Very

1

Us

2

Into

3

Of Course

4

—— ♦♦ ——

1 Very much, very well, very glad, very important, very good.
2 Give us, furnish us, send us, help us, gave us, on us, upon us.
3 Into the, into this, into that, into these, into them, into those.
4 Of course, of course it is, of course it will, of course it will be, of course they have, of course they are.

290 ▸ Frequent Names

1

2

1 Kerr, King, Klein, Larsen, Levy, Lynch.
2 Flora, Florence, Georgiana, Gertrude, Harriet, Henrietta.

BUILDING TRANSCRIPTION SKILLS

291 BUSINESS VOCABULARY BUILDER

demolished Ruined, destroyed.
curtailing Shortening; lessening.
irreparably Beyond repair.

READING AND WRITING PRACTICE

292 Phrase Letter

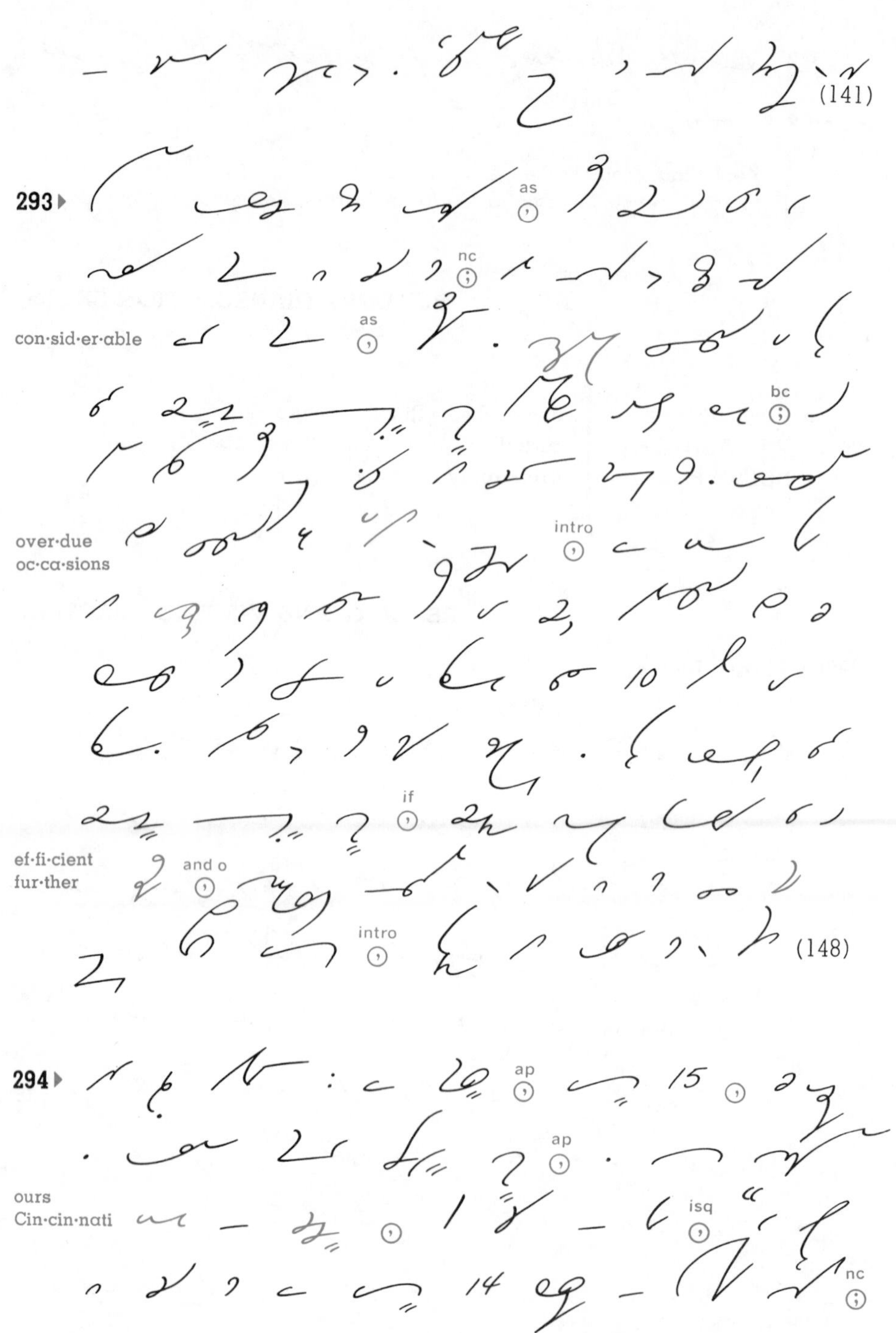

(141)
293
as
nc
con·sid·er·able
as
bc
over·due
oc·ca·sions
intro
if
ef·fi·cient
fur·ther
and o
intro
(148)
294
ap
15
ap
ours
Cin·cin·nati
isq
14
nc

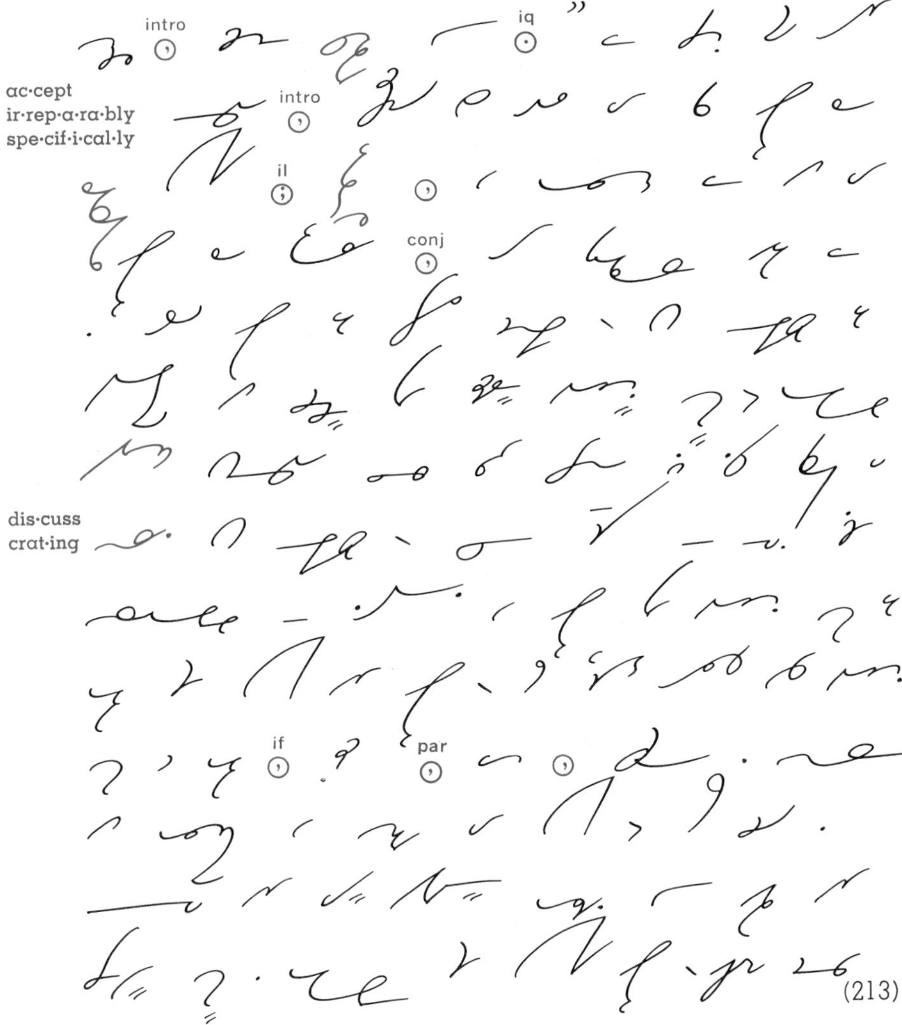

295▸ Transcription Quiz • Up to this stage in the Transcription Quizzes, you have had to supply commas, colons, and semicolons, and obvious missing words.

In the Transcription Quizzes in this and succeeding lessons, you will continue to supply the same types of punctuation, but the missing words will not be obvious; any one of a number of words will make sense at the point of omission. It is your job to supply the word that you think fits best in the sentence. For example:

In the spot where there has been an omission, any one of the following words would be considered correct: *plain, obvious, apparent.* Assuming that the word *obvious* makes the sentence read most smoothly, you would write it in your notebook thus:

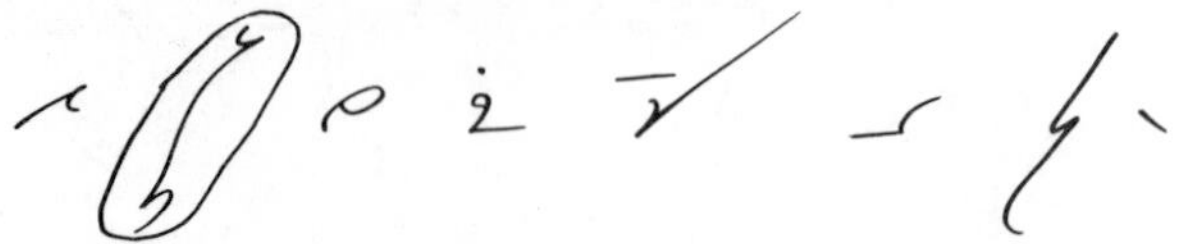

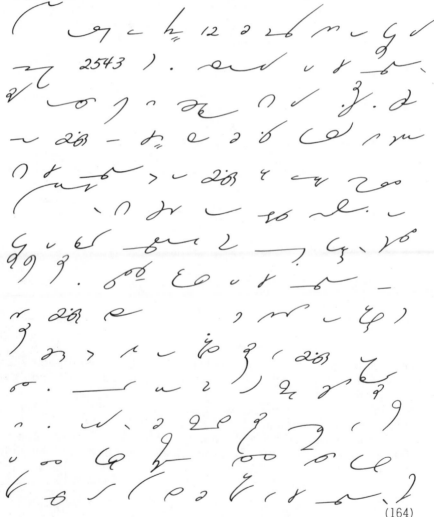

For you to supply: 3 commas – 2 commas parenthetical, 1 comma introductory; 1 semicolon no conjunction, 1 semicolon because of comma; 2 missing words.

(164)

DEVELOPING WORD-BUILDING POWER

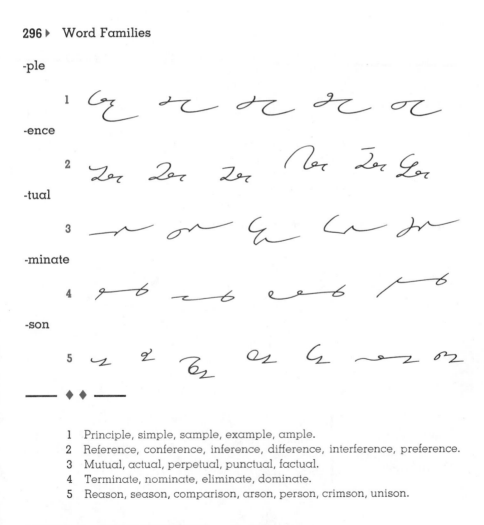

296 ▸ Word Families

-ple

1

-ence

2

-tual

3

-minate

4

-son

5

—— ◆◆ ——

1 Principle, simple, sample, example, ample.
2 Reference, conference, inference, difference, interference, preference.
3 Mutual, actual, perpetual, punctual, factual.
4 Terminate, nominate, eliminate, dominate.
5 Reason, season, comparison, arson, person, crimson, unison.

297▸ SIMILAR-WORDS DRILL principal, principle

principal *(noun)* The amount of money invested or lent on which interest is paid; the head of a school.

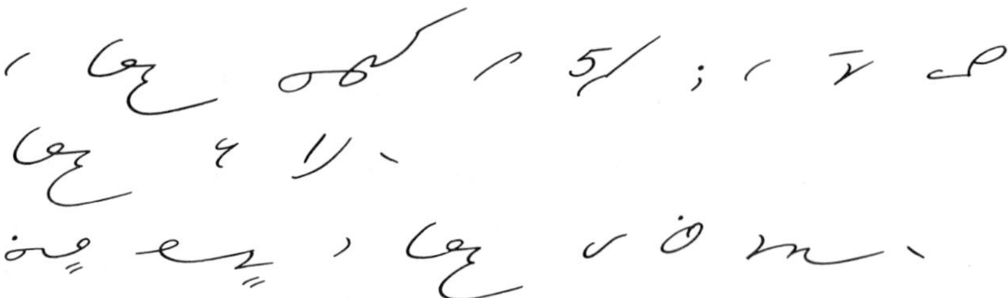

The principal amounted to $5,000; the interest on that principal was $100.
Henry Nelson is principal of the high school.

principal *(adjective)* Main; chief.

My principal job will be addressing high school assemblies.

principle Rule of action; a law of conduct; a fundamental truth.

I cannot give you any definite principles to guide you.
He is a man of high moral principles.

298▸ BUSINESS VOCABULARY BUILDER

terminate End.
vigorous Forceful.
brochures Booklets.

299

at·tempt·ing
prin·ci·ples

world's
prin·ci·pal
oc·curred

intro

prin·ci·pal
en·rolled

(155)

300

intro

il

intro

pledged
year's

intro

re·sponse
wor·thy

if

ex·ceed·ing
Transcribe:
$300,000

par

prin·ci·pal
per·sua·sive
bro·chures

and o

ser

(174)

301▶
Transcribe:
July 15

ser

ap

per·son·al
per·ma·nent

intro

nc

ex·pe·ri·ence
con·fi·dent

intro

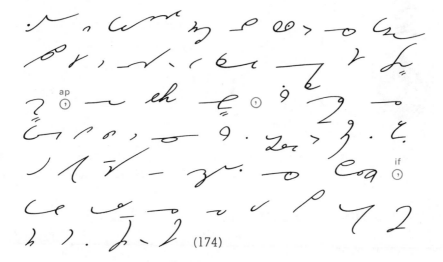

ap

if

(174)

302 ▸ **Transcription Quiz** • For you to supply: 7 commas — 3 commas introductory, 1 comma nonrestrictive, 1 comma apposition, 2 commas parenthetical; 1 semicolon no conjunction; 2 missing words.

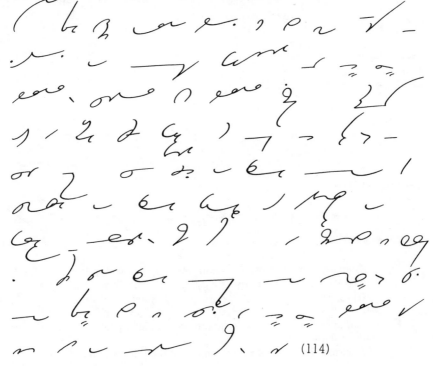

(114)

DEVELOPING WORD-BUILDING POWER

303▸ Word Beginnings and Endings

-sume, -sumption

1

-ily

2

-self, -selves

3

-cient, -ciency

4

-ulate, -ulation

5

—— ♦ ♦ ——

1 Consume, consumer, resume, resumption, presumption, assumed.

2 Steadily, readily, family, easily, necessarily, temporarily, heavily.

3 Themselves, ourselves, yourselves, himself, myself, herself, itself, yourself.

4 Sufficient, sufficiently, efficient, efficiency, proficient, proficiency, patient, patiently.

5 Congratulate, congratulations, tabulate, tabulation, regulated.

304 ▸ Geographical Expressions

1 Ashville, Nashville, Danville, Evansville, Jacksonville, Brownsville, Knoxville.

2 Florida, Georgia, Idaho, Illinois, Indiana, Iowa, Kansas, Kentucky.

3 Bordeaux, Marseilles, Cherbourg, Madrid, Lisbon, Brussels.

BUILDING TRANSCRIPTION SKILLS

305 ▸ SPELLING FAMILIES dis-, des-

People often pronounce the word beginnings *dis* and *des* alike in words such as *discuss* and *despite*. Consequently, pronunciation will not help you decide whether a word is spelled *dis* or *des*. The following list contains words with those word beginnings. Study them carefully.

Words Beginning with Dis-

di·sas·ter	dis·like	dis·pense
dis·close	dis·mayed	dis·pose
dis·cussed	dis·patch	dis·pute
dis·guise	dis·pel	dis·turb

Words Beginning with Des-

de·scribe	de·spair	de·spon·dent
de·scrip·tion	des·per·ate	des·ti·na·tion
de·sir·able	de·spise	des·ig·nate
des·o·late	de·spite	de·stroy

306 ▸ BUSINESS VOCABULARY BUILDER

designate To name.

depict To portray in words; to describe.

motivate To provide with a goal or motive.

307

dis·turb·ing
su·per·in·ten·dent

un·nec·es·sary
suf·fer·ing
mo·rale

Safe·ty
in·ten·sive

as·sis·tance

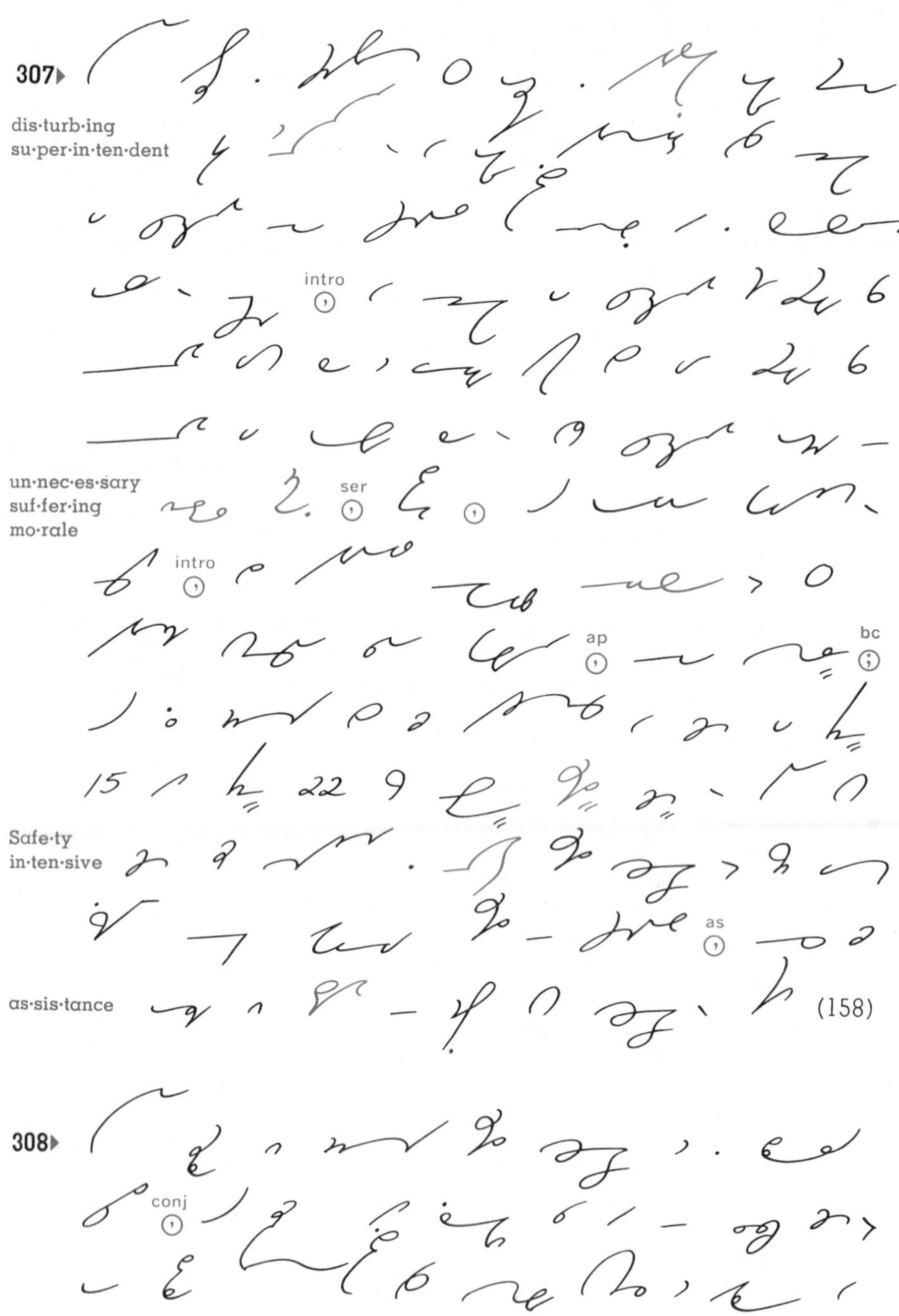

308

intro

and o

well-planned *hyphenated before noun*

oc·cur·ring be·gin·ning

fa·tigue of·fered

il

il

(232)

309▸

ilq

spray·ers
suit·able

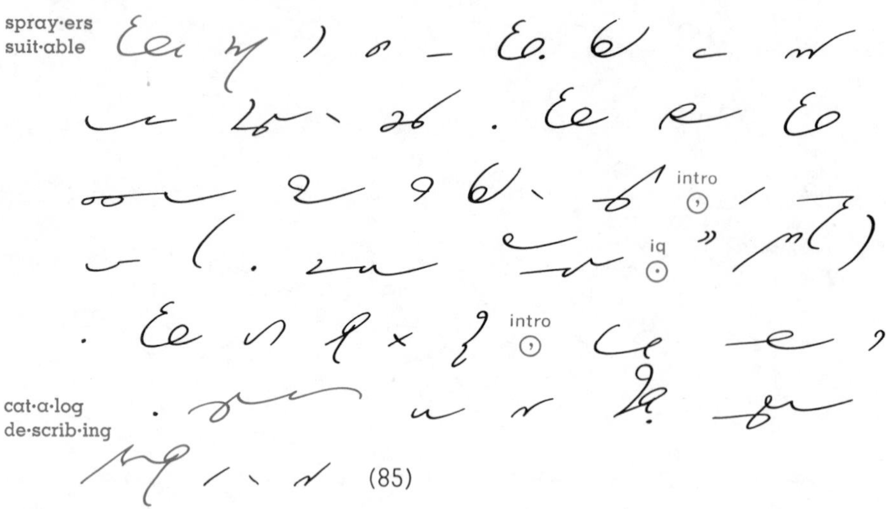

cat·a·log
de·scrib·ing

(85)

310▸ Transcription Quiz • For you to supply: 3 commas—1 comma conjunction, 2 commas introductory; 1 semicolon no conjunction; 1 missing word.

(111)

DEVELOPING WORD-BUILDING POWER

311 ▸ Shorthand Vocabulary Builder

O on Its Side

1 [shorthand outlines]

OO on Its Side

2 [shorthand outlines]

Omission of Short U

3 [shorthand outlines]

Directions

4 [shorthand outlines]

Ort

5 [shorthand outlines]

—— ♦♦ ——

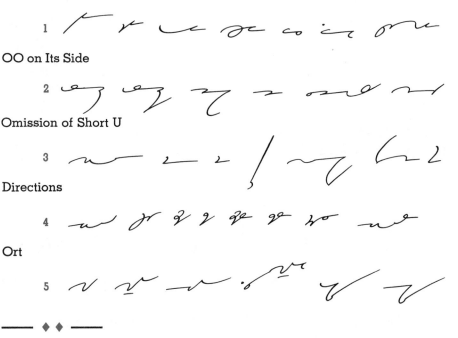

1 Dome, stone, lone, cannon, only, homes, outgrown.
2 Remove, removed, number, noon, enumerate, commute.
3 Column, sum, sun, judges, crumbled, begun, fun.
4 North, south, west, east, western, eastern, southern, northern.
5 Court, quarter, mortal, headquarters, reported, imported.

312▸ Accuracy Practice—Straight Lines • The speed with which you can read your notes will depend in part on the accuracy of your penmanship. The Accuracy Practice exercises in this lesson are intended to improve your ability to write straight lines. With this and the other Accuracy Practice exercises in this volume, follow this procedure:

a Read the entire drill.

b Practice each group separately, writing it once or twice and making a special effort to keep the straight lines absolutely straight.

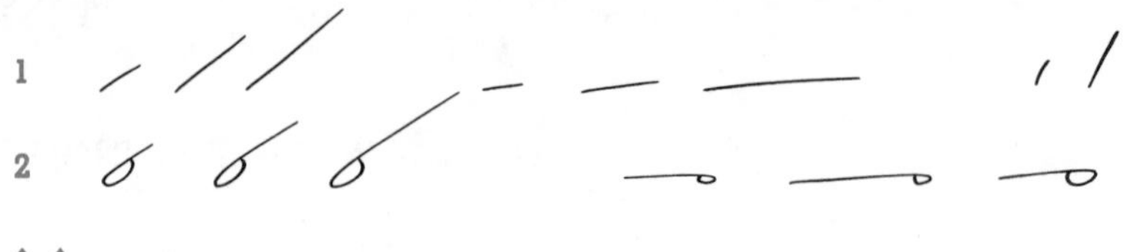

1 It-at, would, debt; in-not, am, men; shall, which.

2 Ate, add, added; me, many, may.

BUILDING TRANSCRIPTION SKILLS

313▸ BUSINESS VOCABULARY BUILDER

destiny Fate.

motifs Themes or main features.

jostled Elbowed; crowded.

READING AND WRITING PRACTICE

314▸ History of the Capitol Building

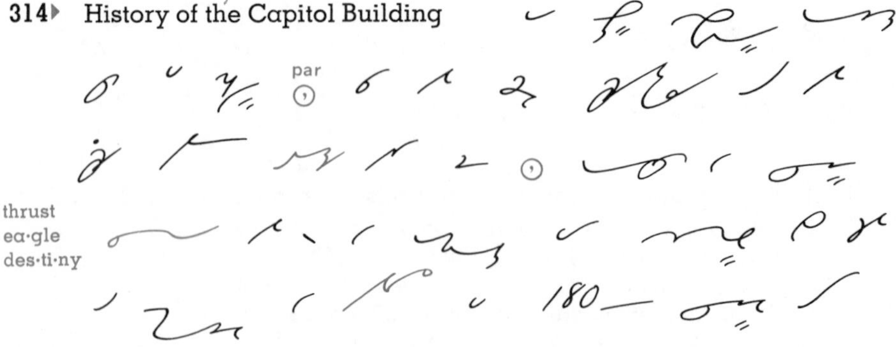

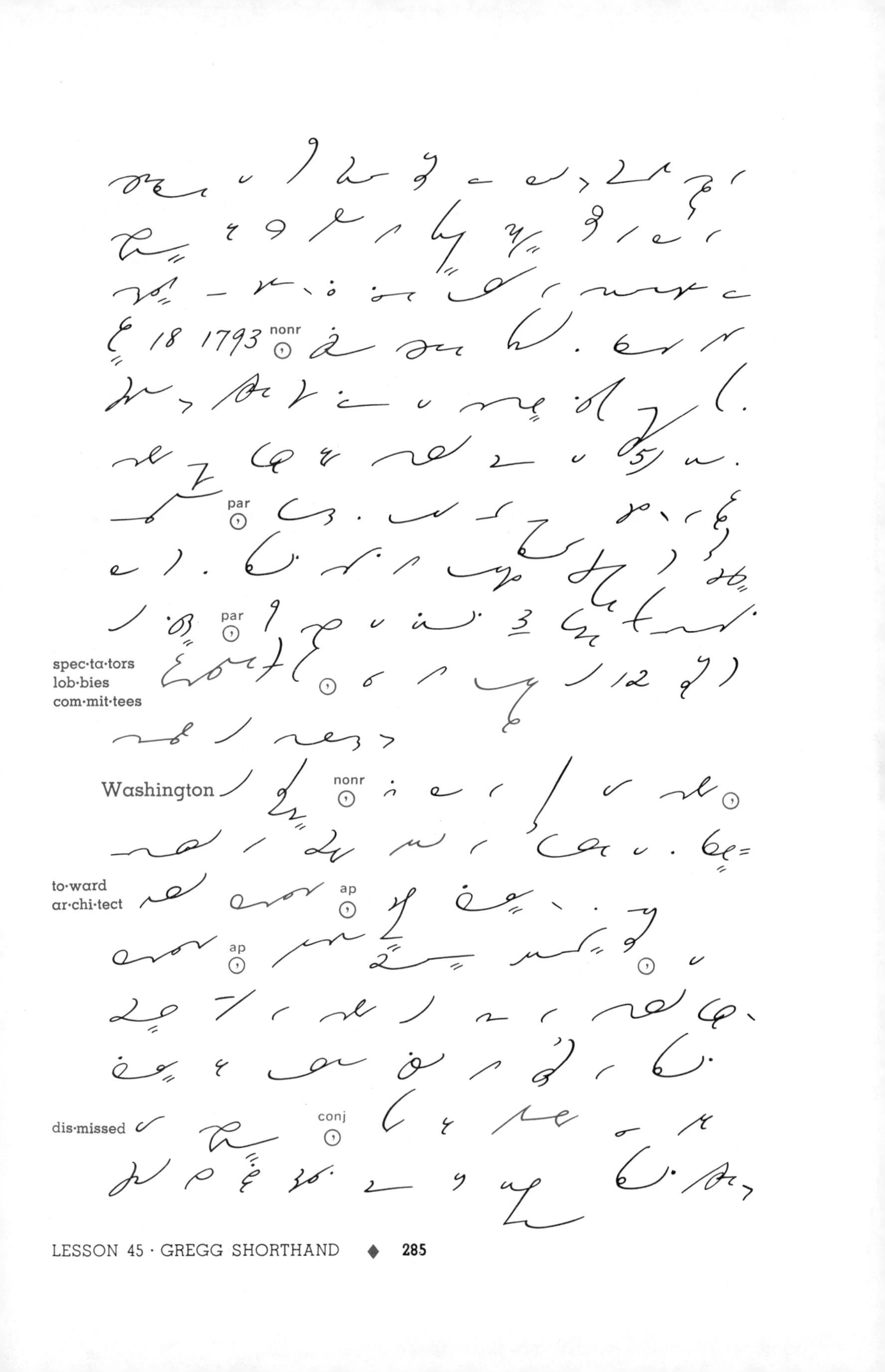

nonr

par

par

spec·ta·tors
lob·bies
com·mit·tees

Washington

nonr

to·ward
ar·chi·tect

ap

ap

dis·missed

conj

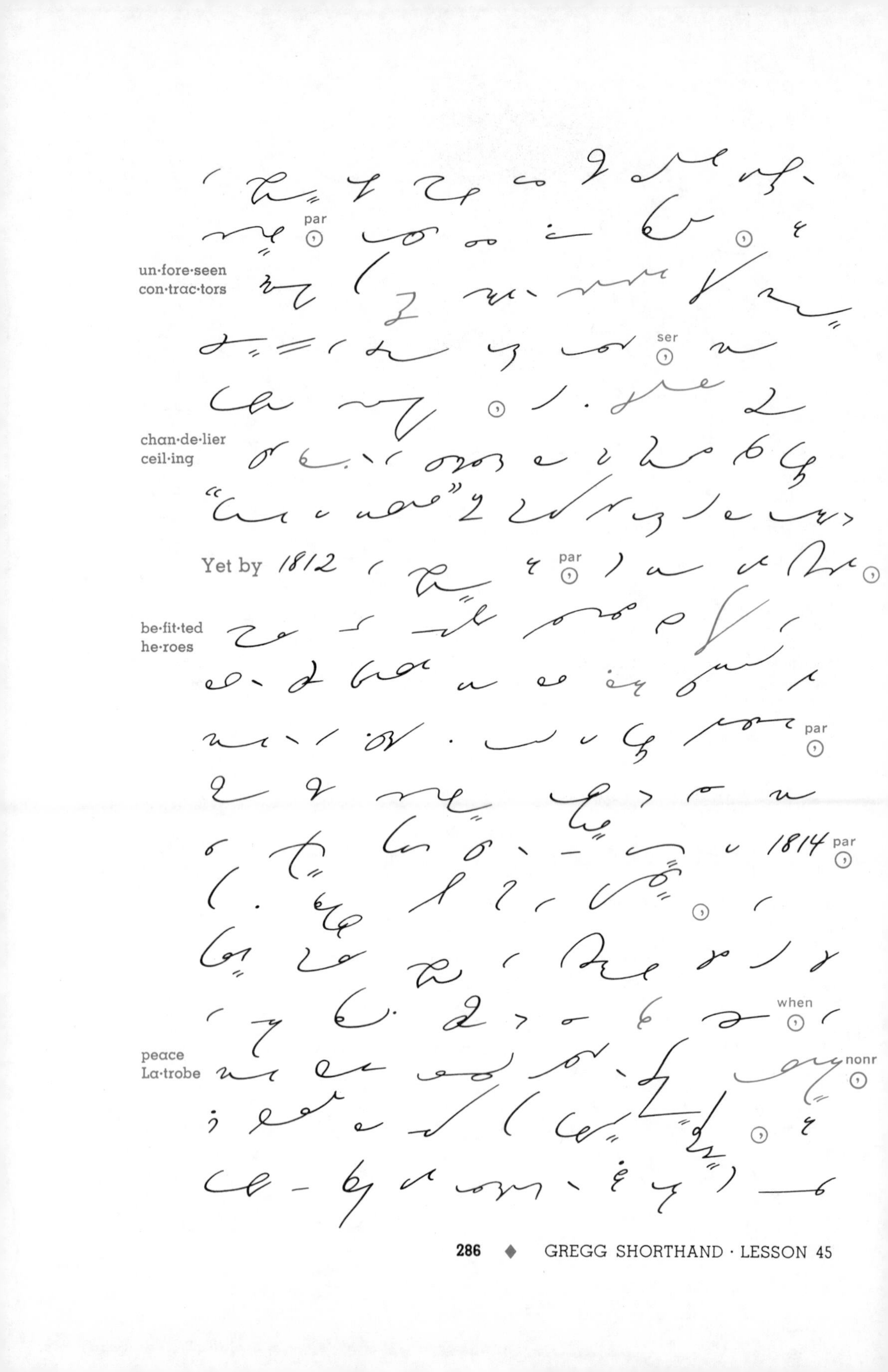

par

un·fore·seen
con·trac·tors

ser

chan·de·lier
ceil·ing

Yet by 1812 par

be·fit·ted
he·roes

par

1814 par

when

peace
La·trobe

nonr

no·ta·bly
mo·tifs

Not long after

intro

par

1851

ser

strug·gles
jos·tled

Li·brary
burst·ing

conj

nonr

par

(604)

CHAPTER TEN

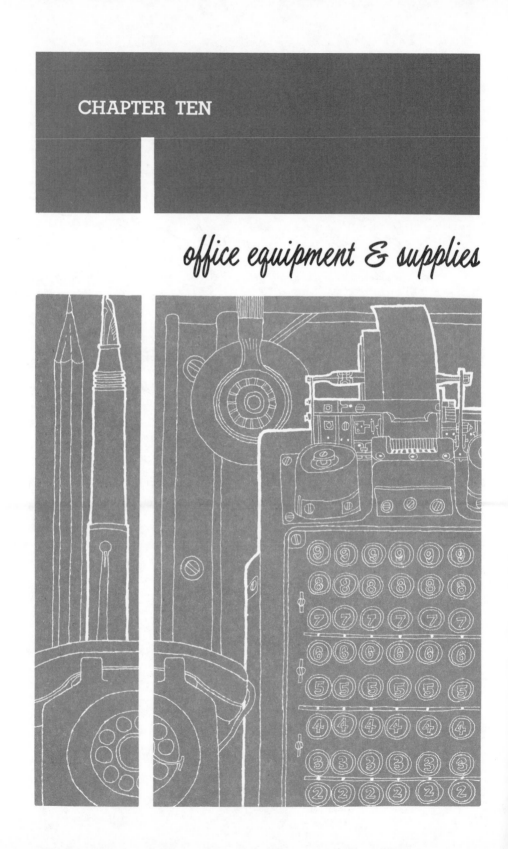

office equipment & supplies

DEVELOPING WORD-BUILDING POWER

315▸ Brief Forms and Derivatives

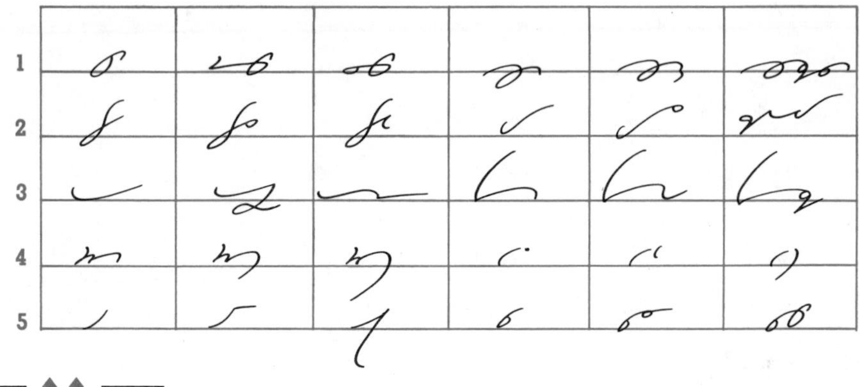

1 How, somehow, anyhow; character, characters, characteristic.
2 Particular, particularly, particulars; ordinary, ordinarily, extraordinary.
3 Well, welfare, welcome; big, bigger, biggest.
4 Success, successful, successive; thank, thanks, thankful.
5 There, therein, thereby; with, within, without.

BUILDING TRANSCRIPTION SKILLS

316▸ BUSINESS VOCABULARY BUILDER

diverted Turned from one course to another.

disrupted Disturbed.

versatility The ability to turn with ease from one thing to another.

READING AND WRITING PRACTICE

317 Brief-Form Letter

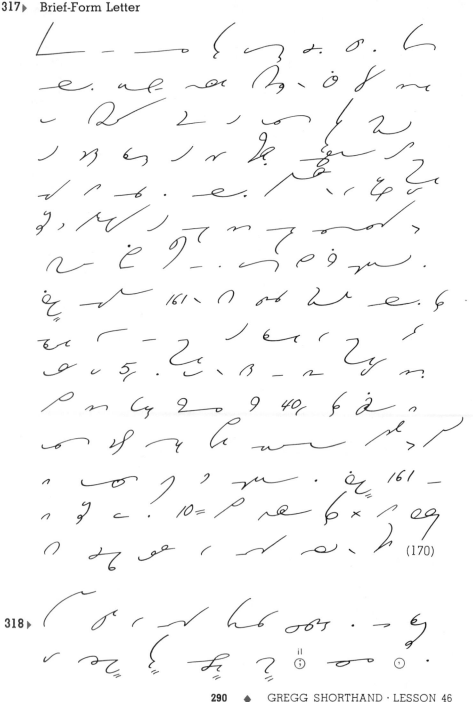

(170)

318

il

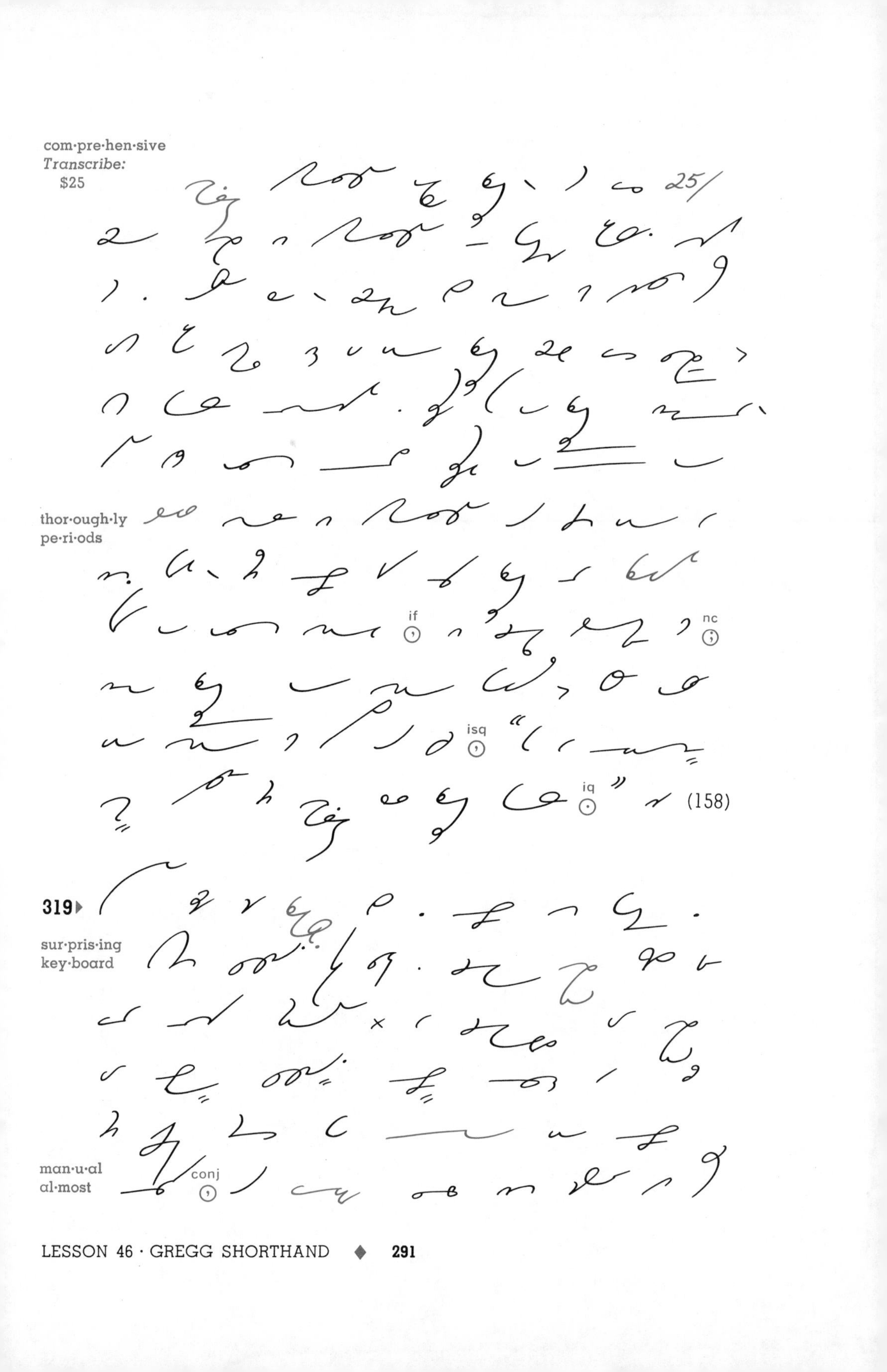

com·pre·hen·sive
Transcribe:
$25

(158)

thor·ough·ly
pe·ri·ods

if

nc

isq

iq

319▸

sur·pris·ing
key·board

man·u·al
al·most

conj

nc

switch
sched·ules
ver·sa·til·i·ty

nonr

in·ter·rupt
rou·tines

and o

if

in·stalled
neigh·bor·hood

when

ap

cr

5:30

intro

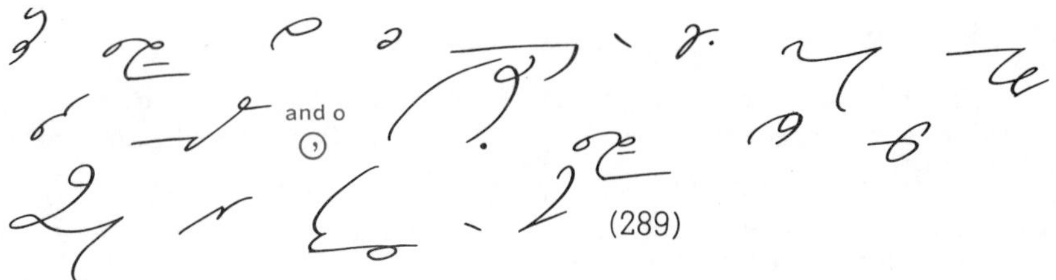

320▸ Transcription Quiz • For you to supply: 5 commas — 2 commas series, 2 commas parenthetical, 1 comma *and* omitted; 1 semicolon because of comma; 2 missing words.

(120)

OFFICE-STYLE DICTATION, 2

Short Insertions

A common change that a businessman makes in his dictation is the insertion of a word or a phrase in a sentence that has already been dictated. The dictator may say:

> Our representative will call on you on Friday, June 16 — make that **our Chicago representative.**

You must be on the alert so that you can quickly find the point at which the addition is to be made. When you find the point, insert the added word or phrase with a caret, just as you would in longhand, thus:

16.

321▸ ILLUSTRATION OF OFFICE-STYLE DICTATION

18 19.

12

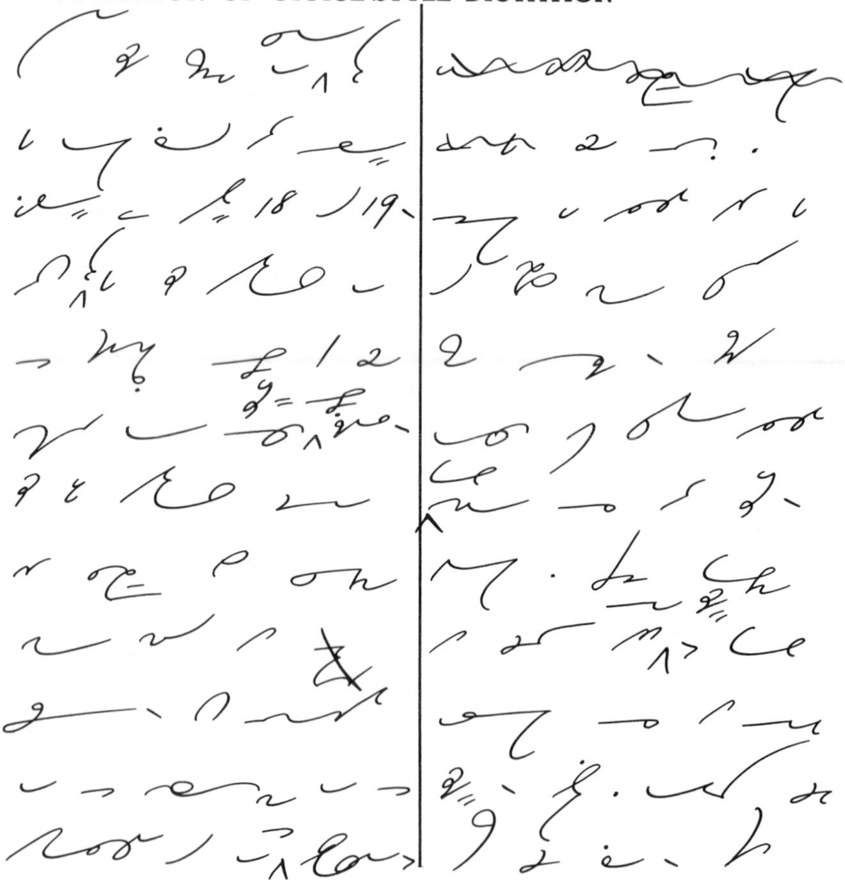

BUILDING PHRASING SKILL

322 Useful Business-Letter Phrases

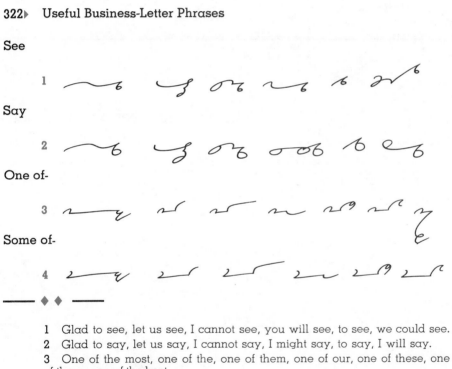

See

1

Say

2

One of-

3

Some of-

4

1 Glad to see, let us see, I cannot see, you will see, to see, we could see.

2 Glad to say, let us say, I cannot say, I might say, to say, I will say.

3 One of the most, one of the, one of them, one of our, one of these, one of those, one of the best.

4 Some of the most, some of the, some of them, some of our, some of these, some of those.

323 Frequent Names

1

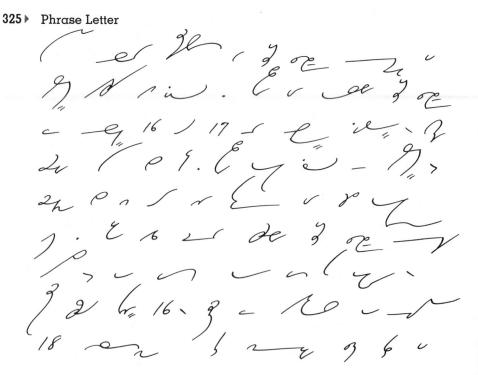

1 Martin, McCarthy, McDonald, McKenzie.
2 Harold, Herbert, Howard, Hugh, Hugo, Isaac, Jacob.

BUILDING TRANSCRIPTION SKILLS

324 BUSINESS VOCABULARY BUILDER

ingenious Cleverly devised; inventive.
ingenuity Cleverness.
subordinates Those who are lesser in rank or importance.

READING AND WRITING PRACTICE

325 Phrase Letter

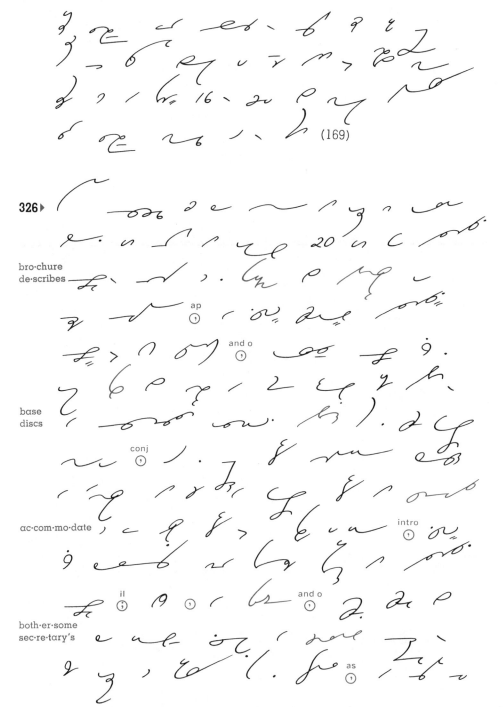

16

20 (169)

326

20

bro·chure
de·scribes

ap

and o

base
discs

conj

ac·com·mo·date

intro

il

and o

both·er·some
sec·re·tary's

as

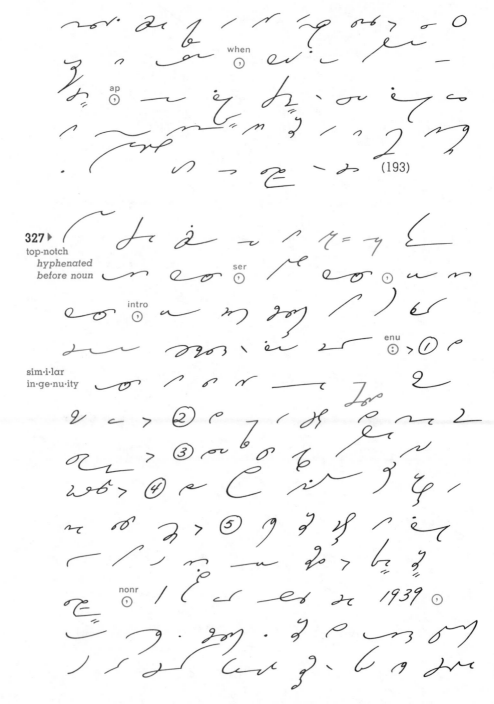

when

ap

(193)

327 top-notch *hyphenated before noun*

ser

intro

enu

sim·i·lar in·ge·nu·ity

nonr

1939

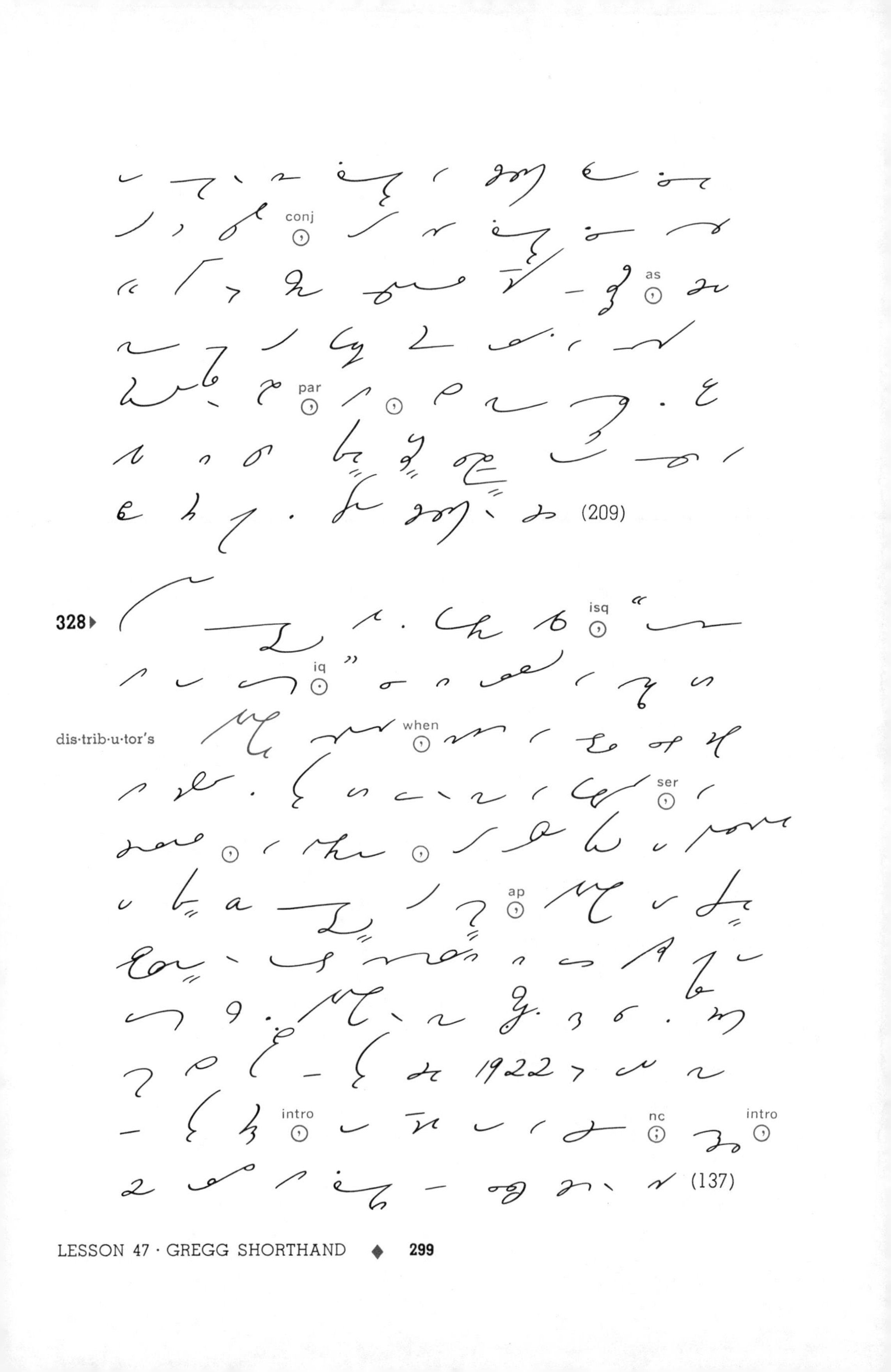

conj

as

par

(209)

328 isq

iq

dis·trib·u·tor's when

ser

ap

intro nc intro

(137)

329▸ Transcription Quiz • For you to supply: 7 commas – 2 commas parenthetical, 2 commas apposition, 1 comma *when* clause, 2 commas series; 2 missing words.

(189)

DEVELOPING WORD-BUILDING POWER

330 ▸ Word Families

-duce

1

-manship

2

Unex-

3

-ct

4

Tem, etc.

5

—— ◆◆ ——

1 Produce, reduce, reproduce, induce, introduce, deduce.
2 Workmanship, salesmanship, penmanship, sportsmanship.
3 Unexcelled, unexplained, unexpected, unexpressed, unexploded.
4 Effect, affect, project, reflect, aspect, perfect, respect.
5 System, item, contemplate, estimate, legitimate, customers.

331 ▸ SIMILAR-WORDS DRILL adverse, averse

adverse Opposing; unfavorable.

Because of adverse weather conditions, it is unlikely that he will be able to meet his class tonight.

averse Unwilling.

I am definitely averse to having him elected president.

332 ▸ BUSINESS VOCABULARY BUILDER

memoranda (plural of memorandum) Informal records or notes.

durable Lasting.

READING AND WRITING PRACTICE

333 ▸

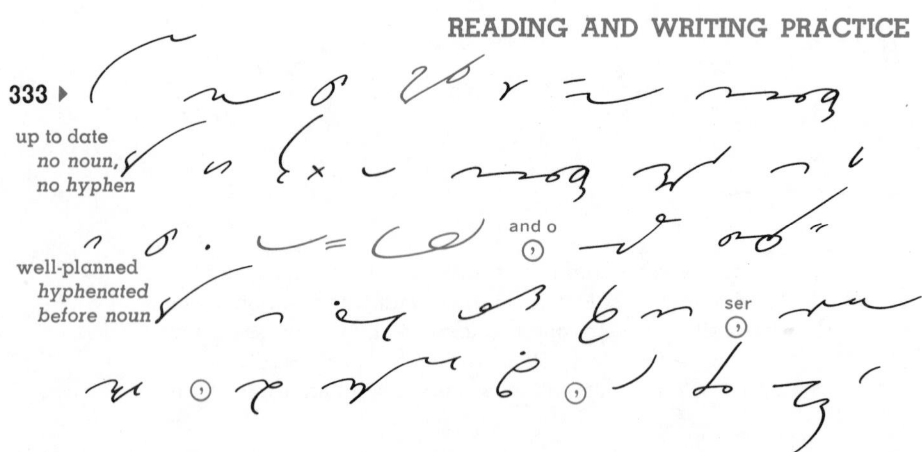

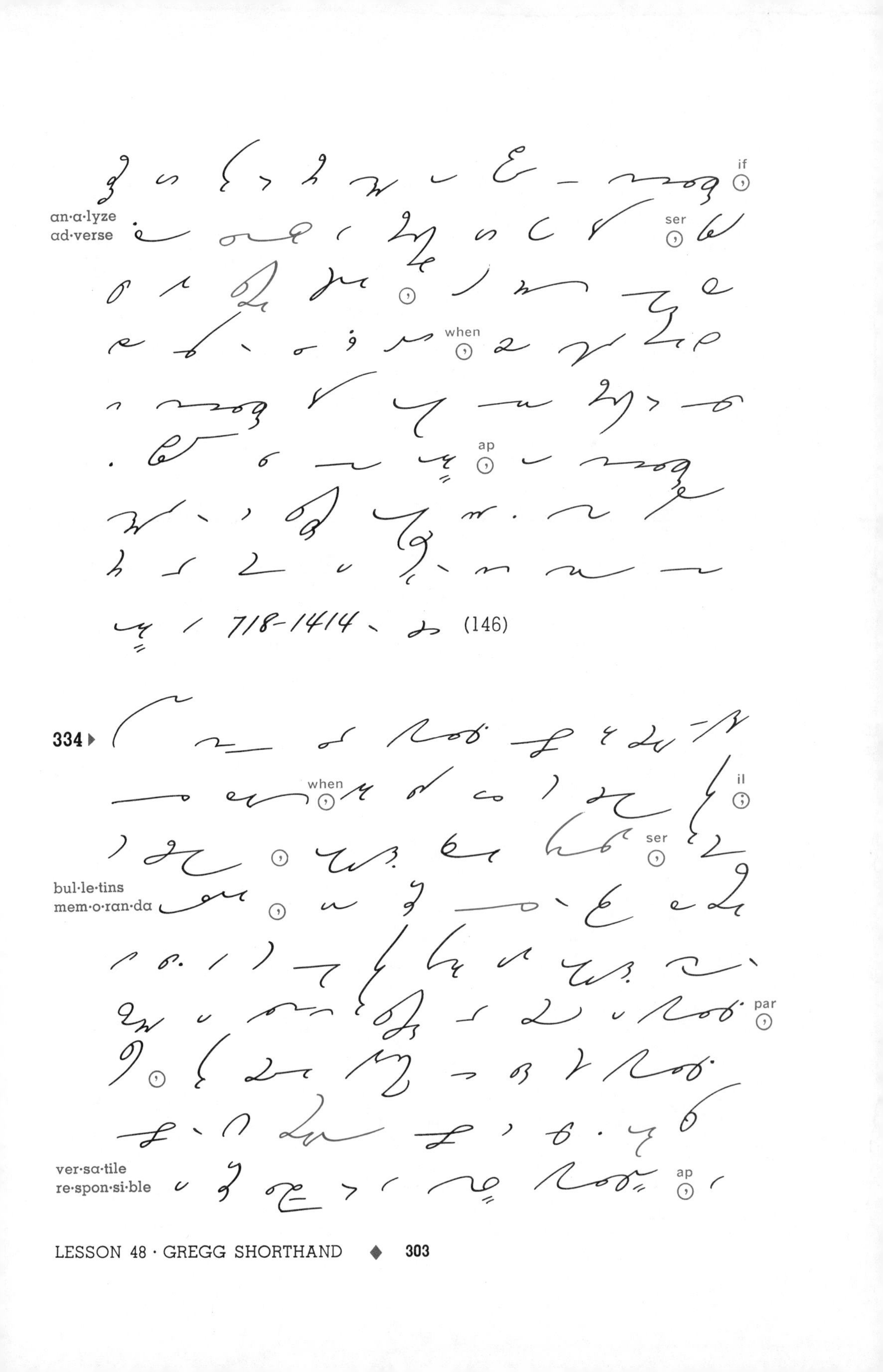

if

an·a·lyze
ad·verse

ser

when

ap

718-1414 (146)

334

when

il

ser

bul·le·tins
mem·o·ran·da

par

ver·sa·tile
re·spon·si·ble

ap

ser

intro

rec·om·mend
fi·ber

(198)

335 four-draw·er *hyphenated before noun*

isq

4 =

842 65/ iq

nc

conj

un·ex·celled
de·spite

intro

conj

as·sis·tance
con·nec·tion

if

well trained
no noun,
no hyphen

conj

(197)

336

par

and o

com·pa·nies
prof·it·ing

par

ser

(93)

337▸ Transcription Quiz • For you to supply: 7 commas – 2 commas *if* clause, 3 commas series, 2 commas parenthetical; 1 semicolon no conjunction; 2 missing words.

(168)

DEVELOPING WORD-BUILDING POWER

338 ▸ Word Beginnings and Endings

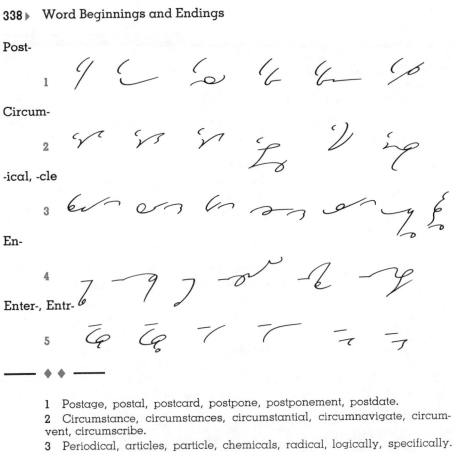

Post-

1

Circum-

2

-ical, -cle

3

En-

4

Enter-, Entr-

5

—— ◆◆ ——

1 Postage, postal, postcard, postpone, postponement, postdate.

2 Circumstance, circumstances, circumstantial, circumnavigate, circumvent, circumscribe.

3 Periodical, articles, particle, chemicals, radical, logically, specifically.

4 Enjoy, engage, envy, encountered, endanger, engraved.

5 Enterprise, enterprisingly, entertain, entertainment, entrance, entrances.

339 ▸ Geographical Expressions

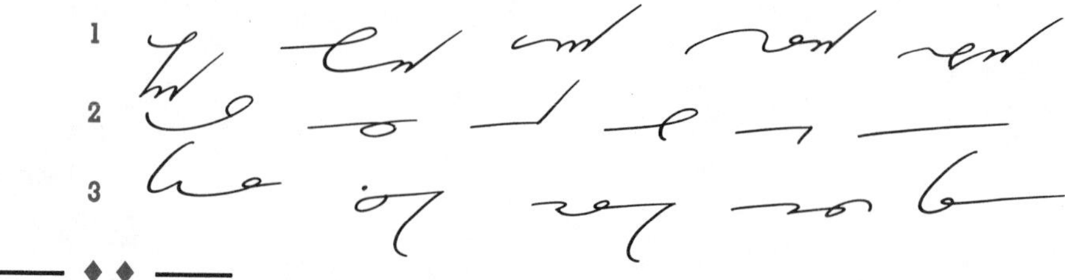

— ♦♦ —

1 Ridgewood, Maplewood, Oakwood, Greenwood, Crestwood.
2 Louisiana, Maine, Maryland, Massachusetts, Michigan, Minnesota.
3 Berlin, Hamburg, Nuremburg, Munich, Bremen.

BUILDING TRANSCRIPTION SKILLS

340 ▸ SPELLING FAMILIES

Forming -ed and -ing Derivatives of Words Ending in L

When the last syllable of a word ending in *l*, preceded by a single vowel, is accented, the *l* is doubled in forming derivatives in *-ed* and *-ing*.

com·pel	**com·pelled**	**com·pel·ling**
dis·pel	**dis·pelled**	**dis·pel·ling**
ex·pel	**ex·pelled**	**ex·pel·ling**
pro·pel	**pro·pelled**	**pro·pel·ling**

When the last syllable is not accented, the *l* is not doubled.

can·cel	**can·celed**	**can·cel·ing**
equal	**equaled**	**equal·ing**
mod·el	**mod·eled**	**mod·el·ing**
ri·val	**ri·valed**	**ri·val·ing**
to·tal	**to·taled**	**to·tal·ing**
trav·el	**trav·eled**	**trav·el·ing**

341 ▸ BUSINESS VOCABULARY BUILDER

acutely Sharply.
transported Carried; shipped.

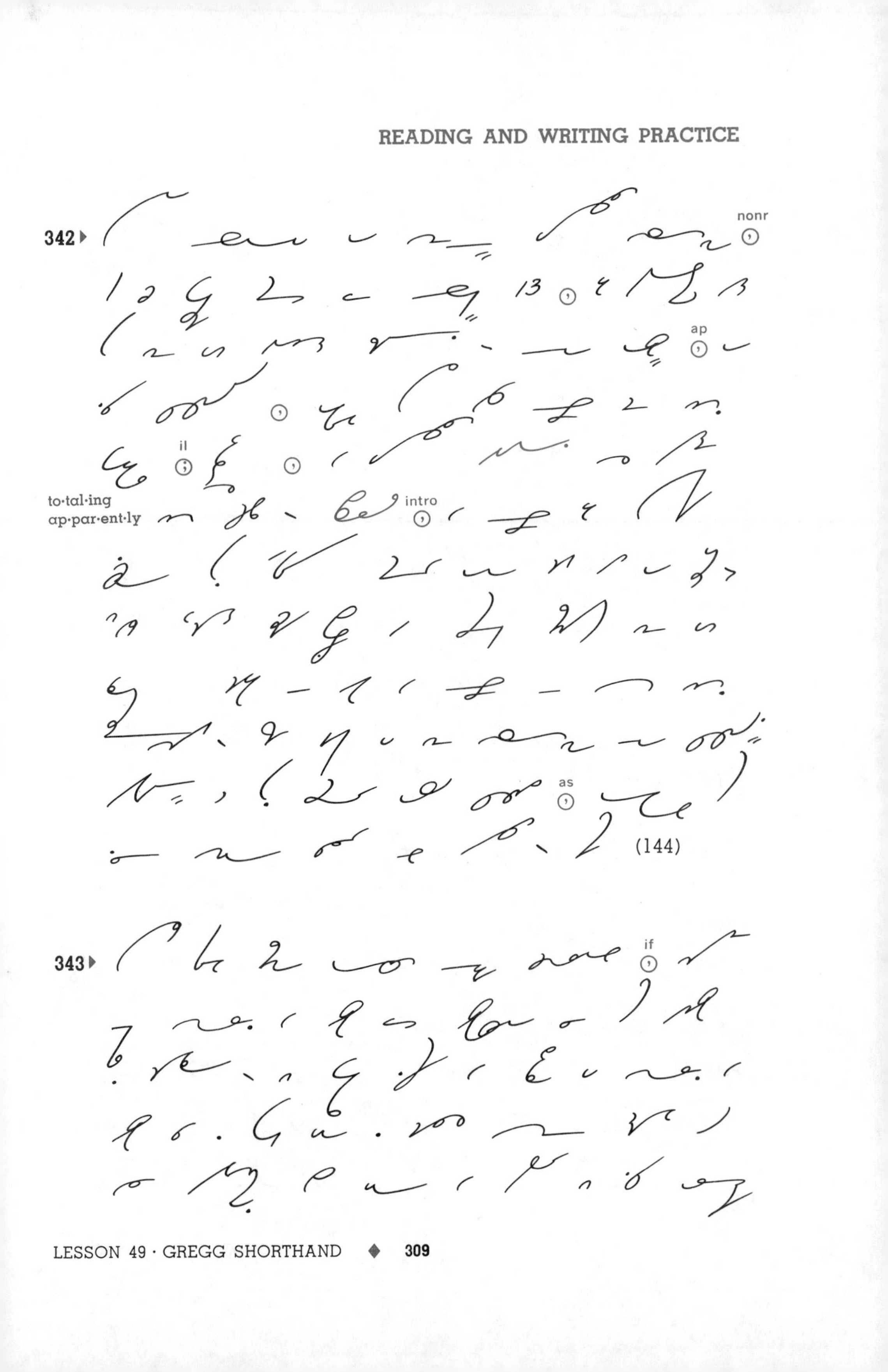

342 nonr ap il to·tal·ing ap·par·ent·ly intro as (144)

343 if

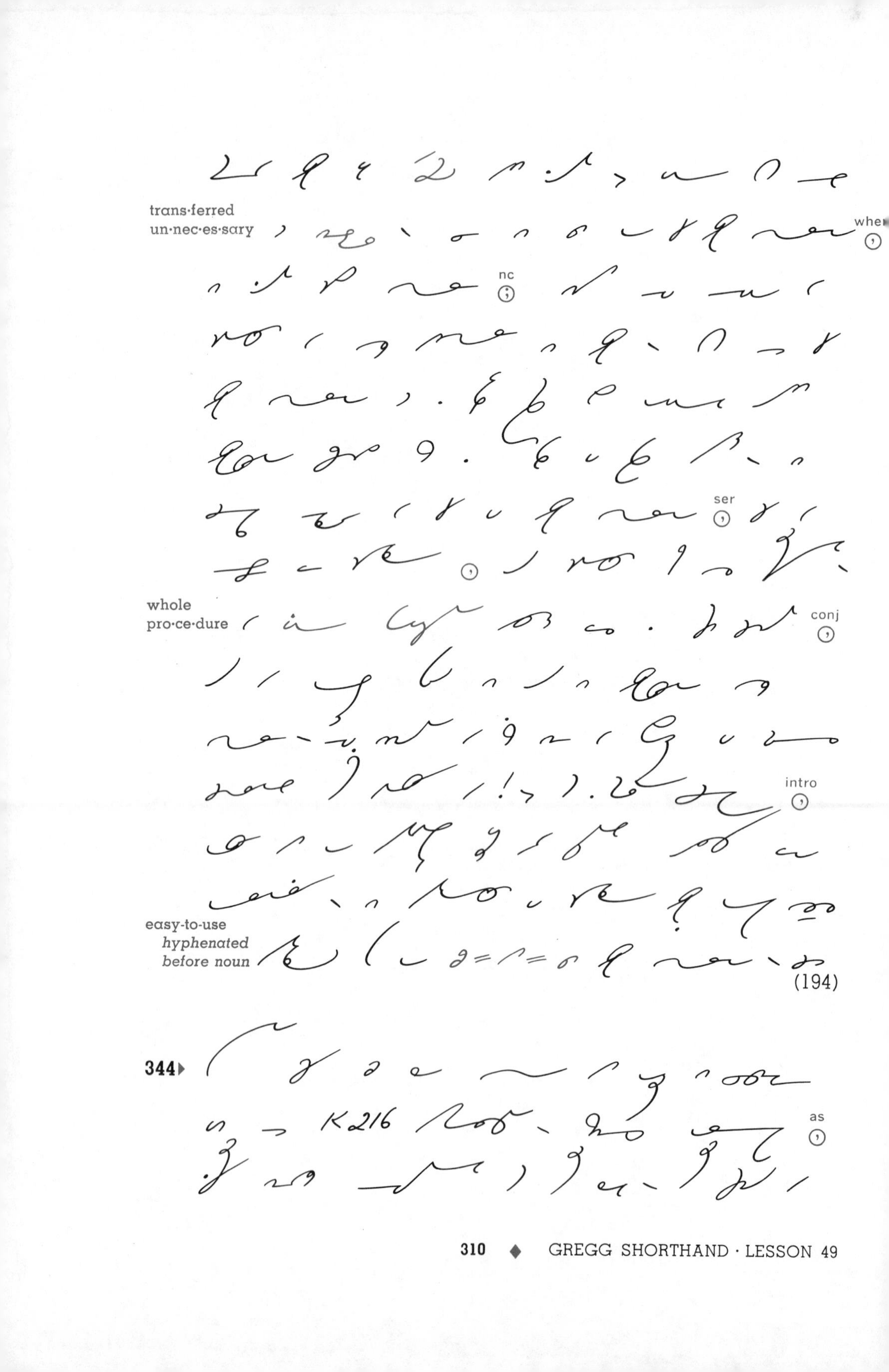

trans·ferred
un·nec·es·sary

when

nc

ser

whole
pro·ce·dure

conj

intro

easy-to-use
hyphenated
before noun

(194)

344▸

as

be·com·ing worn

intro

nc

intro

if

4

Transcribe: 4 p.m.

conj

nonr

(176)

345 ▸ Transcription Quiz · For you to supply: 6 commas—1 comma nonrestrictive, 2 commas apposition, 2 commas series, 1 comma introductory; 1 semicolon no conjunction; 2 missing words.

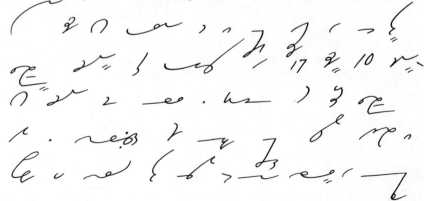

(174)

▸ *Morale in the individual is his zest for living and working—or lack of it. The person with high morale believes in himself, in his future, and in others. He thinks his work is worth doing and that he is doing a good job at it. High morale helps him to take minor irritations in stride, to work under pressure when necessary without blowing up, to get along with people who want to take more than they give. High morale makes a person unbeatable.*—Laird and Laird

DEVELOPING WORD-BUILDING POWER

346▸ Shorthand Vocabulary Builder

Nt

1

U

2

OO

3

Ia

4

Ia

5

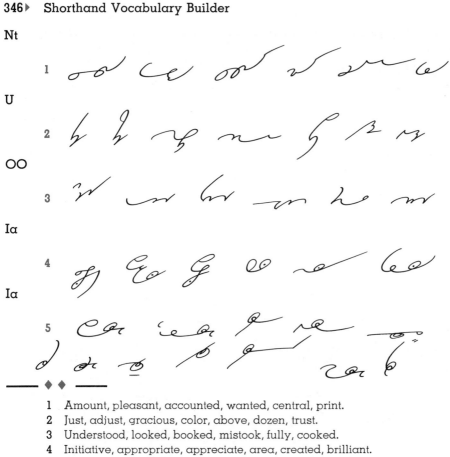

1 Amount, pleasant, accounted, wanted, central, print.
2 Just, adjust, gracious, color, above, dozen, trust.
3 Understood, looked, booked, mistook, fully, cooked.
4 Initiative, appropriate, appreciate, area, created, brilliant.
5 Appliance, self-reliance, dial, trial, Miami, via, science, quiet, diet, diamond, compliance, bias.

347 Accuracy Practice—Circles

1 Air, ail; ache, ago, gay; rate, late.
2 Writ, lead; take, tag; teeth, detain.

BUILDING TRANSCRIPTION SKILLS

348 BUSINESS VOCABULARY BUILDER

primarily In the first place; mainly.
prospective Looking forward to the future.
gracious Full of grace and charm.

READING AND WRITING PRACTICE

349 Secretarial Work

pri·mar·i·ly
glam·our

nc
par
iq

ser

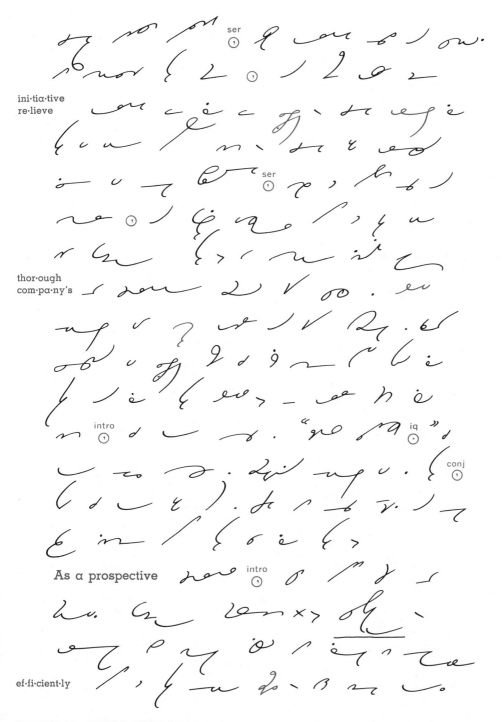

ini·tia·tive
re·lieve

ser

thor·ough
com·pa·ny's

intro

iq

conj

As a prospective

intro

ef·fi·cient·ly

ser

crit·i·cism
tem·per·a·ment

conj

busi·ness·like
over·step·ping

intro

par

ser

and o

self-re·li·ance
gra·cious

par

Good Health.

conj

conj

clothes
col·or

well-mod·u·lated
hyphenated before noun

intro

face-to-face
hyphenated before noun

Sense of Responsibility.

intro

bc

intro

(623)

▸ *There is no substitute for shorthand speed.*—H. H. Green

CHAPTER ELEVEN

personnel

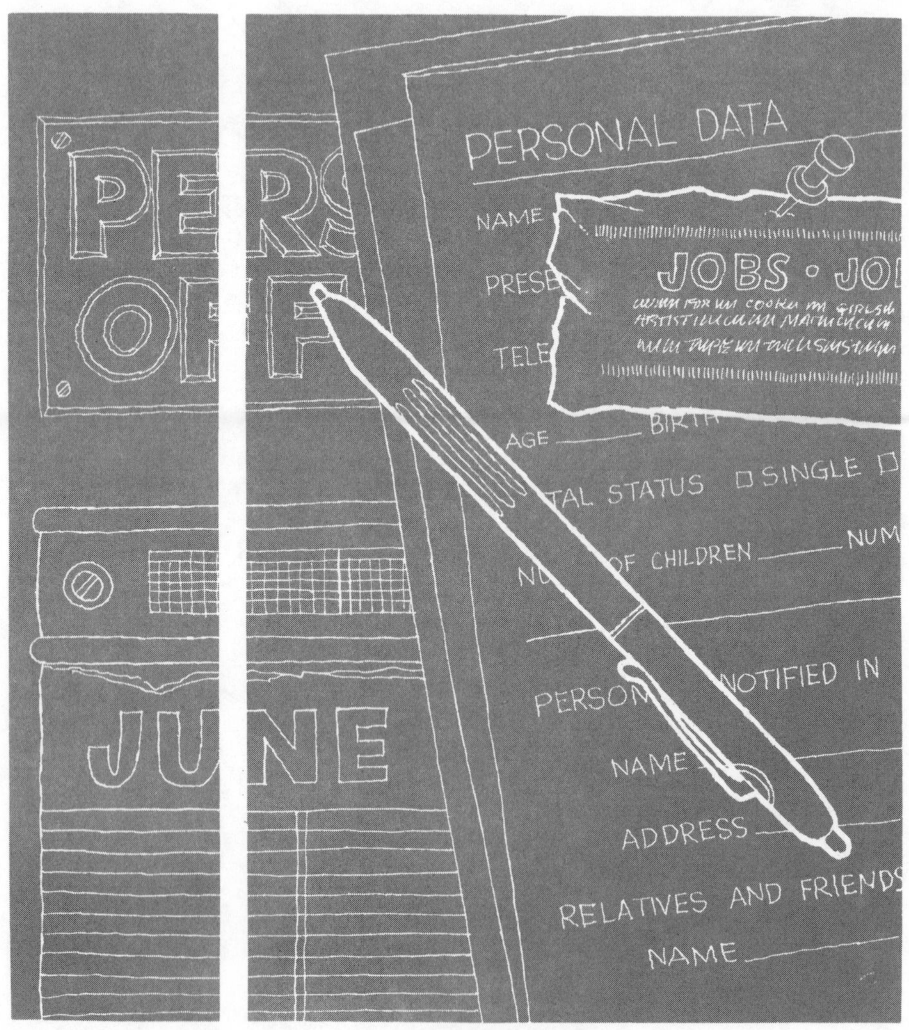

DEVELOPING WORD-BUILDING POWER

350▸ Brief Forms and Derivatives

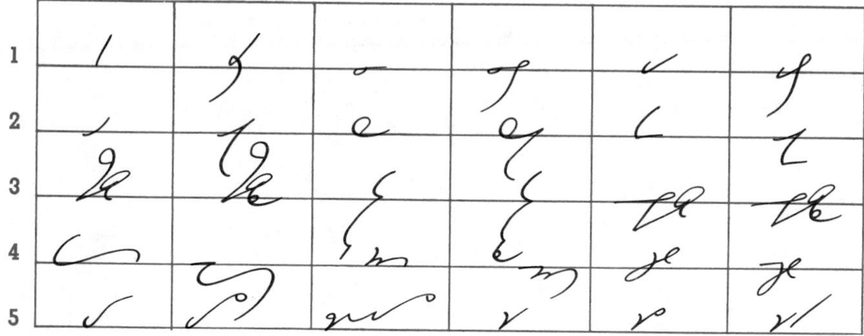

1 Which, whichever; when, whenever; what, whatever.

2 There-their, thereby; where, whereby; upon, thereupon.

3 Advertise, advertiser; publish-publication, publisher; merchandise, merchandiser.

4 Progress, unprogressive; success, unsuccessful; satisfy-satisfactory, unsatisfactory.

5 Ordinary, ordinarily, extraordinarily; state, stately, statehood.

BUILDING TRANSCRIPTION SKILLS

351▸ BUSINESS VOCABULARY BUILDER

inaugurated Observed the beginning of.
potentialities Possibilities.
resented Showed displeasure.

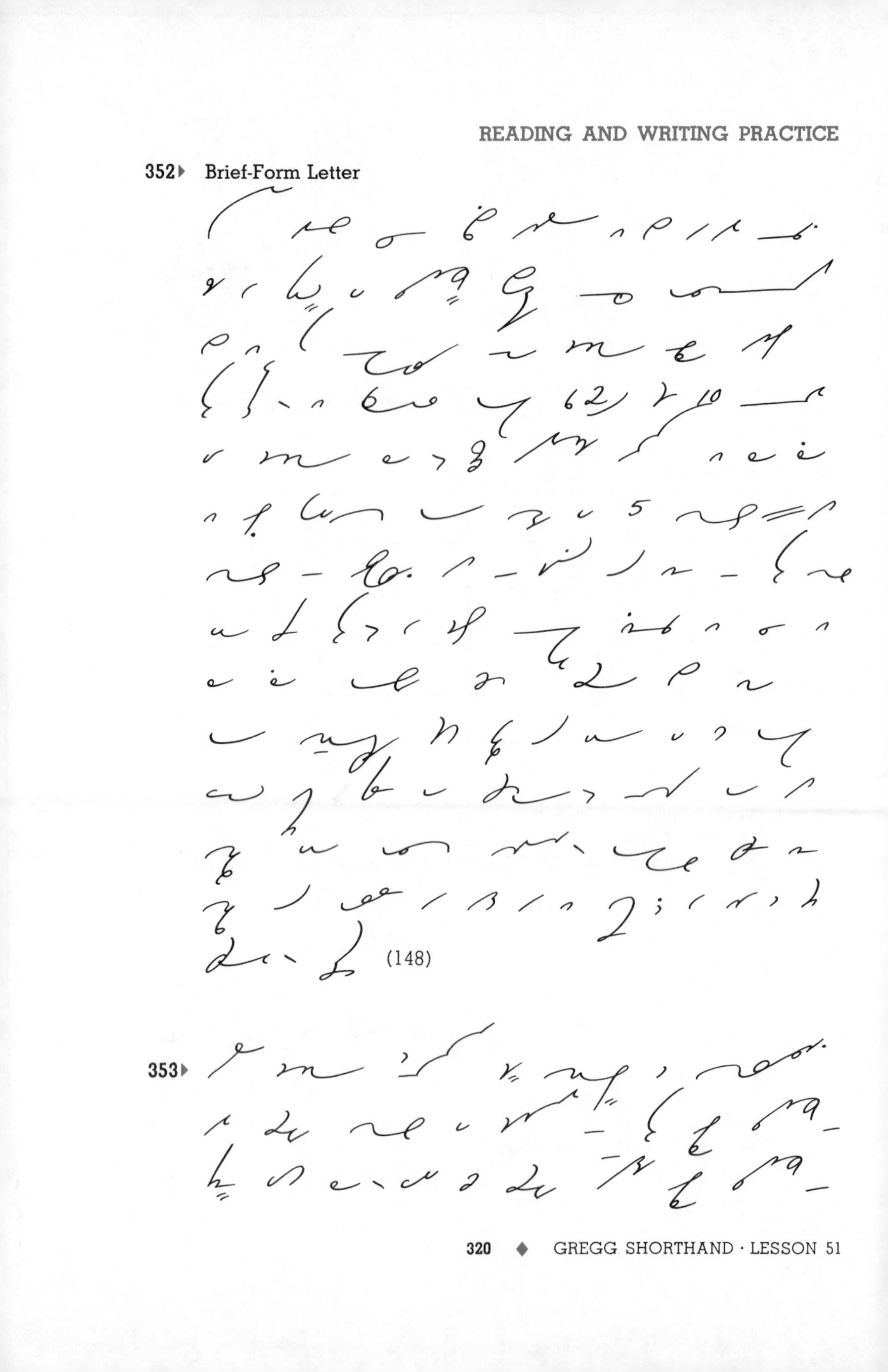

352▸ Brief-Form Letter

(148)

353▸

ed·u·ca·tion 1904 intro

avail·able va·can·cies intro

conj 30 23

po·ten·ti·al·ities con·fi·dent conj

if nc

(181)

354

em·ploy·ees en·thu·si·asm if

iq

and o bc

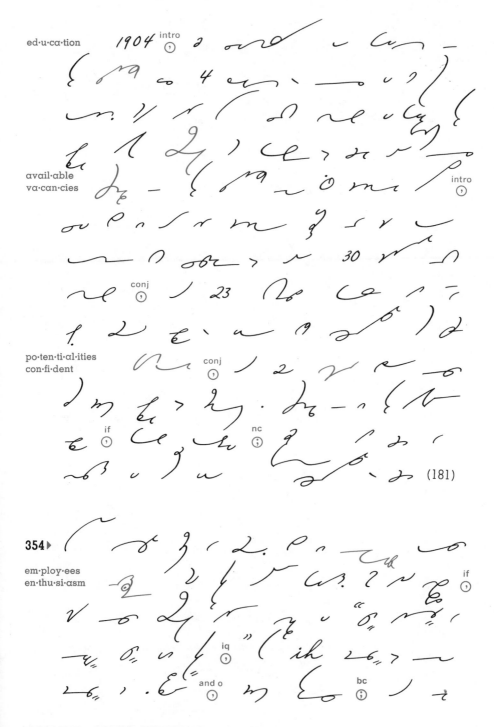

ca·reer
an·a·lyze

intro

Smith's

enu

out·sid·er's
re·sent·ed
de·vel·op

nonr

ser

iq

cr

50 (246)

355 ▸ **Transcription Quiz** • For you to supply: 6 commas—2 commas conjunction, 1 comma introductory, 2 commas series, 1 comma *if* clause; 1 colon enumeration; 2 missing words.

(171)

▸ *The secretary with an eye to the future takes her responsibilities seriously and gives her best to every assignment.*

OFFICE-STYLE DICTATION, 3

Transpositions

A businessman may occasionally decide to transpose words or phrases for emphasis or for some other reason. The dictator may say:

> We are conducting an advertising campaign for our cars in both weekly and monthly magazines—make that **monthly** and **weekly magazines.**

In your notes, you would indicate the transposition thus:

You would then transcribe the word *and* after *monthly.*

356▸ ILLUSTRATION OF OFFICE-STYLE DICTATION

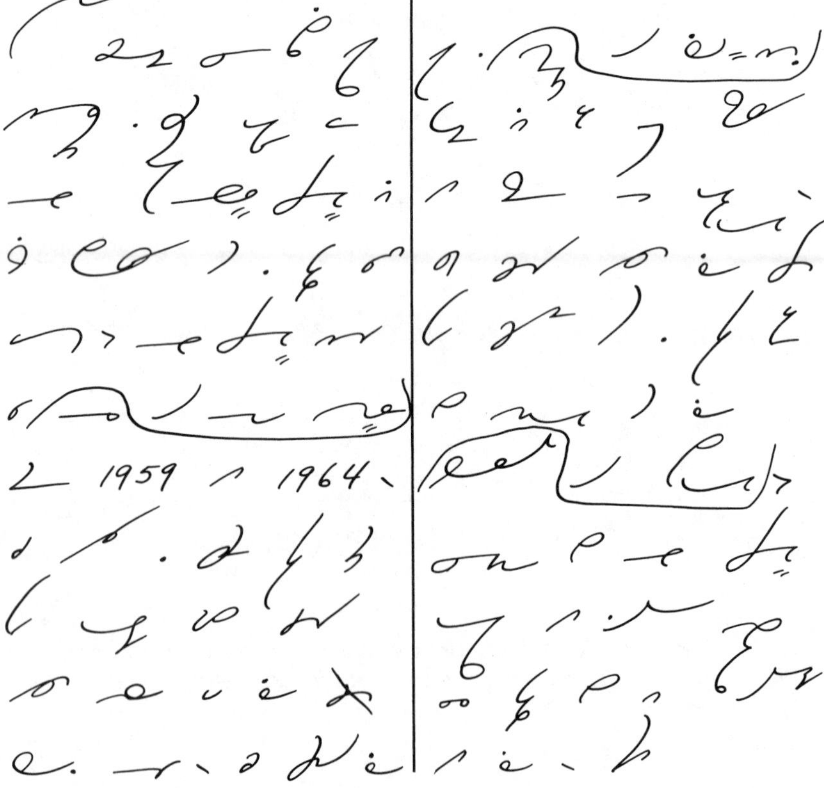

BUILDING PHRASING SKILL

357 ▸ Useful Business-Letter Phrases

We hope

1

Done

2

Think

3

For

4

—— ◆◆ ——

1 We hope, we hope that, we hope you, we hope you will, we hope it will be, we hope you can, we hope it is, we hope that the.

2 Has done, to be done, will be done, should be done, may be done, could be done.

3 I think, you think, we think, who think, if you think, do you think, he thinks.

4 For some time, for a few days, for a moment, for a long time, for your information.

358 ▸ Frequent Names

1

2

1 Miller, Mitchell, Moore, Morgan.
2 Hortense, Ida, Irene, Jean, Jeannette, Josephine, Judith, Julia.

BUILDING TRANSCRIPTION SKILLS

359 BUSINESS VOCABULARY BUILDER

convalescence A period of recovery following an illness.
engaging Drawing favorable attention.
screening Separating into different groups.

READING AND WRITING PRACTICE

360 Phrase Letter

(174)

361

al·ready
schol·ar·ship

as

bc

ex·cel·lent
ini·tia·tive

par

intro

par

ap

ilq

or·ga·niz·ing
les·sons

conj

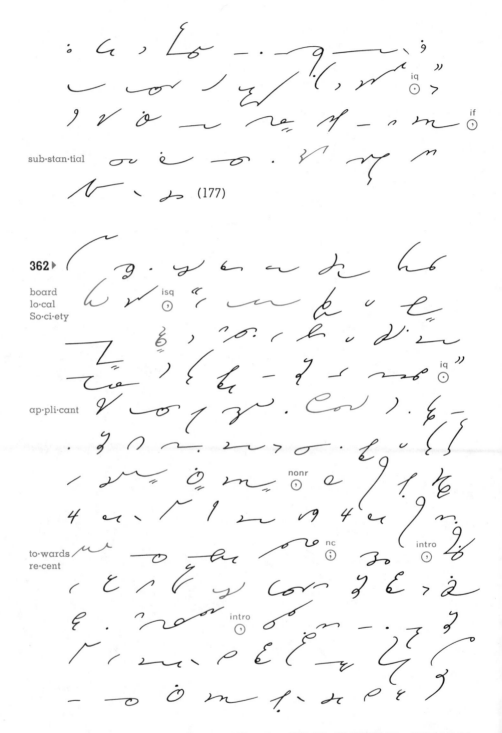

iq

if

sub·stan·tial

(177)

362

board
lo·cal
So·ci·ety

isq

iq

ap·pli·cant

nonr

to·wards
re·cent

nc

intro

intro

par

up to date
no noun,
no hyphen

ap nc intro

ap

ap·prox·i·mate·ly
pri·mar·i·ly

as

(241)

363▸

coun·sel·ing

screen·ing

bc

ser

se·nior
ex·cept

par

conj

(139)

364▸ Transcription Quiz • For you to supply: 7 commas—2 commas series, 1 comma apposition, 1 comma introductory, 1 comma *if* clause, 2 commas parenthetical; 2 missing words.

(162)

DEVELOPING WORD-BUILDING POWER

365▸ Word Families

-ic

1 [shorthand outlines]

-lent

2 [shorthand outlines]

-er

3 [shorthand outlines]

-pen

4 [shorthand outlines]

-uate

5 [shorthand outlines]

—— ◆◆ ——

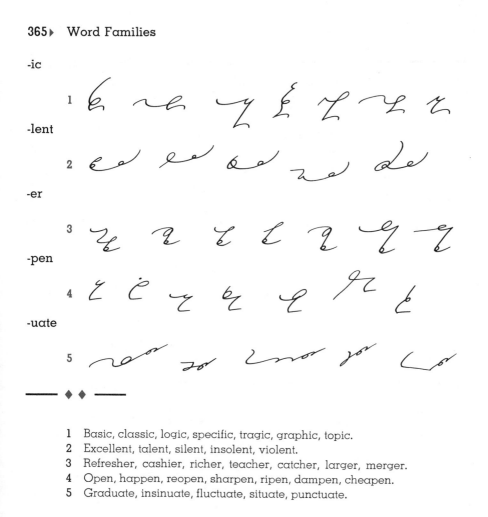

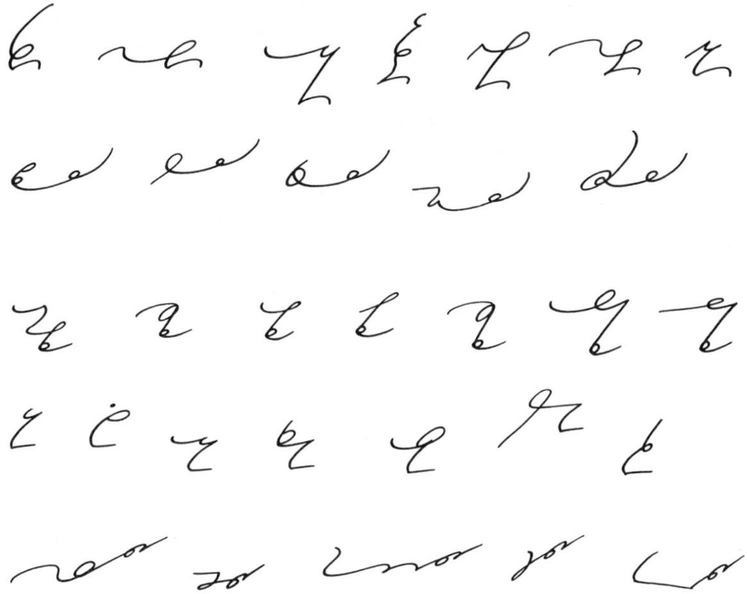

1 Basic, classic, logic, specific, tragic, graphic, topic.
2 Excellent, talent, silent, insolent, violent.
3 Refresher, cashier, richer, teacher, catcher, larger, merger.
4 Open, happen, reopen, sharpen, ripen, dampen, cheapen.
5 Graduate, insinuate, fluctuate, situate, punctuate.

BUILDING TRANSCRIPTION SKILLS

366▸ SIMILAR-WORDS DRILL accept, except

accept To take.

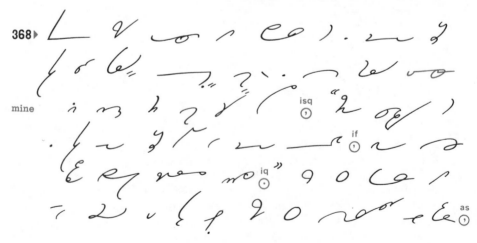

If you will accept these damaged goods, we will give you a discount of 40 percent.

except *(preposition)* Omitted; left out.

All members will attend, except Mr. Jones, who is ill.

367▸ BUSINESS VOCABULARY BUILDER

clients Customers.

utilize Use to advantage.

proceed Go ahead (do not confuse with "precede," which means "come before.")

READING AND WRITING PRACTICE

368▸

mine

isq

if

iq

as

col·lege

(153)

369▸

intro

anx·ious

ap

part-time
hyphenated before noun

nonr

ser

intro

possessing pleasant

and o

bc

if

(195)

370

conj

schedule beginning

ser

nc

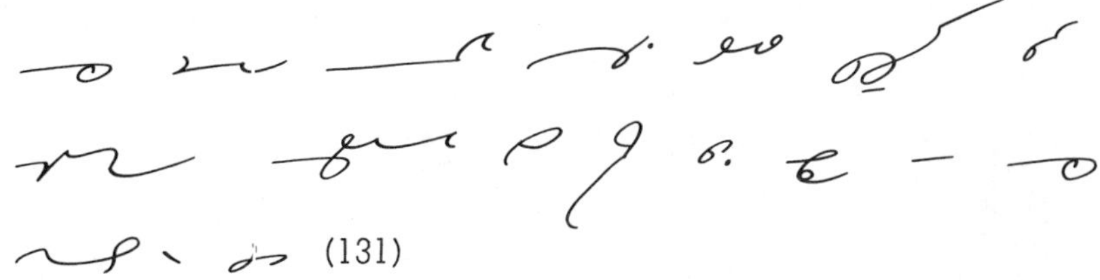

(131)

371▸ Transcription Quiz • For you to supply: 6 commas — 3 commas introductory, 2 commas *if* clause, 1 comma *and* omitted; 1 semicolon no conjunction; 1 colon enumeration; 2 missing words.

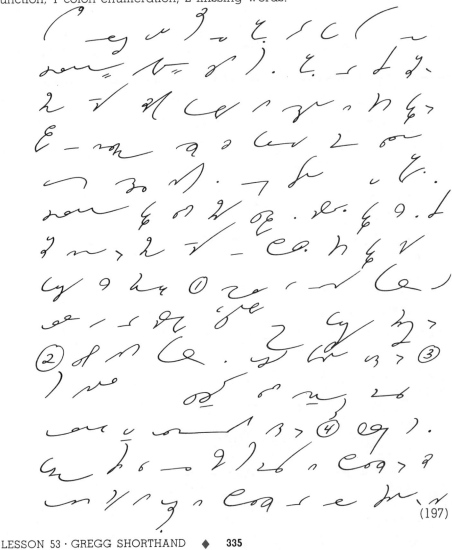

(197)

DEVELOPING WORD-BUILDING POWER

372▸ Word Beginnings and Endings

-lty

1

-gram

2

Super-

3

-lity

4

Inter-

5

—— ◆◆ ——

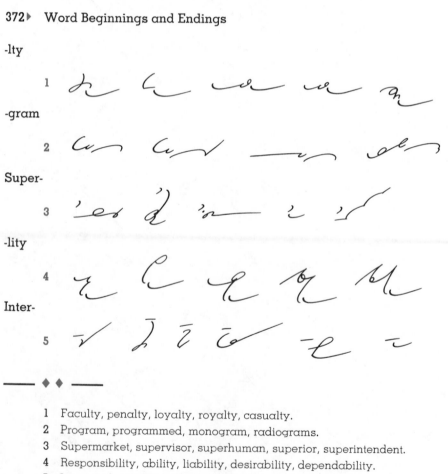

1 Faculty, penalty, loyalty, royalty, casualty.
2 Program, programmed, monogram, radiograms.
3 Supermarket, supervisor, superhuman, superior, superintendent.
4 Responsibility, ability, liability, desirability, dependability.
5 Interested, interview, interrupt, interpreted, international, interior.

373▸ Geographical Expressions

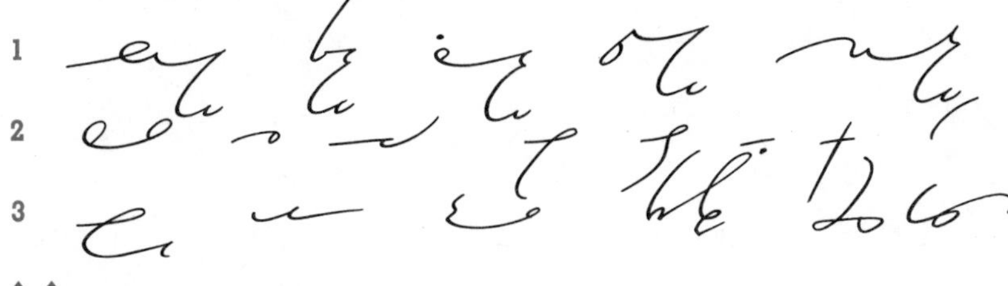

——◆◆——

1 Marlborough, Jonesboro, Hillsboro, Attleboro, Goldsboro.

2 Alabama, Kentucky, Montana, Nebraska, Nevada, New Hampshire, New Jersey, Tennessee.

3 Naples, Rome, Sicily, Budapest, Vienna, Prague.

BUILDING TRANSCRIPTION SKILLS

374▸ SPELLING FAMILIES

Forming -ed and -ing Derivatives of Words Ending in R

When the last syllable of a word ending in *r*, preceded by a single vowel, is accented, the *r* is doubled in forming derivatives in *-ed* and *-ing*.

con·fer	con·ferred	con·fer·ring
in·cur	in·curred	in·cur·ring
oc·cur	oc·curred	oc·cur·ring
pre·fer	pre·ferred	pre·fer·ring
re·fer	re·ferred	re·fer·ring

When the last syllable is not accented, the *r* is not doubled.

dif·fer	dif·fered	dif·fer·ing
flat·ter	flat·tered	flat·ter·ing
hin·der	hin·dered	hin·der·ing
of·fer	of·fered	of·fer·ing

375▸ BUSINESS VOCABULARY BUILDER

gratifying Pleasing.

lucrative Profitable.

aggressive Marked by forceful energy and drive.

376 ▸

hus·tling
world's

ap

ad·ver·tised

Ten·nes·see
Ken·tucky

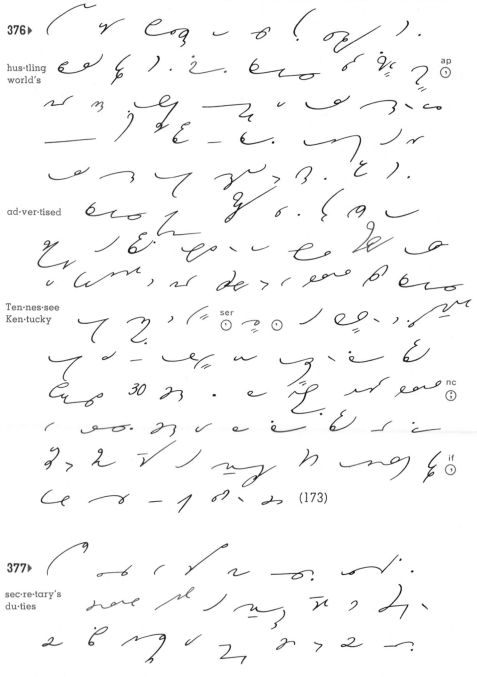

ser

nc

if

(173)

377 ▸

sec·re·tary's
du·ties

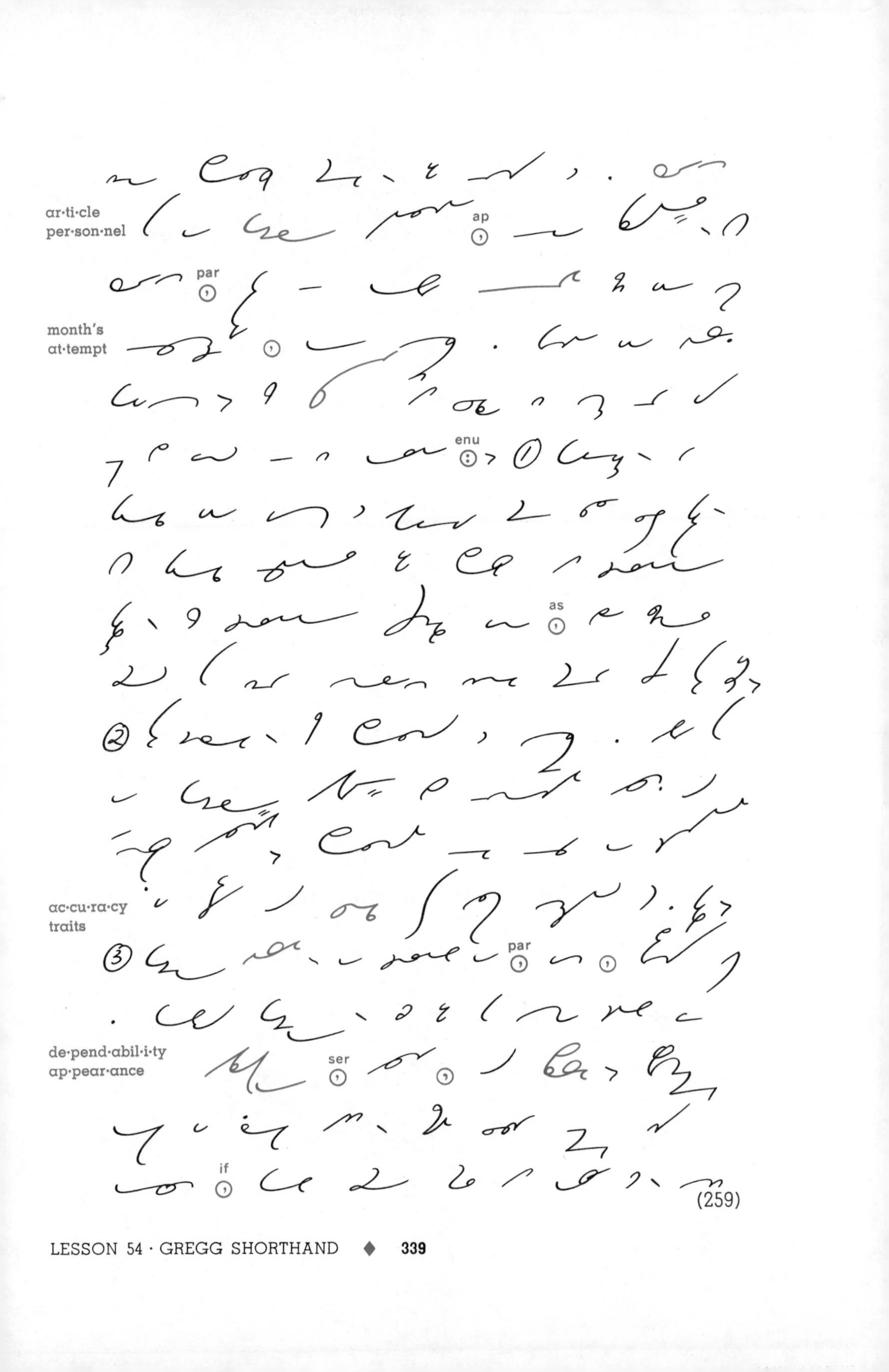

ar·ti·cle
per·son·nel

ap

par

month's
at·tempt

enu

as

ac·cu·ra·cy
traits

par

de·pend·abil·i·ty
ap·pear·ance

ser

if

(259)

378

nonr

and o

dis·trib·u·tor
gro·cery

bc

intro

in·de·pen·dent
ar·ea

and o

ilq

mer·chan·dis·ing

ser

if

il

ser

strict (226)

379▸ Transcription Quiz • For you to supply: 6 commas—2 commas apposition, 2 commas parenthetical, 1 comma *and* omitted, 1 comma introductory; 1 semicolon no conjunction; 2 missing words.

(162)

DEVELOPING WORD-BUILDING POWER

380 ▸ Shorthand Vocabulary Builder

-tition, etc.

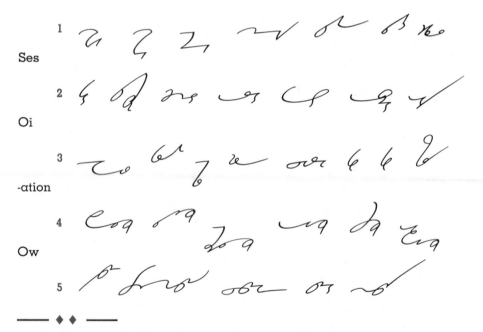

1

Ses

2

Oi

3

-ation

4

Ow

5

1 Competition, combination, information, commissioned, additional, editions, stationery.

2 Possess, advises, weaknesses, lenses, places, licenses, resisted.

3 Employ, points, enjoy, soil, annoyance, poise, choice, avoid.

4 Application, education, investigation, location, vacation, reciprocation.

5 Down, background, announcement, ounces, crowded.

381▸ Accuracy Practice—O Hook

1

2

———— ◆◆ ————

1 Of, was, hope, hobby; row, low; toe, no, mow.
2 What, order; or, coal; bow, saw; of course, organize.

BUILDING TRANSCRIPTION SKILLS

382▸ BUSINESS VOCABULARY BUILDER	
inevitably	Unavoidably.
attainments	Accomplishments.
brevity	Conciseness, shortness.

READING AND WRITING PRACTICE

383▸ Selling Yourself

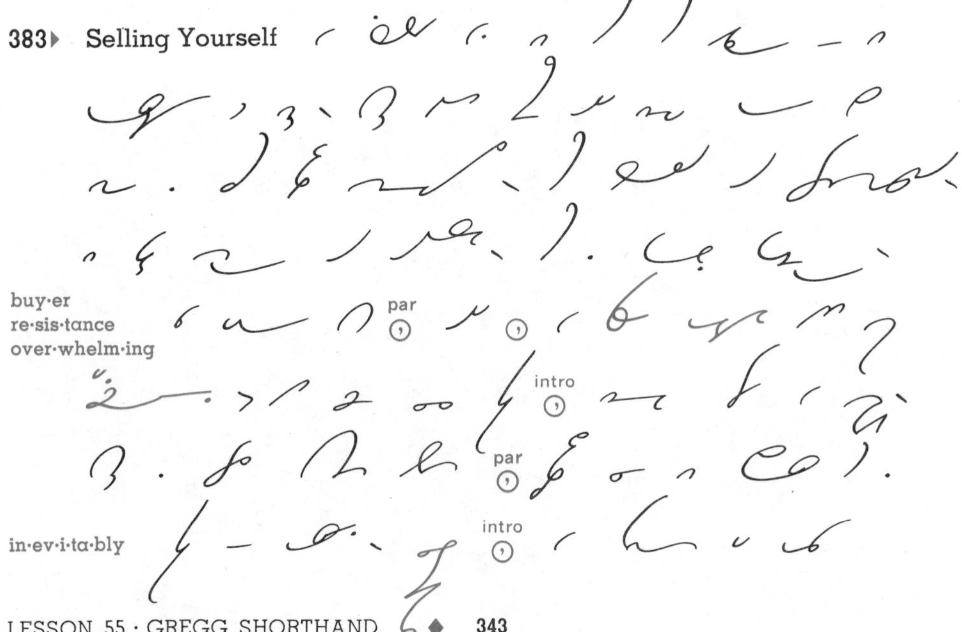

ref·er·ence
dis·tant

346

The formal application.

brev·i·ty
an·swer

pro·spec·tive
em·ploy·er's

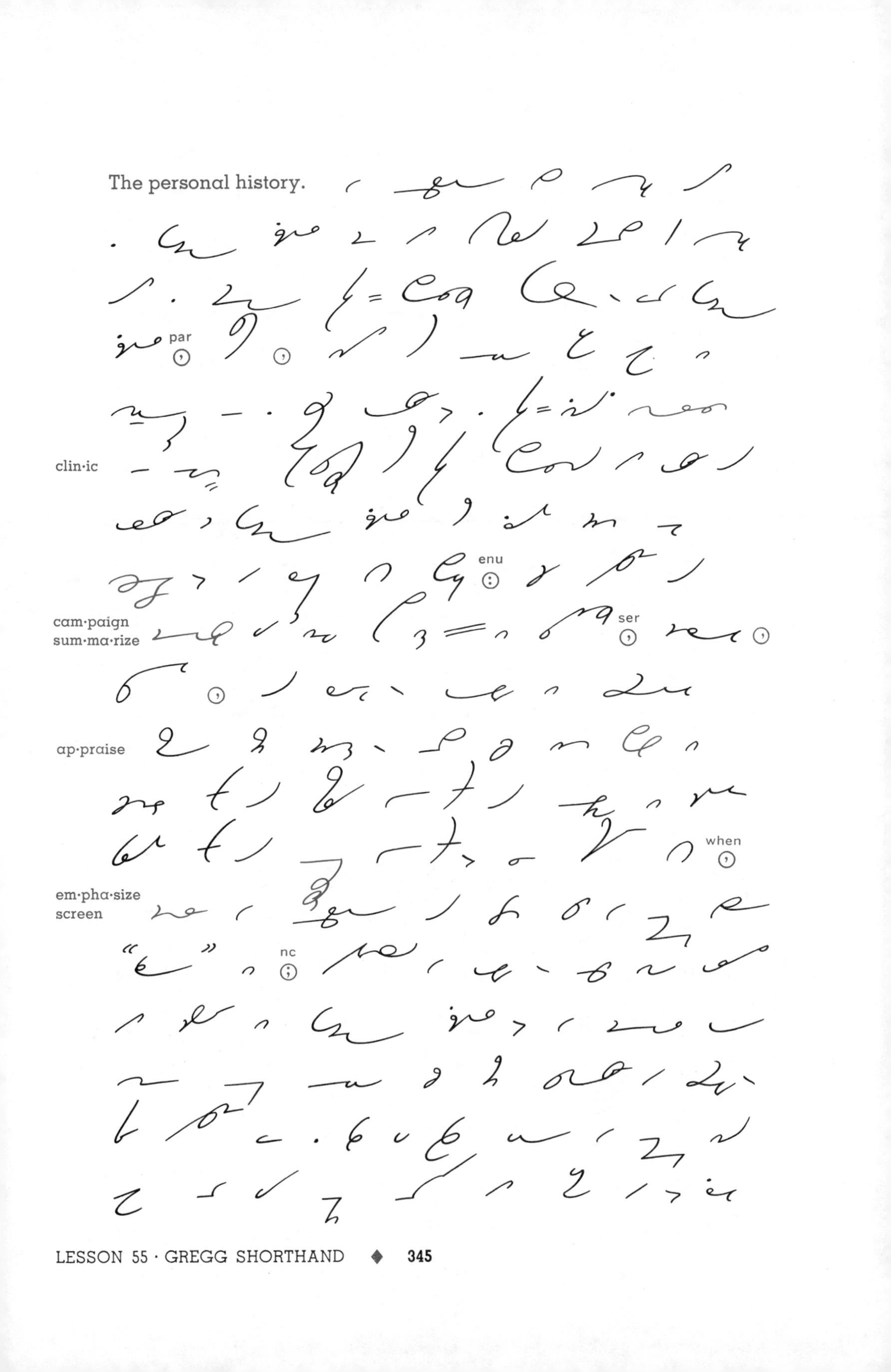

The personal history.

par

clin·ic

enu

cam·paign
sum·ma·rize

ser

ap·praise

when

em·pha·size
screen

nc

enu

ser

ac·com·plish·ments
spe·cial·ized

enu

Keep your

par

par

if

if

intro

if

The letter.

sub·mit·ting
main

par

sin·gle
qual·i·fies

nonr

rou·tine
bus·i·est

intro

intro

(879)

CHAPTER TWELVE

publishing

DEVELOPING WORD-BUILDING POWER

384▸ Brief Forms and Derivatives

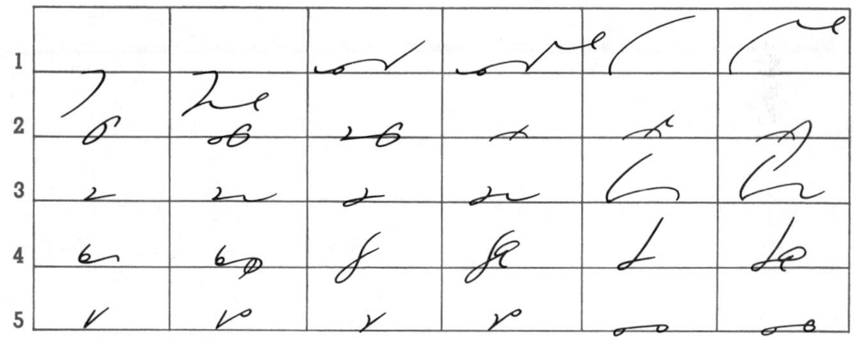

—— ♦♦ ——

1 Never, nevertheless; regard, regardless; time, timeless.
2 How-out, anyhow, somehow; quantity, quantities, quantitative.
3 Soon, sooner; send, sender; big, bigger.
4 Circular, circularize; particular, particularize; general, generalize.
5 Short, shortly; state, stately; immediate, immediately.

BUILDING TRANSCRIPTION SKILLS

385▸ BUSINESS VOCABULARY BUILDER

functional Designed from the standpoint of usefulness.

manifold Marked by variety; many but different.

electrifying Thrilling; exciting.

386 Brief-Form Letter

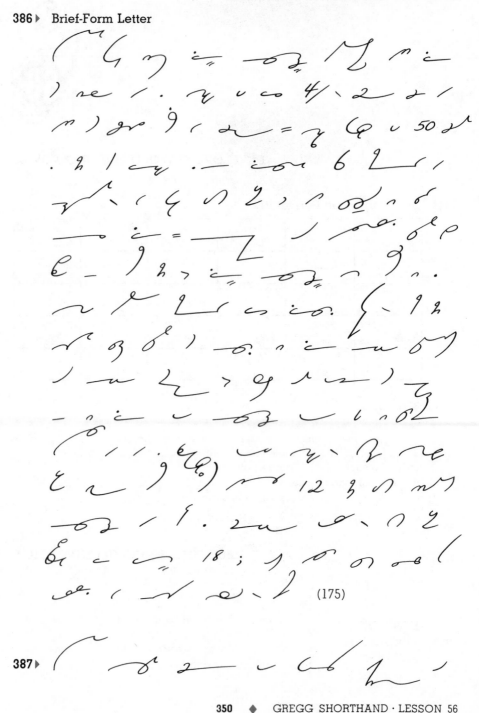

(175)

387

birth·days
Christ·mas

Transcribe:
December 25

en·ve·lope
all ready

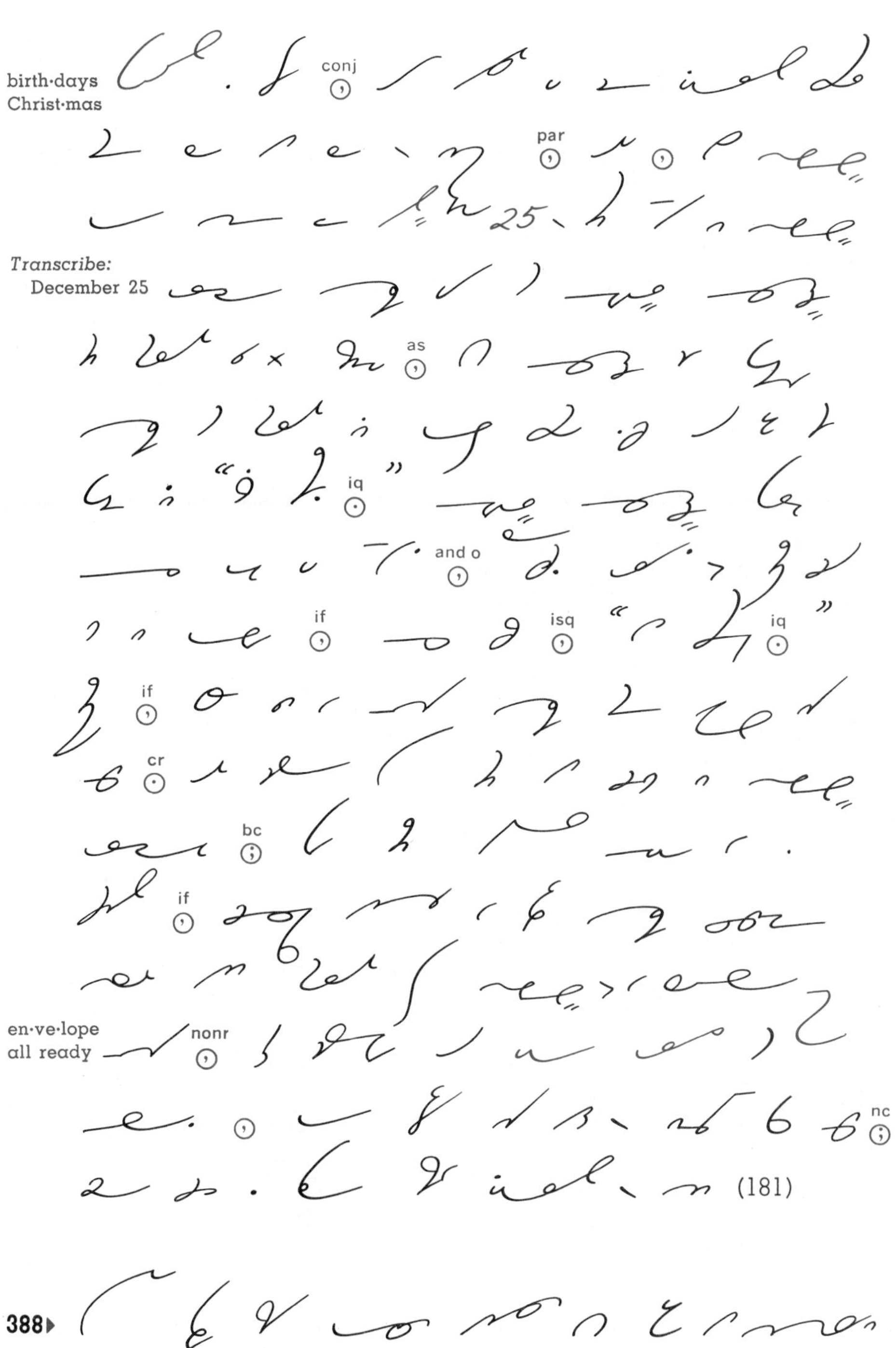

388▸

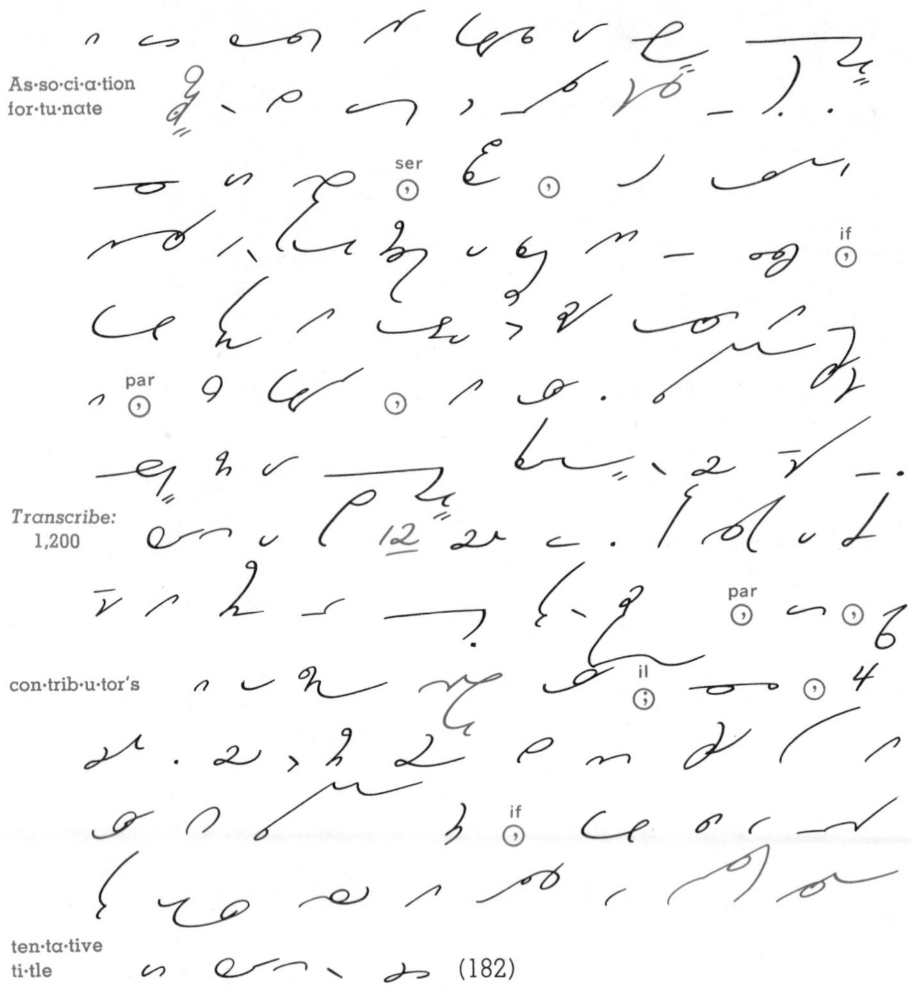

389▸ Transcription Quiz • For you to supply: 6 commas—2 commas introductory, 1 comma *as* clause, 1 comma conjunction, 1 comma *when* clause, 1 comma parenthetical; 1 semicolon no conjunction; 2 missing words.

(193)

▸ *An attractive, neatly typed letter signifies more than a responsible secretary; it becomes a sample of the taste and character of the company. No letter that a secretary mails out should ever be less than perfect.*

Long Transpositions

Occasionally a dictator will decide that an entire sentence or even a paragraph would be more effective if it were transposed to another part of the letter. When this happens, the simplest way to show the transposition is to encircle the material to be transposed and indicate the new position by an arrow.

390 ▸ ILLUSTRATION OF OFFICE-STYLE DICTATION

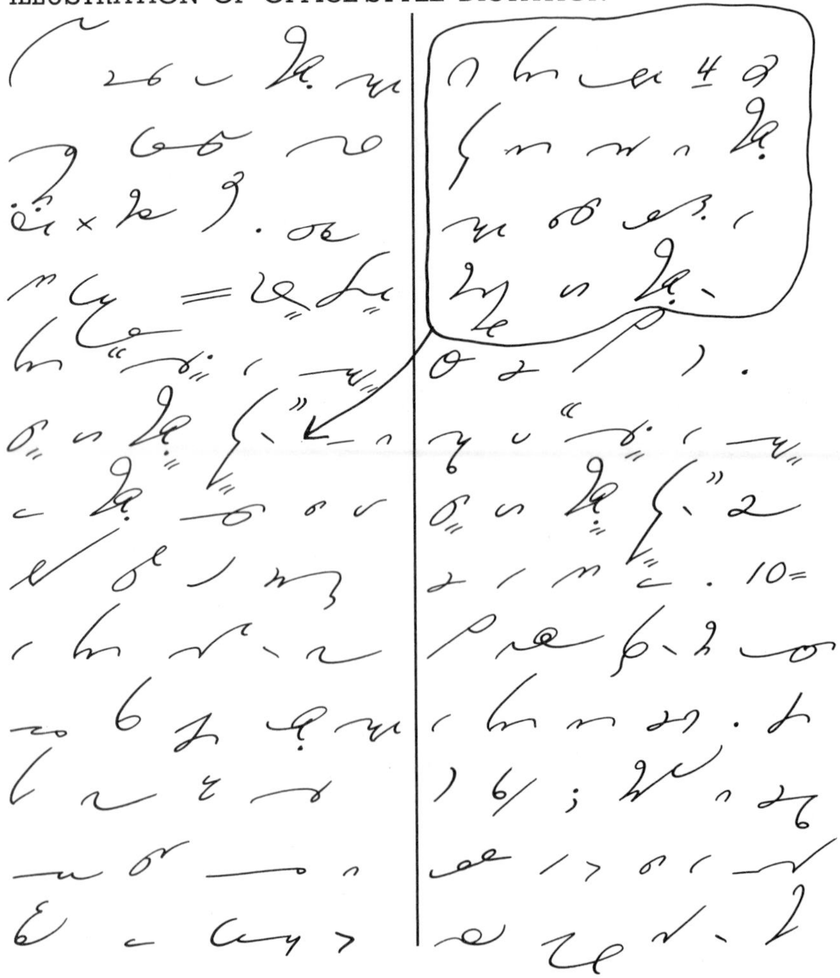

BUILDING PHRASING SKILL

391 ▸ Useful Business-Letter Phrases

Been

1

Any

2

Special Business Phrases

3

Long

4

This

5

— ◆◆ —

1 Has been, it has been, there has been, he would have been, I should have been, you could have been, I might have been, who have been.

2 Any time, any one, any other, any way, any of these, any one of our.

3 Of course, to do, as soon as, as soon as possible, your order, to make, to me, to know.

4 Long ago, long time ago, for a long time, how long.

5 For this, of this, in this, about this, this is, this will, this will be, this can be.

392 ▸ Frequent Names

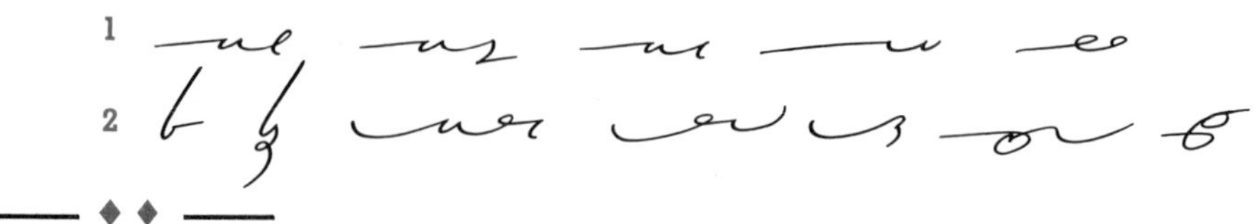

— ♦ ♦ —

1 Morris, Morrison, Morse, Monroe, Murray.
2 John, Joseph, Lawrence, Leonard, Louis, Michael, Nathan.

BUILDING TRANSCRIPTION SKILLS

393 ▸ LANGUAGE STUDY

A knowledge of the more common Greek and Latin word roots is of tremendous value in helping to increase your command of the English language.

In *Gregg Shorthand for Colleges, Volume One,* you studied a number of the more common, simple word roots; in *Gregg Shorthand for Colleges, Volume Two,* you will take up additional, somewhat more advanced word roots.

Read the definition of each word root carefully, and then study the illustrations that follow.

Pro-: In many words in the English language, the prefix *pro-* means *before, ahead, forward, future.*

progressive Moving ahead; going forward.
produce To bring forward; to make.
proceed To go ahead.
program A plan for the future.
prophet One who sees ahead.
prospect A possible future customer.

394 ▸ BUSINESS VOCABULARY BUILDER

formerly Before; in the past. (Do not confuse with "formally," which means "according to established custom or form.")

supplementary Additional; extra.

circulation manager The person in charge of obtaining subscribers to a publication.

395 Phrase Letter

302

(147)

396

as

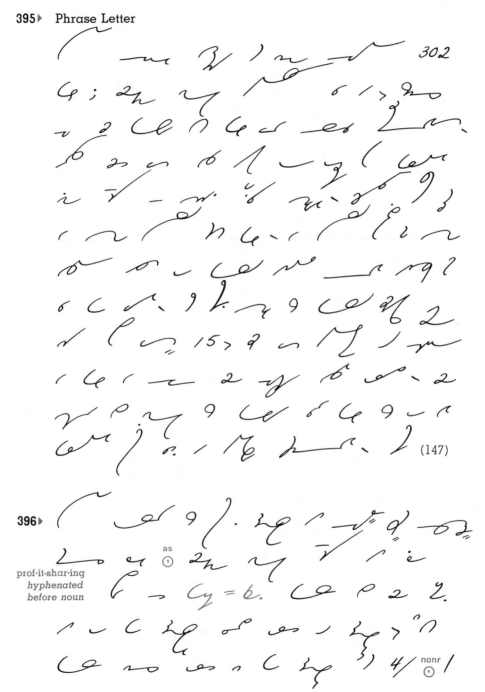

prof·it-shar·ing
hyphenated before noun

nonr

ilq

ris·ing
be·com·ing

conj

nc

iq

par

if

ser

in·ter·rup·tion
cop·ies
re·en·ter·ing

when

(254)

397 ▸

nonr

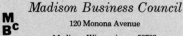

Madison Business Council
120 Monona Avenue
Madison, Wisconsin 53702

February 22, 196-

Mr. Perry R. Strong, President
Harrison Manufacturing Company
4125 North Fifth Avenue
Denver 8, Colorado

Dear Mr. Strong:

Subject: Employees' Handbooks

I am sending you today by express all the material that we have available on how to prepare an employees' handbook.

You will be interested, I am sure, in our experience in helping the Martin Miller Company prepare its latest handbook. When we were called in, that company already had a handbook; but it was out of date. The organization had grown considerably since that handbook was prepared; consequently, the handbook had to be completely rewritten. The new handbook was ready at the end of last year. It benefited by many lessons that had been learned during the work on the first handbook.

While working with Martin Mil
three points are important ir

1. It should not be a t
   should and should nc

2. It should take advar
   satisfaction with wh
   The handbook should
   ing that feeling of

3. It should set down f
   that they are import
   give them informatic
   organization and act

In the first edition of the h
the history of the company.
plished by the time the secor
publication. Consequently, n
history of the company was om

Mr. Perry R. Strong 2 February 22, 196-

These are just a few thoughts that come to me at this time. I am sure that the Martin Miller Company would be glad to send you a copy of their new handbook. I believe that you may find many suggestions in it that you would be able to use when you prepare your handbook.

Needless to say, we are at your service. If you think that a visit with one of our men would be helpful, please call us. We will be glad to arrange an appointment.

Cordially yours,

R. L. Kane

R. L. Kane, Vice-President

RLK:IRT

P. S. I have just learned that Fred Hopkins, the member of our staff who worked with Martin Miller Company, will be in Denver all next week. Would you like to meet him and talk with him?

Two-Page Letter Blocked Style, with Subject Line and Postscript Standard Punctuation

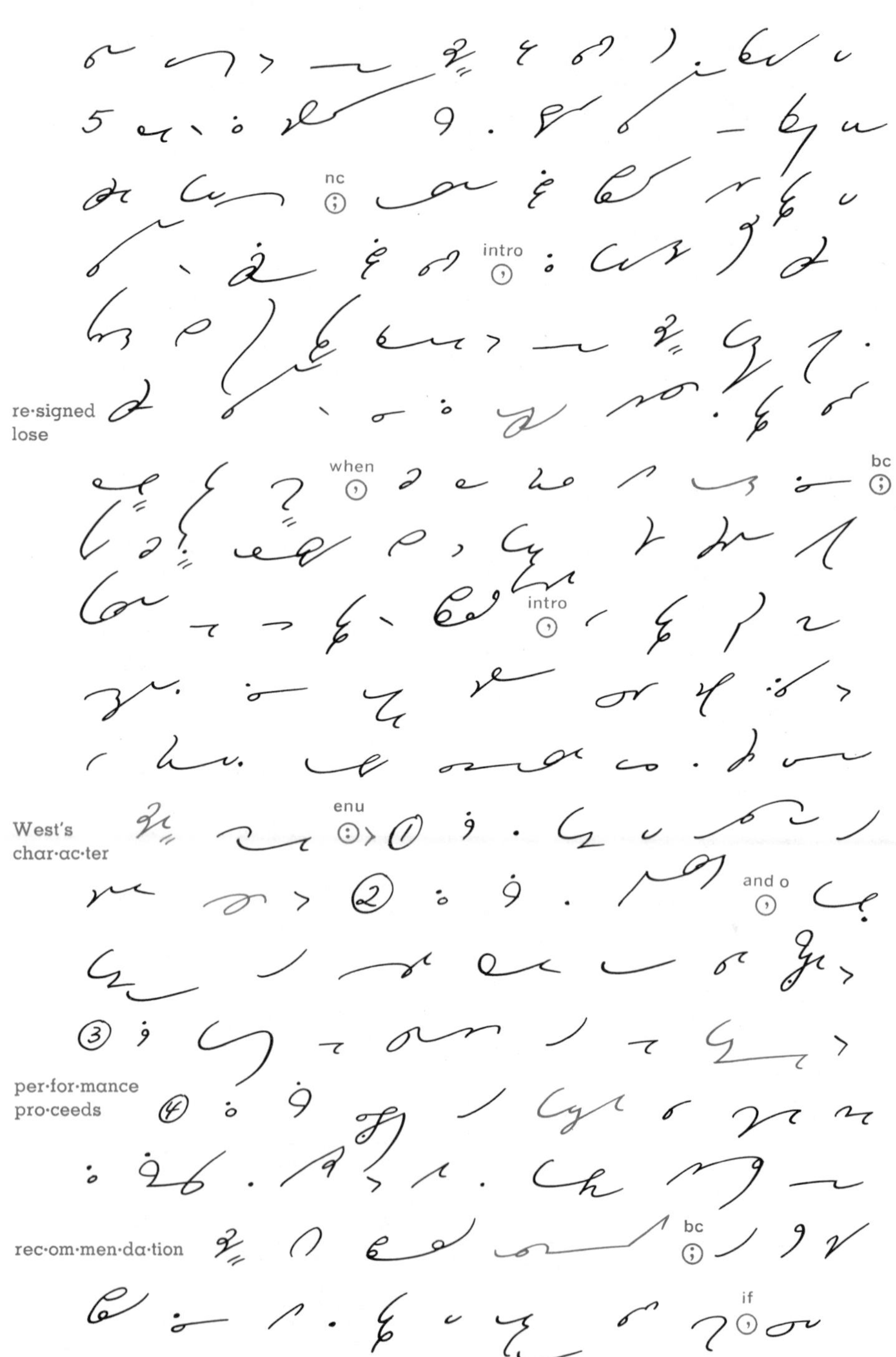
nc
intro
re·signed
lose
when
bc
intro
West's
char·ac·ter
enu
and o
per·for·mance
pro·ceeds
rec·om·men·da·tion
bc
if

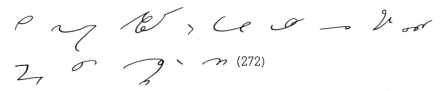

(272)

398▸ Transcription Quiz • For you to supply: 4 commas—1 comma *when* clause, 1 comma introductory, 1 comma nonrestrictive, 1 comma *if* clause; 2 semicolons no conjunction; 2 missing words.

(170)

DEVELOPING WORD-BUILDING POWER

399 Word Families

Rein-

1

Non-

2

-tional

3

-ect

4

-ber

5

1 Reinstate, reinsure, reinsert, reinforcement, reinvest, reinstall.
2 Nonskilled, nonstop, nonsupport, nonessential, nonresident.
3 National, rational, vocational, international, educational.
4 Expect, affect, neglect, respect, aspect, direct.
5 Number, member, rubber, subscriber, remember, chamber, fiber.

400▸ SIMILAR-WORDS DRILL accede, exceed

accede To agree to; to grant.

We are happy to accede to your request for an extension of time.

exceed To go beyond; to be more than.

Some of the classes in this school exceed 40 students.

401▸ BUSINESS VOCABULARY BUILDER

house organ A publication that is written for the employees of an organization.

enlightening Furnishing knowledge or information.

charter member An original member of a group; one who became a member upon the organization of the group.

READING AND WRITING PRACTICE

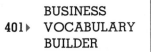

402▸

edi·tion

as

intro

ex·ceeded

nonr

ap

Transcribe:
9 a.m.
5 p.m.

bc

cr

(180)

403

com·mu·ni·ca·tions

intro

ap

ac·cede
re·cent·ly

if

iq

Transcribe:
May, 1965,

1965

ser

en·light·en·ing
typ·i·cal

if

ex·cel·lent

(172)

404▸

ap

intro

bc

par

intro

enu

and o

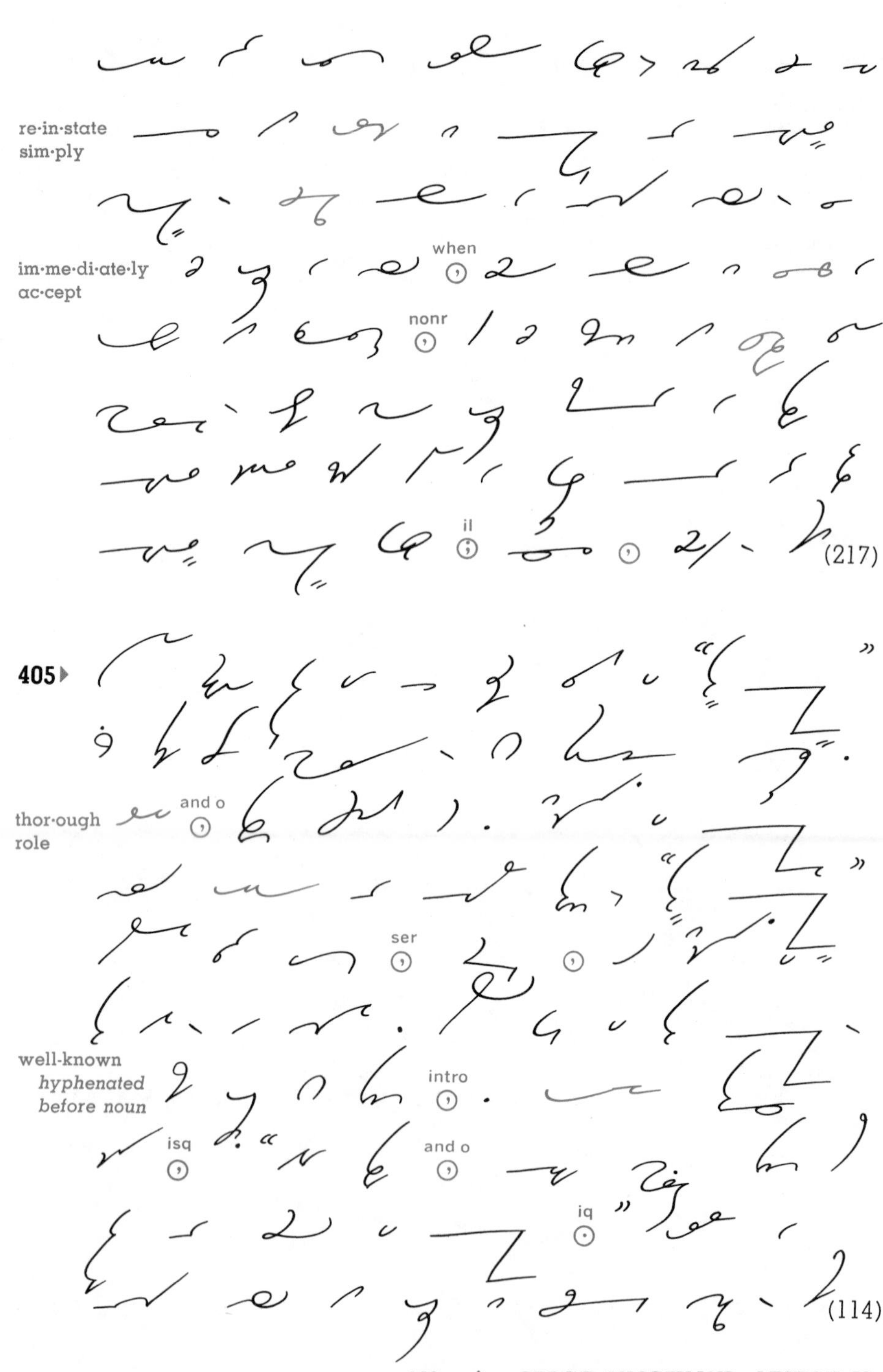

re·in·state
sim·ply
im·me·di·ate·ly
ac·cept
when
nonr
il
(217)
405
thor·ough
role
and o
ser
well-known
hyphenated before noun
intro
isq
and o
iq
(114)

406▸ Transcription Quiz • For you to supply: 4 commas — 2 commas series, 1 comma *when* clause, 1 comma introductory; 1 colon enumeration; 1 semicolon no conjunction; 2 missing words.

(195)

DEVELOPING WORD-BUILDING POWER

407 ▸ Word Beginnings and Endings

Electr-

1

Ul

2

-ment

3

En-

4

In-

5

—— ◆◆ ——

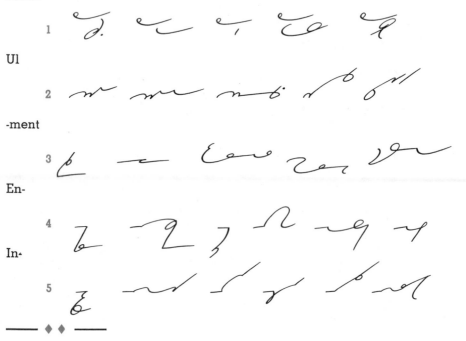

1 Electrifying, electrical, electrician, electroplate, electrotype.
2 Culture, cultural, culminating, ultimate, adulthood.
3 Shipment, moment, supplementary, compliments, fundamental.
4 Enjoyment, engagement, envious, endeavor, enlarge, enrich.
5 Inspire, include, intend, incident, indeed, incredible.

408 ▸ Geographical Expressions

1 Glassport, Bridgeport, Westport, Davenport, Shreveport, Newport.

2 New York, North Carolina, North Dakota, Ohio, Oklahoma, Oregon, Pennsylvania, South Carolina.

3 Bucharest, Athens, Moscow, Oslo, Stockholm, Copenhagen.

BUILDING TRANSCRIPTION SKILLS

409 ▸ SPELLING FAMILIES

Forming -ed and -ing Derivatives of Words Ending in T

When the last syllable of a word ending in *t*, preceded by a single vowel, is accented, the *t* is doubled in forming derivatives in *-ed* and *-ing*.

al·lot	al·lot·ted	al·lot·ting
com·mit	com·mit·ted	com·mit·ting
per·mit	per·mit·ted	per·mit·ting
sub·mit	sub·mit·ted	sub·mit·ting
trans·mit	trans·mit·ted	trans·mit·ting

When the last syllable is not accented, the *t* is not doubled.

ben·e·fit	ben·e·fit·ed	ben·e·fit·ing
cred·it	cred·it·ed	cred·it·ing
prof·it	prof·it·ed	prof·it·ing

When the *t* is preceded by more than one vowel or a consonant, the *t* is not doubled.

ad·just	ad·just·ed	ad·just·ing
cor·rect	cor·rect·ed	cor·rect·ing
greet	greet·ed	greet·ing
in·ter·est	in·ter·est·ed	in·ter·est·ing

410 ▸ BUSINESS VOCABULARY BUILDER

diversity Variety.
procrastinate To delay; to put off.
assume To take for granted.

READING AND WRITING PRACTICE

411 ▸

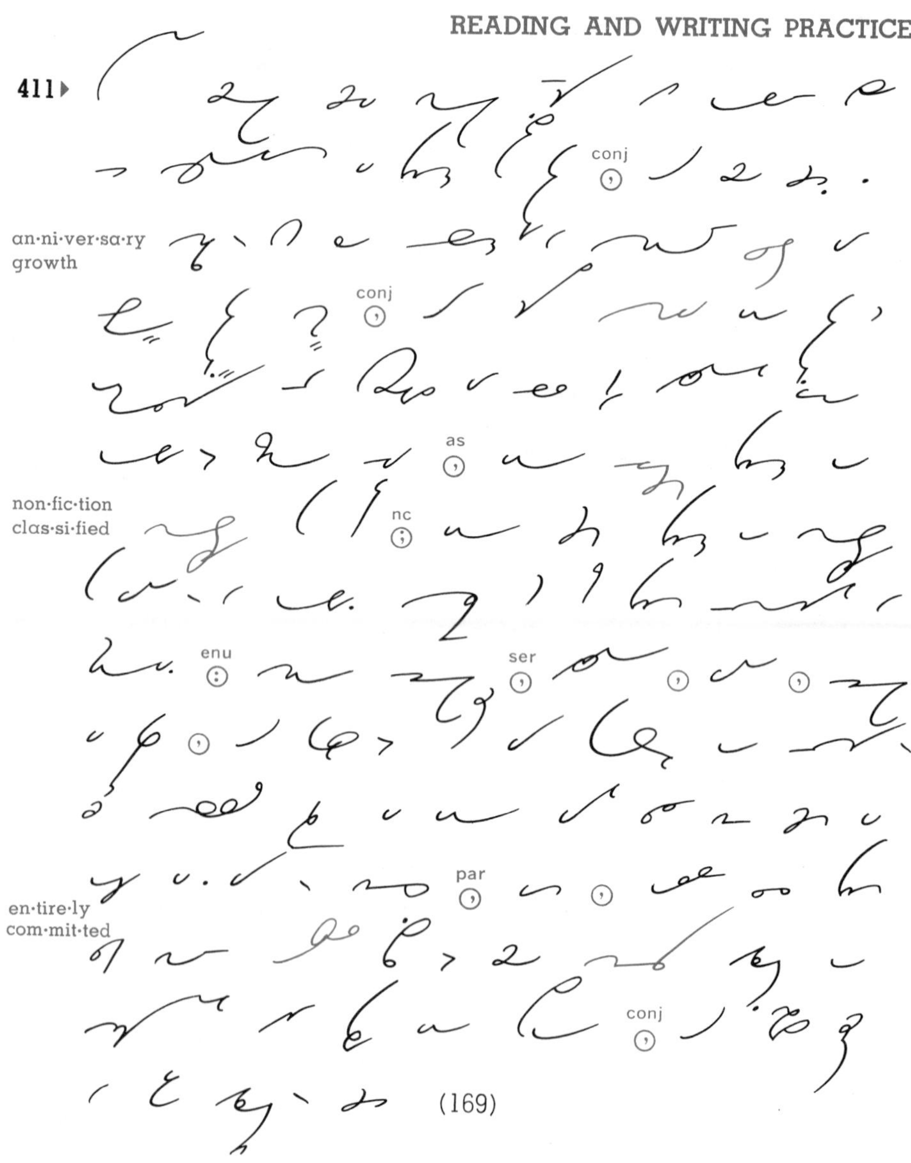

412▸

month's conj

conj

conj

ben·e·fit·ing

48

nov·els
elec·tri·fy·ing
mys·ter·ies

intro

120

il

in·ex·pen·sive
mod·ern

ser

nc

(181)

413▸

5[50]

as isq

80202 iq

enu

3^{50} 5^{50} 7^{25}

intro

bc

ap

when

3^{50} (146)

414 sup·plies sub·scrib·ers

ser

intro

170

35

han·dling
con·fi·dent

intro

(140)

415▸ Transcription Quiz • For you to supply: 5 commas — 4 commas parenthetical, 1 comma introductory; 2 semicolons no conjunction; 1 missing word.

(110)

DEVELOPING WORD-BUILDING POWER

416 ▸ Shorthand Vocabulary Builder

Ia

1

Ngk

2

Ng

3

Ul

4

Nd

5

1 Variation, negotiation, appreciation, depreciation, creation, recreation, appropriation.

2 Frank, rank, blank, trunk, drink, anxious.

3 Wrong, bring, single, anger, long, longer.

4 Result, consult, ultimately, culminate, culture, adults.

5 Respond, lend, imagined, branded, refined, ended.

417 Accuracy Practice—OO Hook

1 You-your, yours truly, you would; other, you want; shoe, woman, do, knew.
2 Into, are you, will you; noon, numb, monument.

BUILDING TRANSCRIPTION SKILLS

418 BUSINESS VOCABULARY BUILDER

patronage Business.
solicitous Full of concern.
conventional According to common usage or practice.
litigation Lawsuit.

READING AND WRITING PRACTICE

419 The Business Letter and Collections

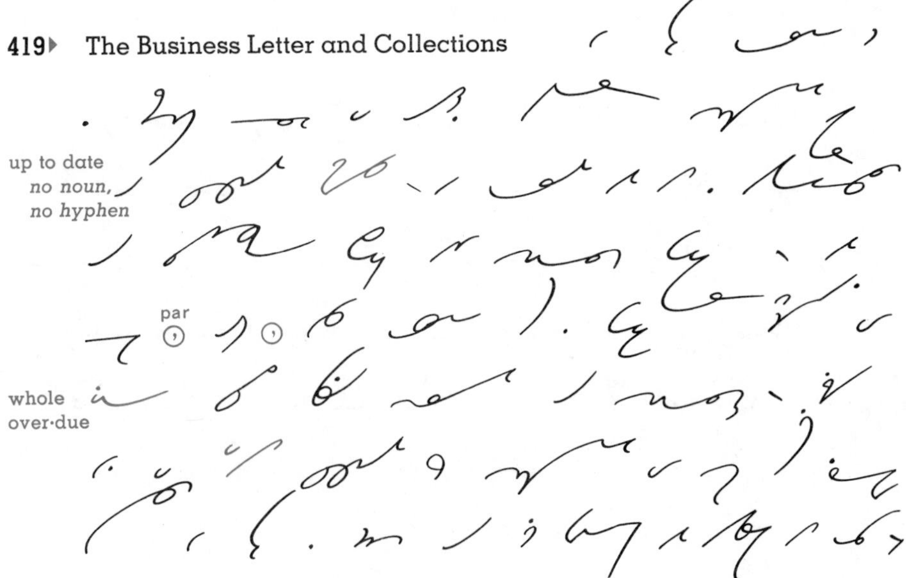

vary·ing
fac·tors

conj

ser

per·son·al
lat·ter

ser

heart
adapt·ed

par

When a customer

when

bc

cap·ture
fan·cy

debt·or
cred·i·tor

when

par

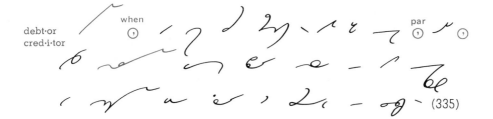

(335)

420 ▸ The Business Letter and Adjustments

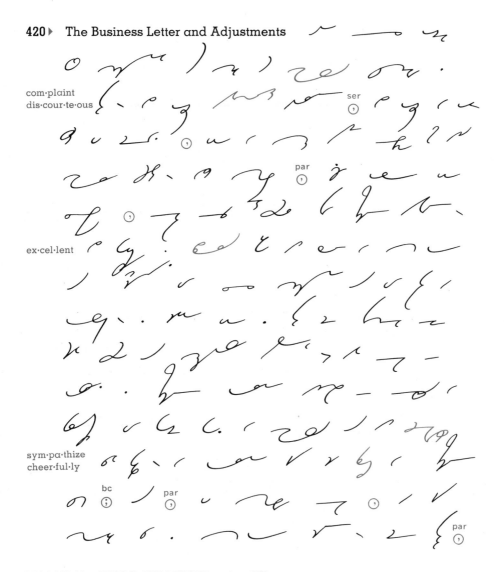

com·plaint
dis·cour·te·ous

ser

par

ex·cel·lent

sym·pa·thize
cheer·ful·ly

bc

par

par

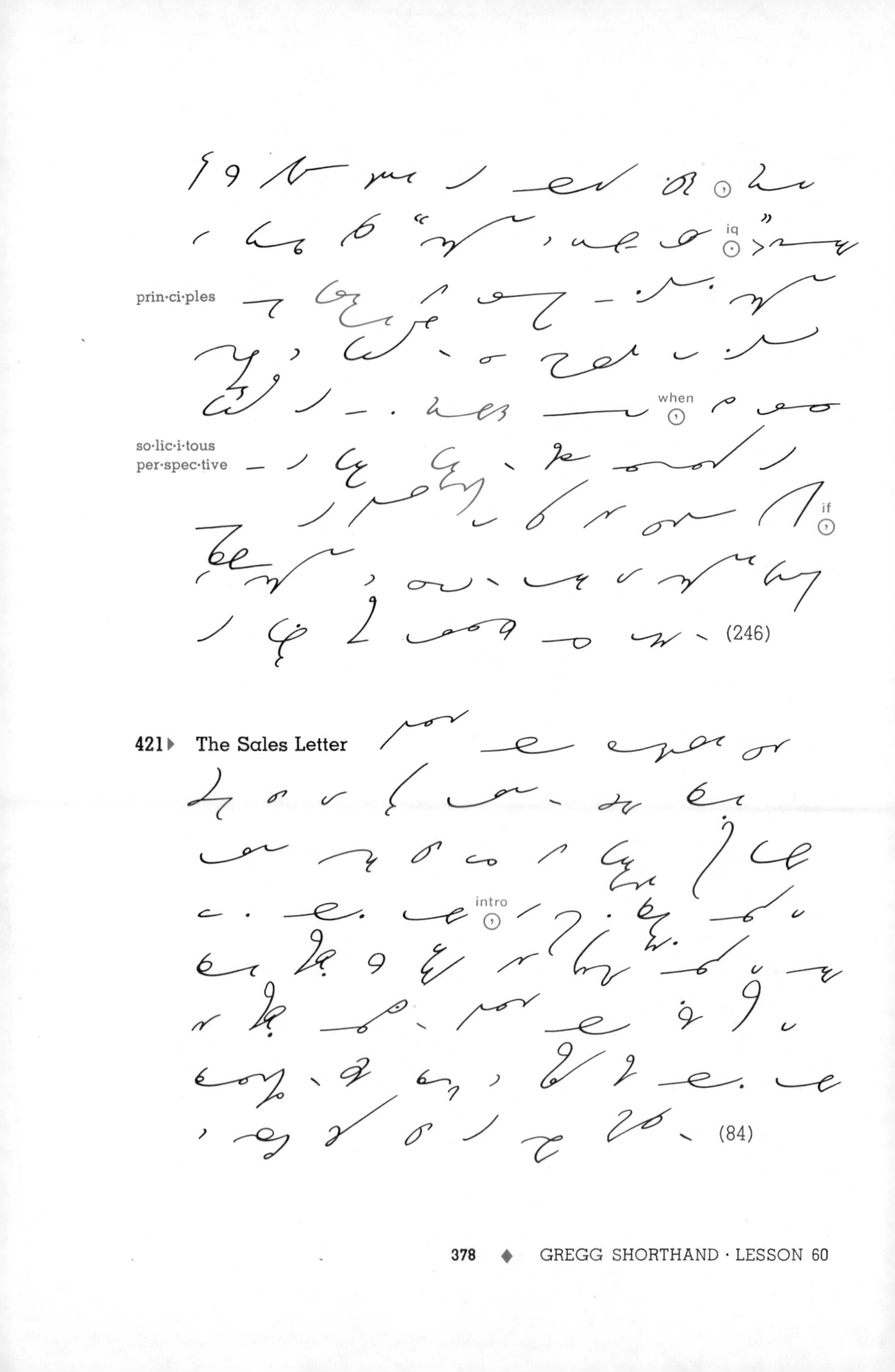

iq

prin·ci·ples

when

so·lic·i·tous
per·spec·tive

if

(246)

421 ▸ The Sales Letter

intro

(84)

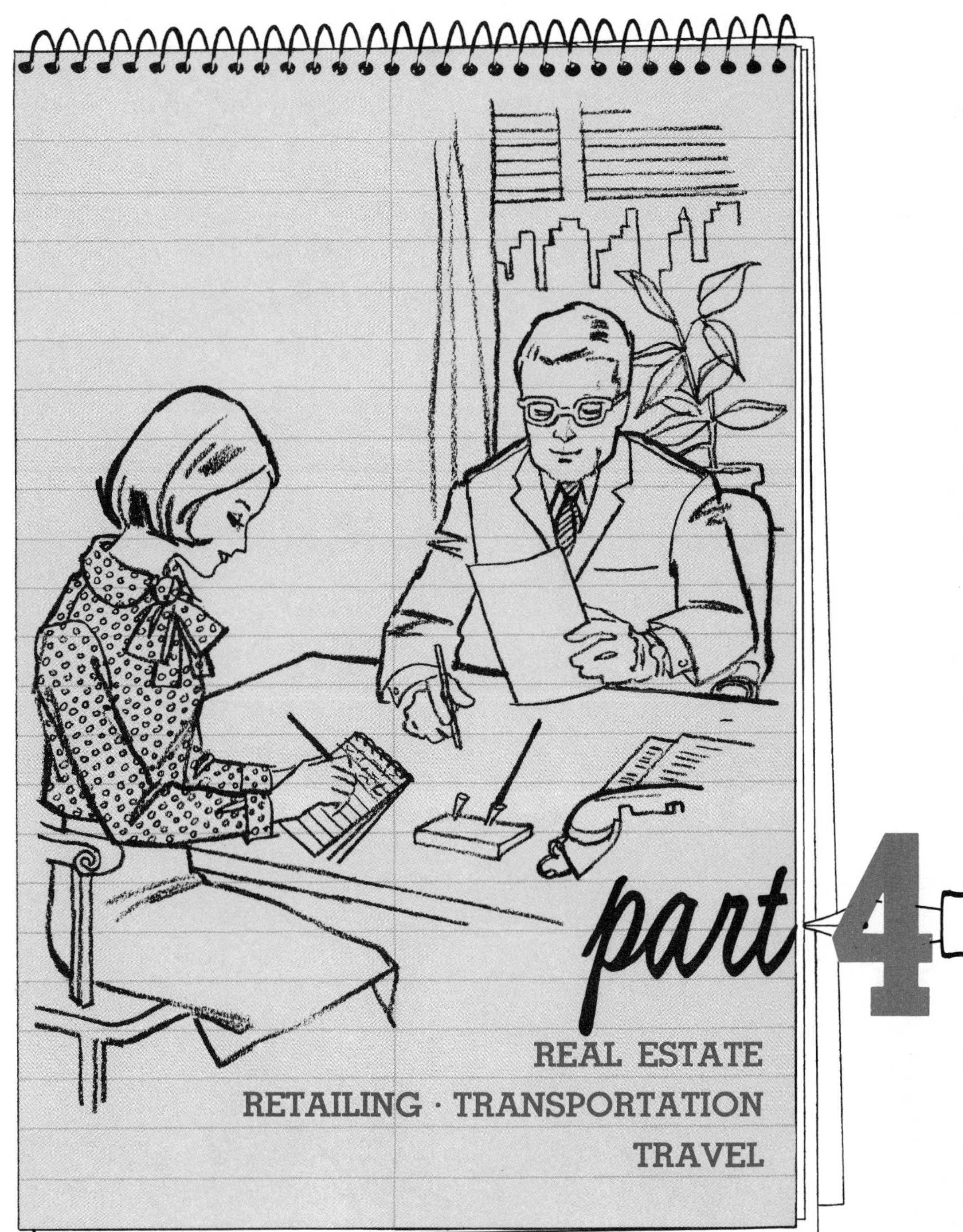

part 4

REAL ESTATE
RETAILING · TRANSPORTATION
TRAVEL

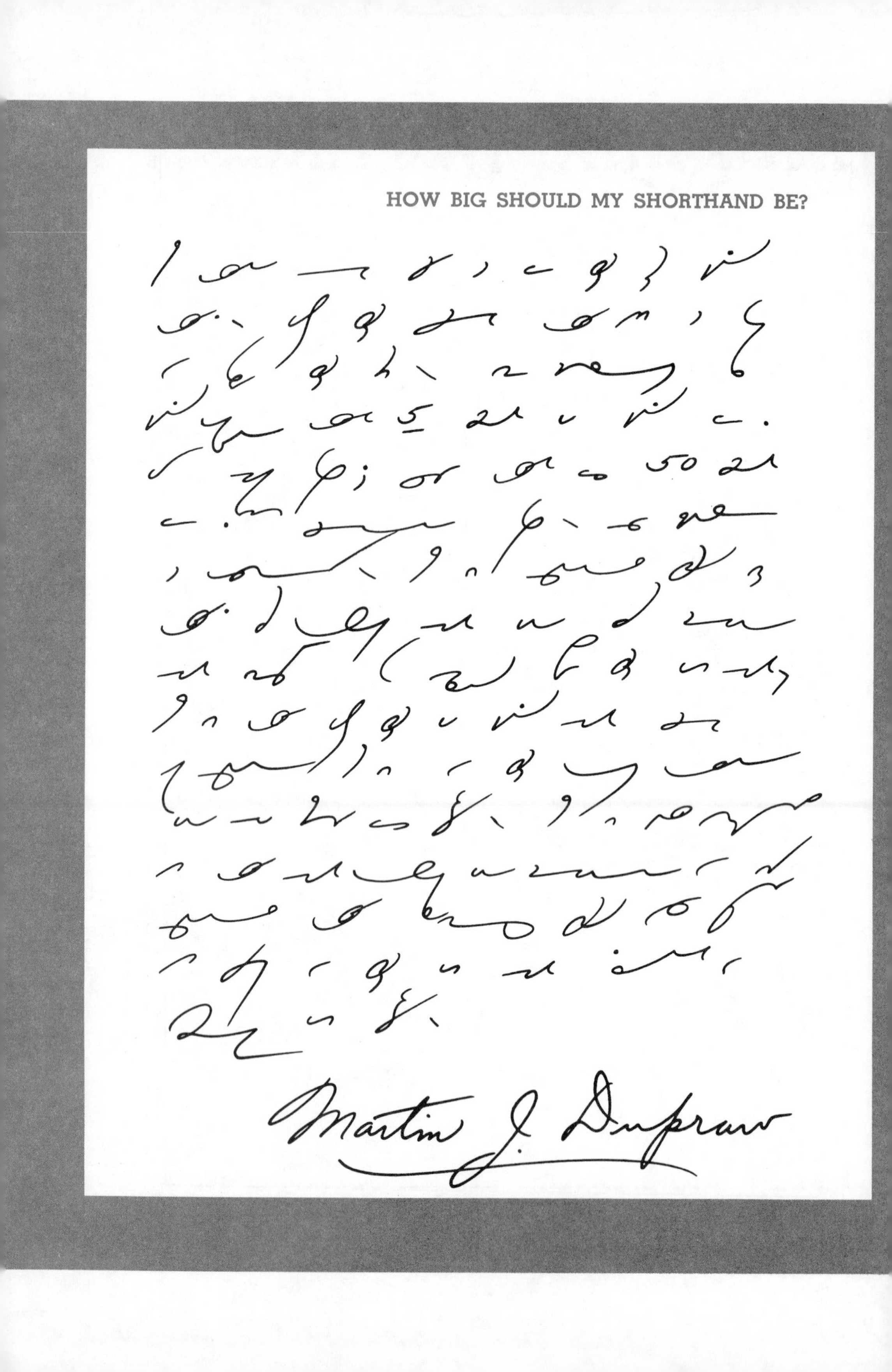

Martin J. Dupraw

advice from a champion

When Martin J. Dupraw won the world's shorthand championship, he established some remarkable records for accuracy. On a speech dictated at 200 words a minute for five minutes, he made only one error. On court testimony dictated at 280 words a minute for five minutes, he made only two errors. These and many other records that he has established are the result, in large measure, of the amazing legibility of his shorthand notes.

When you examine Mr. Dupraw's shorthand notes on the opposite page, one thing will immediately impress you—the careful attention to proportion.

Notice, for example, how large he makes the *a* circles and how small he makes the e circles. Notice, too, how much larger his *l's* are than his *r's*.

Another thing that will strike you is the way he rounds off angles. He does not consciously do this; rounding angles comes naturally to him as a result of his high speed. As your speed increases, you, too, will find that you will naturally round off angles.

In the page that Mr. Dupraw has written in his beautiful shorthand, he discusses the size of notes. Note that he has a fairly large shorthand style, just as he has a large longhand style.

Don't try to imitate Mr. Dupraw's style of writing; take the advice he gives in his article "How Big Should My Shorthand Be?"

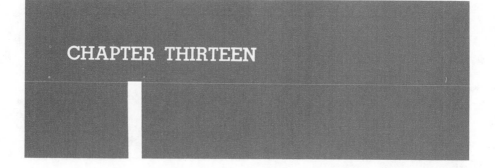

CHAPTER THIRTEEN

real estate

DEVELOPING WORD-BUILDING POWER

422 Brief Forms and Derivatives

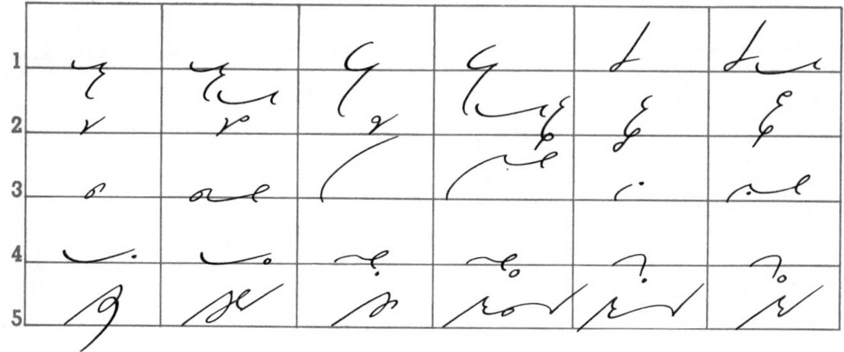

1 Responsible, responsibilities, probable, probabilities, general, generalities.

2 State, stately, estate, special, specially, especial.

3 Use, useless, time, timeless, thank, thankless.

4 Willing, willingly, corresponding, correspondingly, questioning, questioningly.

5 Disadvantage, dissatisfied, disuse, disregard, disorganized, disorder.

BUILDING TRANSCRIPTION SKILLS

423 BUSINESS VOCABULARY BUILDER

tract An indefinite stretch of land. (Be careful not to type "track" when transcribing — a very common mistake that stenographers make.)

envisioned Imagined; thought of.

ad Short for "advertisement." (Be careful not to type "add" when transcribing — another common mistake that stenographers make.)

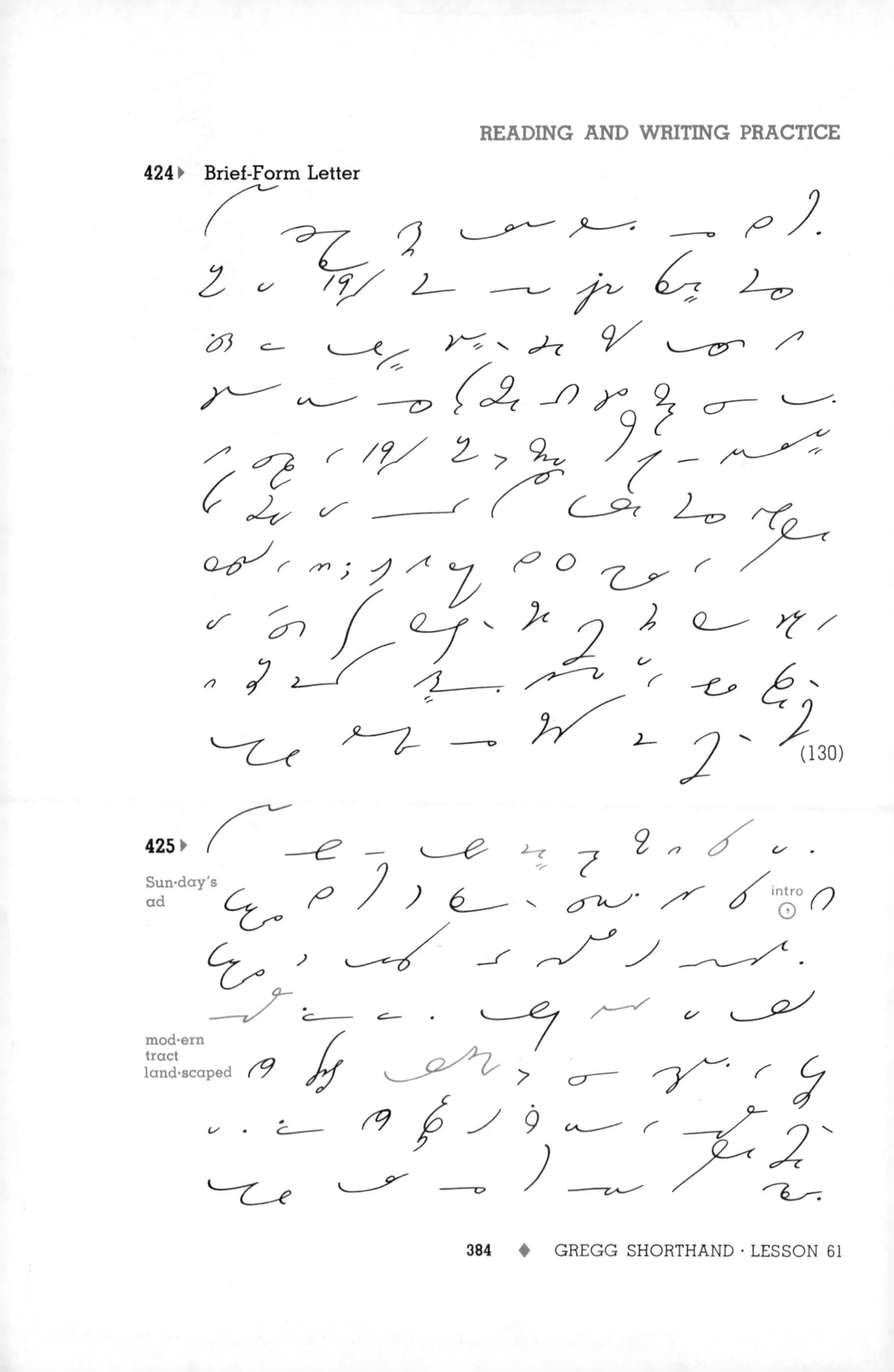

424 Brief-Form Letter

(130)

425

Sun·day's
ad

intro

mod·ern
tract
land·scaped

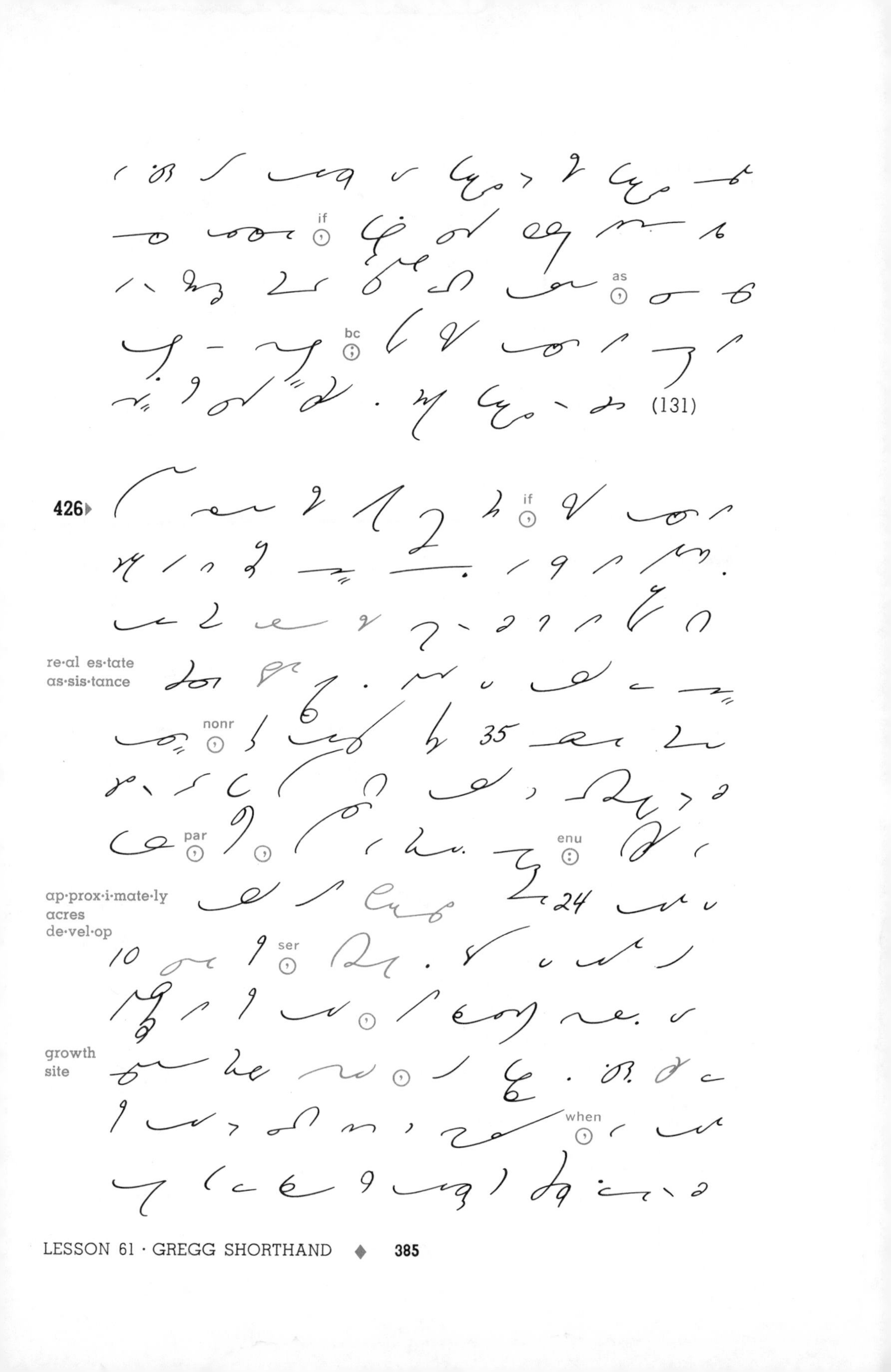

(131)

426

if

as

bc

if

re·al es·tate
as·sis·tance

nonr

35

par

enu

ap·prox·i·mate·ly
acres
de·vel·op

24

10

ser

growth
site

when

be·lieve
Build·er's

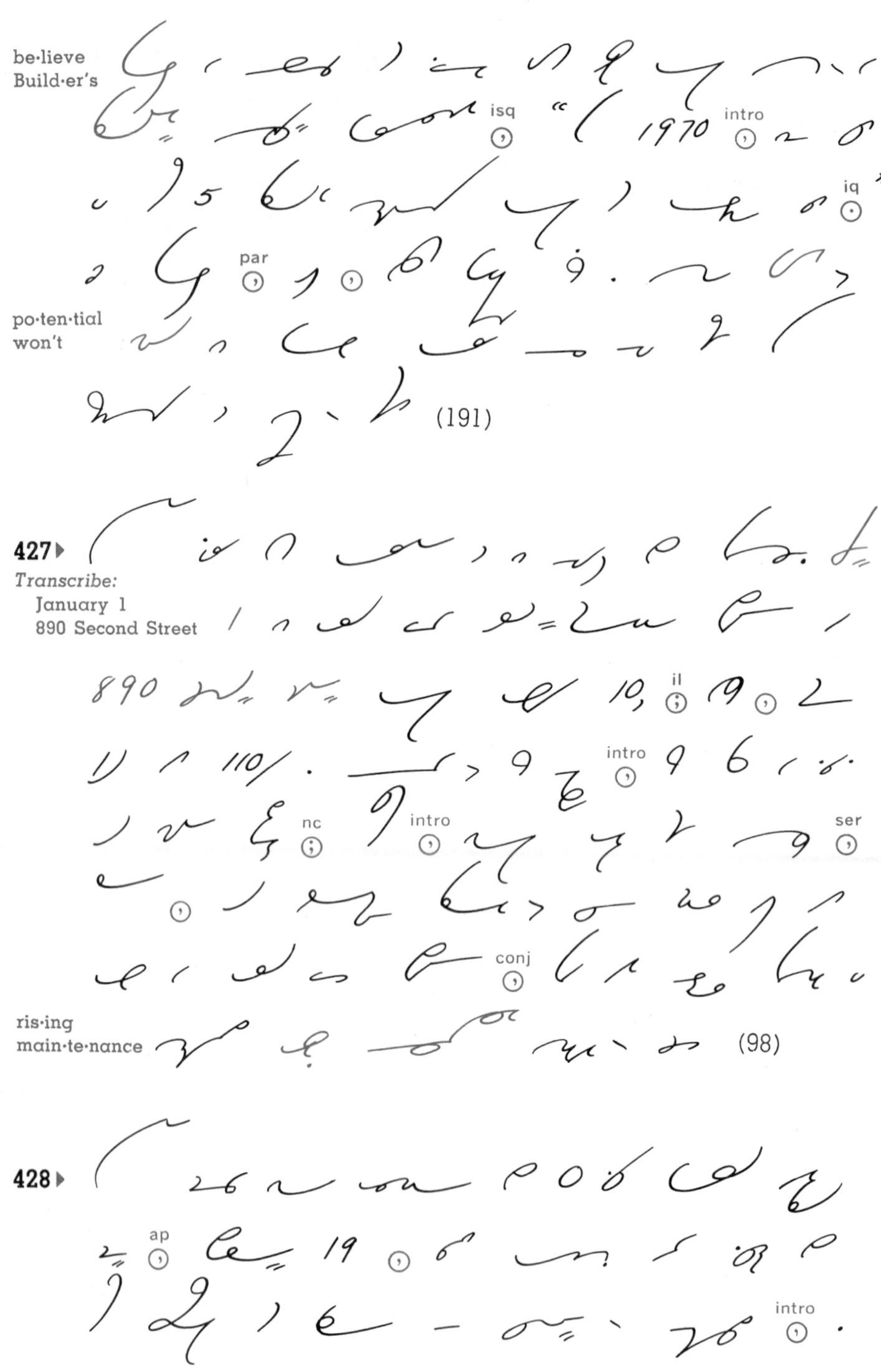

po·ten·tial
won't

(191)

427▸

Transcribe:
January 1
890 Second Street

ris·ing
main·te·nance

(98)

428▸

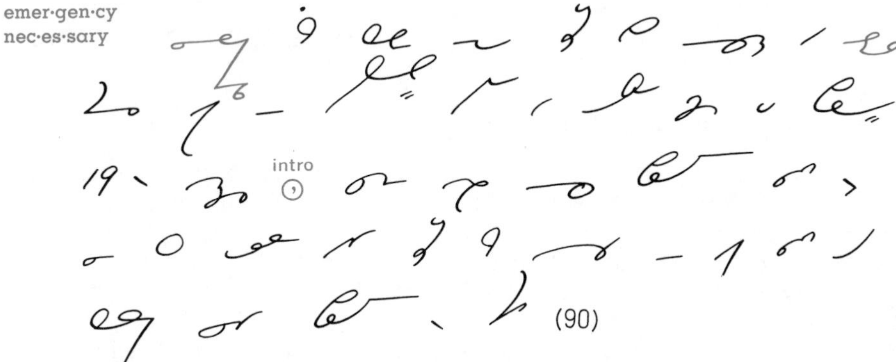

429▸ Transcription Quiz • Up to this point, you have been told the type of punctuation that was necessary to punctuate each Transcription Quiz correctly. You have also been told how many missing words you should supply. Beginning with the following Transcription Quiz, however, it will be your job to discover and supply all missing words and punctuation without any guidance.

OFFICE-STYLE DICTATION, 5

Instructions During Dictation

One of the best ways to emphasize a few lines of typewritten copy is to indent them. If, for example, the letter is typed with a 50-space line, the indented material might be typed on a 40-space line so that it will stand out from the rest of the letter.

If your dictator mentions, *before* he dictates, that the material is to be indented, the shorthand notes can be indented slightly and a large square bracket placed on each side of the material that is to be indented. If he decides on the indention *after* he has dictated the material, you can place the bracket on each side of the section to be indented. That will remind you, when transcribing, to make the necessary change in the margins.

430▸ ILLUSTRATION OF OFFICE-STYLE DICTATION

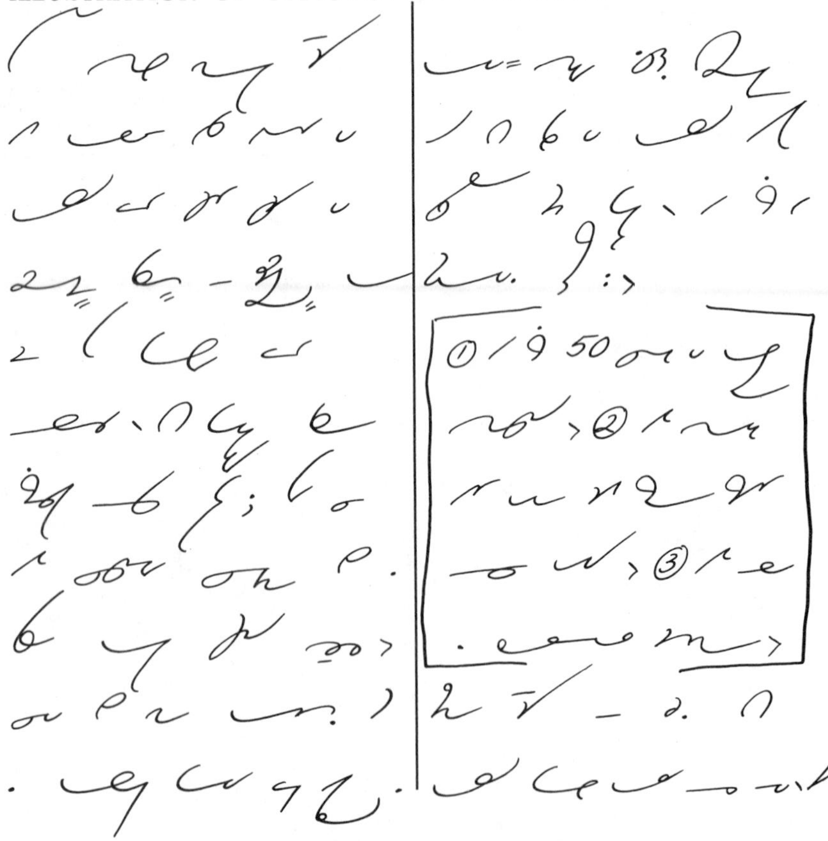

BUILDING PHRASING SKILL

431▸ Useful Business-Letter Phrases

Ago

1

Each

2

Glad

3

Next

4

1 Few days ago, long time ago, some time ago, several months ago, day or two ago, long ago, weeks ago, hours ago, years ago.
2 Each day, each month, each time, each morning, each other, each one.
3 I shall be glad, he will be glad, he would be glad, glad to see.
4 Next month, next time, next morning, next year, next day.

432▸ Frequent Names

1

2

1 O'Brien, O'Donnell, Olsen, Parker, Philips, Quinn, Roberts.
2 Laura, Lillian, Margaret, Marian, Martha.

BUILDING TRANSCRIPTION SKILLS

433▸ LANGUAGE STUDY **dis-:** In many English words, the prefix *dis-* means *not* or *the opposite of* or *the absence of.*

dislike The opposite of "like"; to have an aversion to.
disregard The opposite of "regard"; to pay no attention to.
disloyal Not loyal; unfaithful.
disagreeable Not agreeable; taking a different point of view.
discomfort The opposite of "comfort"; uneasiness.

434▸ BUSINESS VOCABULARY BUILDER

ranch-type house A house in which all the rooms are on one floor.
occupancy The act of taking possession.
vibrating Moving back and forth; shaking.
redecorate To repair and beautify.

READING AND WRITING PRACTICE

435▸ Phrase Letter

10

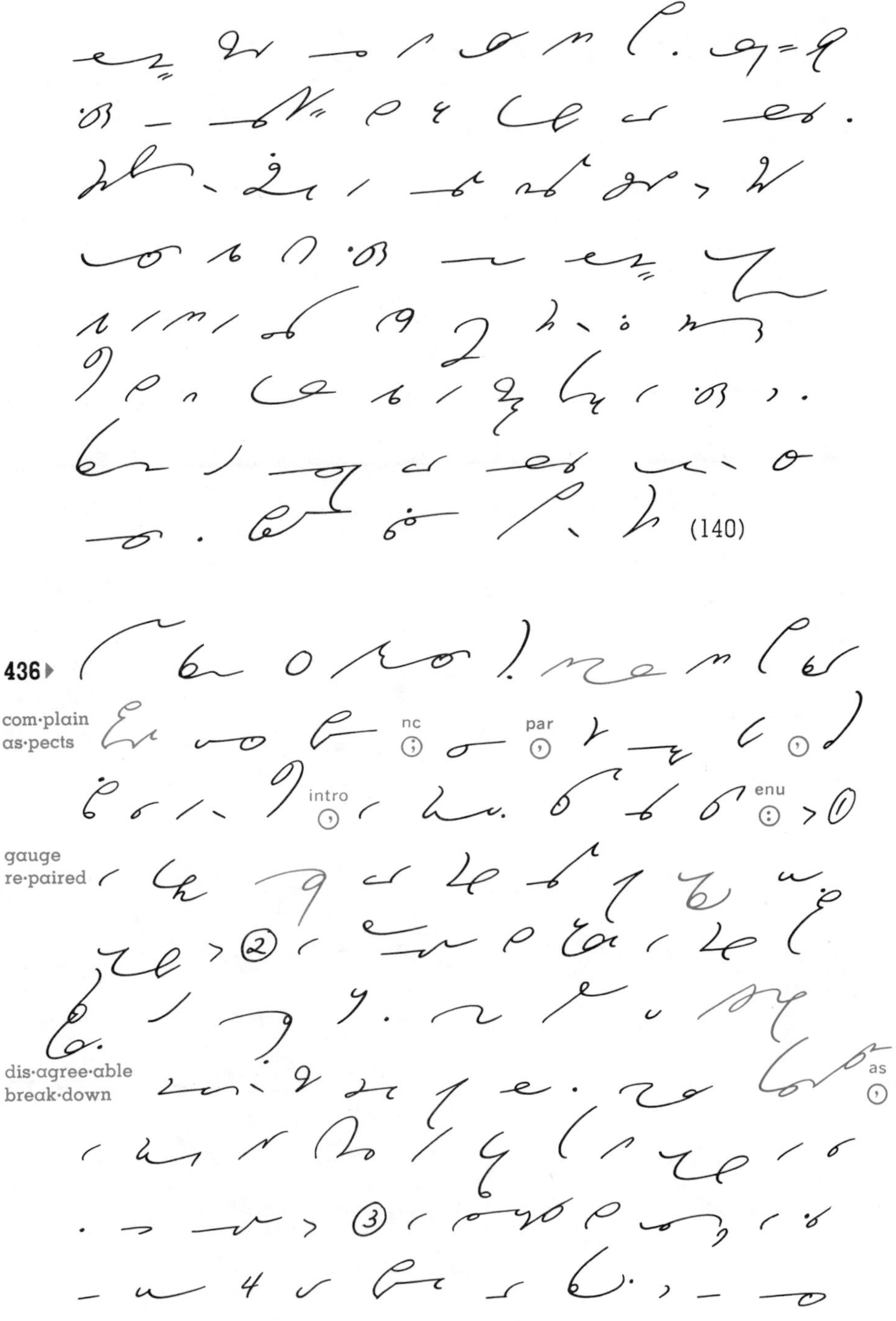
(140)
436
com·plain
as·pects
nc
par
intro
enu
gauge
re·paired
dis·agree·able
break·down
as
②
③

il
par
ther·mo·stat
quite
weath·er
intro
ser
(196)

437

oc·cu·pan·cy
as
ap
nonr
Nel·son's
or·di·nar·i·ly
par
intro

anx·ious
al·ways

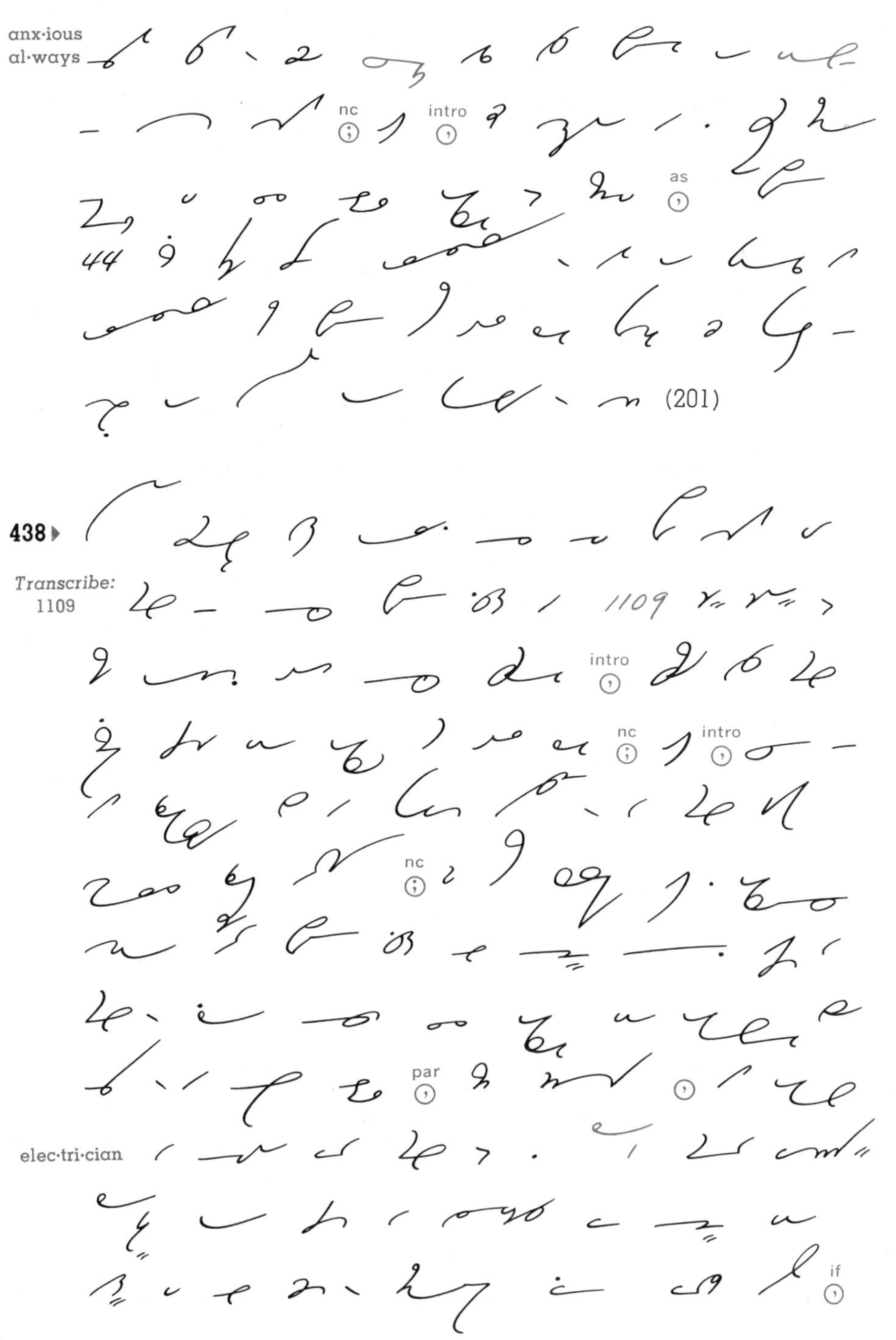

438

Transcribe:
1109

elec·tri·cian

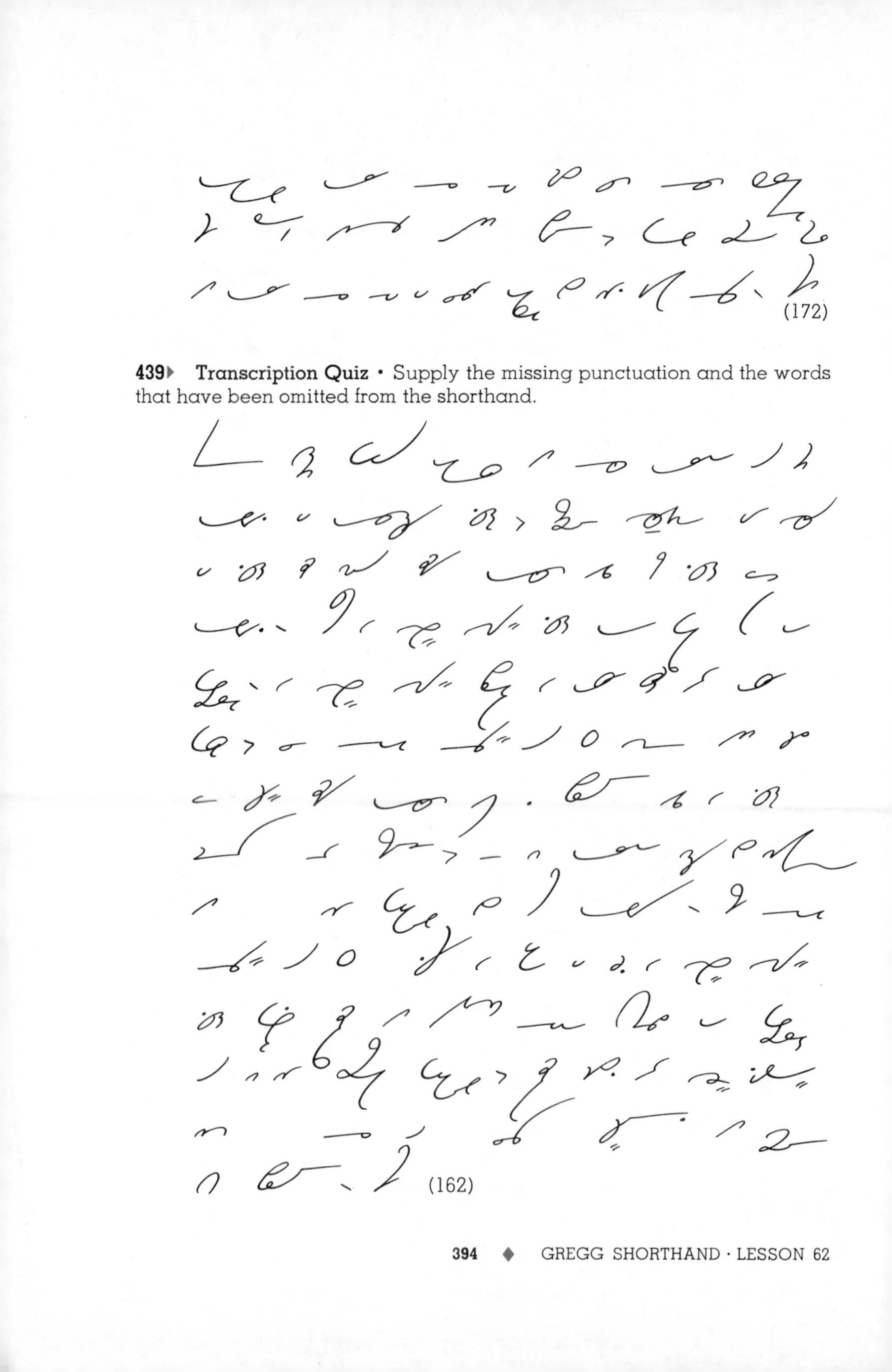

(172)

439▸ Transcription Quiz • Supply the missing punctuation and the words that have been omitted from the shorthand.

(162)

DEVELOPING WORD-BUILDING POWER

440 ▸ Word Families

-sist

1

Able

2

-mentary

3

-ction

4

Field

5

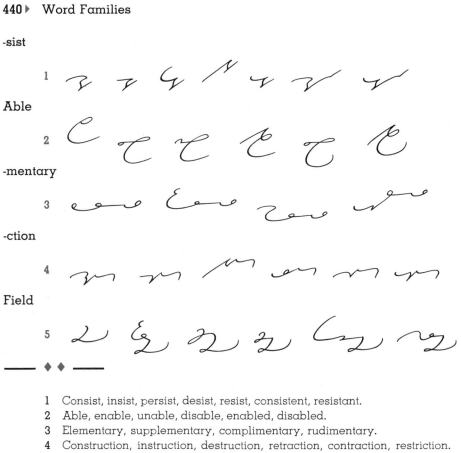

1 Consist, insist, persist, desist, resist, consistent, resistant.
2 Able, enable, unable, disable, enabled, disabled.
3 Elementary, supplementary, complimentary, rudimentary.
4 Construction, instruction, destruction, retraction, contraction, restriction.
5 Field, Springfield, Wakefield, Winfield, Bloomfield, Greenfield.

441 ▸ **SIMILAR-WORDS DRILL** **prominent, permanent**

prominent Noted; standing out.

He is a prominent lawyer in Springfield.

permanent Not subject to change; lasting.

I will make my permanent home in Charleston.

442 ▸ **BUSINESS VOCABULARY BUILDER**

paramount Superior to all others.
commute To travel back and forth regularly.
adapted Fitted to.

READING AND WRITING PRACTICE

443 ▸

prom·i·nent

ser nc intro

conj intro

pref·er·a·bly

ap·pre·ci·ate
de·scrip·tions

(136)

444▸

per·ma·nent
fam·i·ly's

conj

ap

when

par

al·ready
oc·cu·pan·cy

enu

col·or-styled
built-in
hyphenated before noun

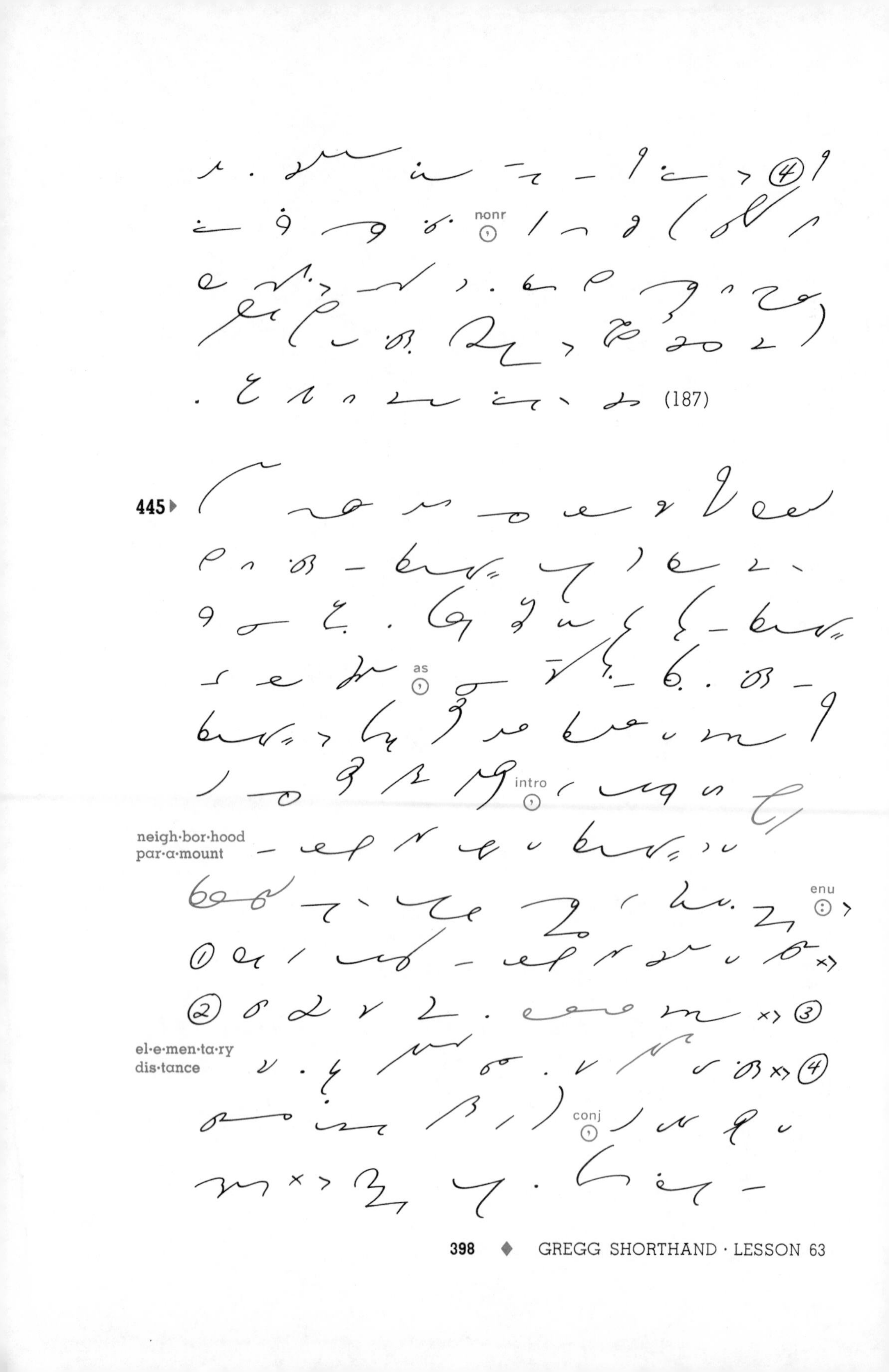

(187)

445

nonr as intro enu conj

neigh·bor·hood
par·a·mount

el·e·men·ta·ry
dis·tance

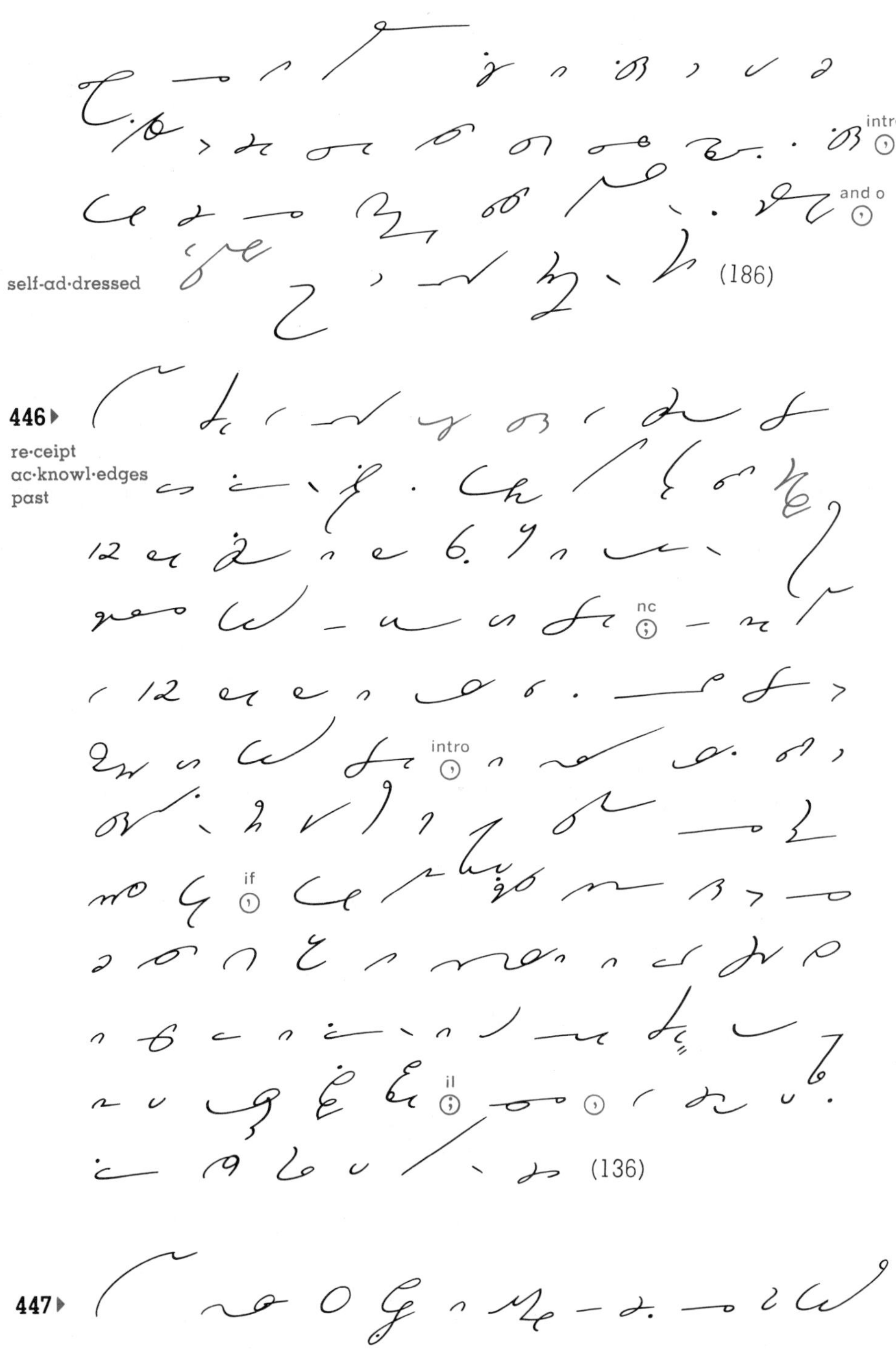
intro
and o
self-ad·dressed
(186)
446
re·ceipt
ac·knowl·edges
past
nc
intro
if
il
(136)
447

(44)

448 ▸ **Transcription Quiz** • Supply the necessary punctuation and the two words omitted from the shorthand. Also watch for a question mark that has been omitted – a frequent error that stenographers make when transcribing.

(184)

DEVELOPING WORD-BUILDING POWER

449 ▸ Word Beginnings and Endings

-ings

1

Con-

2

Dis-

3

-ble

4

-ful

5

— ◆ ◆ —

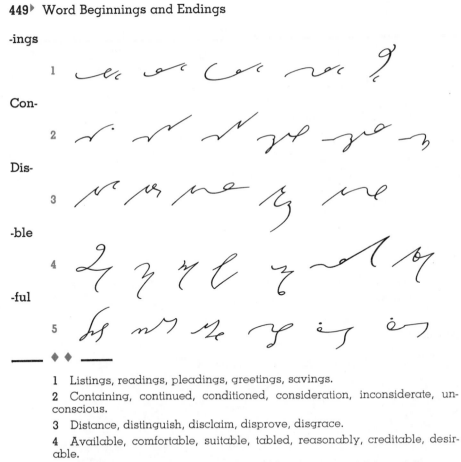

1 Listings, readings, pleadings, greetings, savings.

2 Containing, continued, conditioned, consideration, inconsiderate, unconscious.

3 Distance, distinguish, disclaim, disprove, disgrace.

4 Available, comfortable, suitable, tabled, reasonably, creditable, desirable.

5 Beautiful, wonderful, thoughtfulness, gracefully, helpful, harmful.

450 ▸ Geographical Expressions

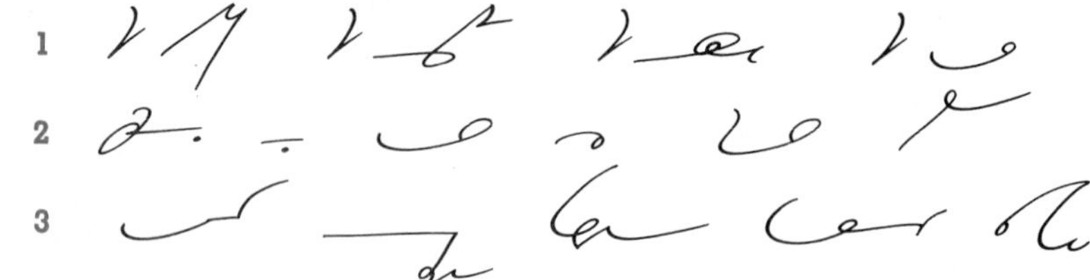

— ♦♦ —

1 Fort Dodge, Fort Madison, Fort Myers, Fort Lee.
2 Wyoming, New Hampshire, Louisiana, Kentucky, Florida, Delaware.
3 London, Manchester, Bristol, Plymouth, Edinburgh.

BUILDING TRANSCRIPTION SKILLS

451 ▸ SPELLING FAMILIES

Double trouble!

Words in which consonants are doubled are a frequent cause of misspelling. This list contains words in which one or more consonants are doubled, words that are repeatedly misspelled by stenographers.

Double M

com·mit·tee
com·mu·ni·ty
im·ma·ture
im·mi·nent
rec·om·mend
sum·ma·ry

Double C

ac·cept
ac·com·mo·date
ac·com·pa·ny
oc·ca·sion
oc·cur·rence
suc·ceed

Double L

ac·ci·den·tal·ly
equal·ly
es·pe·cial·ly
in·ci·den·tal·ly
le·gal·ly
prac·ti·cal·ly

Double G

ag·gra·vate
ag·gre·gate
bag·gage
ex·ag·ger·ate
lug·gage
sug·ges·tion

452 BUSINESS VOCABULARY BUILDER

defray To bear the expenses of.

Realtor A real estate agent who is a member of the National Association of Real Estate Boards.

project A planned undertaking.

READING AND WRITING PRACTICE

453

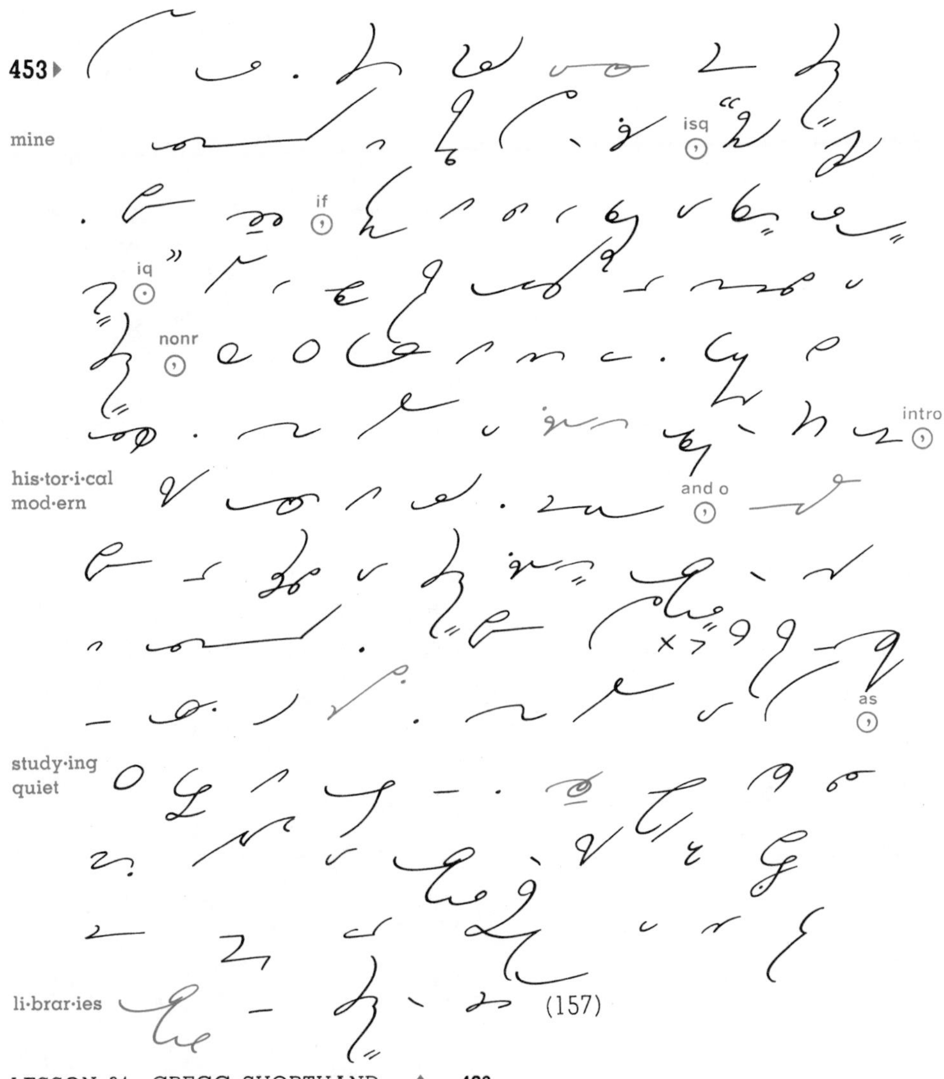

454

grat·i·fy·ing
site

intro

when

acres

tract

wor·thy
sum·mary

intro

(157)

455

nonr

for·mer·ly

as

per·son·nel
col·leagues

ser

if

as·sis·tance
in·ci·den·tal·ly

intro

nine-month
three-month
hyphenated before noun

fi·nan·cial

bc

par

(204)

456

ap

(58)

457 ▸ Transcription Quiz · Supply the necessary punctuation and the missing words.

(187)

DEVELOPING WORD-BUILDING POWER

458 ▸ Shorthand Vocabulary Builder

Geographical Expressions

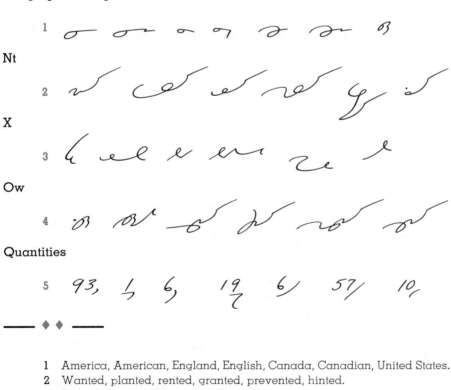

1 [shorthand]

Nt

2 [shorthand]

X

3 [shorthand]

Ow

4 [shorthand]

Quantities

5 [shorthand]

— ◆◆ —

1 America, American, England, English, Canada, Canadian, United States.
2 Wanted, planted, rented, granted, prevented, hinted.
3 Box, relax, text, textiles, complex, index.
4 House, thousands, mounted, founded, grounded, counted.
5 93 percent, 100 percent, 6 feet, 1,900 pounds, $600, $57, 10,000.

459 ▸ Accuracy Practice—Curves

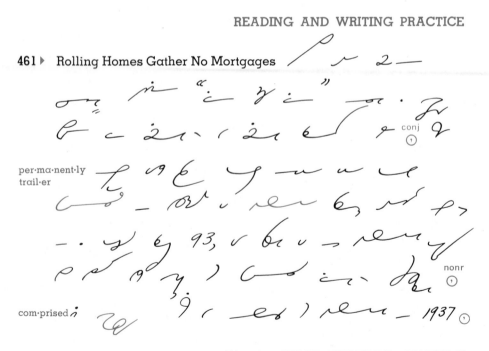

1 Present, please; brain, blame; free, value.
2 Pay, bay; see, fee, very; about, as, half, advantage; ease, if, ever-every.

BUILDING TRANSCRIPTION SKILLS

460 ▸ BUSINESS VOCABULARY BUILDER

compact Pressed closely together.
conveyance A means of carrying; a vehicle.
contraption A gadget.

READING AND WRITING PRACTICE

461 ▸ Rolling Homes Gather No Mortgages

conj

per·ma·nent·ly
trail·er

nonr

com·prised

1937

at·tempts
Cur·tiss

par

ve·hi·cles

bc

ser

fam·i·lies
gear

iq

Among the

intro

break·ing

Sher·man's
con·vey·ance

par

up·right
rem·e·died
ax·le

when
ser

cou·ple
ex·hib·it·ing

1930 intro

117 conj

1933

The early

17

steel
weighed

19

645

fore·saw
choose

conj

par

intro

par

par

hitch

One of the

enu

nonr

nonr

isq

iq

(650)

CHAPTER FOURTEEN

retailing

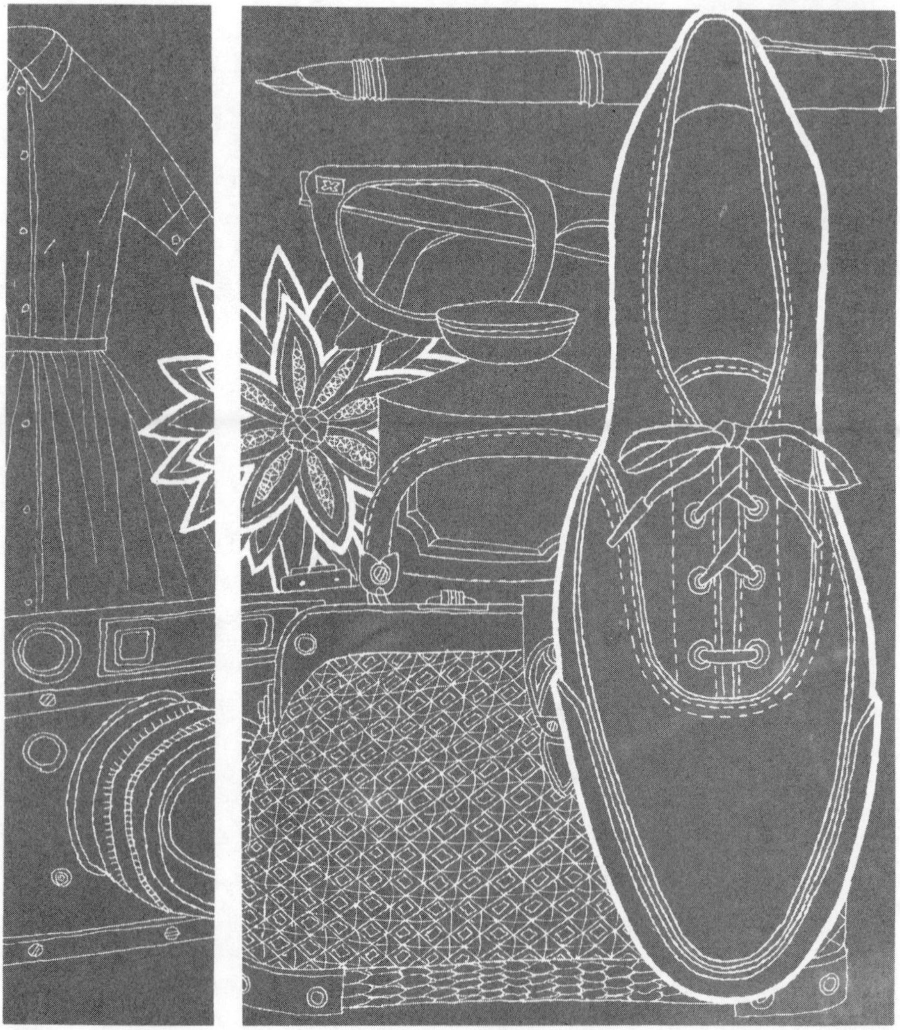

DEVELOPING WORD-BUILDING POWER

462▸ Brief Forms and Derivatives

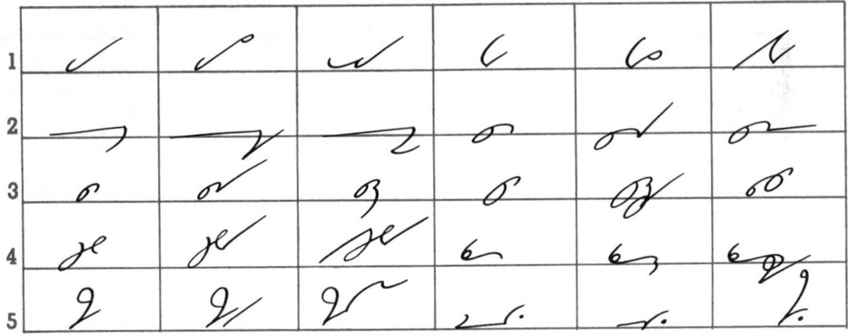

—— ♦♦ ——

1 Order, orderly, reorder; part, partly, depart.

2 Manufacture, manufactured, manufacturer; acknowledge, acknowledged, acknowledgment.

3 Use, used, useful; out, outside, without.

4 Satisfy, satisfied, dissatisfied; circular, circulars, circularized.

5 After, afterward, afterdinner; something, nothing, everything.

BUILDING TRANSCRIPTION SKILLS

463▸ BUSINESS VOCABULARY BUILDER

soliciting Approaching with a request; asking for.

furriers Those dealing in the buying and selling of furs.

make amends To compensate for a loss or injury.

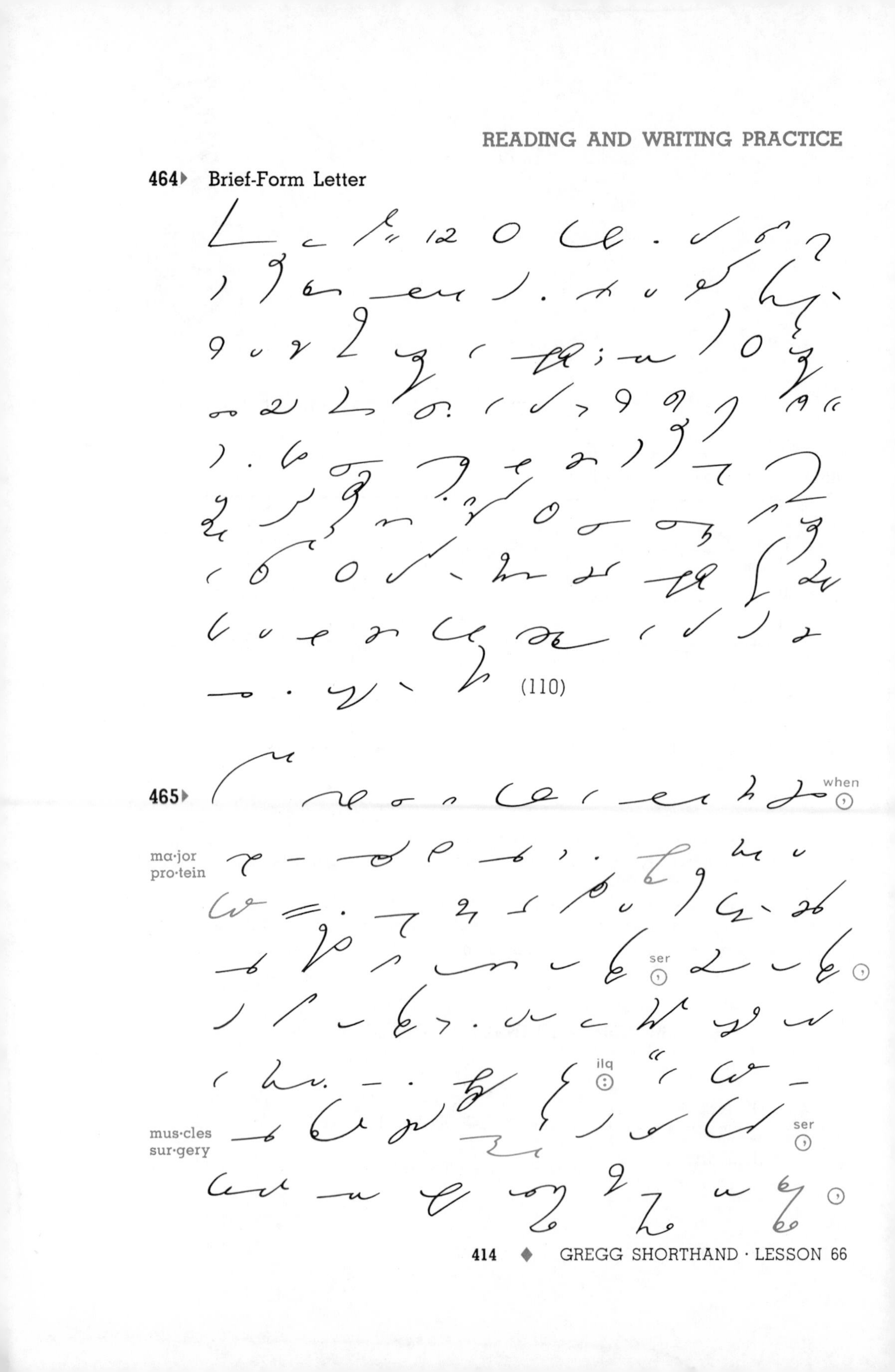

464 Brief-Form Letter

(110)

465

when

ma·jor
pro·tein

ser

ilq

mus·cles
sur·gery

ser

fa·tigue

iq

when

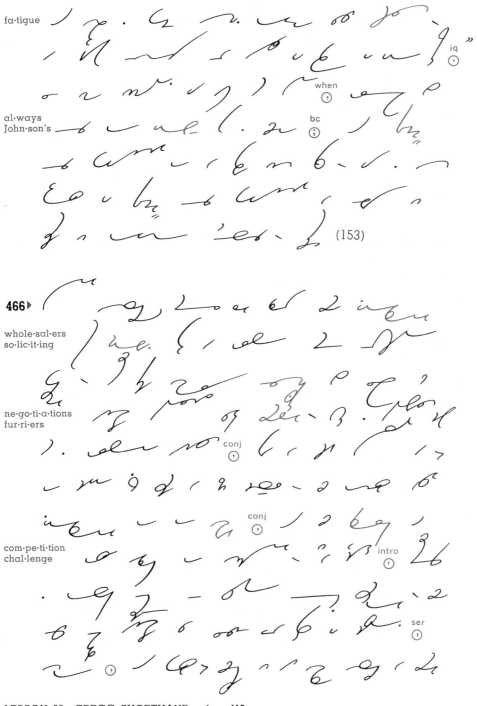

al·ways
John·son's

bc

(153)

466

whole·sal·ers
so·lic·it·ing

ne·go·ti·a·tions
fur·ri·ers

conj

conj

com·pe·ti·tion
chal·lenge

intro

ser

racks

(168)

467

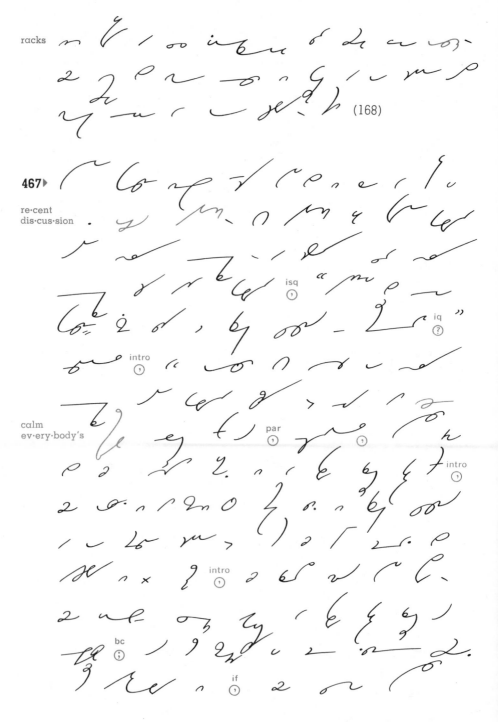

re·cent
dis·cus·sion

isq

iq

intro

calm
ev·ery·body's

par

intro

intro

bc

if

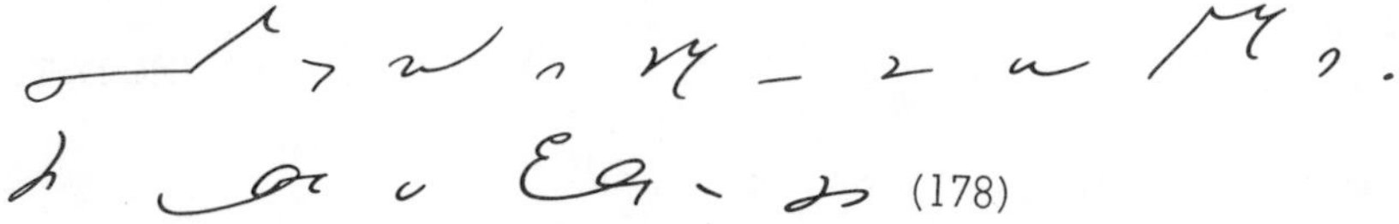

468▸ Transcription Quiz • Supply the necessary punctuation and the missing word.

(108)

▸ *Cheerfulness is contagious! Even over the telephone a pleasant disposition and a friendly tone of voice are easily communicated to the invisible person at the other end of the wire.*

Instructions During Dictation *(Continued)*

Some dictators interrupt their dictation to give instructions about spelling, punctuation, and other details of transcription. Always record these instructions, no matter how elementary they may seem to you.

If your dictator spells a proper name or a word, record the spelling in longhand immediately above your shorthand outline. If he dictates punctuation, place the marks in your notes, encircling them so that you do not try to read them as shorthand outlines.

469▸ ILLUSTRATION OF OFFICE-STYLE DICTATION

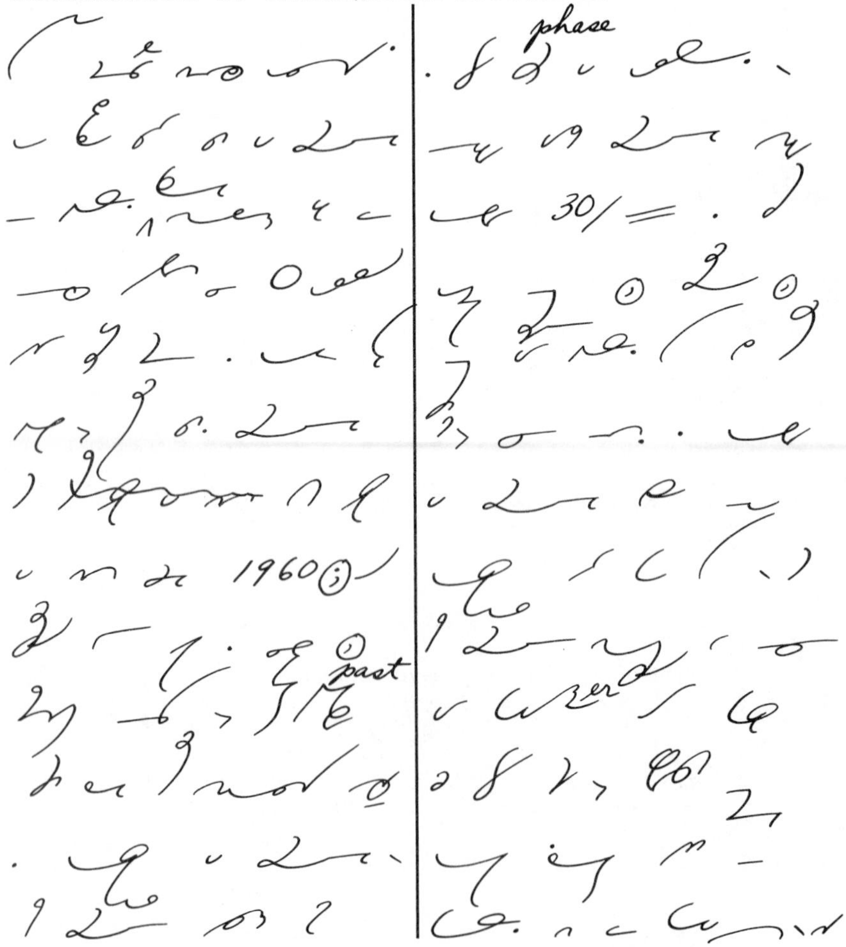

BUILDING PHRASING SKILL

470 Useful Business-Letter Phrases

For

1

Month, Months

2

To Omitted

3

Or Omitted

4

1 For a long time, for many days, for a few days, for a moment, for some time.

2 This month, few months, several months, months ago.

3 In addition to the, glad to see, in order to be able, able to say, ought to be, up to date.

4 Day or two, day or two ago, one or two, two or three, three or four, once or twice, week or two.

471 Frequent Names

1

2

1 Robertson, Robinson, Rogers, Russell, Ryan, Schmidt, Schneider, Scott.
2 Norman, Oliver, Owen, Patrick, Peter, Philip, Rudolph.

BUILDING TRANSCRIPTION SKILLS

472▸ LANGUAGE STUDY **ex-**: In a great many words, *ex-* means *from, out, out of.*

extract Something taken out; a selection from a piece of writing.
extended Stretched out; lengthened.
exterior The outside.
exceedingly Going out or beyond the measure of.
expend To pay out.
exhaust To tire out; to run out of.

473▸ BUSINESS VOCABULARY BUILDER

axiom A statement accepted as truth.
indestructible Incapable of being destroyed.
deterioration The act of growing worse.

READING AND WRITING PRACTICE

474▸ Phrase Letter

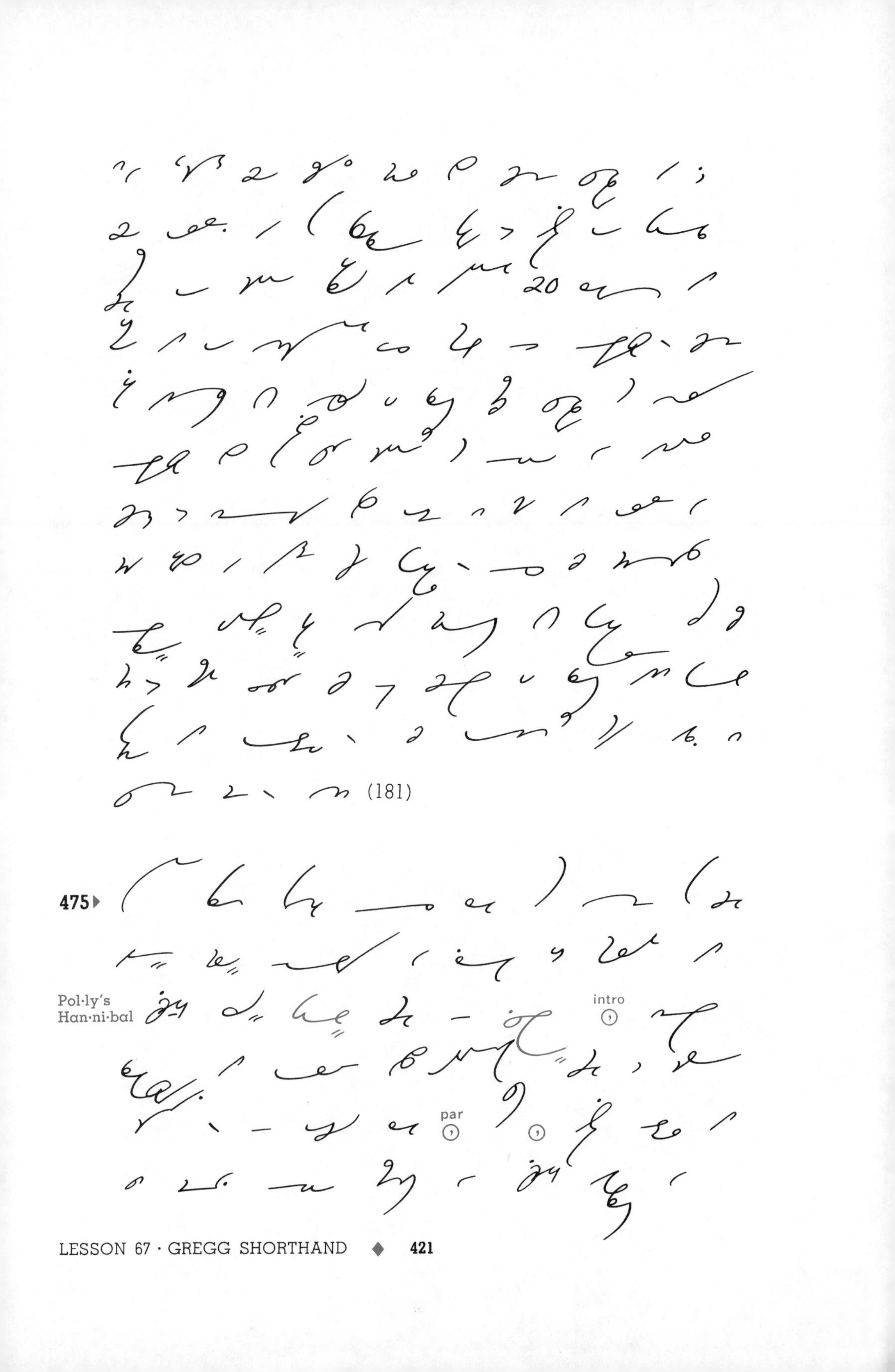

20

(181)

475

Pol·ly's
Han·ni·bal

intro

par

chem·i·cal
de·vel·op·ing

nonr

de·te·ri·o·ra·tion
his·tor·i·cal·ly

conj

ap·ply·ing
ap·plied
Saw·yer's

in·te·ri·or
ex·te·ri·or

if

(194)

476

fi·nan·cial
ax·i·om

clothes

par

buy·ing
clear·ance

conj

par

ad·vance

pre·sea·son
cloth·ing

ser

(193)

477▸

30 if

par

(51)

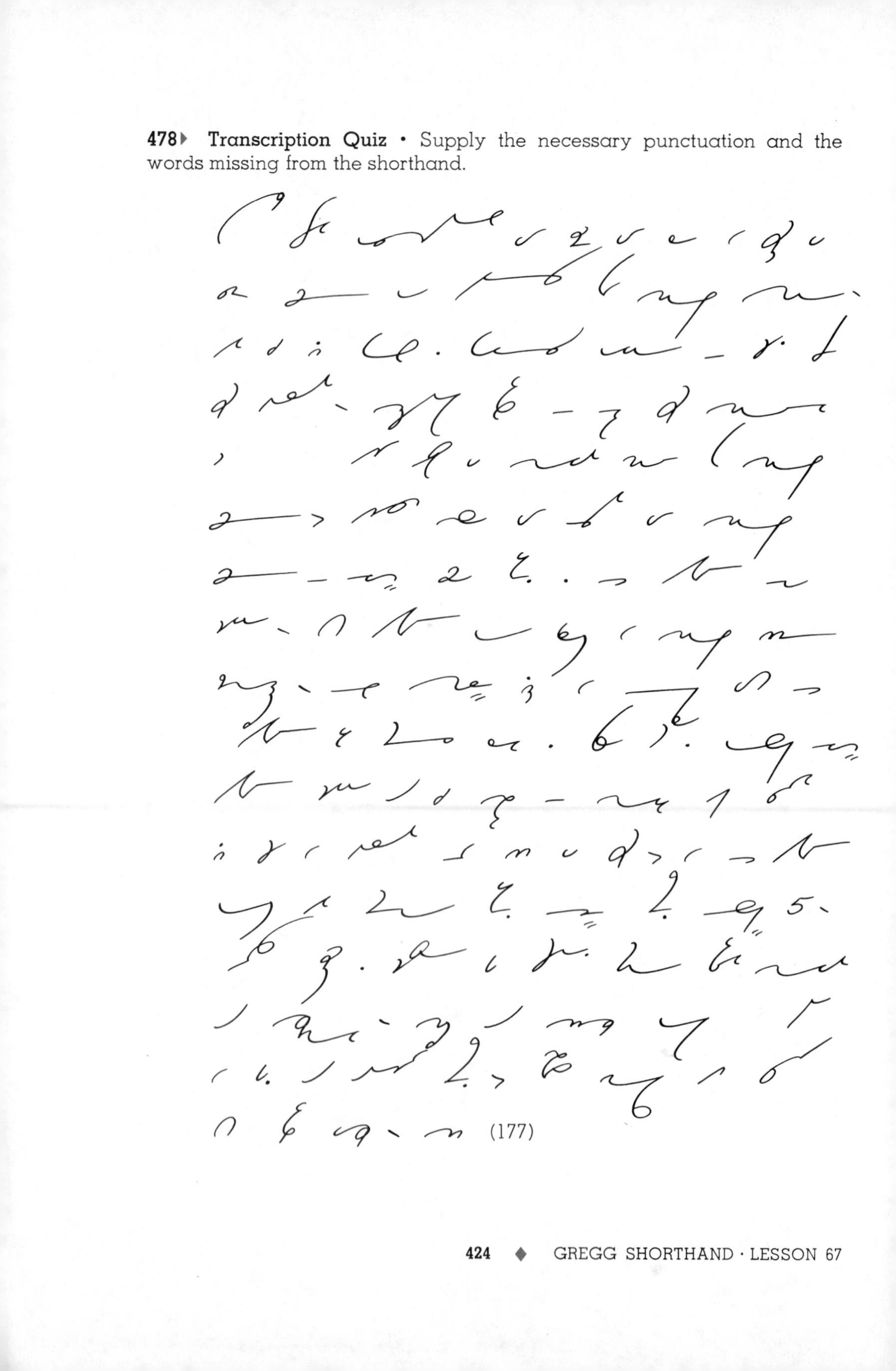

478▸ Transcription Quiz • Supply the necessary punctuation and the words missing from the shorthand.

(177)

DEVELOPING WORD-BUILDING POWER

479 ▸ Word Families

Unt-

1

-fied

2

Rise

3

Room

4

Body

5

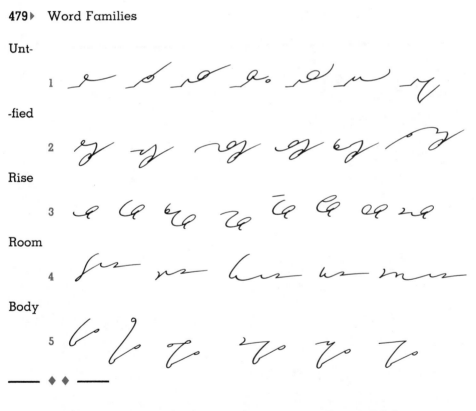

1 Until, untied, untried, untiringly, untrained, untold, untroubled.
2 Terrified, notified, gratified, ratified, certified, dignified.
3 Rise, prize, surprise, comprise, enterprise, apprise, arise, sunrise.
4 Bedroom, stateroom, ballroom, showroom, schoolroom.
5 Body, everybody, anybody, somebody, nobody, embody.

480▸ SIMILAR-WORDS DRILL **wares, wears**

wares Goods.

The wares were attractively displayed.

wears Has on; stands up under use or time.

She always wears smart clothes.
We must determine how well the cloth wears before we can use it for our suits.

481▸ BUSINESS VOCABULARY BUILDER

emporium A store; a market.

logic Sound reasoning.

skeptics Persons who approach a situation or problem with doubt.

READING AND WRITING PRACTICE

482▸

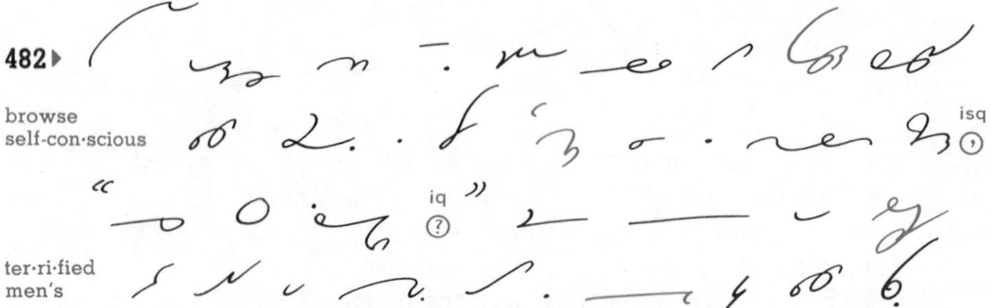

browse
self-con·scious
ter·ri·fied
men's

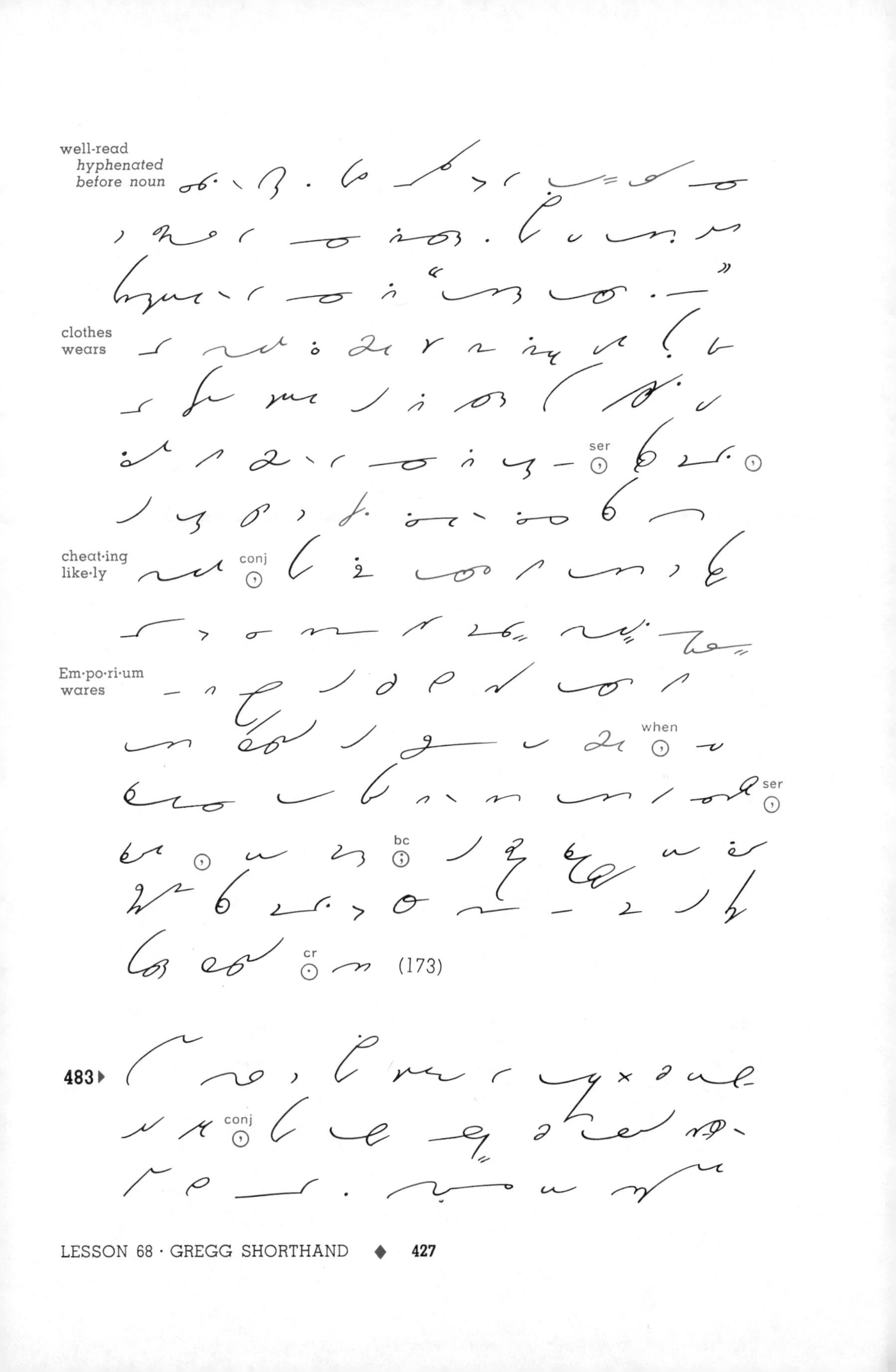

well-read
hyphenated before noun

clothes
wears

ser ser

cheat·ing
like·ly

conj

Em·po·ri·um
wares

when

ser

bc

cr

(173)

483

conj

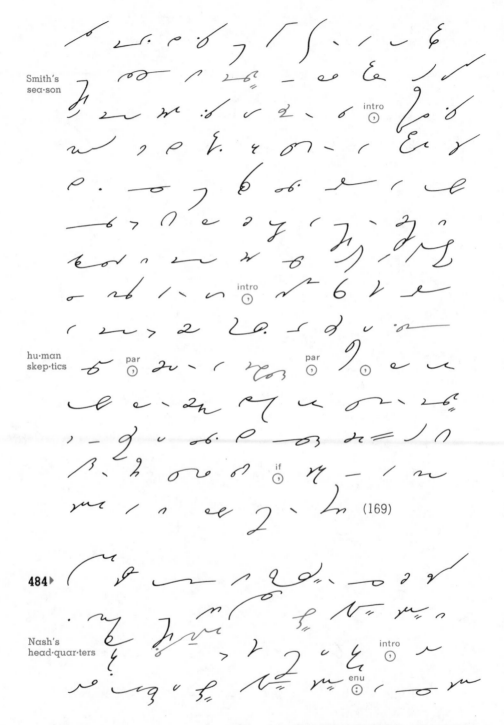

Smith's sea·son

intro

intro

hu·man skep·tics

par

par

if

(169)

484

Nash's head·quar·ters

intro

enu

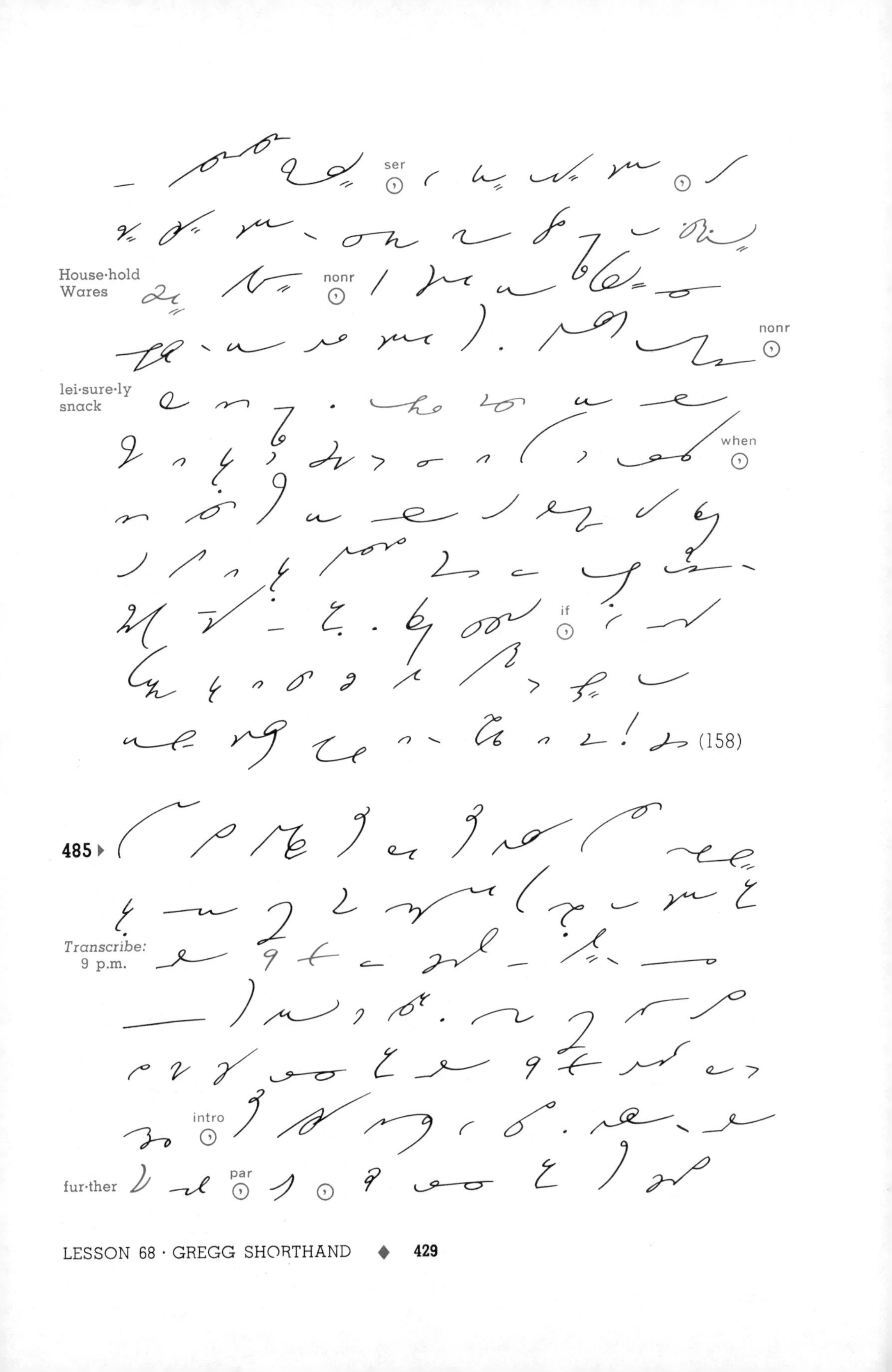

ser

House·hold Wares

nonr

nonr

lei·sure·ly snack

when

if

(158)

485 ▸

Transcribe: 9 p.m.

intro

fur·ther

par

486▸ Transcription Quiz • Supply the necessary punctuation and the words missing from the shorthand.

(167)

DEVELOPING WORD-BUILDING POWER

487 ▸ Word Beginnings and Endings

-ship

1

-ily

2

Post-

3

De-

4

Mis-

5

— ♦♦ —

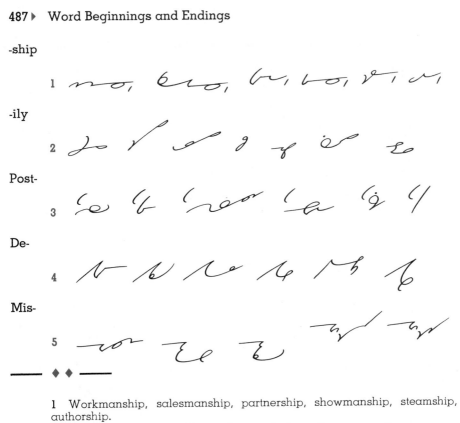

1 Workmanship, salesmanship, partnership, showmanship, steamship, authorship.

2 Family, steadily, readily, easily, noisily, heartily, necessarily.

3 Postcard, postpone, postgraduate, postmaster, posthaste, postage.

4 Department, depend, deplete, depression, delicious, debase.

5 Mistaken, misplace, misspelled, misunderstand, misunderstood.

488 ▸ Geographical Expressions

——— ♦♦ ———

1 St. Charles, St. John, St. Paul, St. Lawrence, St. Louis.

2 Wisconsin, Rhode Island, California, Nebraska, Nevada, Maryland, Massachusetts.

3 Russia, Hungary, Tunis, Iran, Iraq, Africa, Asia.

BUILDING TRANSCRIPTION SKILLS

489 ▸ SPELLING FAMILIES

More double trouble!

Here are additional words that are often misspelled because they contain double consonants.

Double R

ar·range	em·bar·rass	re·ferred
con·ferred	in·ter·rupt	oc·curred

Double N

in·no·va·tion	per·son·nel	ques·tion·naire

Double F

sher·iff	tar·iff	traf·fic

Double S

mis·spell	per·mis·sion	pro·cess
nec·es·sary	pos·ses·sion	suc·cess·ful

490▸ BUSINESS VOCABULARY BUILDER

evolution An unfolding; a process of opening out.

contemporary Living in the same period of time.

custom-made suit A suit made for a specific individual, according to his measurements.

READING AND WRITING PRACTICE

491▸

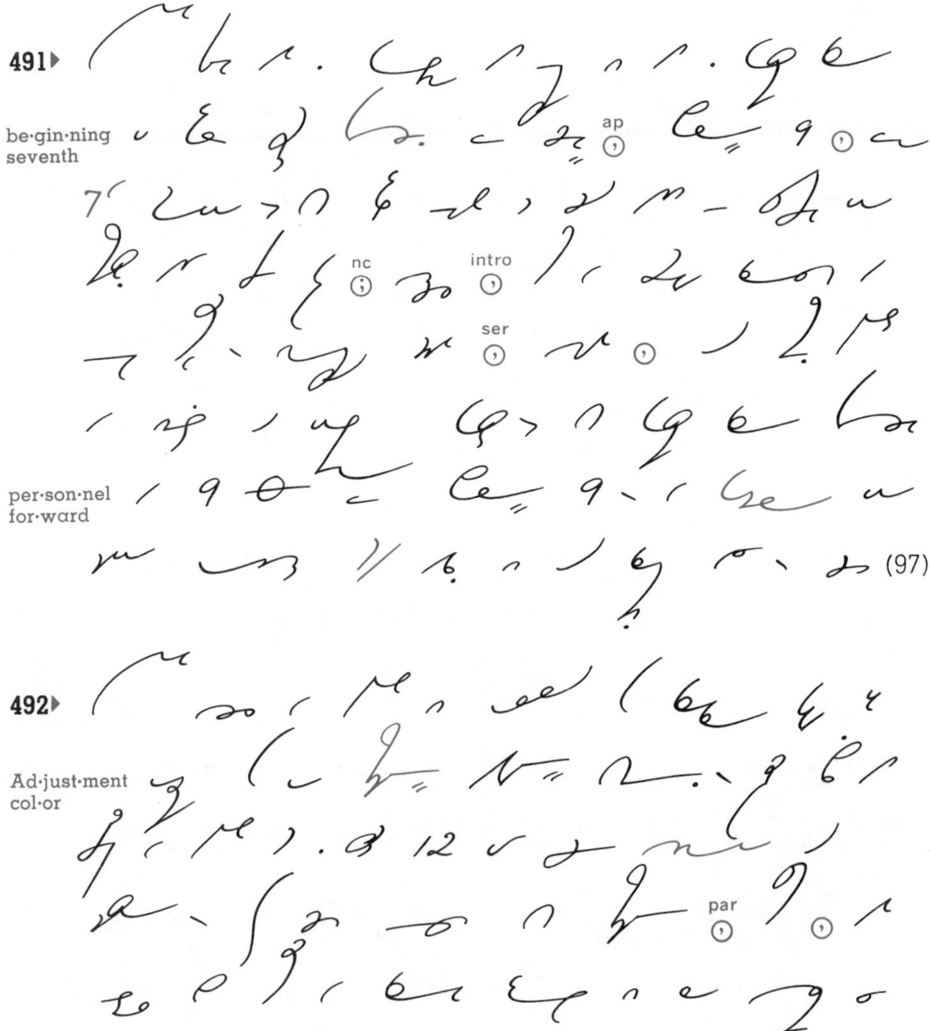

15 intro

60

cel·e·brate
oc·ca·sion

intro

evo·lu·tion
to·day's
vogue

60

par

con·tem·po·rary
de·sign·ers

nc (167)

493 ▸

intro

raise
over·head

ser

ab·sorb
rais·ing

nc intro 15

15

nonr

(146)

494▸ Transcription Quiz • Supply the necessary punctuation and the word missing from the shorthand.

(120)

DEVELOPING WORD-BUILDING POWER

495 ▸ Shorthand Vocabulary Builder

W

1 [shorthand]

Th

2 [shorthand]

Abbreviation

3 [shorthand]

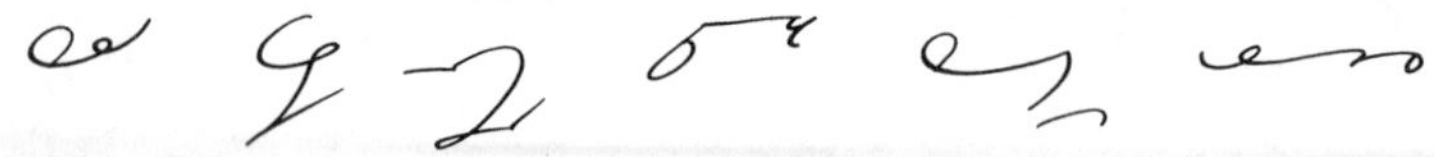

U Expressed by OO

4 [shorthand]

Oi

5 [shorthand]

—— ◆◆ ——

1 Washing, wear, worrying, winter, weekly, wait, wall, wool.

2 Clothes, moths, healthy, thermometer, width, lengthy.

3 Arithmetic, privileged, inconvenienced, atmosphere, alphabetical, reluctantly.

4 Suitable, reduce, producing, numerous, newsstand, absolutely.

5 Lawyers, soiled, appointment, boiler, destroyed.

496 Accuracy Practice—Diphthongs

1 Use, few, human, fuel; out-how, ounce, now, power.
2 Point, toil, oil, royal, boil, soil, annoy.
3 Tie, pile, fine, nice, dine, wire, guide, height.

BUILDING TRANSCRIPTION SKILLS

497 BUSINESS VOCABULARY BUILDER

wardrobe A collection of wearing apparel.
boon A timely benefit or favor.
incredible Difficult to believe.

READING AND WRITING PRACTICE

498 Science and the Traveler

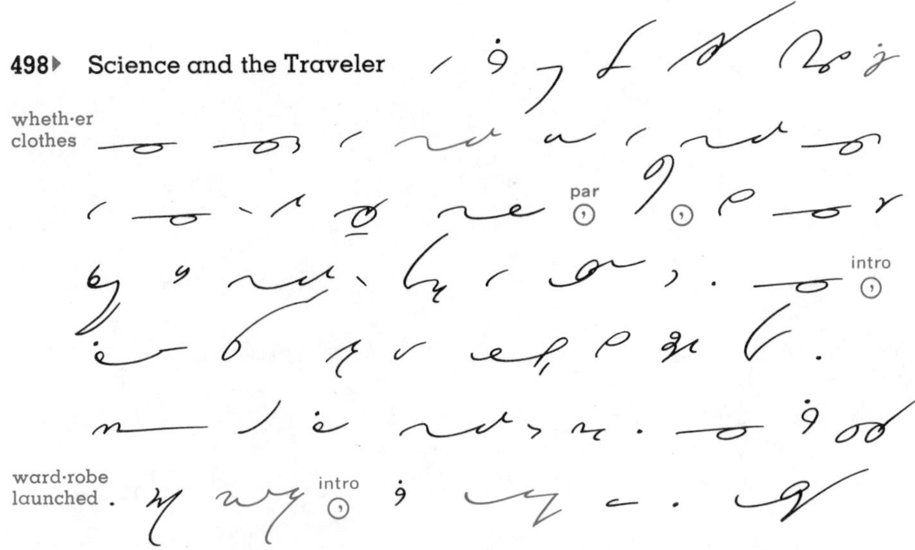

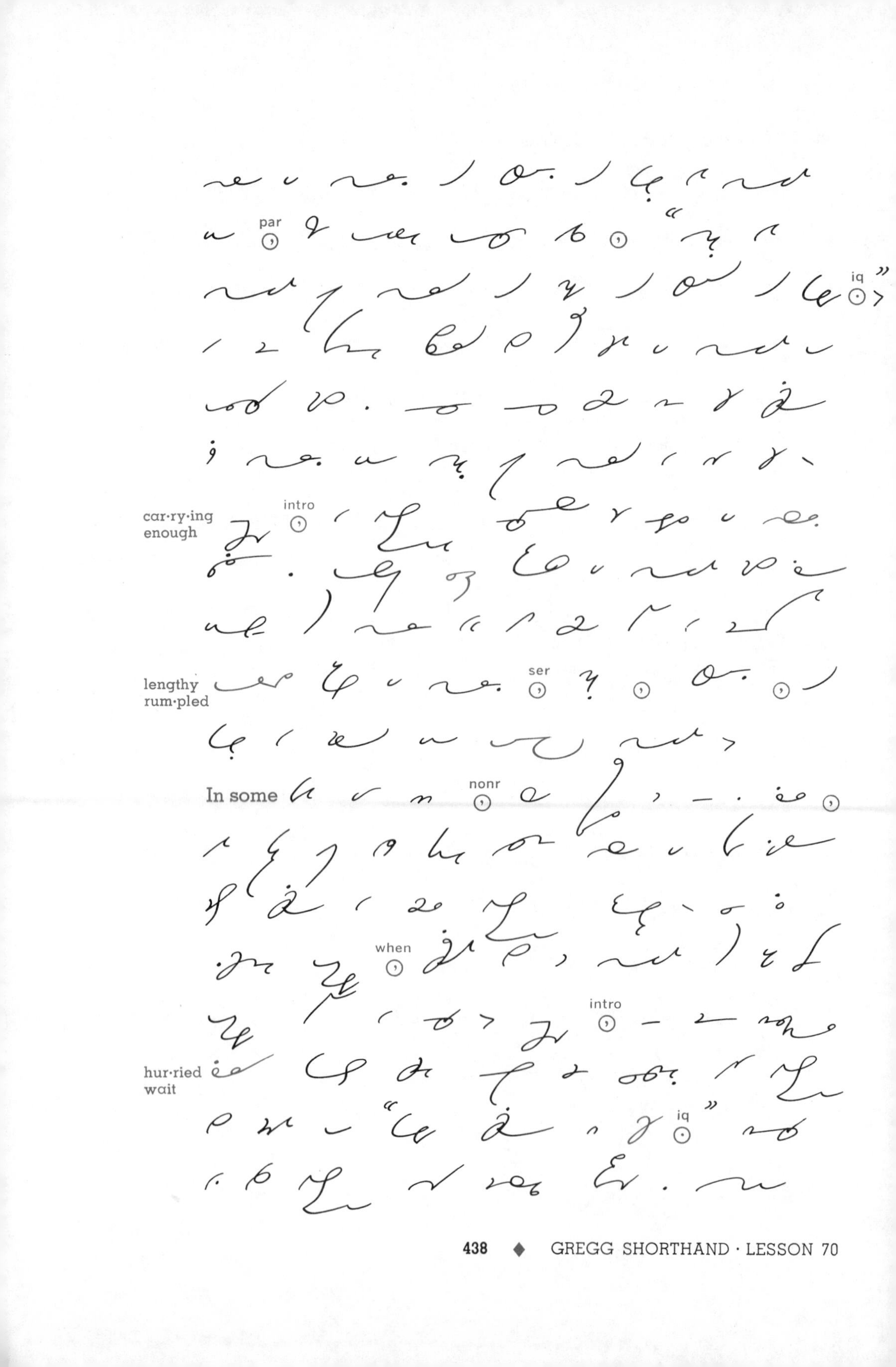

par

iq

intro

carrying enough

ser

lengthy rumpled

In some

nonr

when

intro

hurried wait

iq

conj as

intro

lei·sure·ly par

par

sim·ple
arith·me·tic

par

two-week
hyphenated before noun

Laundry par

cy·cle

lat·ter
un·til

week-long
three-week
hyphenated before noun

par

intro

al·ready

par

Our first

intro

par

nonr

intro

nonr

iq

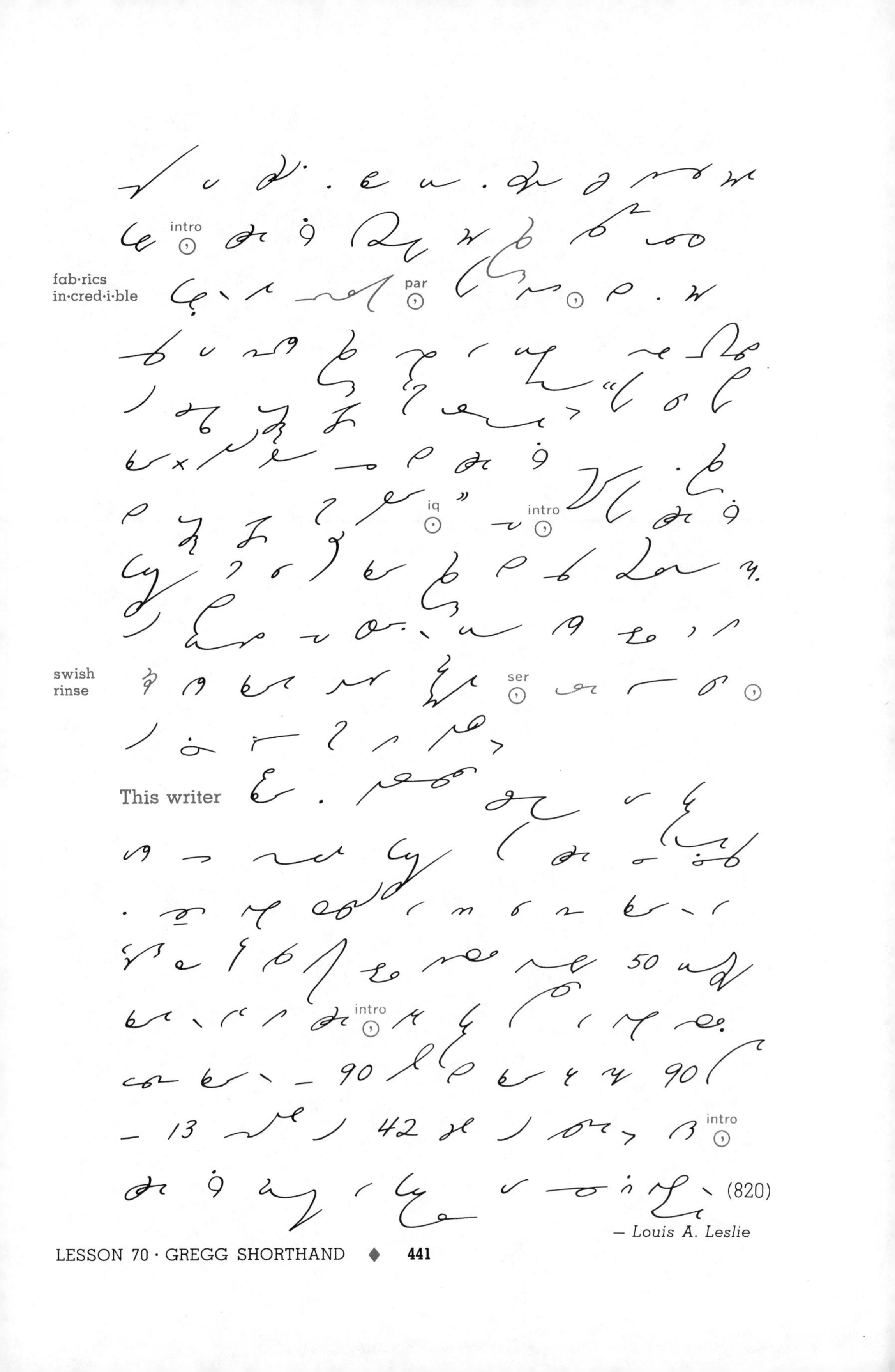

intro

fab·rics
in·cred·i·ble

par

iq

intro

swish
rinse

ser

This writer

50

intro

90 90

13 42

intro

(820)

— *Louis A. Leslie*

CHAPTER FIFTEEN

transportation

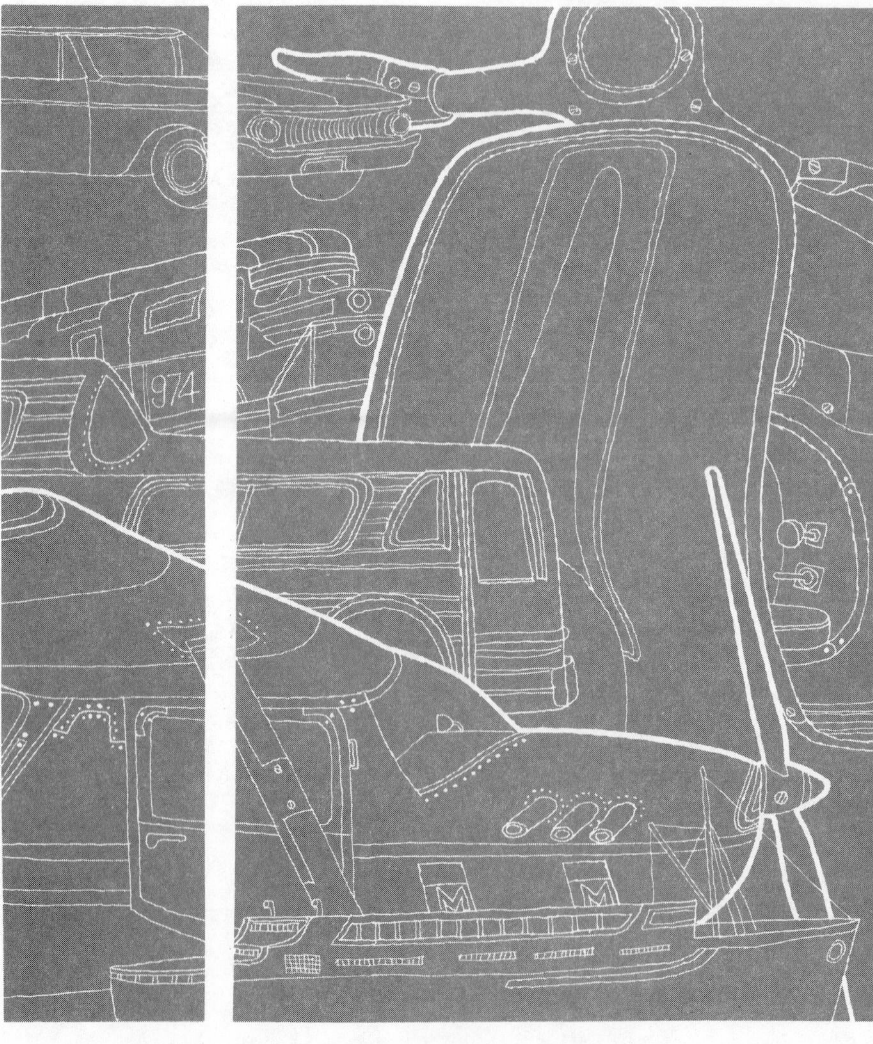

DEVELOPING WORD-BUILDING POWER

499▸ Brief-Forms and Derivatives

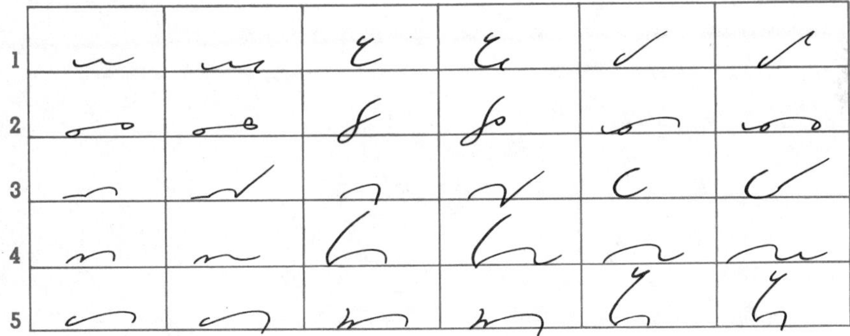

—— ♦♦ ——

1 Railroad, railroads; opportunity, opportunities; order, orders.
2 Immediate, immediately; particular, particularly; regular, regularly.
3 Enclose, enclosed; question, questioned; present, presented.
4 Work, worker; big, bigger; great, greater.
5 Organize, organization; suggest, suggestion; object, objection.

BUILDING TRANSCRIPTION SKILLS

500▸ BUSINESS VOCABULARY BUILDER

debris Rubbish.

agenda A memorandum of things to be done.

proxy A document that empowers one person to act for another.

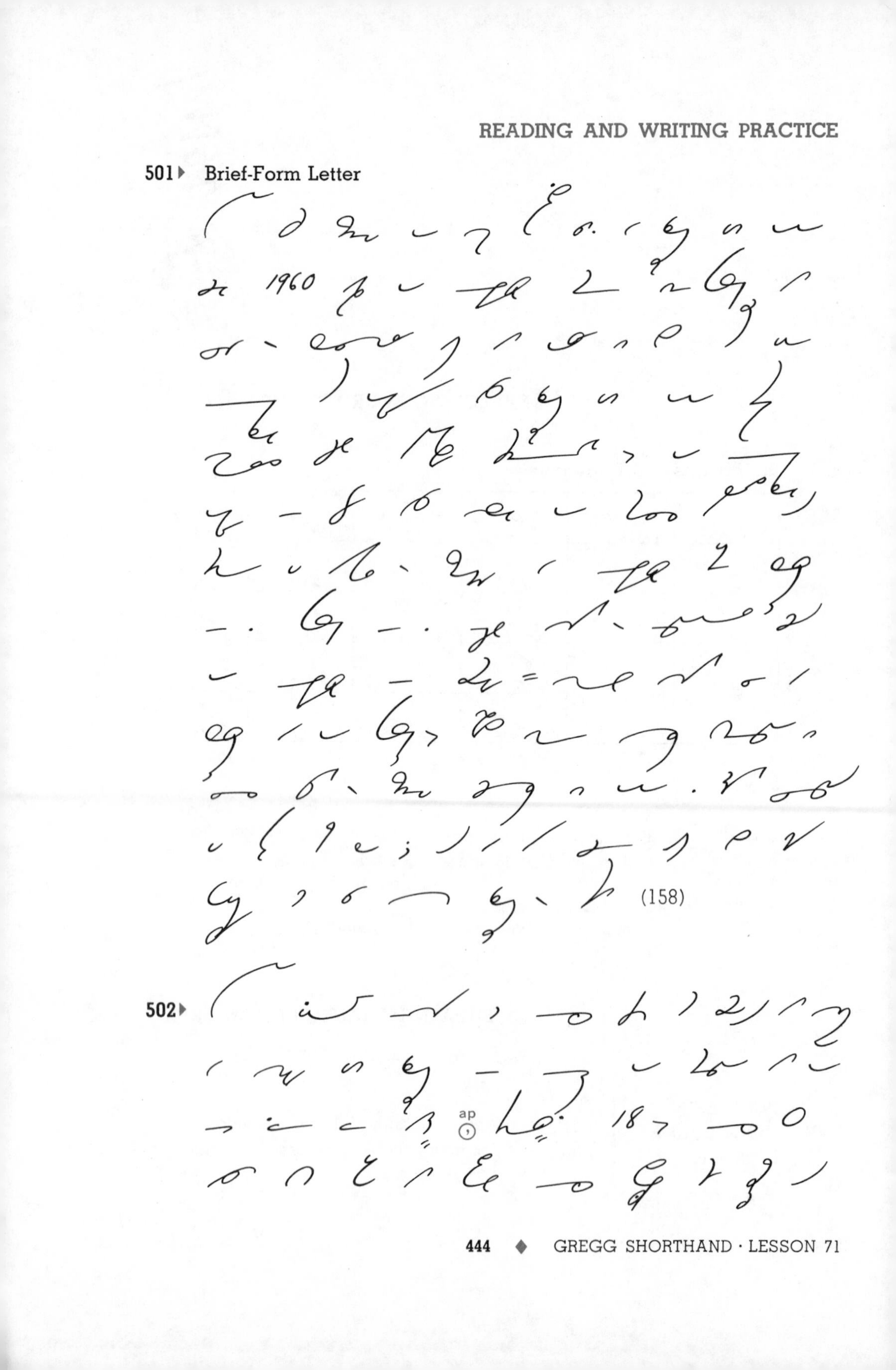

501 Brief-Form Letter

1960

(158)

502

18

ap

thought·ful·ness
mov·ing

when

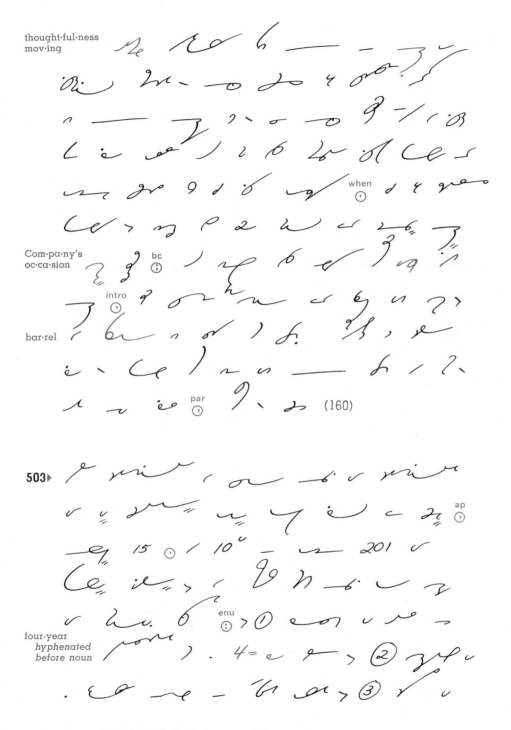

Com·pa·ny's
oc·ca·sion

bc

intro

bar·rel

par

(160)

503

ap

15 10 201

enu

four-year
hyphenated before noun

4=

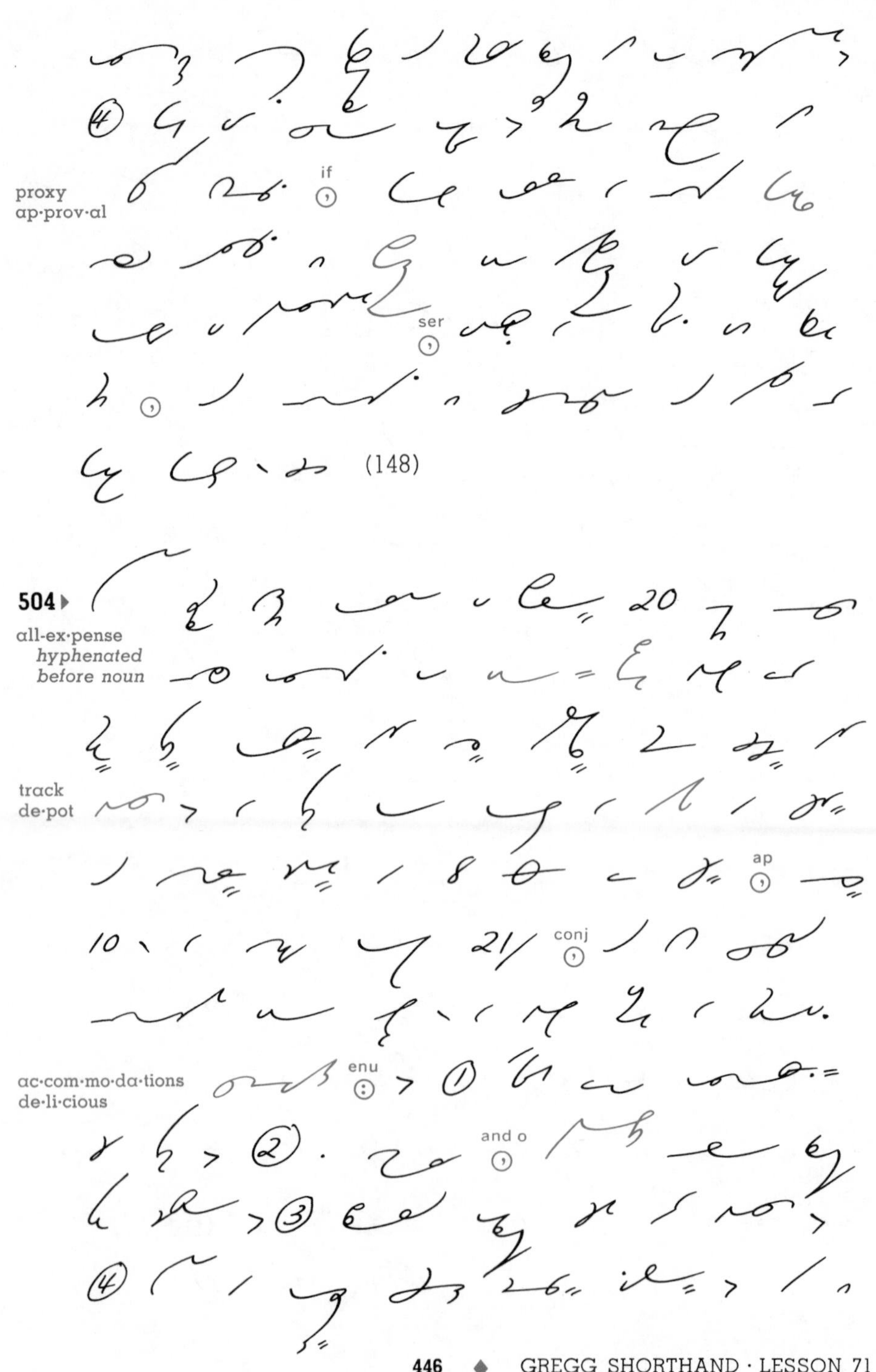

proxy
ap·prov·al
if
ser
(148)
504
all-ex·pense
hyphenated before noun
track
de·pot
ap
conj
ac·com·mo·da·tions
de·li·cious
enu
and o

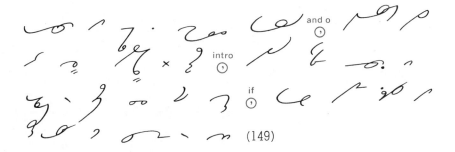

and o

intro

if

(149)

505▸ Transcription Quiz • Supply the necessary punctuation and the missing word.

15

(119)

OFFICE-STYLE DICTATION, 7

Instructions During Dictation *(Concluded)*

The types of instructions to which you should pay very close attention are those that require you to do something *before* you transcribe. In the middle of a letter, for example, the dictator may say, "Send a carbon of this letter to Jones." You must have this information *before* you start transcribing the letter; therefore, when this happens you must record the fact that you are to send Jones a carbon at the *beginning of your notes for that letter*.

You can see the importance of leaving a few blank lines at the head of each letter.

506 ▸ ILLUSTRATION OF OFFICE-STYLE DICTATION

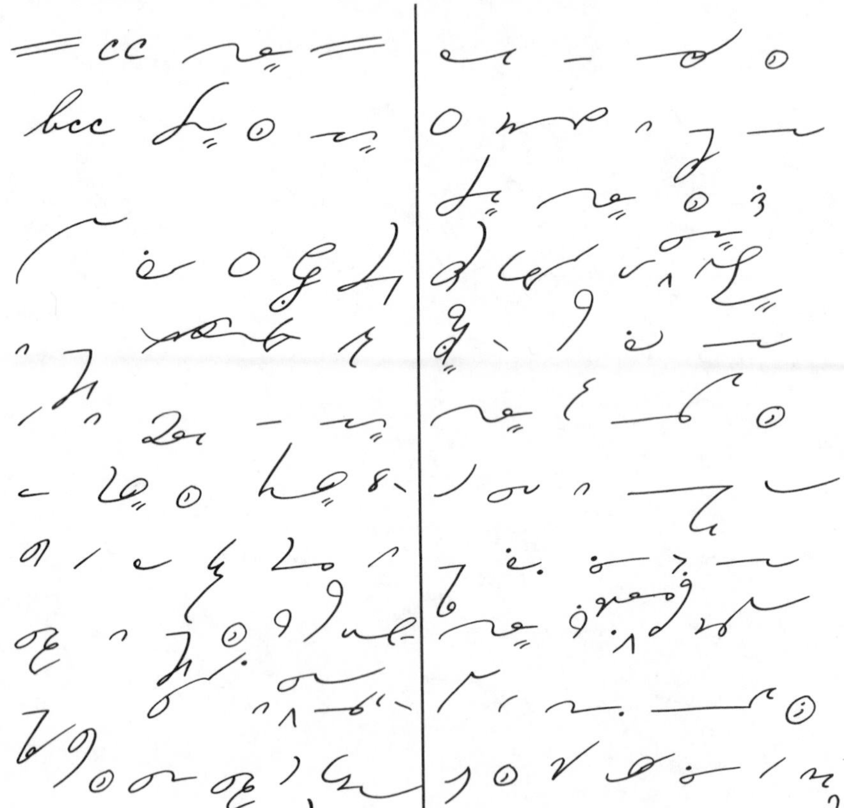

DEVELOPING WORD-BUILDING POWER

507▸ Useful Business-Letter Phrases

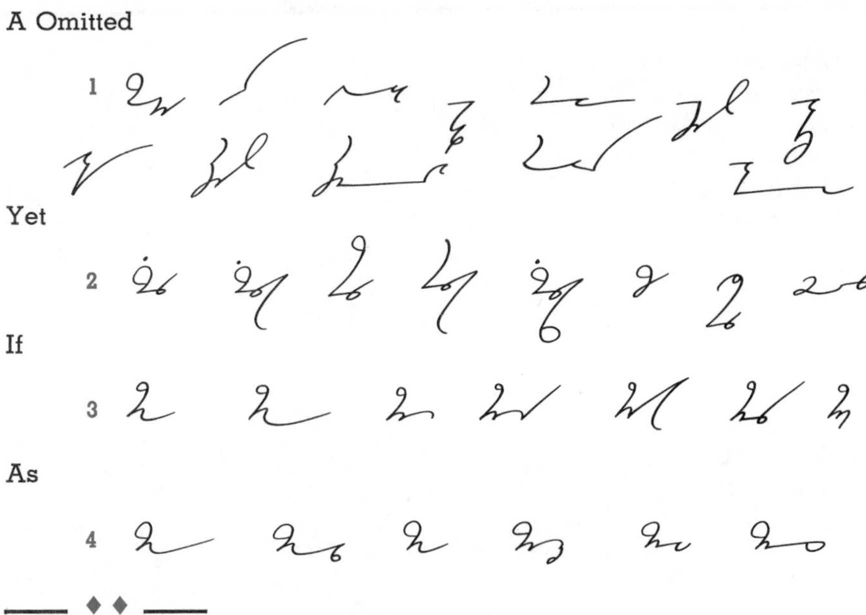

A Omitted

Yet

If

As

1 As a result, at a time, at a loss, in a position, for a moment, in a few days, in such a way, at such a time, for a few days, for a few months, for a long time, in such a manner.

2 Has not yet, has not yet been, I have not yet, have not yet been, has not yet been able, as yet, they have not yet, we are not yet.

3 If you are, if you will, if you can, if you could, if you would be, if you need, if you wish.

4 As you will, as you will see, as you are, as you can see, as you know, as you may.

508 ▸ Frequent Names

1 Shaw, Shea, Simpson, Snyder, Stevens, Stewart, Sullivan, Taylor.
2 Pauline, Phyllis, Rachel, Rebecca, Ruth, Sarah, Sylvia.

BUILDING TRANSCRIPTION SKILLS

509 ▸ LANGUAGE STUDY **in-**: The syllable *in* has several meanings. It is very frequently used as the prefix meaning *not*.

informal Not formal; casual.
inconvenient Not suitable.
incomplete Not finished; partially finished.
incapable Not able.
incompetent Not proficient.
insufficient Not enough; too little.

510 ▸ BUSINESS VOCABULARY BUILDER

irreparable Beyond repair.
knotty Difficult; perplexing; puzzling. (Caution: The shorthand outline for "knotty" is the same as the one for "naughty." Your employer might be quite disturbed if he dictated "knotty problem" and you transcribed "naughty problem"!)
fleet A number of cars or trucks operated by the same individual or company.

READING AND WRITING PRACTICE

511 ▸ Phrase Letter

5 . 4

15

(167)

512 as

in·suf·fi·cient
cap·i·tal
knot·ty

fleet
avail·able

Interoffice Memorandum

TO	F. J. Marvin	FROM	A. R. Smith
LOCATION	Personnel Department	LOCATION	Foreign Department
SUBJECT	Job Replacement	DATE	May 20, 19--

My secretary, Miss Helen A. Hicks, has just informed me that she is to be married on June 15. She plans to leave on June 1.

If it is possible, I should like to get someone to fill the vacancy immediately, so that Miss Hicks can help in the training of the new girl.

As you know, most of my correspondence is with customers in South and Central America. Consequently, it would be a great help to me if you could find a girl who has some degree of proficiency in Spanish.

I shall be in Cleveland on May 21 and 22, but I shall be back on the morning of May 23. I shall, therefore, be able to interview any girls you send me any time after May 22.

A. R. S.

ARS:HH

Interoffice Memorandum

bad·ly needed
no noun,
no hyphen

when

of·fered
ma·jor

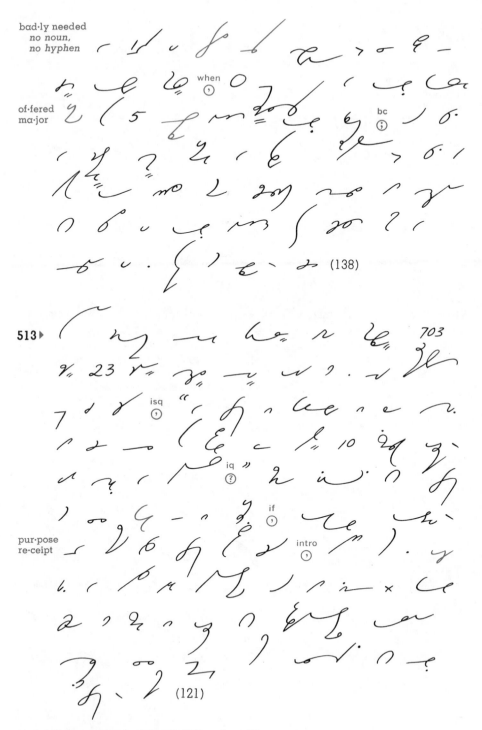

bc

(138)

513 703

23

isq

10

iq

if

pur·pose
re·ceipt

intro

(121)

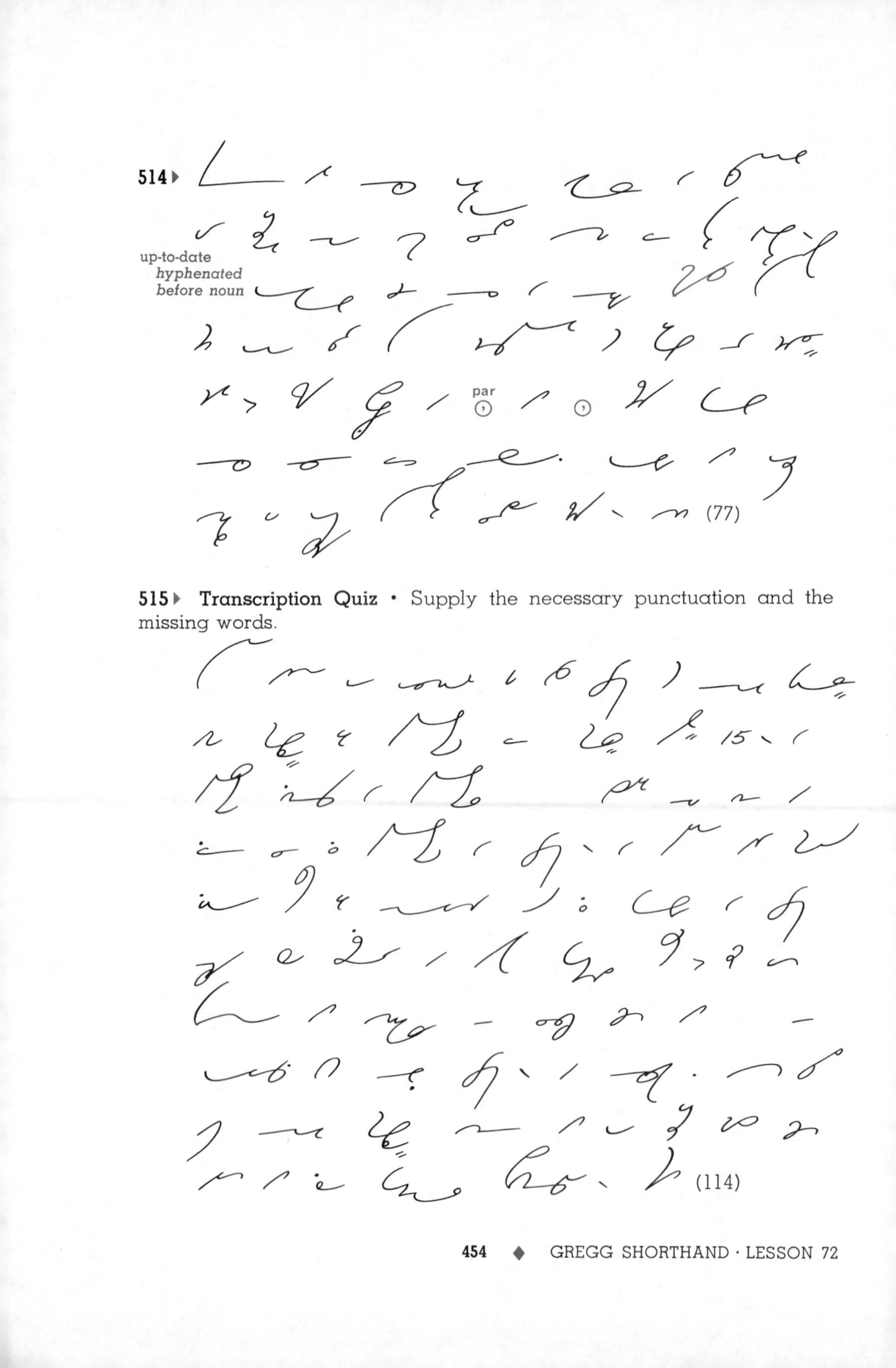

514 ▸

up-to-date *hyphenated before noun*

par

(77)

515 ▸ **Transcription Quiz** • Supply the necessary punctuation and the missing words.

15

(114)

DEVELOPING WORD-BUILDING POWER

516 ▸ Word Families

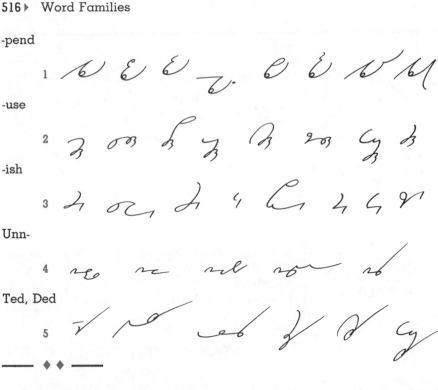

-pend

1

-use

2

-ish

3

Unn-

4

Ted, Ded

5

—— ◆◆ ——

1 Depend, expend, spend, impending, append, suspend, dependent, dependable.

2 Confuse, accuse, abuse, refuse, defuse, excuse, profuse, fuse.

3 Finish, accomplish, vanish, selfish, abolish, furnish, punish, astonish.

4 Unnecessary, unknown, unnoticed, unnatural, unneeded.

5 Interested, delighted, limited, visited, divided, provided.

BUILDING TRANSCRIPTION SKILLS

517 ▸ SIMILAR-WORDS DRILL   past, passed

past *(noun)* A former time. (*Past* is also used as an adjective.)

The program has been very successful in the past.

Please take care of your past-due account.

passed Moved along; went by; transferred.

I passed him on the street.

Before many days had passed, he took care of his account.

I passed the report on to him.

518 ▸ BUSINESS VOCABULARY BUILDER

10 Downing Street The home of the Prime Minister of England.

disembark Get off.

itinerary An outline of travel routes.

READING AND WRITING PRACTICE

519 ▸

spon·sor·ing
Eu·rope

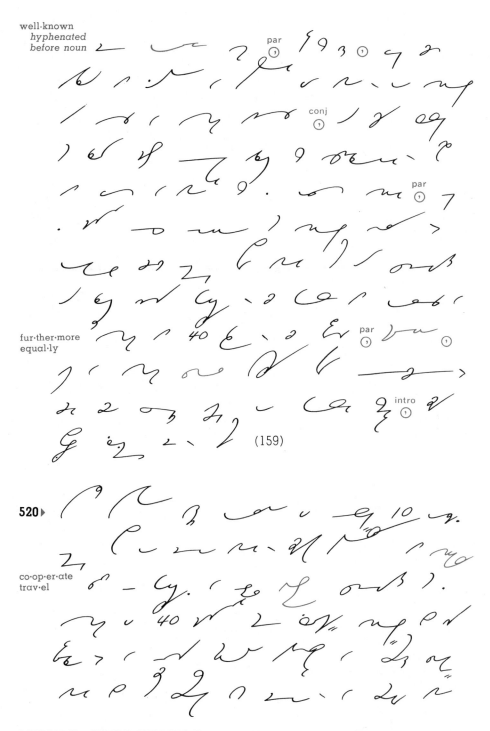

well-known
hyphenated before noun

par

conj

par

fur·ther·more
equal·ly

par

intro

(159)

520

co·op·er·ate
trav·el

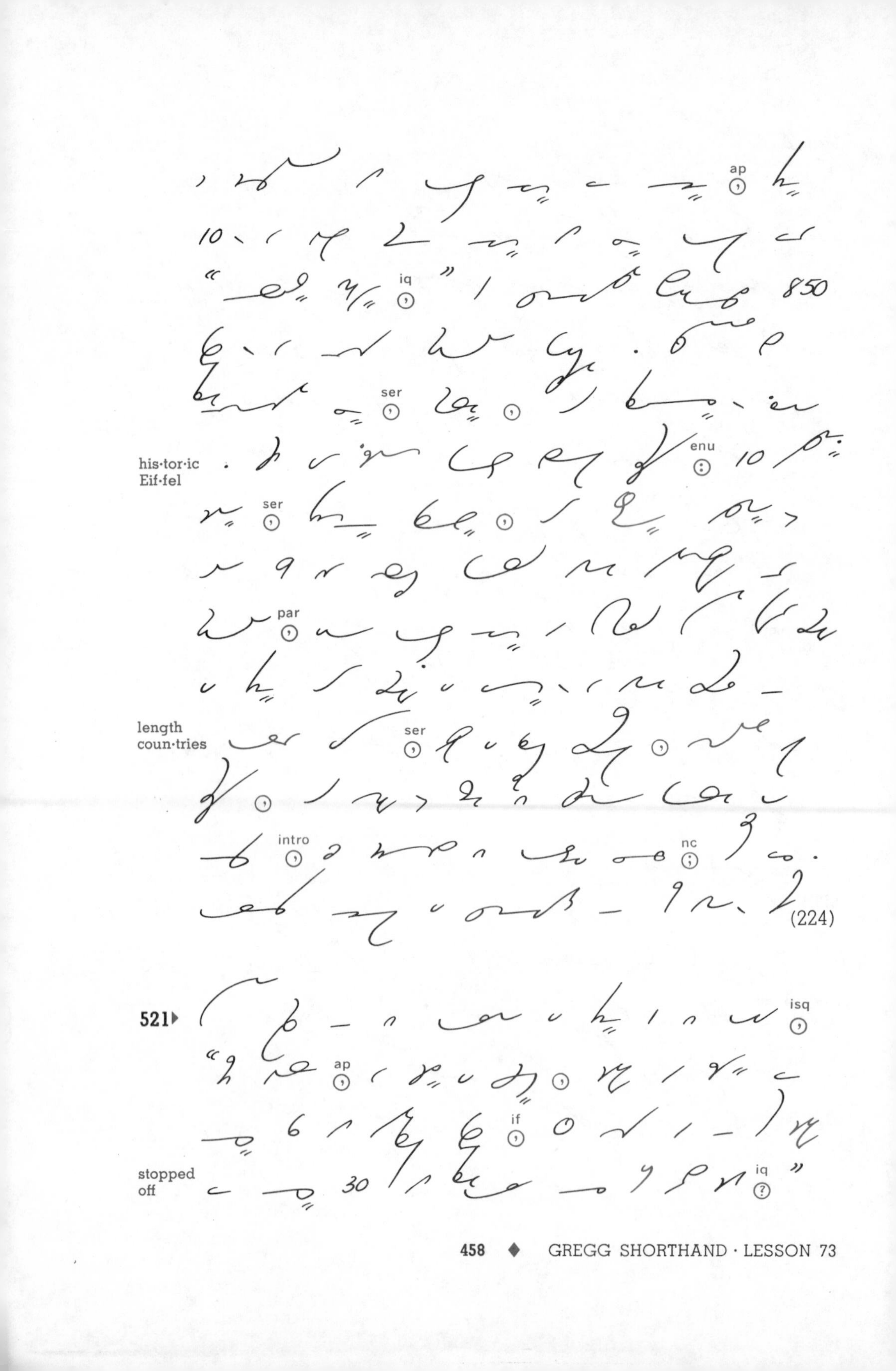

ap

10 850

iq

ser

his·tor·ic
Eif·fel

enu 10

ser

par

length
coun·tries

ser

intro

nc

(224)

521▸

isq

ap

if

stopped
off

30

iq

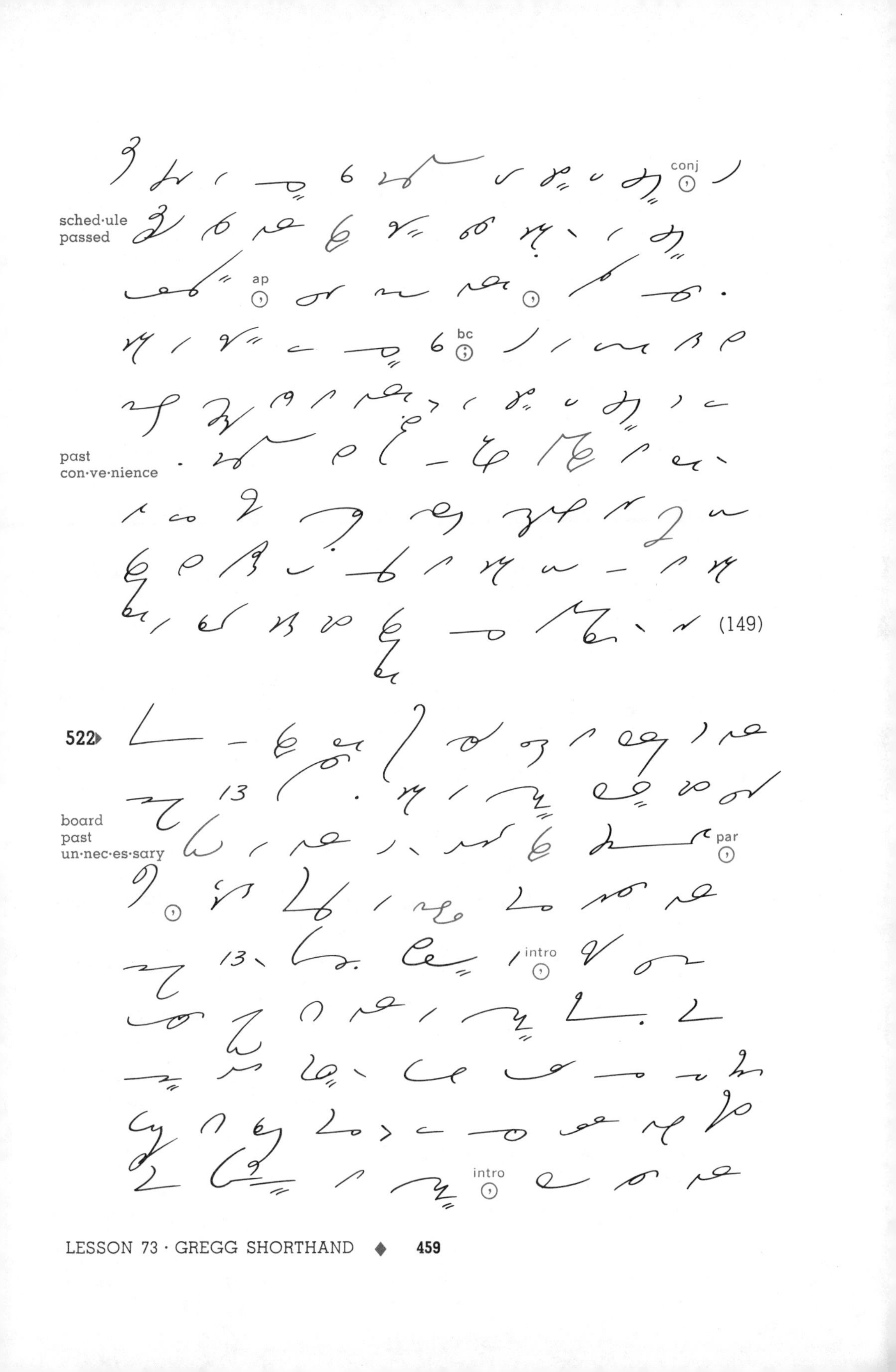

conj

sched·ule
passed

ap

bc

past
con·ve·nience

(149)

522

13

board
past
un·nec·es·sary

par

13

intro

intro

cour·te·ous
ex·cel·lent

(143)

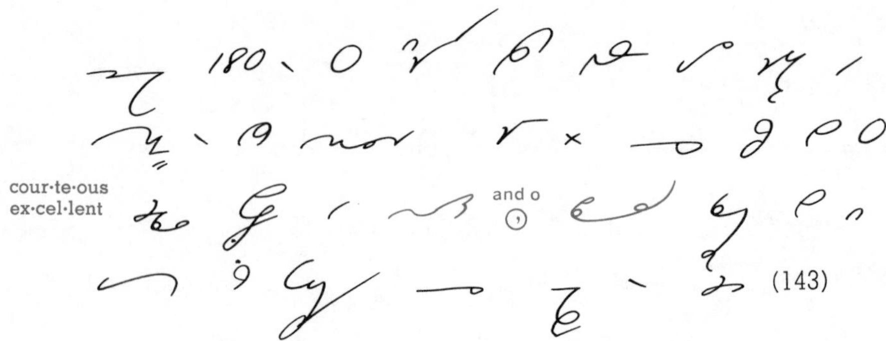

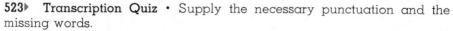

523▸ Transcription Quiz • Supply the necessary punctuation and the missing words.

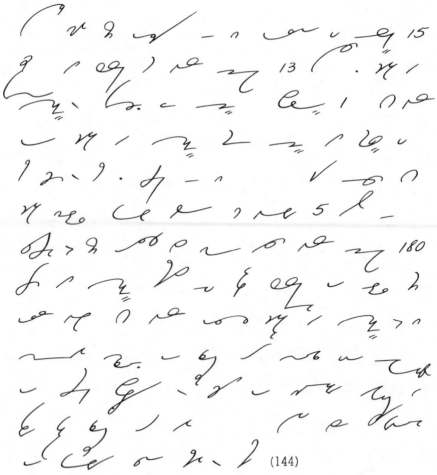

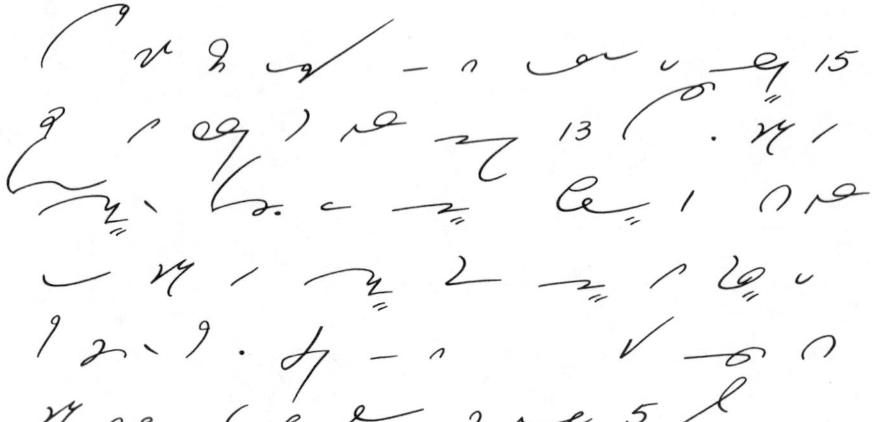

(144)

DEVELOPING WORD-BUILDING POWER

524 Word Beginnings and Endings

Trans-

1

Inter-

2

Sub-

3

For, Fore

4

-ful

5

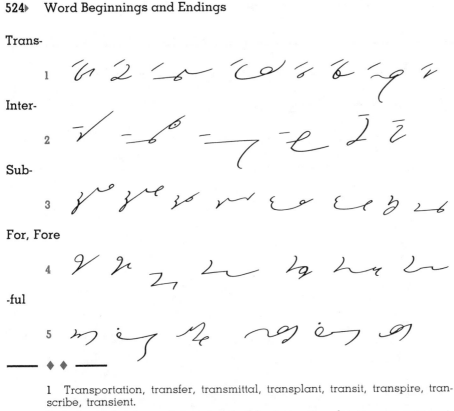

1 Transportation, transfer, transmittal, transplant, transit, transpire, transcribe, transient.

2 Interested, intermediate, interminable, international, intervene, interrupt.

3 Subsidiary, subsidiaries, substitute, subtract, sublet, sublease, subway, submit.

4 Afford, efforts, information, formal, forecast, foreclose, forerunner.

5 Successful, helpful, thoughtfulness, gratefully, harmful, rightful.

525 Geographical Expressions

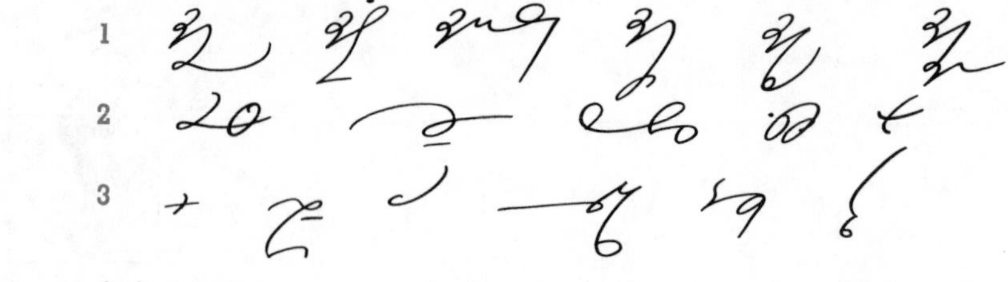

1 Westfield, West Haven, West Orange, Westview, West Bend, Westchester.

2 Philippine Islands, Guam, Alaska, Hawaii, Puerto Rico.

3 Nova Scotia, Quebec, Ontario, Manitoba, Saskatchewan, British Columbia.

BUILDING TRANSCRIPTION SKILLS

526 SPELLING FAMILIES -el, -al, -le

Always think twice when you start to transcribe a word that ends with the sound of *l;* the word may be spelled *-el, -al,* or *-le.*

When in doubt, look it up!

Words Ending in -el

an·gel	la·bel	pan·el
bar·rel	trav·el	par·cel
can·cel	nick·el	mod·el

Words Ending in -al

fi·nal	met·al	sig·nal
lo·cal	in·for·mal	vi·tal
scan·dal	le·gal	med·al

Words Ending in -le

an·gle	mid·dle	set·tle
cir·cle	sim·ple	sprin·kle
gam·ble	sam·ple	un·cle
gen·tle	chuck·le	han·dle

527 BUSINESS VOCABULARY BUILDER

roomette A small private single bedroom in a Pullman car.

effects (noun) Goods, possessions.

subsidiaries Companies owned by other companies that own at least a majority of its shares.

READING AND WRITING PRACTICE

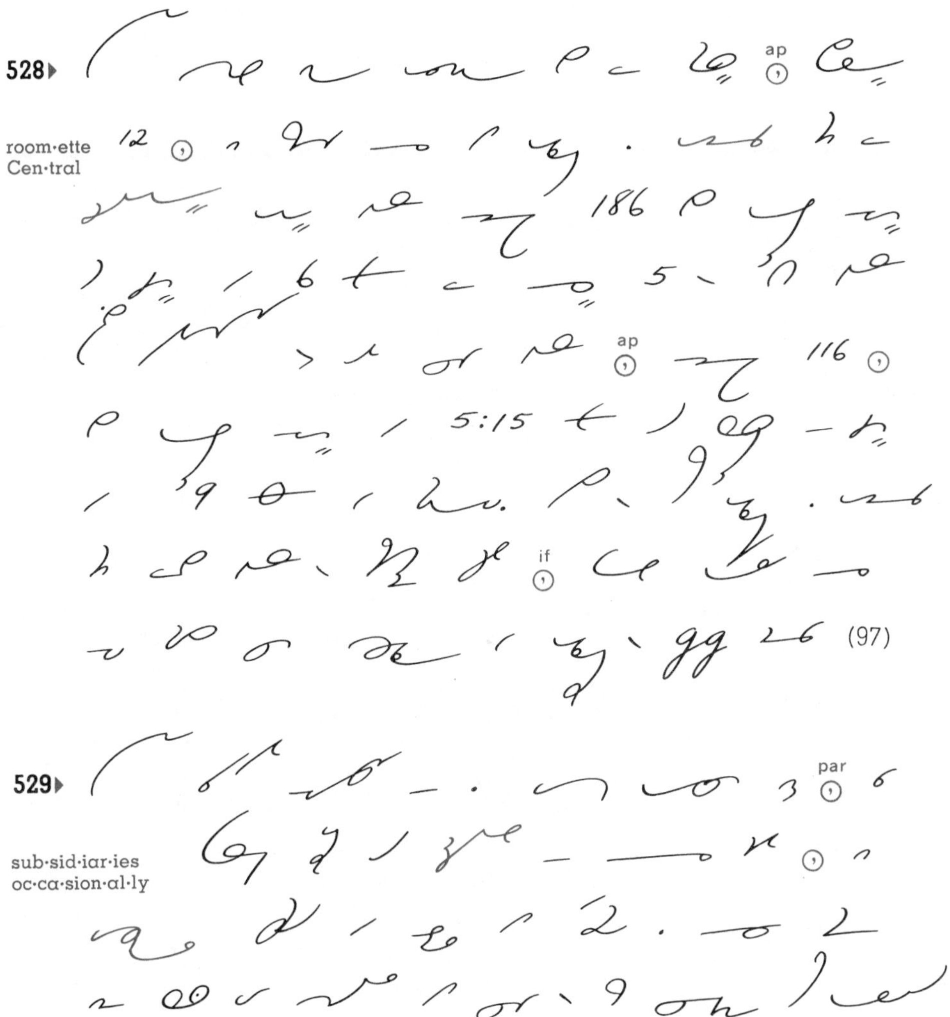

ex·pe·ri·ence
ex·pen·sive

as

par

bc

suit·able
min·i·mum

il

when

enu

trans·ferred
set·tle

intro

bc

intro

ef·fects
ef·fi·cient·ly

ser

intro

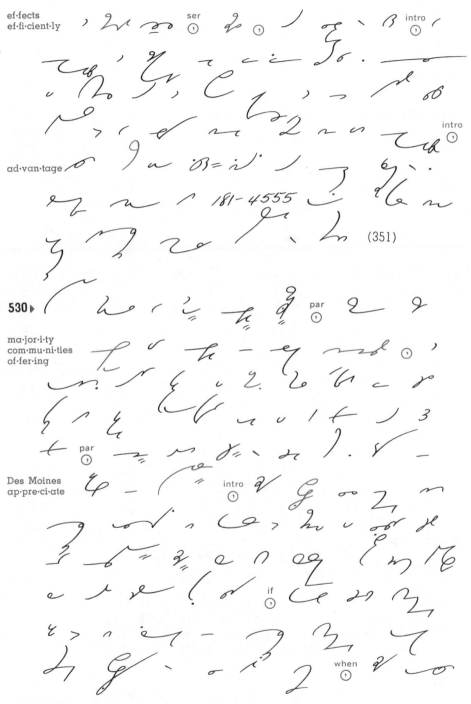

intro

ad·van·tage

181-4555

(351)

530

par

ma·jor·i·ty
com·mu·ni·ties
of·fer·ing

par

Des Moines
ap·pre·ci·ate

intro

if

when

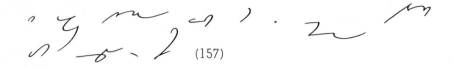

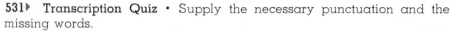

(157)

531▸ Transcription Quiz • Supply the necessary punctuation and the missing words.

(122)

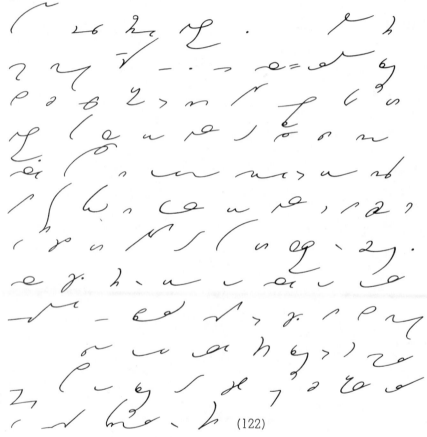

▸ *In meeting the public, your best approach is a polite, interested manner; and your best technique is to smile. A smile has an amazing effect, even over the phone.*

DEVELOPING WORD-BUILDING POWER

532 Shorthand Vocabulary Builder

Def, Dev, etc.

1

-ure

2

-tition, etc.

3

Mem

4

-quire

5

1 Difference, defense, devote, division, individual, dividend.

2 Culture, nature, failure, stature, departure, temperature.

3 Vaccination, recommendation, transportation, information, stationed, commissioner.

4 Memories, remember, memorandum, member, membership.

5 Inquire, require, requirement, acquire, acquirement, esquire.

533▸ Accuracy Practice—Similar Outlines

1 You-your, this, way, say, we, see, you will, it will, you are.
2 They, to me, that, with, when, yet, I think, I can, he can.

BUILDING TRANSCRIPTION SKILLS

534▸ BUSINESS VOCABULARY BUILDER

carriers Persons or companies in the transportation business.

embassies The offices or residences of ambassadors.

literature Any kind of printed advertising matter, such as booklets, circulars, brochures, etc.

READING AND WRITING PRACTICE

535▸ Travel Know-How

conj

par

par

ig·no·rance
car·ri·ers
phase

wear
tear

conj

enu

ser

sce·nic
com·pa·nies

Travel agents

em·bas·sies
con·sul·ar

for·eign

if

bar·ri·er
it's

④

conj

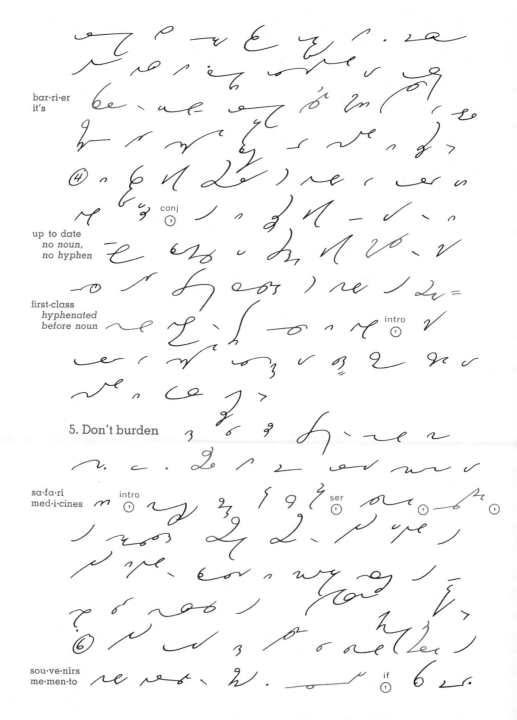

up to date
no noun, no hyphen

first-class
hyphenated before noun

intro

5. Don't burden

sa·fa·ri
med·i·cines

intro

ser

⑥

sou·ve·nirs
me·men·to

if

conj

nc

over·tire
stren·u·ous

conj

8. Keep your

best·made
hyphenated before noun

guid·ance
as·sis·tance

when

par

nonr

per·mits
doc·u·ments

ser

if

(671) — *Frances G. Knight*

CHAPTER SIXTEEN

travel

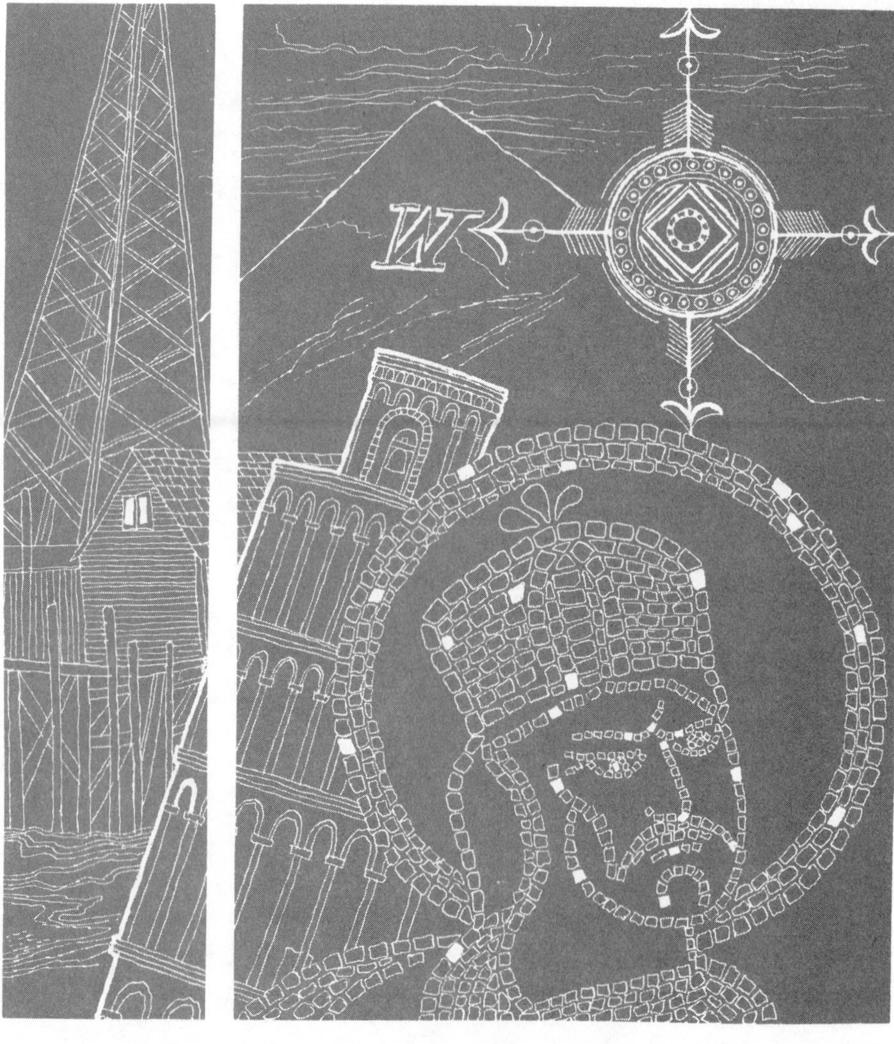

DEVELOPING WORD-BUILDING POWER

536 ▸ Brief Forms and Derivatives

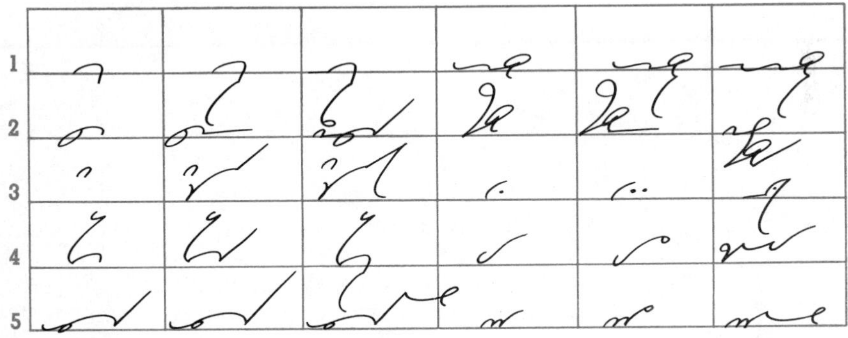

— ♦♦ —

1 Question, questionable, unquestionably; recognize, recognizable, unrecognizable.

2 Acknowledge, acknowledgment, unacknowledged; advertise, advertisement, unadvertised.

3 Under, understand, understandable; think, thinking, unthinkable.

4 Object, objected, objectionable; ordinary, ordinarily, extraordinary.

5 Regard, regarded, regardless; worth, worthy, worthless.

BUILDING TRANSCRIPTION SKILLS

537 ▸ BUSINESS VOCABULARY BUILDER

exposition A public exhibition or show.

en route On the way.

Scandinavian countries Norway, Sweden, Denmark, Iceland, and Finland.

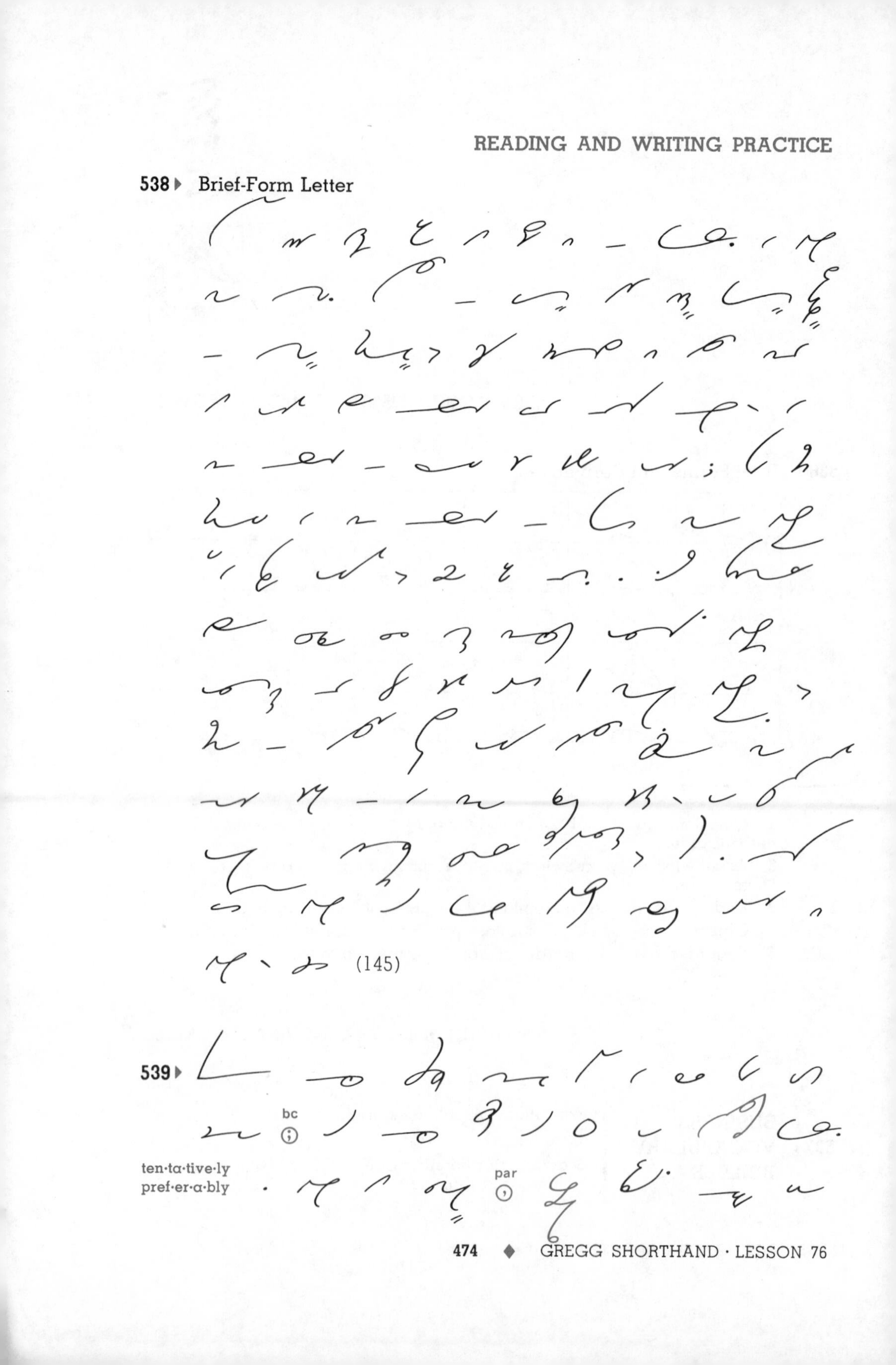

538 ▸ Brief-Form Letter

(145)

539 ▸

bc

ten·ta·tive·ly
pref·er·a·bly

par

ser

ser

spe·cial·izes
guided

de·scrip·tion
itin·er·ary

enu

ser

lodg·ing
wheth·er
fi·nanc·ing

(167)

540

in·quir·ing
Scan·di·na·vian

il

ser

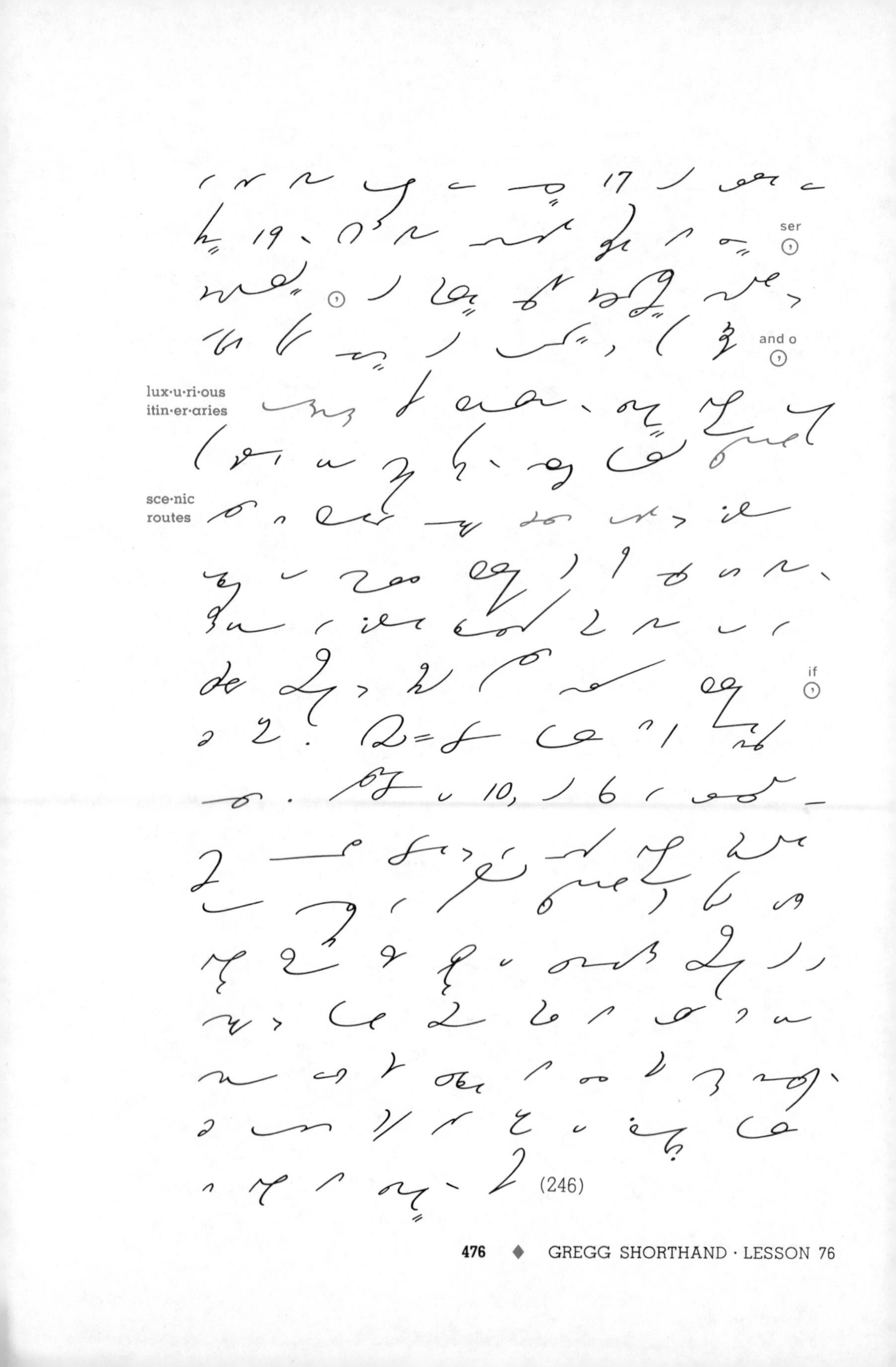

ser

and o

lux·u·ri·ous
itin·er·aries

sce·nic
routes

if

(246)

541 ▸ **Transcription Quiz** • Supply the necessary punctuation and the words omitted from the shorthand.

(153)

▸ *Many young people who have special talents or interest in drama, music, art, journalism, politics, and so on have found that secretarial training works almost like magic in gaining entrance to these areas of work.*—John Robert Gregg

Extensive Changes

Most dictators make only an occasional change in their dictation. Some, however, make so many changes that it is advisable to write in only one column of the notebook, leaving the second column for insertions or changes.

542▸ ILLUSTRATION OF OFFICE-STYLE DICTATION

BUILDING PHRASING SKILL

543 ▸ Useful Business-Letter Phrases

Many

1

Let Us

2

And

3

Salutations and Closings

4

— ◆◆ —

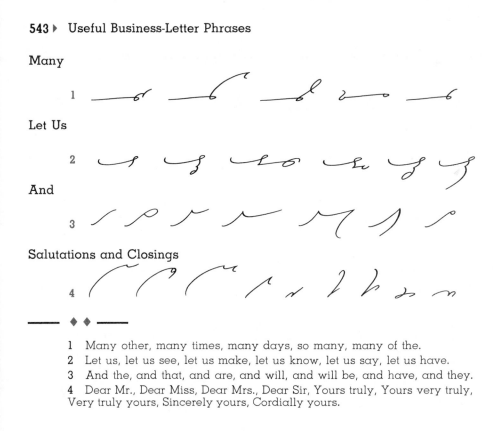

1 Many other, many times, many days, so many, many of the.
2 Let us, let us see, let us make, let us know, let us say, let us have.
3 And the, and that, and are, and will, and will be, and have, and they.
4 Dear Mr., Dear Miss, Dear Mrs., Dear Sir, Yours truly, Yours very truly, Very truly yours, Sincerely yours, Cordially yours.

544 ▸ Frequent Names

1

2

1 Thomas, Thompson, Thomson, Turner, Walker, Walsh.
2 Samuel, Stephen, Vincent, Walter, William.

BUILDING TRANSCRIPTION SKILLS

545 LANGUAGE STUDY **inter-:** *Between; among; in the midst.*

international Between or among nations.

interview A face-to-face meeting; in business, a consultation between an employer and a prospective employee.

interrupt To break into or between.

intercollegiate Between or among colleges.

intervene To come in between.

intermediate Coming or done between.

546 BUSINESS VOCABULARY BUILDER

tracer An inquiry about an article that has been lost.

wistfully Hopefully; wishfully.

amiable Having a pleasant disposition; friendly.

rigid Unyielding; inflexible.

READING AND WRITING PRACTICE

547 Phrase Letter

280

(108)

548 if

ad·ver·tise·ments
wist·ful·ly

isq

conj iq

par

ad·ven·ture
re·al·i·ty

bud·get
re·al·is·ti·cal·ly

par

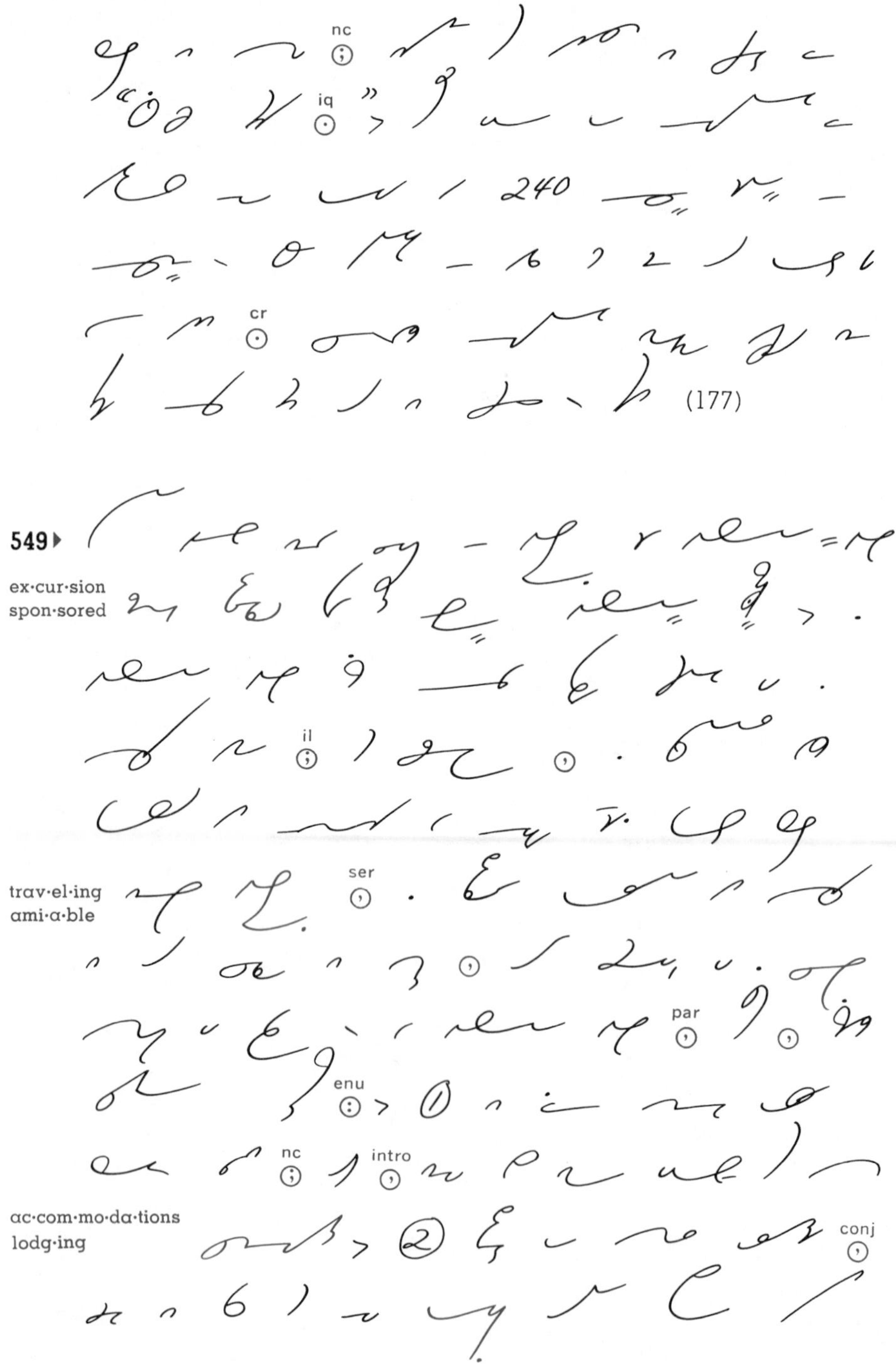
nc
iq
240
cr
(177)
549
ex·cur·sion
spon·sored
il
trav·el·ing
ami·a·ble
ser
par
enu
nc
intro
ac·com·mo·da·tions
lodg·ing
conj

③

au·then·tic
neigh·bor·ly

ser

④

when

rig·id
in·ter·rupt
pur·sue

ilq

faint
heart

intro

par

knowl·edge
ca·su·al

iq

when

par

(324)

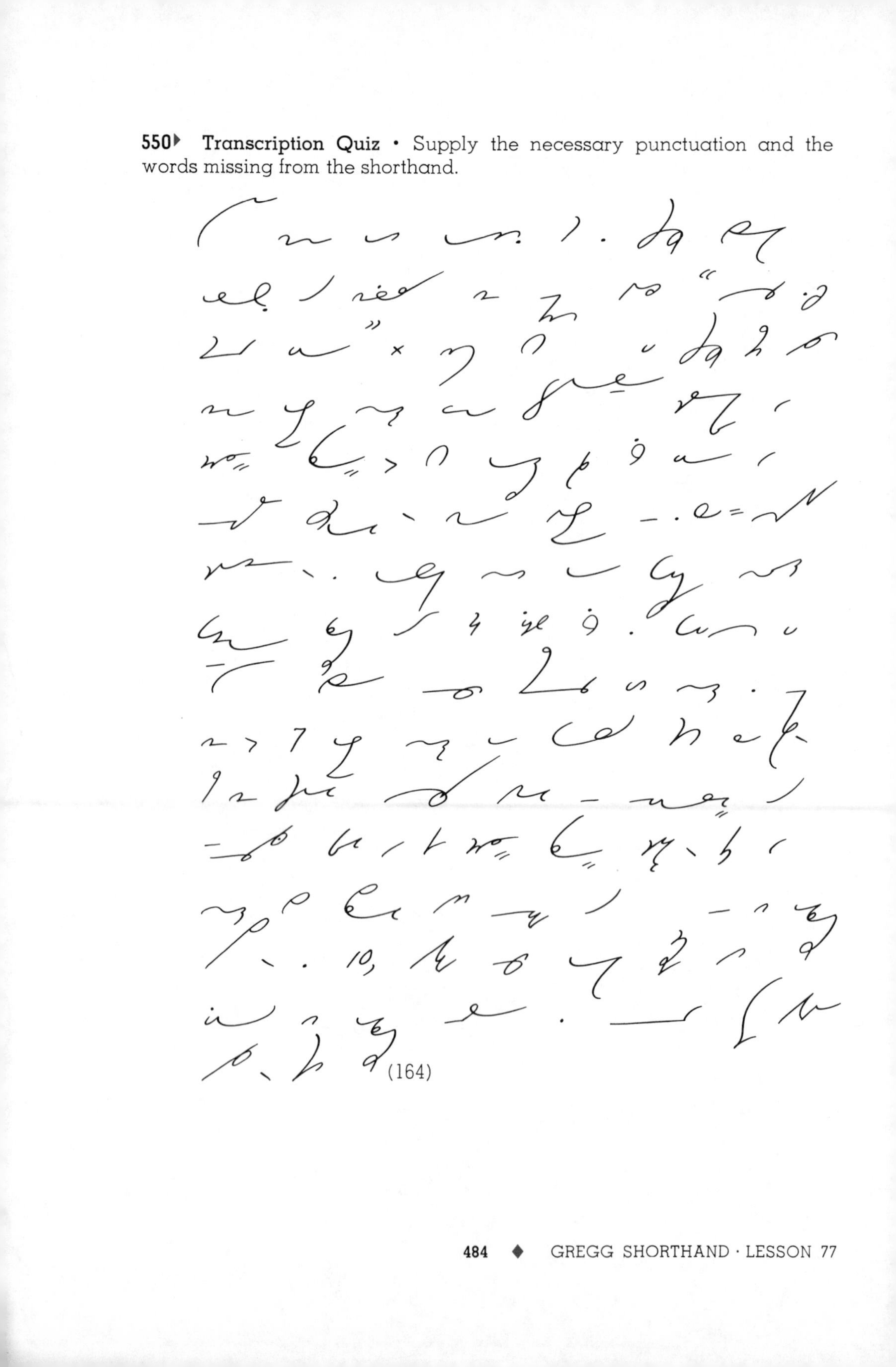

550▸ Transcription Quiz • Supply the necessary punctuation and the words missing from the shorthand.

(164)

DEVELOPING WORD-BUILDING POWER

551 ▸ Word Families

-tic

1

-ery

2

-nion

3

-rt

4

-tion

5

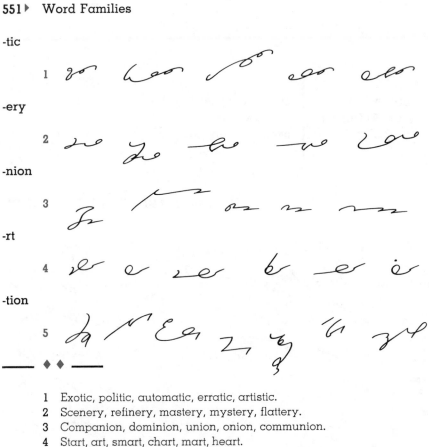

1 Exotic, politic, automatic, erratic, artistic.
2 Scenery, refinery, mastery, mystery, flattery.
3 Companion, dominion, union, onion, communion.
4 Start, art, smart, chart, mart, heart.
5 Vacation, destination, explanation, information, reservations, transportation, consideration.

BUILDING TRANSCRIPTION SKILLS

552▸ SIMILAR-WORDS DRILL **aboard, abroad**

aboard On, or within, a ship, railroad car, or passenger vehicle.

Travel aboard our vessels is a wonderful experience.

abroad Outside the United States.

While he was abroad, he visited France and England.

553▸ BUSINESS VOCABULARY BUILDER

exotic Excitingly different.
gratuities Tips.
genial Kindly; friendly.

READING AND WRITING PRACTICE

554▸

abroad
ac·tu·al·ly

far·away
ex·ot·ic

bc

gra·tu·ities ser

when

par

ser

com·pan·ions
fas·ci·nat·ing

conj

choose
rough

intro

ex·pe·ri·enc·ing when

ser

if

first class
no noun,
no hyphen

bane
bud·get

par

ser

intro

(348)

555

intro

ca·noe·ing
an·nu·al

sce·nery
leaves

intro

nonr

as

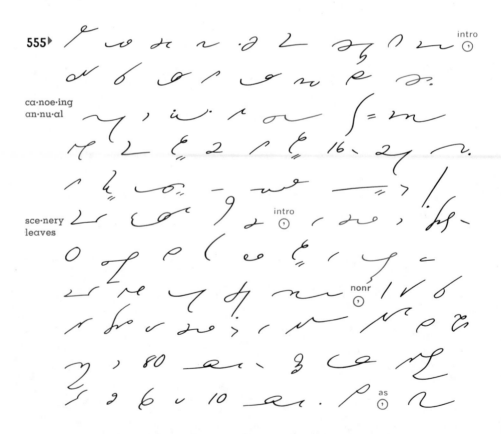

556 ▸ Transcription Quiz • Supply the necessary punctuation and the word missing from the shorthand.

(104)

PAGE FROM A SECRETARY'S NOTEBOOK

On page 491 you will find a page from an efficient secretary's notebook. Let us examine some of the techniques that she used when she wrote that page.

NOTE: The numbers of the following paragraphs correspond to the encircled numbers on page 491.

1▸ She indicated the end of a letter with a double line.

2▸ She left several blank spaces before she started the next letter. In these spaces she writes any instructions she may receive from her dictator either during or after the dictation.

3▸ Her employer inserted a word in a sentence he had previously dictated. She indicated the point of the insertion with a caret and wrote the word directly above it.

4▸ Her employer dictated the punctuation he wanted in this sentence. She always inserts, in a circle, any punctuation that her employer dictates.

5▸ She indicated with a heavy colored pencil mark down the side of this letter that the letter is to be transcribed first, after her employer completes his dictation. She always has a colored pencil handy for this purpose.

6▸ She always places the date at the bottom of the page. (In the Gregg Official Shorthand Notebook a place is provided for the date.)

7▸ This shorthand outline represents the expression "Basic College Accounting," an expression that occurs again and again in her dictation. She has devised a timesaving shortcut for it.

8▸ Her employer spelled out this name for her. Whenever he spells a name or a word for her, she writes the name or word in longhand in her notes.

9▸ Her employer decided to make a long insertion in a paragraph that he had already dictated. She placed a large *a* at the point of the insertion.

10▸ She drew a double line after the last sentence that had been dictated.

11▸ She wrote a large *a* underneath the double line and wrote the new material to be inserted.

12▸ She drew another double line to indicate the end of the insertion and continued taking the rest of the dictation.

13▸ Her employer decided to transpose two adjectives because he felt the sentence would read better that way.

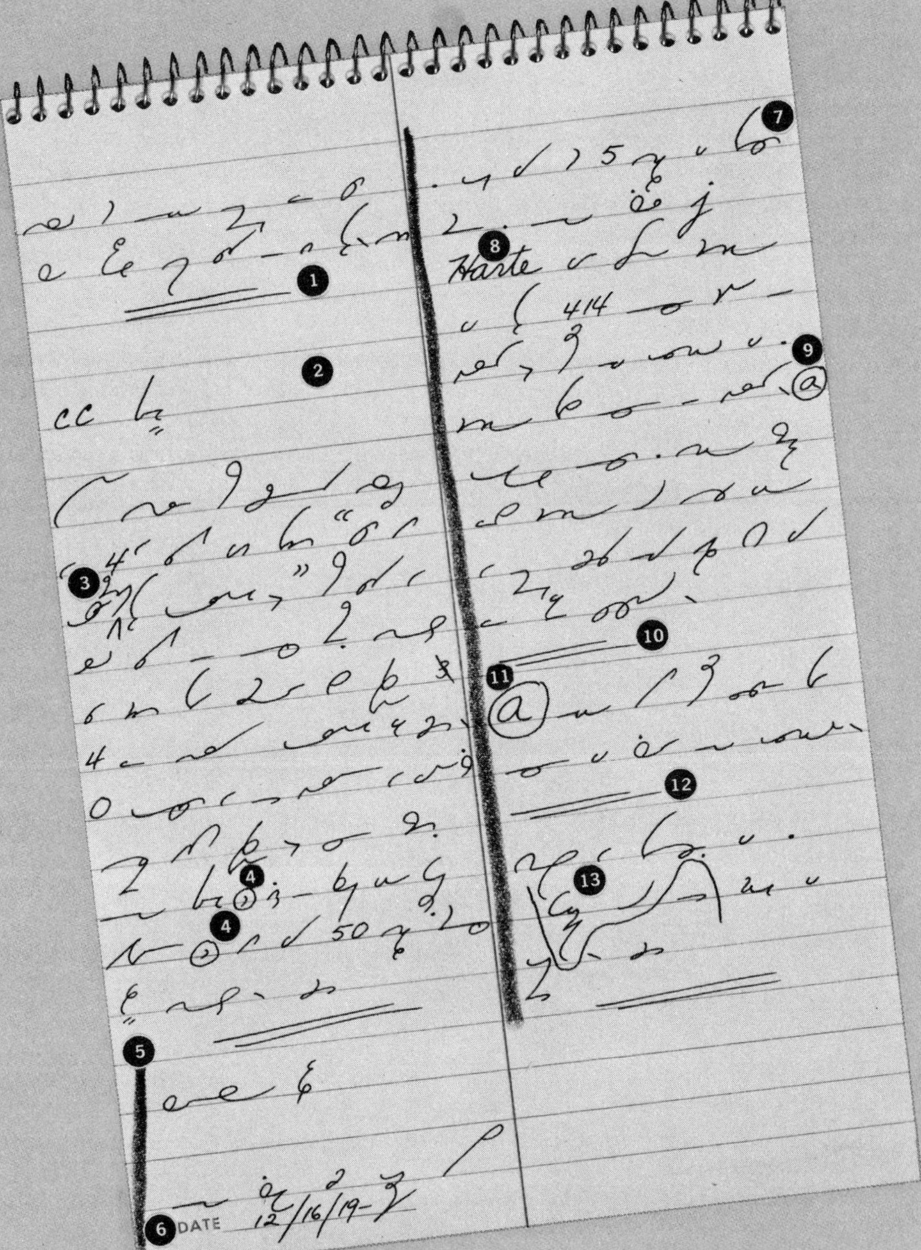

A page from a secretary's notebook. The encircled numbers correspond to the numbered explanations on page 490.

DEVELOPING WORD-BUILDING POWER

557▸ Word Beginnings and Endings

Over-

1

-gram

2

-ward

3

-ment

4

Ul

5

—— ♦♦ ——

1 Overseas, overhead, overcoat, overpower, overworked, overcomes, overpaid.

2 Program, telegrams, monograms, radiogram.

3 Reward, forwarded, awkwardly, eastward, outward, onward, inward.

4 Refreshments, enjoyment, appointment, fundamental, experimental, shipment.

5 Result, cultured, culminate, adult, consulted, insults.

BUILDING TRANSCRIPTION SKILLS

558 ▸ SPELLING FAMILIES -an, -on, -en

Words ending with an *n* that is preceded by *a*, *o*, or *e* have always been a source of spelling difficulty for stenographers.

Practice each of the following groups.

Words Ending in -an

met·ro·pol·i·tan	par·ti·san	slo·gan
or·gan	pu·ri·tan	sub·ur·ban
or·phan	ur·ban	vet·er·an

Words Ending in -on

but·ton	lun·cheon	rib·bon
cot·ton	par·don	sur·geon
les·son (instruction)	per·son	wag·on

Words Ending in -en

broad·en	giv·en	less·en (decrease)
bur·den	hid·den	spo·ken
cit·i·zen	kitch·en	writ·ten

A number of these words appear in the Reading and Writing Practice. Watch for them.

559 ▸ BUSINESS VOCABULARY BUILDER

amended Changed by an addition or modification.
reimburse Repay.

READING AND WRITING PRACTICE

560 ▸

Ho·ri·zons

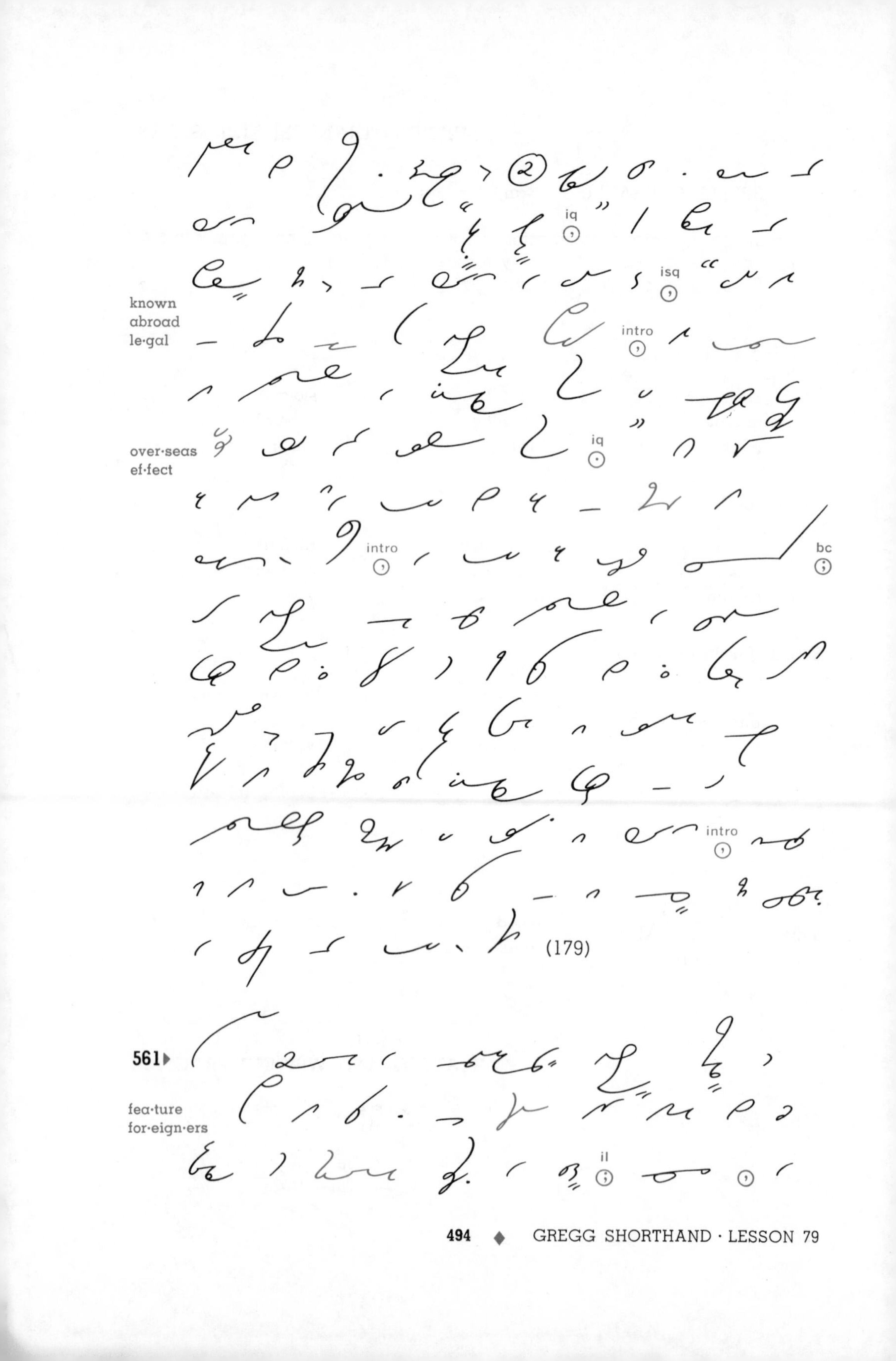

known
abroad
le·gal

iq

isq

intro

over·seas
ef·fect

iq

intro

bc

intro

(179)

561▸

fea·ture
for·eign·ers

il

cit·i·zens

as

par·tic·i·pate

lun·cheon
flex·i·ble

nc

guests'
re·im·burse

par

bc

and o

if

(239)

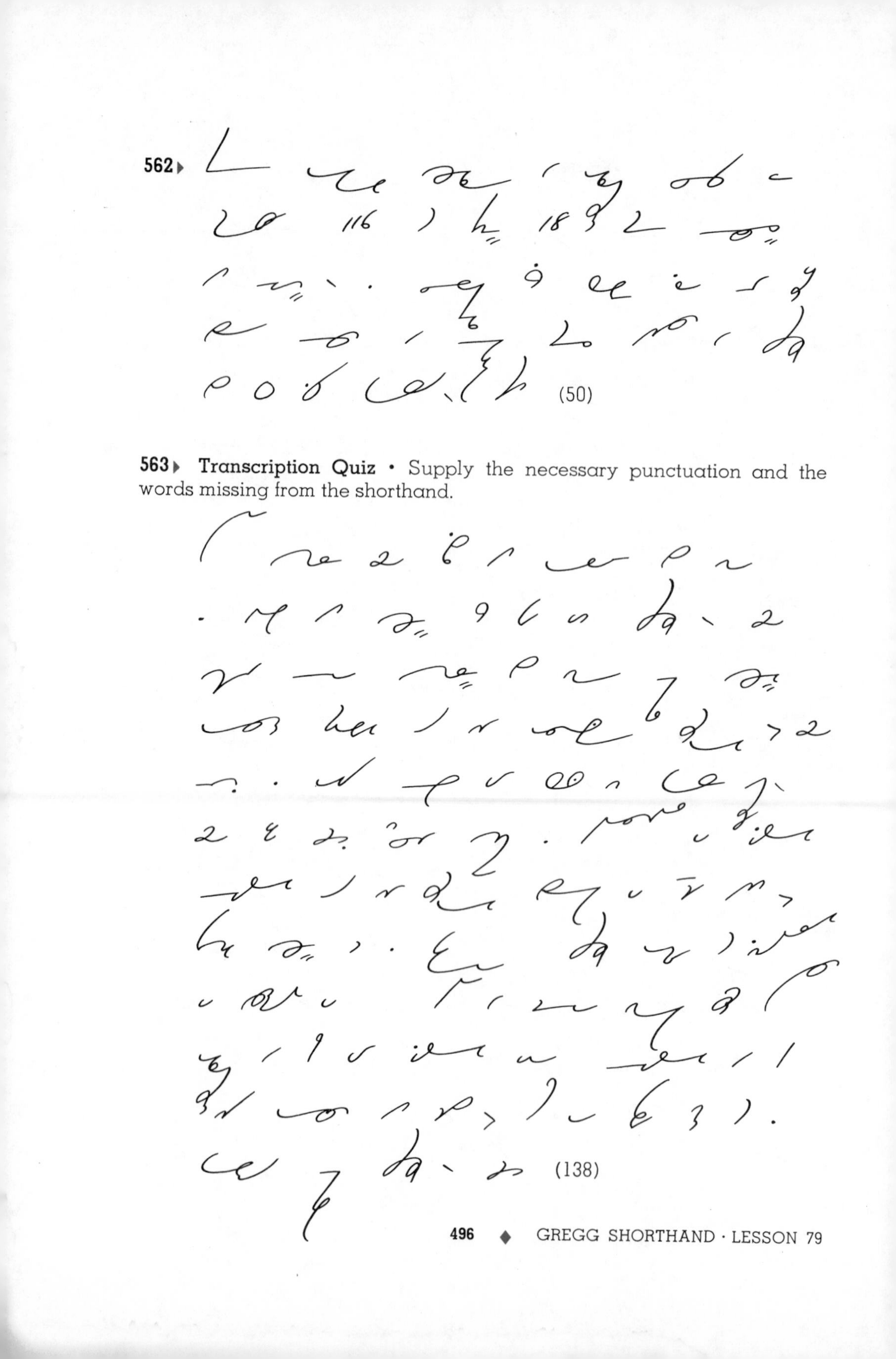

562▸ 116 18 (50)

563▸ Transcription Quiz · Supply the necessary punctuation and the words missing from the shorthand.

(138)

DEVELOPING WORD-BUILDING POWER

564 ▸ Shorthand Vocabulary Builder

Ses

1

Ah, Aw

2

Omission of Short U

3

Oi

4

Geographical Expressions

5

— ♦♦ —

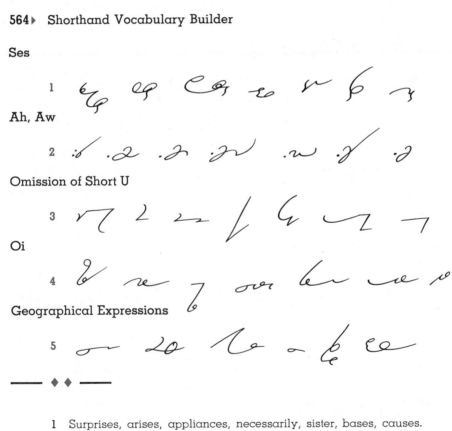

1 Surprises, arises, appliances, necessarily, sister, bases, causes.
2 Ahead, aware, awake, awakened, award, awaited, away.
3 Stumble, fun, someone, judged, brushed, luncheon, much.
4 Avoid, coil, enjoy, annoyance, boiler, lawyer, toy.
5 American, Philippine Islands, Dublin, England, Japanese, Israel.

565 BUSINESS VOCABULARY BUILDER

stereotype A fixed or conventional notion, character, or pattern.

passé Out of date; old-fashioned.

alien Strange to; not natural to.

READING AND WRITING PRACTICE

566 Etiquette Abroad

ste·reo·type
un·couth
par
cus·toms
alien
par
lapse
apol·o·gies
par
bc
per·mis·si·ble
lo·cal
if
guest

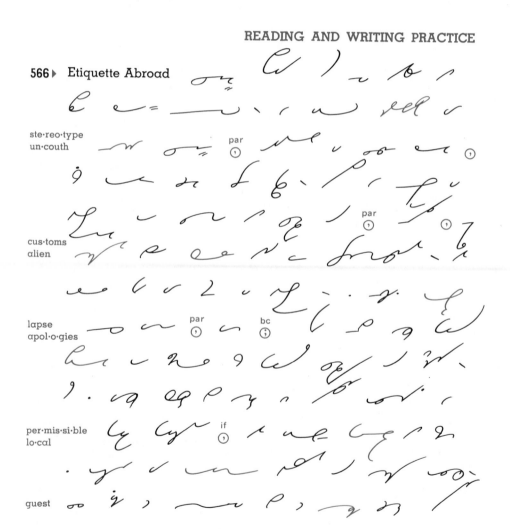

em·bar·rass·ment
na·tion's

par

well known
no noun,
no hyphen

bc

par

par

de·scends
steep

par

In the

intro

9 5:30 6:30

par

sur·prised
is·sue
of·fered

conj

intro

tran·sis·tor

par ,

ser , , ,

re·sis·tance
adapt·er

ser , , ,

The only

nc ; intro ,

Is·ra·el
en·cour·aged

intro , bc ; par ,

,

nonr ,

nonr ,

first-class
hyphenated before noun

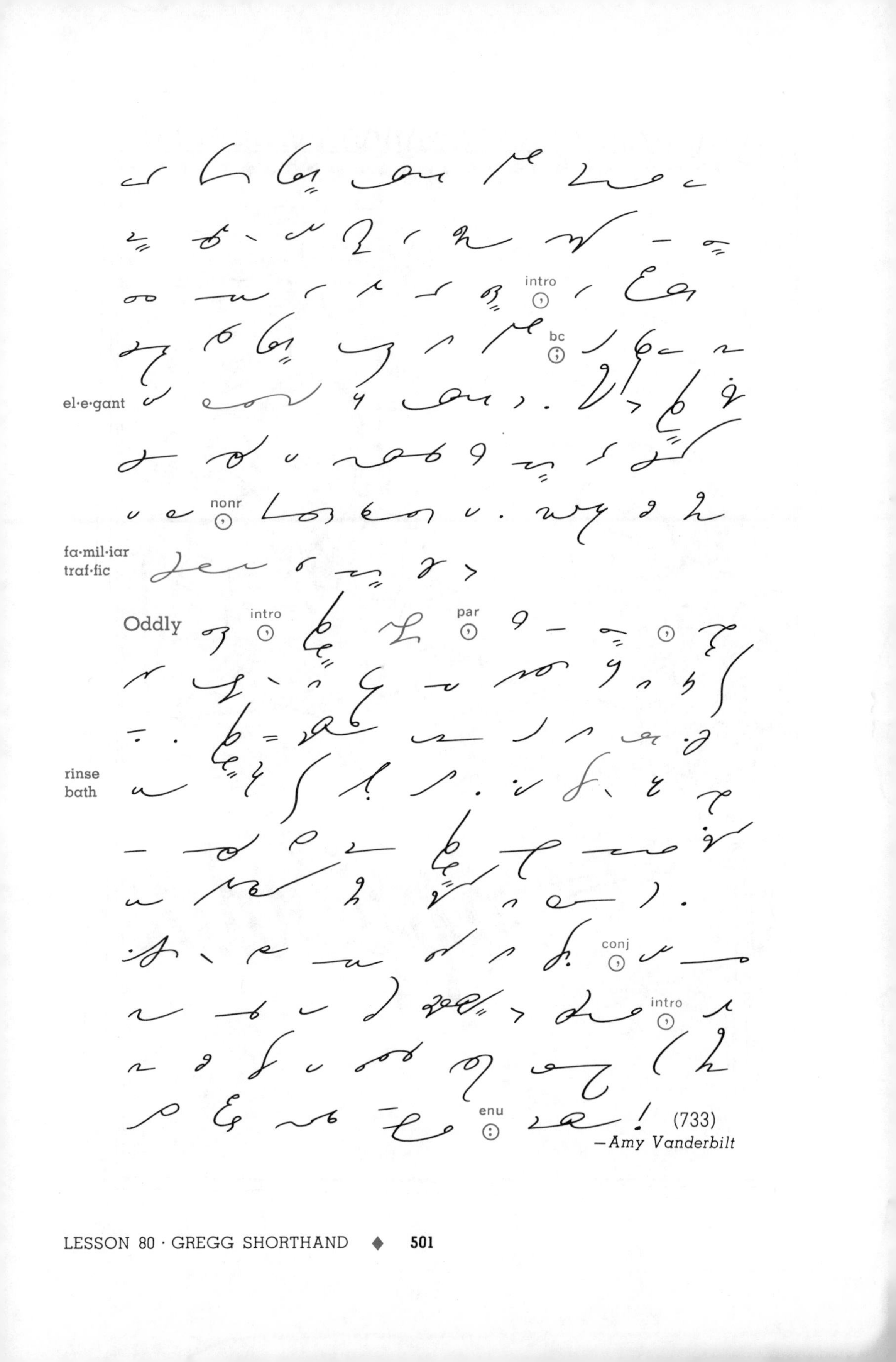

el·e·gant

intro

bc

nonr

fa·mil·iar
traf·fic

Oddly

intro

par

rinse
bath

conj

intro

enu

(733)

—*Amy Vanderbilt*

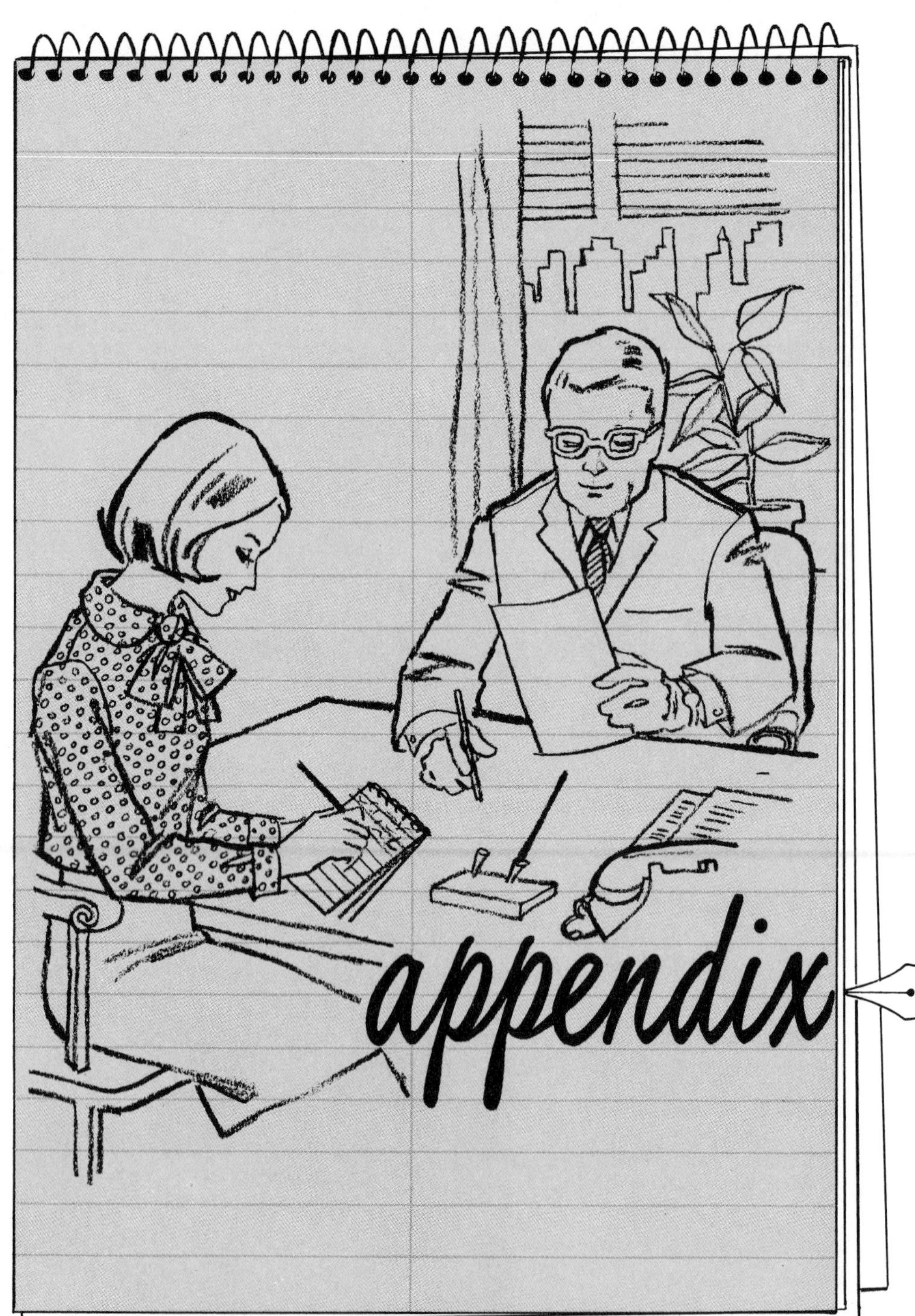
appendix

LIST OF JOINED WORD ENDINGS

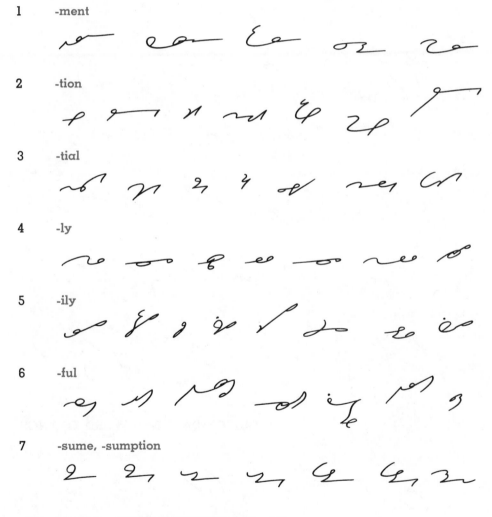

1 -ment

2 -tion

3 -tial

4 -ly

5 -ily

6 -ful

7 -sume, -sumption

8 -ble

9 -ther

10 -ual

11 -ure

12 -self, -selves

13 -ort

14 -tain

15 -cient, -ciency

LIST OF DISJOINED WORD ENDINGS

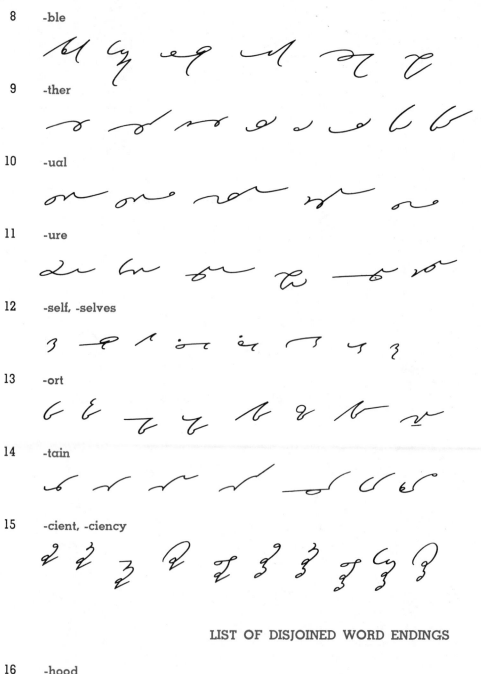

16 -hood

17 -ward

18 -ship

19 -cle, -cal

20 -ulate

21 -ingly

22 -ings

23 -gram

24 -ification

25 -lity

26 -lty

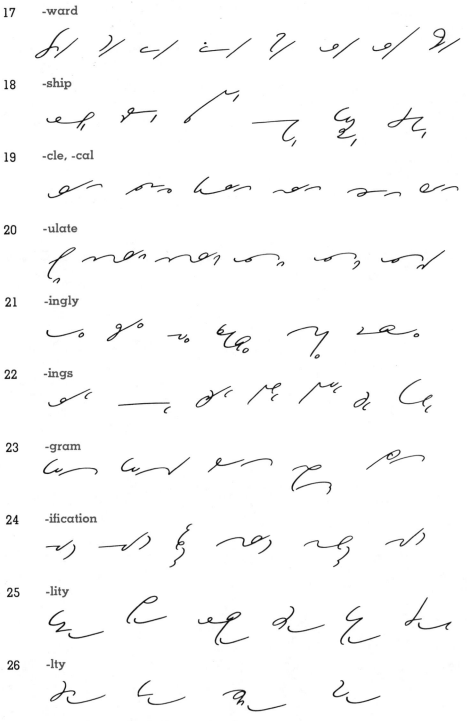

27 -rity

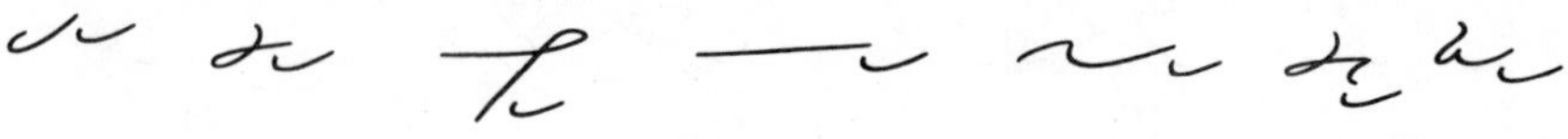

LIST OF JOINED WORD BEGINNINGS

28 Per-, Pur-

29 Em-

30 Im-

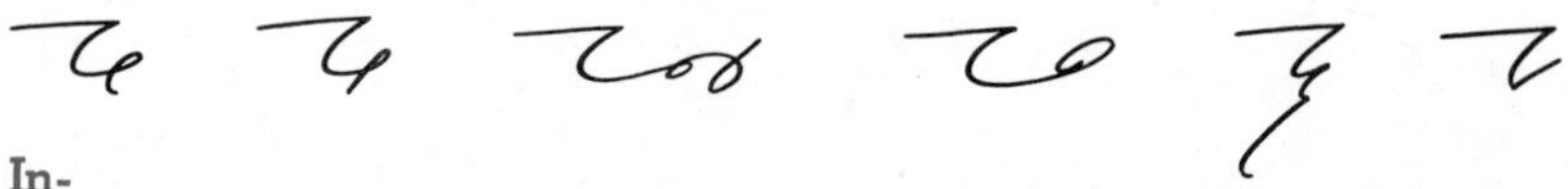

31 In-

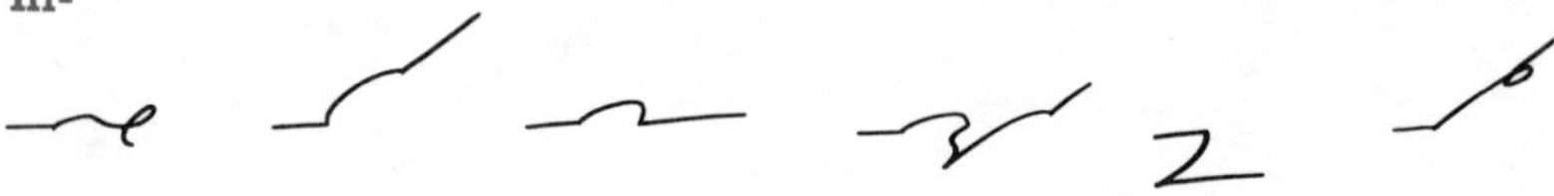

32 En-

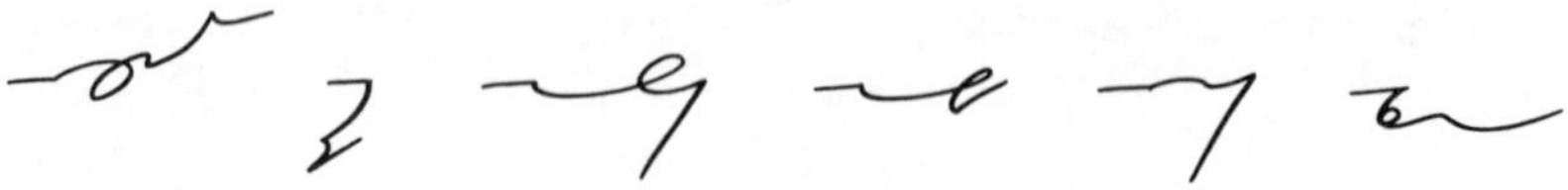

33 Un-

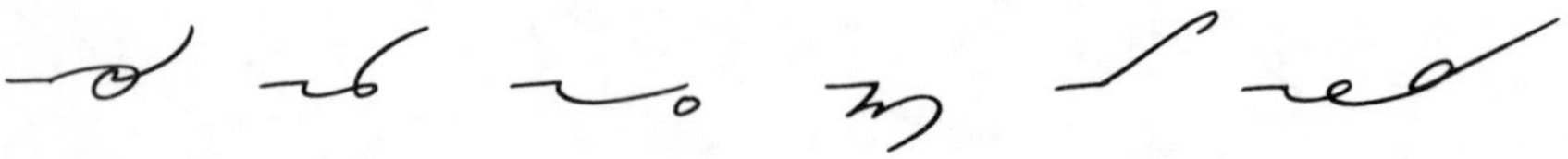

34 Re-

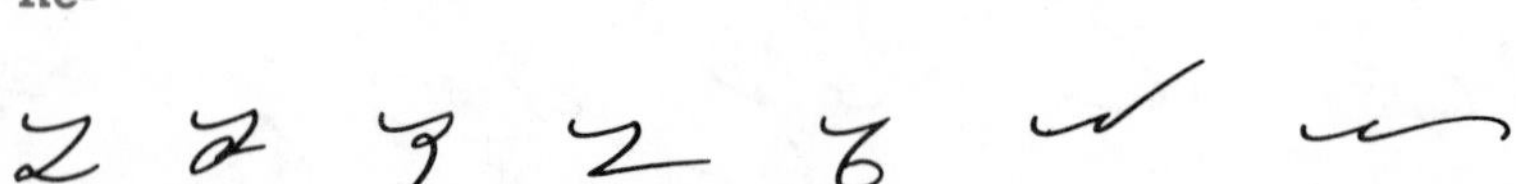

35 Be-

36 De-, Dĭ-

37 Dis-, Des-

38 Mis-

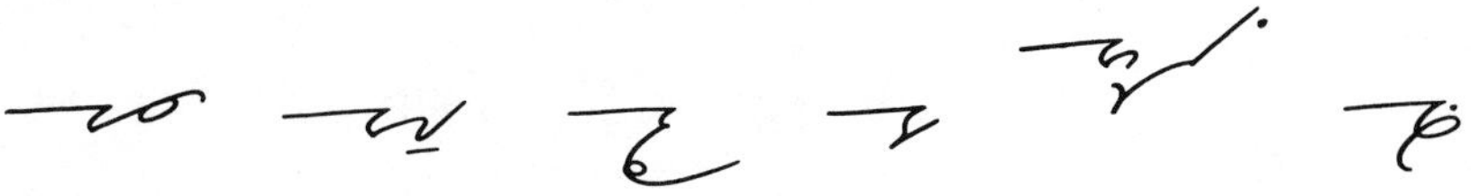

39 Ex-

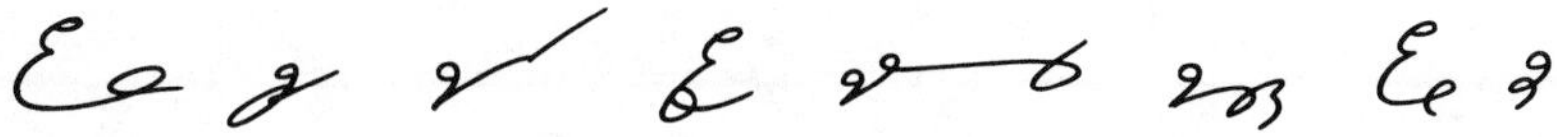

40 Com-

41 Con-

42 Sub-

43 Al-

44 For-, Fore-

45 Fur-

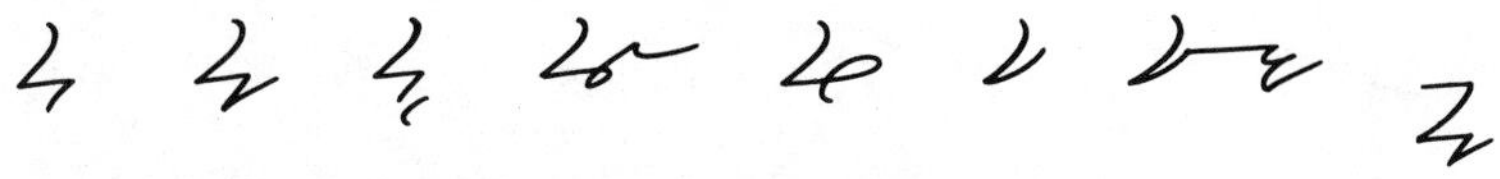

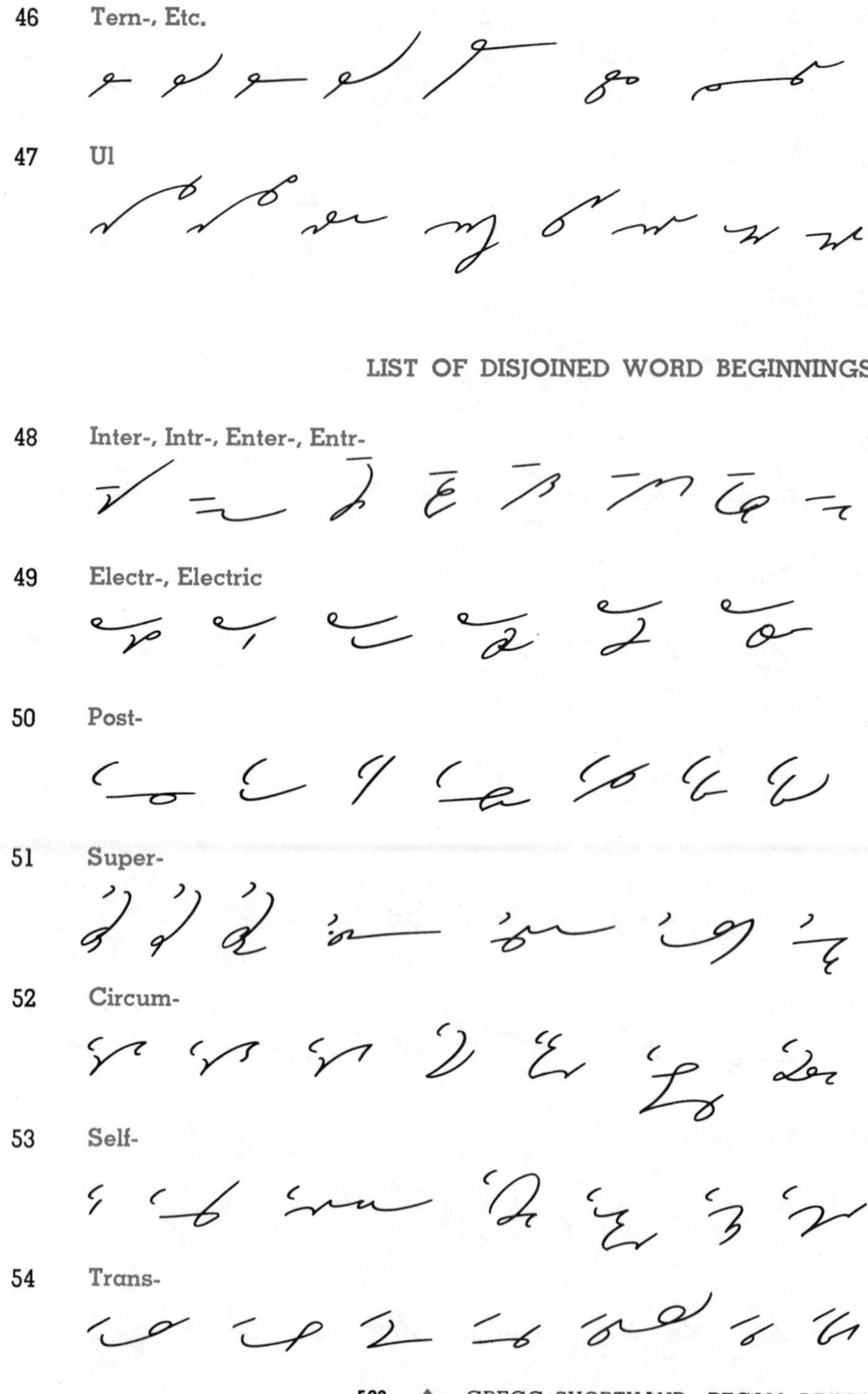

46 Tern-, Etc.

47 Ul

LIST OF DISJOINED WORD BEGINNINGS

48 Inter-, Intr-, Enter-, Entr-

49 Electr-, Electric

50 Post-

51 Super-

52 Circum-

53 Self-

54 Trans-

55 Under-

56 Over-

LIST OF SPECIAL PHRASES

57 T for To in Phrases

58 Been Represented by B

59 Able Represented by A

60 Want Preceded by Pronoun

61 Ago Represented by G

62 To Omitted in Phrases

63 The Omitted in Phrases

64 Of Omitted in Phrases

65 A Omitted in Phrases

66 Intersected Phrases

67 Special Phrases

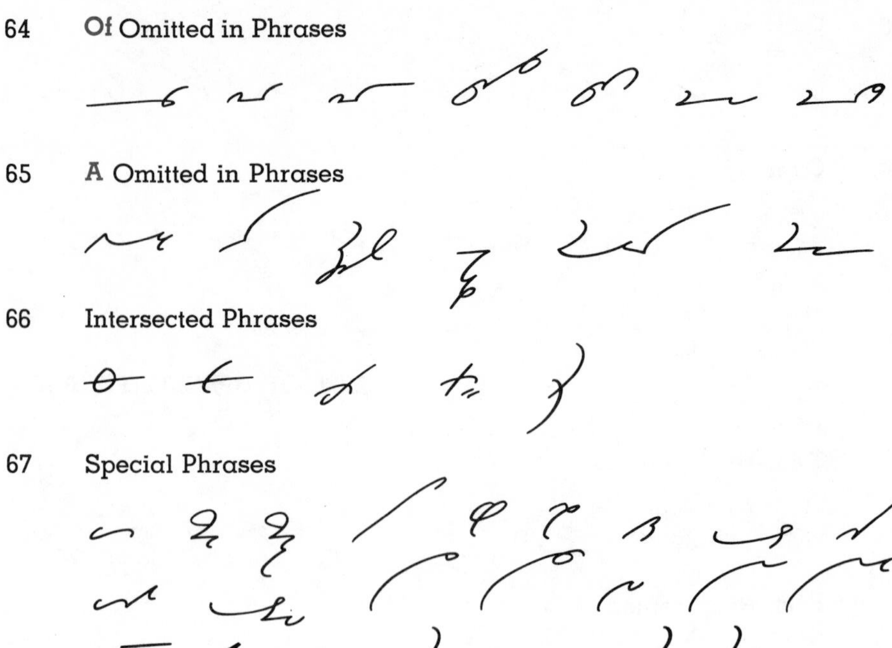

index

BUILDING YOUR TRANSCRIPTION SKILLS

The number next to each entry refers to the page in the text in which the entry appears.

SIMILAR WORDS

SPELLING FAMILIES

TYPING-STYLE STUDIES

FREQUENTLY USED PHRASES
OF GREGG SHORTHAND

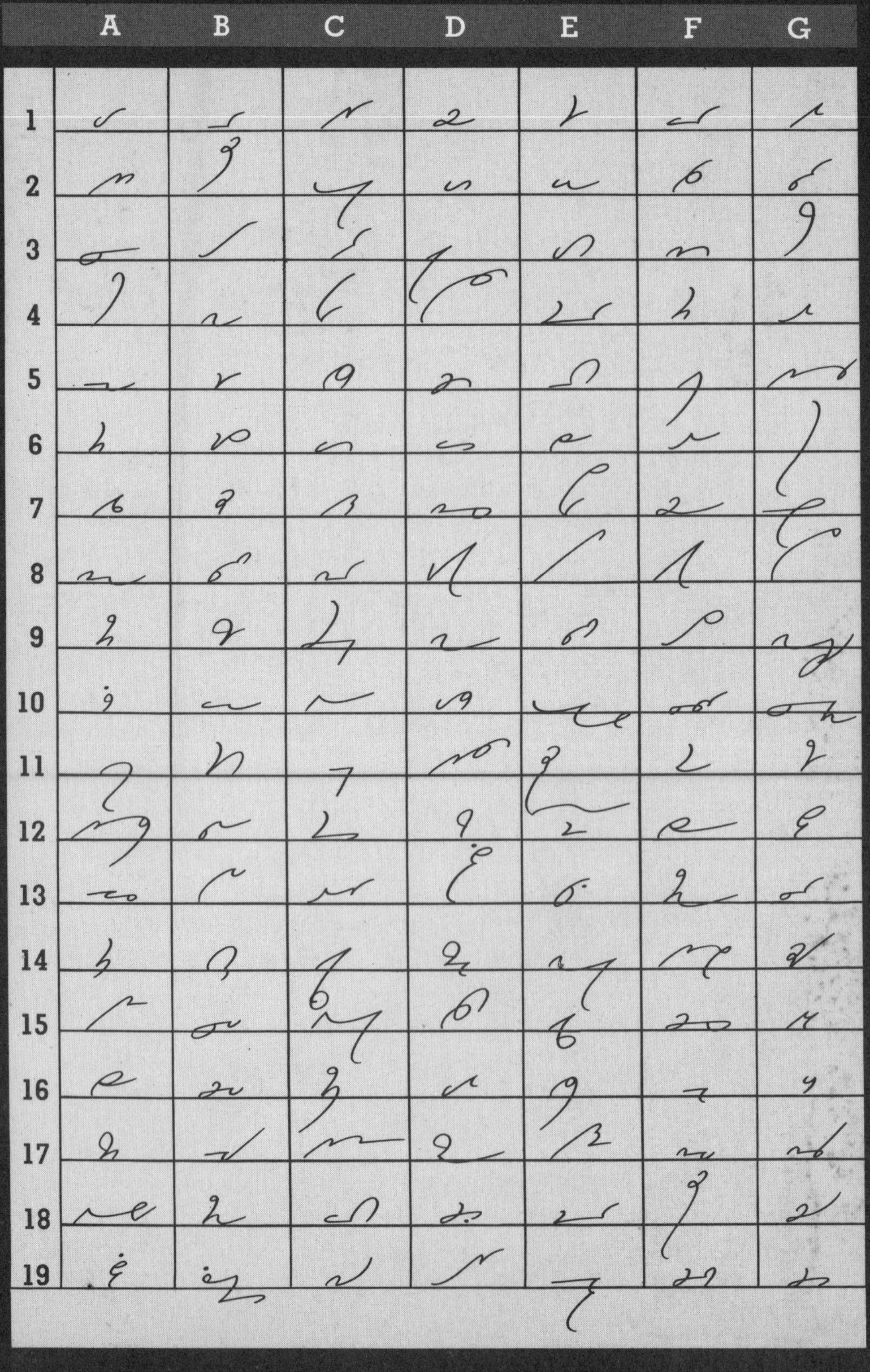

	A	B	C	D	E	F	G
1							
2							
3							
4							
5							
6							
7							
8							
9							
10							
11							
12							
13							
14							
15							
16							
17							
18							
19							